T0350458

Advances in Malware and Data–Driven Network Security

Brij B. Gupta
National Institute of Technology, Kurukshetra, India

A volume in the Advances in Information Security,
Privacy, and Ethics (AISPE) Book Series

Published in the United States of America by
IGI Global
Information Science Reference (an imprint of IGI Global)
701 E. Chocolate Avenue
Hershey PA, USA 17033
Tel: 717-533-8845
Fax: 717-533-8661
E-mail: cust@igi-global.com
Web site: http://www.igi-global.com

Copyright © 2022 by IGI Global. All rights reserved. No part of this publication may be reproduced, stored or distributed in any form or by any means, electronic or mechanical, including photocopying, without written permission from the publisher. Product or company names used in this set are for identification purposes only. Inclusion of the names of the products or companies does not indicate a claim of ownership by IGI Global of the trademark or registered trademark.

Library of Congress Cataloging-in-Publication Data

Names: Gupta, Brij, 1982- editor.
Title: Advances in malware and data-driven network security / Brij B.
  Gupta, editor.
Description: Hershey, PA : Information Science Reference, [2021] | Includes
  bibliographical references and index. | Summary: "This book describes
  some of the recent notable advances in threat-detection using
  machine-learning and artificial-intelligence with a focus on malwares,
  covering the current trends in ML/statistical approaches to detecting,
  clustering or classification of cyber-threats extensively"-- Provided by
  publisher.
Identifiers: LCCN 2021010790 (print) | LCCN 2021010791 (ebook) | ISBN
  9781799877899 (h/c) | ISBN 9781799877905 (s/c) | ISBN 9781799877912
  (ebook)
Subjects: LCSH: Computer networks--Security measures. | Malware (Computer
  software) | Machine learning. | Digital forensic science.
Classification: LCC TK5105.59 .A3828 2021 (print) | LCC TK5105.59 (ebook)
  | DDC 005.8--dc23
LC record available at https://lccn.loc.gov/2021010790
LC ebook record available at https://lccn.loc.gov/2021010791

This book is published in the IGI Global book series Advances in Information Security, Privacy, and Ethics (AISPE) (ISSN: 1948-9730; eISSN: 1948-9749)

British Cataloguing in Publication Data
A Cataloguing in Publication record for this book is available from the British Library.

All work contributed to this book is new, previously-unpublished material. The views expressed in this book are those of the authors, but not necessarily of the publisher.

For electronic access to this publication, please contact: eresources@igi-global.com.

Advances in Information Security, Privacy, and Ethics (AISPE) Book Series

Manish Gupta
State University of New York, USA

ISSN:1948-9730
EISSN:1948-9749

MISSION

As digital technologies become more pervasive in everyday life and the Internet is utilized in ever increasing ways by both private and public entities, concern over digital threats becomes more prevalent.

The **Advances in Information Security, Privacy, & Ethics (AISPE) Book Series** provides cutting-edge research on the protection and misuse of information and technology across various industries and settings. Comprised of scholarly research on topics such as identity management, cryptography, system security, authentication, and data protection, this book series is ideal for reference by IT professionals, academicians, and upper-level students.

COVERAGE

- Risk Management
- Technoethics
- Data Storage of Minors
- Information Security Standards
- Global Privacy Concerns
- CIA Triad of Information Security
- Security Information Management
- Telecommunications Regulations
- Privacy-Enhancing Technologies
- Cookies

IGI Global is currently accepting manuscripts for publication within this series. To submit a proposal for a volume in this series, please contact our Acquisition Editors at Acquisitions@igi-global.com or visit: http://www.igi-global.com/publish/.

The Advances in Information Security, Privacy, and Ethics (AISPE) Book Series (ISSN 1948-9730) is published by IGI Global, 701 E. Chocolate Avenue, Hershey, PA 17033-1240, USA, www.igi-global.com. This series is composed of titles available for purchase individually; each title is edited to be contextually exclusive from any other title within the series. For pricing and ordering information please visit http://www.igi-global.com/book-series/advances-information-security-privacy-ethics/37157. Postmaster: Send all address changes to above address. Copyright © 2022 IGI Global. All rights, including translation in other languages reserved by the publisher. No part of this series may be reproduced or used in any form or by any means – graphics, electronic, or mechanical, including photocopying, recording, taping, or information and retrieval systems – without written permission from the publisher, except for non commercial, educational use, including classroom teaching purposes. The views expressed in this series are those of the authors, but not necessarily of IGI Global.

Titles in this Series

For a list of additional titles in this series, please visit: www.igi-global.com/book-series

Modern Day Surveillance Ecosystem and Impacts on Privacy
Ananda Mitra (Wake Forest University USA)
Information Science Reference • © 2022 • 242pp • H/C (ISBN: 9781799838470) • US $195.00

Ethical Hacking Techniques and Countermeasures for Cybercrime Prevention
Nabie Y. Conteh (Southern University at New Orleans USA)
Information Science Reference • © 2021 • 168pp • H/C (ISBN: 9781799865049) • US $225.00

NATO and the Future of European and Asian Security
Carsten Sander Christensen (Billund Municipaly's Museums, Denmark) and Vakhtang Maisaia (Caucasus International University, Georgia)
Information Science Reference • © 2021 • 331pp • H/C (ISBN: 9781799871187) • US $195.00

Handbook of Research on Advancing Cybersecurity for Digital Transformation
Kamaljeet Sandhu (University of New England, Australia)
Information Science Reference • © 2021 • 460pp • H/C (ISBN: 9781799869757) • US $275.00

Enabling Blockchain Technology for Secure Networking and Communications
Adel Ben Mnaouer (Canadian University Dubai, UAE) and Lamia Chaari Fourati (University of Sfax, Tunisia)
Information Science Reference • © 2021 • 339pp • H/C (ISBN: 9781799858393) • US $215.00

Multidisciplinary Approach to Modern Digital Steganography
Sabyasachi Pramanik (Haldia Institute of Technology, India) Mangesh Manikrao Ghonge (Sandip Foundation's Institute of Technology and Research Centre, India) Renjith V. Ravi (MEA Engineering College, India) and Korhan Cengiz (Trakya University, Turkey)
Information Science Reference • © 2021 • 380pp • H/C (ISBN: 9781799871606) • US $195.00

Strategic Approaches to Digital Platform Security Assurance
Yuri Bobbert (ON2IT BV, The Netherlands & Antwerp Management School, University of Antwerp, Belgium) Maria Chtepen (BNP Paribas Group, Belgium) Tapan Kumar (Cognizant, The Netherlands) Yves Vanderbeken (DXC, Belgium) and Dennis Verslegers (Orange Cyberdefense, Belgium)
Information Science Reference • © 2021 • 394pp • H/C (ISBN: 9781799873679) • US $195.00

Security and Privacy Solutions for the Internet of Energy
Mohamed Amine Ferrag (Guelma University, Algeria)
Information Science Reference • © 2021 • 325pp • H/C (ISBN: 9781799846161) • US $195.00

701 East Chocolate Avenue, Hershey, PA 17033, USA
Tel: 717-533-8845 x100 • Fax: 717-533-8661
E-Mail: cust@igi-global.com • www.igi-global.com

Dedicated to my wife Varsha Gupta, daughter Prisha, and son Divit
for their constant support during the course of this Book.
Brij B. Gupta

Editorial Advisory Board

Ammar Almomani, *Al-Balqa Applied University, Jordan*
Nalin A. G. Arachchilage, *University of New South Wales, Australia*
V. C. Bhavsar, *UNB, Canada*
Mohd Anuaruddin Bin Ahmadon, *Yamaguchi University, Japan*
Arcangelo Castiglione, *University of Salerno, Italy*
Xiaojun Chang, *Monash University, Clayton, Australia*
Francisco José García Peñalvo, *University of Salamanca, Spain*
Deepak Gupta, *LoginRadius Inc., Canada*
Ching-Hsien Hsu, *Asia University, Taiwan*
Jin Li, *Guangzhou University, China*
Yining Liu, *Guilin University of Electronic Technology, China*
Ahmad Manasrah, *Yarmouk University, Jordan*
Gregorio Martinez Perez, *University of Murcia, Spain*
Melody Moh, *San Jose State University, USA*
Nadia Nedjah, *State University of Rio de Janeiro, Brazil*
Dragan Peraković, *University of Zagreb, Croatia*
T. Perumal, *Universiti Putra Malaysia (UPM), Malaysia*
Raffaele Pizzolante, *University of Salerno, Italy*
Konstantinos Psannis, *University of Macedonia, Greece*
Imran Razzak, *Deakin University, Australia*
Michael Sheng, *Macquarie University, Australia*
Shingo Yamaguchi, *Yamaguchi University, Japan*

Table of Contents

Detailed Table of Contents

    Krishna Yadav, National Institute of Technology, Kurukshetra, India
    Aarushi Sethi, National Institute of Technology, Kurukshetra, India
    Mavneet Kaur, National Institute of Technology, Kurukshetra, India
    Dragan Perakovic, University of Zagreb, Croatia

Companies and organizations are collecting all sorts of data ranging from nominal feedback like customer reviews to highly classified data like medical records. With data being such a critical aspect of most of the operations around us, cybercriminals are looking for an opportunity to misuse this information. One such device that cybercriminals use to further their malicious intent is malware. Over the years, these cybercriminals have become immensely powerful using the knowledge of previous attacks. Hence, malware analysis and methods to troubleshoot the problems arising due to malware attacks is the need of the hour. Over time, different new approaches have been developed to defend malware. However, in recent times, machine learning-based malware analysis has gained popularity. The capacity to detect possible future malware by learning from existing malware patterns makes this method very popular. In this chapter, the authors have introduced different malware and the machine learning-based approach that has been developed in recent times to mitigate malware.

    Santosh Kumar Smmarwar, National Institute of Technology, Raipur, India
    Govind P. Gupta, National Institute of Technology, Raipur, India
    Sanjay Kumar, National Institute of Technology, Raipur, India

With more uses of internet-based services, the risk of cyberattacks is growing continuously. To analyze these research trends for malware and intrusion detection, the authors applied the topic modeling approach in the study by using the LDA (latent dirichlet allocation) and calculating the maximum and minimum probability of the words, which appears in the large collection of text. The LDA technique is useful in finding the hidden topics for further research in the areas of network and cybersecurity. In this chapter, they collected the abstract of two thousand papers from the Scopus library from 2014 to 2021. These collected papers are from reputed publications such as Elsevier, Springer, and IEEE Transactions. The main aim of this study is to find research trends based on keywords that are untouched or on which less research work has been done. To the best of the authors' knowledge, this will be the first study done by using the LDA technique for topic modeling in the areas of network security to demonstrate the research gap and trends for malware and intrusion detection systems.

    Praneeth Gunti, National Institute of Technology, Kurukshetra, India
    Brij B. Gupta, National Institute of Technology, Kurukshetra, India
    Francisco José García Peñalvo, University of Salamanca, Spain

A never-ending fight is taking place among malware creators and security experts as the advances in malware are daunting. The machine learning strategies are indeed the new mode of researching malware. The purpose of this chapter is to explore machine learning methods for malware recognition and in general deep learning methods. The chapter gives complete explanations of the techniques and resources used in a standard machine learning process for detecting malware. It examines the study issues that are posed by existing study methods and introduces the potential avenues of study in future. By administering a study to the participants, scholars have a better knowledge of the malware detections. The authors start by discussing simple dynamic modelling methods, their importance to the data analytics of malware, and their implementations. They use open access resources such as virustotal.com that review sample of dynamic analysis in reality.

    Kwok Tai Chui, Hong Kong Metropolitan University, Hong Kong
    Patricia Ordóñez de Pablos, The University of Oviedo, Spain
    Miltiadis D. Lytras, Deree College — The American College of Greece, Greece
    Ryan Wen Liu, Wuhan University of Technology, China
    Chien-wen Shen, National Central University, Taiwan

Software has been the essential element to computers in today's digital era. Unfortunately, it has experienced challenges from various types of malware, which are designed for sabotage, criminal money-making, and information theft. To protect the gadgets from malware, numerous malware detection algorithms have been proposed. In the olden days there were shallow learning algorithms, and in recent years there are deep learning algorithms. With the availability of big data for training of model and affordable and high-performance computing services, deep learning has demonstrated its superiority in many smart city applications, in terms of accuracy, error rate, etc. This chapter intends to conduct a systematic review on the latest development of deep learning algorithms for malware detection. Some future research directions are suggested for further exploration.

Ángel Luis Perales Gómez, University of Murcia, Spain

Lorenzo Fernández Maimó, University of Murcia, Spain

Alberto Huertas Celdrán, University of Zurich, Switzerland

Félix Jesús García Clemente, University of Murcia, Spain

In the last decades, factories have suffered a significant change in automation, evolving from isolated towards interconnected systems. However, the adoption of open standards and the opening to the internet have caused an increment in the number of attacks. In addition, traditional intrusion detection systems relying on a signature database, where malware patterns are stored, are failing due to the high specialization of industrial cyberattacks. For this reason, the research community is moving towards the anomaly detection paradigm. This paradigm is showing great results when it is implemented using machine learning and deep learning techniques. This chapter surveys several incidents caused by cyberattacks targeting industrial scenarios. Next, to understand the current status of anomaly detection solutions, it analyses the current industrial datasets and anomaly detection systems in the industrial field. In addition, the chapter shows an example of malware attacking a manufacturing plant, resulting in a safety threat. Finally, cybersecurity and safety solutions are reviewed.

Priyanka Ahlawat, National Institute of Technology, Kurukshetra, India

Pranjil Singhal, National Institute of Technology, Kurukshetra, India

Khushi Goyal, National Institute of Technology, Kurukshetra, India

Kanak Yadav, National Institute of Technology, Kurukshetra, India

Rohit Bathla, National Institute of Technology, Kurukshetra, India

Considering the situation when the node which is entering in the network is a malicious node, it can check and record the various operations of the network which could be responsible for some serious security issues. In order to safeguard the network, the author propose an approach which is in view of the advanced encoding strategy, termed as convolution coding approach. According to the requirement of network, the initial bits are assigned, and by applying the convolution technique, the final code is generated for each and every node. Considering the fact that it is a digital method, the codes can be represented by using the binary number system. All the nodes that are a part of the network will be having their corresponding final binary code, say C. The verification of each node is carried out by matching the generated code C with the security code within a particular time period before transmitting the data. This process enables the detection of malicious or attacker node. Furthermore, to enhance the versatility and execution, the system is organized into clusters.

In the real scenario, there is a large multicast group where nodes leave and join frequently, and also the number of nodes leaving and joining is also not proportionate. Hence, scalable rekeying process is an important issue that needs to be concerned for the secured group communication for dynamic groups. In basic rekeying scheme, which is based on the logical key hierarchy, the rekeying cost depends on the logarithm of the size of group for a join or depart request by the user. However, the memory efficiency of this group rekeying protocol (GREP) is a huge storage overhead over the system. The authors aim to provide a survey of various group key management schemes and then propose an efficient scalable solution based on linked LKH and the linked list data structure. Results have shown that the Linked LKH algorithm has a very low effective cost for rekeying the LKH as compared to the basic LKH algorithm (i.e., based on the number of new joined and departure requests).

This chapter introduces a new kind of cybersecurity system named botnet defense system (BDS) that defends an IoT system against malicious botnets. This chapter consists of two parts. The former part describes the concept and design of the BDS. The concept is "fight fire with fire." To realize the concept, the BDS uses bot technology. The BDS builds a white-hat botnet on the IoT system by itself and uses it to exterminate the malicious botnets. The white-hat botnet autonomously spreads over the IoT system and thus drastically increases the defense ability. The latter part explains the strategy of the BDS. The white-hat botnet is a so-called double-edged sword. It defends the IoT system against malicious botnet but wastes the system's resources. Therefore, the BDS should strategically use the white-hat botnet. Some strategies have been proposed. Their characteristics are discussed through the simulation with the agent-oriented petri nets.

The internet of things is a cutting-edge technology that is vulnerable to all sorts of fictitious solutions. As a new phase of computing emerges in the digital world, it intends to produce a huge number of smart gadgets that can host a wide range of applications and operations. IoT gadgets are a perfect target for cyber assaults because of their wide dispersion, availability/accessibility, and top-notch computing power. Furthermore, as numerous IoT devices gather and investigate private data, they become a gold mine for hostile actors. Hence, the matter of fact is that security, particularly the potential to diagnose compromised nodes, as well as the collection and preservation of testimony of an attack or illegal activity, have become top priorities. This chapter delves into the timeline and the most challenging security and privacy issues that exist in the present scenario. In addition to this, some open issues and future research directions are also discussed.

Enrique Tomás Martínez Beltrán, University of Murcia, Spain
Mario Quiles Pérez, University of Murcia, Spain
Sergio López Bernal, University of Murcia, Spain
Alberto Huertas Celdrán, University of Zürich, Switzerland
Gregorio Martínez Pérez, University of Murcia, Spain

In recent years, the growth of brain-computer interfaces (BCIs) has been remarkable in specific application fields, such as the medical sector or the entertainment industry. Most of these fields use evoked potentials, like P300, to obtain neural data able to handle prostheses or achieve greater immersion experience in videogames. The natural use of BCI involves the management of sensitive users' information as behaviors, emotions, or thoughts. In this context, new security breaches in BCI are offering cybercriminals the possibility of collecting sensitive data and affecting subjects' physical integrity, which are critical issues. For all these reasons, the fact of applying efficient cybersecurity mechanisms has become a main challenge. To improve this challenge, this chapter proposes a framework able to detect cyberattacks affecting one of the most typical scenarios of BCI, the generation of P300 through visual stimuli. A pool of experiments demonstrates the performance of the proposed framework.

Santosh Kumar Smmarwar, National Institute of Technology, Raipur, India
Govind P. Gupta, National Institute of Technology, Raipur, India
Sanjay Kumar, National Institute of Technology, Raipur, India

Blockchain since 2009 has been gaining more popularity in various fields to use in numerous applications to overcome the security issues such as privacy, transparency, and mutability of data in the process of data sharing. Process of data sharing has many addressed and unaddressed challenges such as information encryption and decryption, data authentication, storage security, latency time, transfer speed of data, detecting malicious nodes, prevent the computer system from attacks, trust in the sharing process. In this chapter, the authors have reviewed the data sharing paper based on blockchain technology and presented the analysis of various techniques used in the information sharing process. The comprehensive analysis is categorizing in the following areas like incentive mechanism-based work, IoT-based data sharing, healthcare data sharing, and internet of vehicle data sharing using blockchain.

Priyanka Ahlawat, National Institute of Technology, Kurukshetra, India
Mukul Goyal, National Institute of Technology, Kurukshetra, India
Rishabh Sethi, National Institute of Technology, Kurukshetra, India
Nitish Gupta, National Institute of Technology, Kurukshetra, India

Node capture attack is one of the crucial attacks in wireless sensor networks (WSN) that seizes the node physically and withdraws the confidential data from the node's memory. The chapter exploits the adversarial behavior during a node capture to build an attack model. The authors also propose a fruit fly optimization algorithm (FFOA) that is a multi-objective optimization algorithm that consists of a number of objectives for capturing a node in the network: maximum node contribution, maximum key contributions are some examples of the same. The aim is to demolish the maximum part of the network while minimizing the cost and maximizing attacking efficiency. Due to the multi-objective function, the authors attain a maximum fraction of compromised traffic, lower attacking rounds, and lower energy cost as contrasted with other node capture attack algorithms. They have developed an algorithm, which is an enhanced version of FFOA and has even better efficiency than FFOA.

Brain-computer interfaces (BCIs) have experienced a considerable evolution in the last decade, expanding from clinical scenarios to sectors such as entertainment or video games. Nevertheless, this popularization makes them a target for cyberattacks like malware. Current literature lacks comprehensive works focusing on cybersecurity applied to BCIs and, mainly, publications performing a rigorous analysis of the risks and weaknesses that these interfaces present. If not studied properly, these potential vulnerabilities could dramatically impact users' data, service availability, and, most importantly, users' safety. Because of that, this work introduces an evaluation of the risk that each BCI classification already defined in the literature presents to raise awareness between the readers of this chapter about the potential threat that BCIs can generate in the next years if comprehensive measures, based on standard mechanisms, are not adopted. Moreover, it seeks to alert academic and industrial stakeholders about the impact these risks could have on future BCI hardware and software.

Preface

Every day approximately three-hundred thousand to four-hundred thousand new malware are registered, many of them being adware and variants of previously known malware. Anti-virus companies and researchers cannot deal with such a deluge of malware to analyze and build patches. The only way to scale the efforts is to build algorithms to enable machines to analyze malware and classify and cluster them to such a level of granularity that it will enable humans (or machines) to gain critical insights about them and build solutions that are specific enough to detect and thwart existing malware and generic-enough to thwart future variants.

Advances in Malware and Data-Driven Network Security comprehensively covers data-driven malware security with an emphasis on using statistical, machine learning, and AI as well as the current trends in ML/statistical approaches to detecting, clustering, and classification of cyber-threats. Providing information on advances in malware and data-driven network security as well as future research directions, it is ideal for graduate students, academicians, faculty members, scientists, software developers, security analysts, computer engineers, programmers, IT specialists, and researchers who are seeking to learn and carry out research in the area of malware and data-driven network security.

This book contains chapters dealing with different aspects of Malware analysis, Intrusion Detection on Network System, Data-driven Network Security, Anti-Virus Vendors, Botnet Defense Systems, Malicious Node Detection, Brain-Computer Interfaces Classifications, Cybersecurity Risks, Data-Driven Network Security, Deep Learning Techniques, Blockchain Systems, Linked LKH Algorithms, WSN Security, Machine Learning, Malicious Node Detection, Malware Algorithms, Malware Detection, SecBrain.

Specifically, this book contains discussion on the following topics:

- Machine Learning for Malware Analysis: Methods, Challenges, and Future Directions
- Research Trends for Malware and Intrusion Detection on Network System: A Topic Modelling Approach
- Deep-Learning and Machine-Learning-Based Techniques for Malware Detection and Data-Driven Network Security
- The Era of Advanced Machine Learning and Deep Learning Algorithms for Malware Detection
- Malware Detection in Industrial Scenarios Using Machine Learning and Deep Learning Techniques
- Malicious Node Detection using Convolution Technique: Authentication in Wireless Sensor Network (WSN)
- Scalable Rekeying Using Linked LKH Algorithm for Secure Multicast Communication
- Botnet Defense System and White-Hat Worm Launch Strategy in IoT Network
- A Survey on Emerging Security Issues, Challenges and Solutions for Internet of Things (IoTs)

- SecBrain: A Framework to Detect Cyberattacks Revealing Sensitive Data in Brain-Computer Interfaces
- A Study on Data Sharing using Blockchain System and Its Challenges and Applications
- Fruit Fly Optimization-Based Adversarial Modeling for Securing Wireless Sensor Network (WSN): Fruit Fly Optimization
- Cybersecurity Risks Associated With Brain-Computer Interfaces Classifications

ORGANIZATION OF BOOK

Chapter 1: Nowadays companies and organizations are collecting all sorts of data ranging from nominal feedback like customer reviews to highly classified data like medical records. With data being such a critical aspect of most of the operations around us, cybercriminals are looking for an opportunity to misuse this information. One such device that cybercriminals use to further their malicious intent is malware. Over the years, these cybercriminals have become immensely powerful using the knowledge of previous attacks. Hence malware analysis and methods to troubleshoot the problems arising due to malware attacks is the need of the hour. Over time, different new approaches have been developed to defend malware. However, in recent times, machine learning-based malware analysis has gained enough popularity. The capacity to detect possible future malware by learning from existing malware patterns makes this method very popular. In this chapter, we have introduced different malware and the machine learning-based approach that has been developed in recent times to mitigate these malware.

Chapter 2: With more uses of internet-based services, the risk of cyberattacks is growing continuously, to analyze these research trends for malware and intrusion detection, we applied the topic modeling approach in our study by using the LDA (Latent Dirichlet Allocation) and calculate the maximum and minimum probability of the words, which appears in the large collection of text. The LDA Technique is useful in finding the hidden topics for further research in the areas of network and cybersecurity. In this paper, we collected the abstract of two thousand papers from the Scopus library from 2014 to 2021. These collected papers are from reputed publications such as Elsevier, Springer, and IEEE Transaction, etc. The main aim of this study is to find out research trends based on keywords that are untouched or less research work has been done on that. To the best of our knowledge, this will be the first study done by using the LDA technique for topic modeling in the areas of network security to demonstrate the research gap and trends for malware and intrusion detection systems.

Chapter 3: A never-ending fight is taking place among malware creators and security experts as the advances in malware are daunting. The machine learning strategies are indeed the new mode of researching malware. The purpose of this chapter is to explore machine learning methods for malware recognition and in general, deep learning methods. The chapter gives complete explanations of the techniques and resources used in a standard machine learning process for detecting malware. It examines the study issues that are posed by existing study methods and introduces the potential avenues of study in future. By administering a study to the participants, scholars have a better knowledge of the malware detections. We start by discussing simple dynamic modelling methods, their importance to the data analytics of malware, and their implementations. We use open access resources such as virustotal.com which review sample of dynamic analysis in reality.

Chapter 4: Software has been the essential element to computers in today's digital era. Unfortunately, it has experienced challenges from various types of malwares which are designed for sabotage, criminal money-making, and information theft. To protect the gadgets from malware, numerous malware detection algorithms have been proposed in the olden days there were shallow learning algorithms and recent years there are deep learning algorithms. With the availability of big data for training of model and affordable and high-performance computing services, deep learning has demonstrated its superiority in many smart city applications, in terms of accuracy, error rate, etc. This chapter intends to conduct a systematic review on the latest development of deep learning algorithms for malware detection. Some future research directions are suggested for further exploration.

Chapter 5: In the last decades, factories have suffered a significant change in automation, evolving from isolated towards interconnected systems. However, the adoption of open standards and the opening to the Internet have caused an increment in the number of attacks. In addition, traditional Intrusion Detection Systems relying on a signature database, where malware patterns are stored, are failing due to the high specialization of industrial cyberattacks. For this reason, the research community is moving towards the Anomaly Detection paradigm. This paradigm is showing great results when it is implemented using Machine Learning and Deep Learning techniques. This chapter surveys several incidents caused by cyberattacks targeting industrial scenarios. Next, to understand the current status of anomaly detection solutions, it analyses the current industrial datasets and anomaly detection systems in the industrial field. In addition, the chapter shows an example of malware attacking a manufacturing plant, resulting in a safety threat. Finally, cybersecurity and safety solutions are reviewed.

Chapter 6: Considering the situation when the node which is entering in the network is an a malicious node then it can check and record the various operations of the network which could be responsible for some serious security issues. In order to safeguard the network we are hereby proposing an approach which is in view of the advanced encoding strategy, termed as Convolution coding approach. According to the requirement of network, the initial bits are assigned and by applying the convolution technique, the final code is generated for each and every node. Considering the fact that it is a digital method, the codes can be represented by using the binary number system. All the nodes which are a part of the network will be having their corresponding final binary code, say C. The verification of each node is carried out by matching the generated code C with the security code within a particular time period before transmitting the data. This process enables the detection of malicious or attacker node. Furthermore to enhance the versatility and execution, the system is organized into clusters.

Chapter 7: In real-scenario, we have a large multicast group where node leaves and joins occur frequently, and also the number of nodes leaving and joining is also not proportionate. Hence Scalable rekeying process is an important issue that needs to be concerned for the Secured Group communication for dynamic groups. In basic rekeying scheme which is based on the logical key hierarchy, the rekeying cost depends on the logarithm of the size of group for a join or depart request by the user. However, the memory efficiency of this Group Rekeying protocol (GREP) is a huge storage overhead over the system. We aim to provide a survey of various group key management schemes and then propose an efficient scalable solution based on linked LKH and the linked List data structure. Results have shown that show that the Linked LKH algorithm has a very low effective cost for rekeying the LKH as compared to the basic LKH algorithm i.e. based on the number of new joined and departure requests.

Chapter 8: This chapter introduces a new kind of cybersecurity system named Botnet Defense System (BDS) that defends an IoT system against malicious botnets. This chapter consists of two parts. The former part describes the concept and design of the BDS. The concept is "fight fire with fire". To realize the concept, the BDS uses bot technology. The BDS builds a white-hat botnet on the IoT system by itself and uses it to exterminate the malicious botnets. The white-hat botnet autonomously spreads over the IoT system and thus drastically increases the defense ability. The latter part explains the strategy of the BDS. The white-hat botnet is a so-called double-edge sword. It defends the IoT system against malicious botnet but wastes the system's resources. Therefore, the BDS should strategically use the white-hat botnet. Some strategies have been proposed. Their characteristics are discussed through the simulation with the agent-oriented Petri nets.

Chapter 9: The Internet of Things is a cutting-edge technology that is vulnerable to all sorts of fictitious solutions. As a new phase of computing emerges in the digital world, it intends to produce a huge number of smart gadgets that can host a wide range of applications and operations. IoT gadgets are a perfect target for cyber assaults because of their wide dispersion, availability/accessibility and top-notch computing power. Furthermore, as numerous IoT devices gather and investigate private data, they become a gold mine for hostile actors. Hence, the matter of fact is that security, particularly the potential to diagnose compromised nodes, as well as the collection and preservation of testimony of an attack or illegal activity, have become top priorities. This article delves into the timeline and the most challenging security and privacy issues that exist in the present scenario. In addition to this, some open issues and future research directions are also discussed.

Chapter 10: In recent years, the growth of Brain-Computer Interfaces (BCIs) has been remarkable in specific application fields, such as the medical sector or the entertainment industry. Most of these fields use evoked potentials, like P300, to obtain neural data able to handle prostheses or achieve greater immersion experience in videogames. The natural use of BCI involves the management of sensitive users' information as behaviors, emotions or thoughts. In this context, new security breaches in BCI are offering cybercriminals the possibility of collecting sensitive data and affecting subjects' physical integrity, which are critical issues. For all these reasons, the fact of applying efficient cybersecurity mechanisms has become a main challenge. To improve this challenge, this chapter proposes a framework able to detect cyberattacks affecting one of the most typical scenarios of BCI, the generation of P300 through visual stimuli. A pool of experiments demonstrates the performance of the proposed framework.

Chapter 11: Blockchain since 2009 has been gaining more popularity in various fields to use in numerous applications to overcome the security issues such as privacy, transparency, and mutability of data in process of data sharing. Process of data sharing has many addressed and unaddressed challenges such as information encryption and decryption, data authentication, storage security, latency time, transfer speed of data, detecting malicious nodes, prevent the computer system from attacks, trust in the sharing process. In this paper, we have reviewed the data sharing paper based on blockchain technology and presented the analysis of various techniques used in the information sharing process. Our comprehensive analysis is categorizing in the following areas like incentive mechanism-based work, IoT-based data sharing, healthcare data sharing, and Internet of vehicle data sharing using blockchain

Chapter 12: Node capture attack is one of the crucial attacks in wireless sensor network (WSN) that seizes the node physically and withdraws the confidential data from the node's memory. The chapter exploits the adversarial behavior during a node capture to build an attack model. We also propose a Fruit Fly Optimization Algorithm (FFOA) that is a multi-objective optimization algorithm that consists of a number of objectives for capturing a node in the network: maximum node contribution, maximum key contributions are some examples of the same. The aim is to demolish the maximum part of the network while minimizing the cost and maximizing attacking efficiency. Due to the multi-objective function, we attain a maximum fraction of compromised traffic, lower attacking rounds, and lower energy cost as contrasted with other node capture attack algorithms. We have developed an algorithm, which is an enhanced version of FFOA and has even better efficiency than FFOA

Chapter 13: Brain-Computer Interfaces (BCIs) have experienced a considerable evolution in the last decade, expanding from clinical scenarios to sectors such as entertainment or video games. Nevertheless, this popularization makes them a target for cyberattacks like malware. Current literature lacks comprehensive works focusing on cybersecurity applied to BCIs and, mainly, publications performing a rigorous analysis of the risks and weaknesses that these interfaces present. If not studied properly, these potential vulnerabilities could dramatically impact users' data, service availability, and, most importantly, users' safety. Because of that, this work introduces an evaluation of the risk that each BCI classification already defined in the literature presents to raise awareness between the readers of this chapter about the potential threat that BCIs can generate in the next years if comprehensive measures, based on standard mechanisms, are not adopted. Moreover, it seeks to alert academic and industrial stakeholders about the impact these risks could have on future BCI hardware and software.

Acknowledgment

Many people have contributed greatly to this book on Advances in Malware and Data-Driven Network Security. We, the editors, would like to acknowledge all of them for their valuable help and generous ideas in improving the quality of this book. With our feelings of gratitude, we would like to introduce them in turn. The first mention is the authors and reviewers of each chapter of this book. Without their outstanding expertise, constructive reviews and devoted effort, this comprehensive book would become something without contents. The second mention is the IGI Global staff for their constant encouragement, continuous assistance and untiring support. Without their technical support, this book would not be completed. The third mention is the editor's family for being the source of continuous love, unconditional support and prayers not only for this work, but throughout our life. Last but far from least, we express our heartfelt thanks to the Almighty for bestowing over us the courage to face the complexities of life and complete this work.

Brij B. Gupta
October 1, 2021

Chapter 1
Machine Learning for Malware Analysis:
Methods, Challenges, and Future Directions

Krishna Yadav
National Institute of Technology, Kurukshetra, India

Aarushi Sethi
National Institute of Technology, Kurukshetra, India

Mavneet Kaur
National Institute of Technology, Kurukshetra, India

Dragan Perakovic
(iD) https://orcid.org/0000-0002-0476-9373
University of Zagreb, Croatia

ABSTRACT

Companies and organizations are collecting all sorts of data ranging from nominal feedback like customer reviews to highly classified data like medical records. With data being such a critical aspect of most of the operations around us, cybercriminals are looking for an opportunity to misuse this information. One such device that cybercriminals use to further their malicious intent is malware. Over the years, these cybercriminals have become immensely powerful using the knowledge of previous attacks. Hence, malware analysis and methods to troubleshoot the problems arising due to malware attacks is the need of the hour. Over time, different new approaches have been developed to defend malware. However, in recent times, machine learning-based malware analysis has gained popularity. The capacity to detect possible future malware by learning from existing malware patterns makes this method very popular. In this chapter, the authors have introduced different malware and the machine learning-based approach that has been developed in recent times to mitigate malware.

DOI: 10.4018/978-1-7998-7789-9.ch001

Copyright © 2022, IGI Global. Copying or distributing in print or electronic forms without written permission of IGI Global is prohibited.

INTRODUCTION

Malware or malicious software is an umbrella term that comprises all the software that is designed with the purpose of corrupting or harming any program, device, service, or network. Once malware penetrates through the network and gets access to the files, it may infect or corrupt the data, steal the data or even use it for identity thefts. With IoT rapidly becoming a reality, more and more devices are being connected, which means that if one device in a system gets infected (Sharmeen, Shaila, 2019), all the other devices are at risk of being infected as well. The trend of the number of major cyberattacks over the years is pretty sporadic. However, with the introduction of machine learning models, there has been quite a downfall for the past two years (2019 and 2020), with the drop in the number of malware attacks going down by 43.3%. These machine learning models range from probabilistic to decision tree-based to deep neural networks. Over the years, numerous types of malware have been created that work in different ways to harm your files. Knowing what type of malware has infected your network is extremely helpful in order to find suitable techniques for patching.

There are various kinds of malware available these days. Figure 1 gives a pictorial representation of different types of malware. One of them is a computer virus (UCCI, Daniele, 2019). Computer viruses are one of the most common malware. They usually come attached to a file. Once the file is opened, it corrupts the system by transferring from one programme to another. It can transfer through programmes, computers, and even networks. Computer viruses can spread by email, text message attachments, audio files, etc. The next category of malware is worms. Unlike viruses, worms do not require any action by the victim; they replicate themselves by finding loopholes in the security of the software or operating system. The main purpose of worms is to destroy the files that it has access to and make them unusable by using certain encryption or corruption techniques.

Figure 1. Types of malware

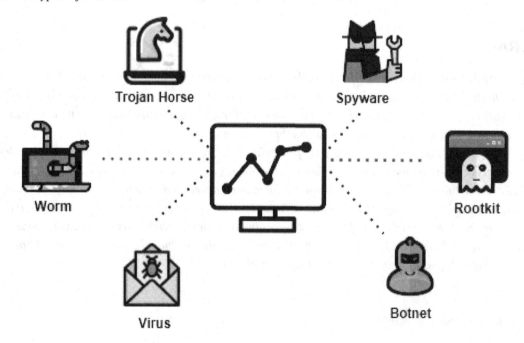

Further knowledge of specific footprints of each malware can be useful. These footprints or signatures of a malware lead to the detection of patterns which can be picked up by machine learning algorithms. This topic is beyond the scope of this chapter but G. Cabau, M. Buhu (2016) can be referred for more information.

These days every nation is growing rapidly in terms of technologies, transportation, health, etc. Organizations are competing against each other and are very curious to know what others are doing. Some organizations develop malware to spy on other systems, which are known as Trojans. Trojans disguise themselves as harmless files, but once it gains access to your files, it can spy on the victim's activities, steal data from the device or crash entire programmes. It can affect the performance of the computer system by slowing it down, increasing the number of pop-ups, installation of new, unfamiliar software, increase in the number of spam, etc. Another form of malware is spyware which is not as harmful as trojan, and the main objective is to spy on its victim's activities. Even the most menial tasks like the webpages that a user uses can be highly valuable data for an attacker. Further, it can send back sensitive financial, medical, or personal information that may be used for fraud, stealing, identity theft, etc. These software are usually installed onto the devices without explicit permission or knowledge of the user.

When an attack is performed to infect a wide range of systems connected in a network, then botnets are used. Botnets are malware that taps into the network of connected devices like mobile phones, computers, and other smart devices that are connected through IoT technology. It then gains remote access to all these devices, and the hacker may use it for malpractices. Several DoS/DDoS attacks in history have been carried out with botnets. Another type of malware is a rootkit which is programmed in such a way that it penetrates the network easily to get access to the computer system and then allows access to other, more dangerous malware. If a computer is infected with rootkit malware, then hackers can execute commands remotely and change the configuration of the system. As data is a very important part of any organization, these days, hackers are targeting the data of different organizations. A malware called ransomware is widely being used to infect a system and encrypt all its data. The data can only be recovered if the key is entered, which is provided by the hackers if the organization becomes ready to pay an amount known as ransom to these hackers.

In the rest of the section, section 2 describes various malware detection approaches that have been developed till now. Section 3 discusses various machine learning algorithms, the feature extraction process, and required datasets for malware analysis. Section 4 discusses the challenges involved in using machine learning algorithms in malware analysis. Section 5 discusses the future directions, and finally, section 6 discusses possible integration of recent emerging topics in AI for malware detection. Finally, section 7 concludes the paper.

MALWARE DETECTION APPROACH

Since malware can inversely infect the health of a computer system or network, it is important to invest in quality anti-virus softwares. These anti-virus softwares are based on the two major malware detection methods namely - signature based detection and heuristic based detection. Another technique for memory based detection is also being developed, but it is a relatively novel concept.

Signature Based Detection

Currently, the majority of the antivirus available use signature-based methods for malware detection (Sathyanarayan, V. Sai, 2008). This technique comprises capturing a typical signature from the malware and using this knowledge to handle similar malwares. A signature is a unique footprint or pattern used by a malware to attack the system. This may be a unique sequence of bytes or a file hash. This technique has been used since the development of the first antivirus softwares, but it has its share of advantages and disadvantages. One of the major advantages that play a pivotal role in making this technique so popular is that it is very fast and efficient. The pre-existing knowledge of this footprint also factors into a low false positive rate in general. The main disadvantage of such an approach is that it does not work well with newly released malware, and it is not effective against obfuscation. Obfuscation (Wroblewski, Gregory, 2002) is a process adopted by attackers to render the pre-existing code illegible or hard to read while maintaining its functionality. It prevents the malware from being detected but at the same time disrupts the execution of the victim's programme. Some of the obfuscation techniques are - changing the look of the programme while keeping the same functionality using dead code insertion, integrating the malware in the victim's programme using code insertion methods, switching or reassigning the registers.

Heuristic Based Detection

Heuristic based detection techniques were developed as a response to signature based detection techniques, specifically its shortcomings (Bazrafshan, Zahra, 2013). Unlike signature based detection, which is developed on the concept of comparison, heuristic based detection mechanisms run the files in a carefully orchestrated and/or monitored environment to detect anomalies and malwares. It is also effective against polymorphic viruses because of the aforementioned property. In this method, the behaviour of the malware is analyzed during the training or learning process, and the files are categorized as malicious or legitimate based on the learning. This is the testing phase. This concept of training and testing incorporates well with the training-testing structure of machine learning. The ability to learn and adapt gives this technique an edge when it comes to zero-day malwares. However, the same property can be disadvantageous as well as it has higher false positive rates. This technique also takes way longer than signature based detection.

Heuristic based detection makes use of machine learning models to predict the malicious or corrupt components. This process and steps involved in it are discussed in great detail.

MACHINE LEARNING FOR MALWARE ANALYSIS

Since malware is a diverse term, machine learning can be used to uncover various hidden patterns, and various deductions can be made by making use of the same data but different features. Machine learning-based malware analysis comprises three different steps, which are represented in figure 2. In the first step, i.e., Malware detection (Idiaka, Nwokedi, 2007) and (Siddiqui, Muazzam, 2008), the goal is to determine whether a given sample is malicious or benign. Such models form the basis of many complex machine learning solutions as the very first step to analyse malware analysis is determining whether a file poses any threat to the security of a system. Malware category detection (Siddiqui, Muazzam, 2008) is determining what type of malware has been encountered. This is one of the most important types of malware analysis as each malware needs to be handled differently depending on its mode of operation and method of attack. Each malware has different footprints which can be utilized to detect its type. Malware comparison, as the name suggests, is comparing how different or similar a sample is to a certain type of malware or is it a variant of a type of malware or not. It is especially useful against new malwares as any similarity to certain malware may be useful for developing a patch against it.

Figure 2. Common objectives for malware analysis

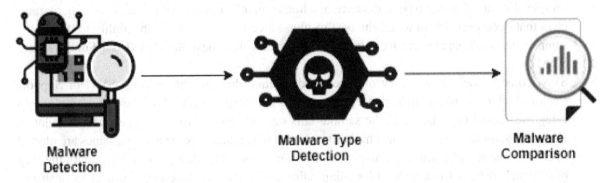

Malware
Detection

Malware Type
Detection

Malware
Comparison

Machine Learning Methods

In machine learning, the dataset is used to train a model using an algorithm that helps in predicting the outcome of a proposed sample. This is a little different than rule-based classification because the model is not a set of predefined rules, rather it is adaptive, and it learns with each new sample. Given the objectives, classification models (Liu, 2017) are a clear choice. The classification can either be malicious or benign files for malware detection, classifying the malwares into types or simply classifying a sample into high, medium, low categories based on its similarity or difference to specific type of malware. The possibilities are endless, and the categories can be modified based on the need. However, the three examples mentioned above are by far the most common types of classification prevalent in researches that focus on malware analytics. The three main types of machine learning are - supervised, unsupervised and reinforcement learning, out of which the first two are more popular at the moment. Supervised machine learning comprises a set of training and testing data with the output of the training data labeled. Whereas in unsupervised machine learning, the output sets are not labeled. Many machine learning algorithms and their effectiveness in this scenario are discussed below. These techniques include KNN, SVM, Logistic regression, Random Forest, Naive-Bayes, Gradient Boosting decision trees, etc. for supervised machine learning and for unsupervised machine learning, k-means clustering, hierarchical clustering, etc. are described. Apart from these machine learning algorithms, deep learning algorithms like Artificial Neural Network, Convolutional Neural Network, and Recurrent Neural Network are being used for complex purposes like malware similarity and difference as they are efficient when it comes to working with non-linear, images or sequential data.

A few common machine learning algorithms and how they are used for malware detection are discussed down below.

1. **KNN**

   This is a supervised machine learning algorithm. KNN or K Nearest Neighbours model is based on the concept of clustering using distance. In this method, imagine the features to be the axes of a multidimensional plane. Each of the samples is plotted on the multidimensional plane. The proximity of these samples is used to define their clusters or categories in which the output is divided. The criteria of proximity is calculated by the distance. The distance of a sample to the cluster is measured between the sample and the centroid of the cluster, which is also called the cluster head. In this method, K i.e., the number of neighbours to be considered for assigning a cluster to a given sample, distance, i.e., the type of distance- euclidean, manhattan etc. are some of the hyperparameters that need to be tuned to get the best results. Since this process has the ability to divide the samples into multiple clusters, it can be used to determine the type of malware (Choi, Sunoh, 2020).

2. **SVM**

   SVM comes under the category of supervised machine learning algorithms. SVM or Support Vector Machine is based on the concept of defining a hyperplane and classifying the samples into categories based on which side the sample falls on with respect to said hyperplane. Similar to KNN, the samples are plotted on a multidimensional plane, and optimized hyperplanes are plotted to classify the samples into categories. The division is done into multiple categories with the help of a kernel. A kernel is a method for using a linear classifier to solve non-linear classifications. In SVM, the main hyperparameters are type of kernel- polynomial, linear, rbf, etc and C, i.e., the penalty parameter. This is also a method capable of effective multi-class classification and can be used for malware type, similarity, difference, etc.

3. **Logistic Regression**

   This is a supervised machine learning algorithm. Logistic Regression is a model that is more often than not used for binary classification. It predicts the output in the form of the probability of class 0 using the log probability formula. Since this model is generally used for binary classification, it can be effective only in malware detection of benign and malicious classes.

4. **K-Means Clustering**

   K-means clustering is loosely related to K Nearest Neighbour, i.e., it classifies a sample based on its proximity with the centroid of a cluster, but this is an unsupervised machine learning algorithm, i.e., inferences are only made based on the input vectors and not the labels assigned to them. In this algorithm, K, which is the number of clusters, is a hyperparameter. Since output labels are not necessary for such algorithms to function, such models can be effective in scenarios where the output is uncertain or unavailable. Such scenarios are common in context to new variants, and types of malwares as their effect on the environment have not already been analyzed properly (Feizollah, Ali, 2014).

   Other popular algorithms are naive-bayes, decision trees based, ensemble, hierarchical clustering, etc. All of these algorithms can be useful in various aspects of malware detection using machine learning. Algorithms like KNN and SVM are extremely effective when it comes to the types and variance in malware. Logistic Regression comes in handy when we want to differentiate between malicious and benign files. Unsupervised learning algorithms like K-Means clustering can be used for critical and unknown files. Authors at (Shhadat, Ihab, Amena Hayajneh, 2020) have used different machine learning algorithms for malware detection on the same benchmark dataset. The results obtained is presented in table 1.

Although machine learning algorithms are very successful in detecting malware, these days, different deep learning algorithms like CNN(Convolution Neural Network) and autoencoders have also been very efficient. Authors at (Ganesh, Meenu, 2017) have presented that information can be obtained from the application of smartphones to and can be converted to images for applying CNN. They have scanned several apk files and decompiled using a parser and disassembler. The disassemble file is a .xml file which is later used to make an image of vector size 12*12. This image acts as an input for the CNN algorithm. They have obtained an accuracy of 95%. Finding good features to prepare a dataset to train deep learning algorithms can sometimes be time-consuming. Additionally, ineffective features might be generated through some poor feature engineering processes. To solve the problem, authors at (M. Yousefi-Azar, 2017) have used autoencoders to generate machine-generated features. Autoencoder generates features by distributing the dataset into some lower-dimensional space and trying to reconstruct the original data from the learned features set. Authors, with the help of experiments, have demonstrated that unsupervised algorithms like autoencoders can generate better discriminative features than traditional feature engineering processes.

Table 1. Comparison of machine learning algorithms

Classifier	Binary Classification Accuracy	Multiclass Classification Accuracy
K Nearest Neighbours	96.1%	88%
Support Vector Machine	96.1%	88.6%
Bernoulli Naive - Bayes	91%	91.8%
Random Forest	97.8%	95.8%
Hard Voting	97%	92%
Logistic Regression	95%	90%
Decision Trees	97.8%	92%

After defining a model and compiling it, it is trained on the dataset. After training the model, it can be used to predict the outcome.

Figure 3 represents an end-to-end approach (Kaspersky, 2021) to using machine learning to build a model for malware analysis. Usually, a large amount of raw data needs to be extracted and processed if the process of analyzing starts from scratch. The raw data is still in the form of complex data structures. These features can be sandbox logs, disassembler logs, etc. These features can be extracted in a pre-execution phase and should be done in a high-computation environment. These 'heavy-computation' features are highly effective in predicting the presence or absence of a model in file. A large-scale model can be created that predicts the same. The large scale or general model is used to divide the files into harmful and benign. Once they are broadly categorised, 'lighter' features from the suspicious files are extracted for further inspection. The light-computation features are fille structure, content statistics, API, etc. The outcome of these models can be used for specific, more objective driven purposes like detecting the type or class of malware, whether it is a variant or not, etc., to make a new model. Once this model is created and trained, it can be used for the purpose of prediction. This model is updated regularly and is adaptable as new malware requires new information. Machine learning provides a holistic product as our model is not just dependent on predefined information. It learns as new files are encountered.

Figure 3. Depicting the high-level steps for a machine learning analysis

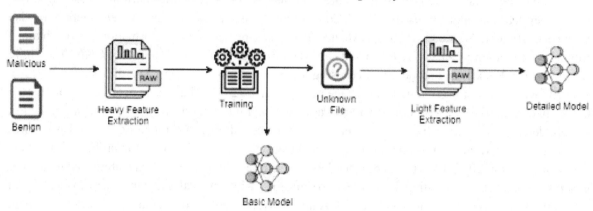

Datasets

The datasets used for malware can be structured in such a way that they classify a sample as malicious or benign, or it can be used to classify the type of malware that has attacked/ is being observed. The datasets can be obtained from public sources, security setup providers, sandboxed analysis service providers like Malware DB, VX Heaven, or VirusShare repository. Various organizations do machine-learning-based malware analysis by creating their own datasets. Due to such problems, there are very few malware based-datasets available publicly. However, institutes like UNB have made various efforts to publicly share such datasets. Malware in android mobiles is increasing at an alarming rate. Considering this situation, UNB has developed CCCS-CIC-AndMal-2020 dataset that comprises 200K benign and 200K malware samples that further includes 14 prominent malware with 191 eminent malware families (D. Sean, B. Li, 2021). The CICMalDroid 2020 is a dataset that contains over 17,341 malware samples (S. Mahdavifar, A.Firtriah, 2020). The dataset was collected between December 2017 to December 2018. It contains five different categories of malware, i.e., Adware, Banking malware, SMS malware, Riskware and Benign. CIC-InvesAndMal2019 is another malware dataset created that includes permissions and intents as static features and API calls along with generated log files as dynamic features (Laya Taheri, 2019). Besides those features, they have also added features such as battery states, packages, process logs, log states, etc. Another CIC-AndMal2017 is an android-based malware dataset that contains more than 10, 854 samples (A.H Lashkari, 2018). Researchers have collected around six thousand apps from google play and extracted the features that contain four different malware classes, i.e., Adware, Ransomware, Scareware, SMS Malware.

If large companies with huge data repositories are developing a model, they prefer to use the in-house data to train the model while simultaneously keeping a check on the security of their own network. E.g., Microsoft created a dataset of more than 500,000 malicious files and shared it as a public dataset. The most popular types of datasets are malware detection datasets that classify a given sample as malicious or benign (A.H Lashkari, 2018). The benign samples are the harmless, legitimate files or programmes. However, Internet Service Providers (ISPs), honeypots, and Computer Emergency Response Teams (CERTs) developed both benign and malicious datasets for the public in order to analyze the other aspects and properties of malware as well. When it comes to malware detection datasets, the ratio of number of benign samples to number of malware samples is quite large, which may lead to the development of a biased model. To overcome this problem, techniques such as undersampling or oversampling (Pang, Ying, 2019), the latter more than the former, may be made use of to balance the number of samples. Authors at (D.Gavrilut, 2009), have categorized malware dataset into, training, test and scale-up dataset. The categorized dataset is represented in table 2.

Table 2. Categorization of dataset

Database	Files		Unique Combinations	
	Malware	Clean	Malware	Clean
Training	27475	273133	7822	415
Test	11605	6522	506	130
Scale - up	approx. 3M	approx. 180M	12817	16437

Feature Extraction

When it comes to extracting features (Sihawal, 2018) that are best suited for a specific problem, there are three types of feature extraction methods - static, dynamic, and hybrid analysis.

Static

For such analysis, PE or Portable Executable files do not need to be run in order for features to be extracted from them. For a PE file to be examined and analysed for feature extraction, tools like IDA Pro, OllyDbg, Exeinfo PE, PEstudio are used to disassemble them and extract information about the malware, receive instructions and pick up on patterns. Some of the static features that are commonly used are API calls, string signature, control flow graph (CFG), opcode (operation codes) frequency, and byte sequence n-grams. These have been discussed further in detail later on.

Dynamic

In such analysis, the PE files do not need to be disassembled for analysis. They are analyzed by running them in a controlled, monitored environment. This is really effective against obfuscated and polymorphic or zero-day viruses that use methods that are different or variations of pre-existing malwares. However, as the model is constantly being developed or updated, it takes a long time and a lot of computation to train the model. Hence, such a setup can be problematic in time sensitive environments. Features like API calls, API sequences or file system registry can be obtained using dynamic techniques like function call monitoring, function parameter analysis, instruction traces, and information flow tracking. As mentioned before, for dynamic analysis the files are monitored in a controlled and monitored environment. This environment can be generated with the help of emulators, debuggers, simulators or virtual machines. The challenges faced during the creation of the environment are discussed in a later section.

Hybrid

Hybrid analysis is performed by making use of both, static and dynamic features. This approach has been proved more effective than static and dynamic analysis as it makes use of the advantages and disadvantages of static and dynamic features to create a balanced model for the proposed problem.

Features Description

A good set of features can boost the accuracy of machine learning algorithms for malware analysis. The popular features (11) used for malware analysis are discussed below.

Byte Sequence

Byte sequence is a static feature. While searching for footprints of a malware, specific byte sequences that are found in a sequence can lead to the recognition of a corrupted or malicious file. The distinction can be based on the byte size or certain characteristic strings called n-grams.

N-Gram

N-gram is a static feature. It is a subsequence of a prominent sequence that has been divided into chunks of size n. The number of n-grams that are present in a sequence are extracted as a feature for analysis. Malwares can be identified based on the number of n-grams found in a suspicious sample in combination with other features. N-grams of size no more than three are preferred by researchers.

Opcode

Opcodes are extracted through static analysis. Opcodes or operation codes are designed to identify the machine level operations that are executed by the PE files. Opcodes are a very common feature as they extract the frequency of opcodes in a sample or its similarity and difference to another sequence to detect the presence or absence of malware. These machine level operations can further be divided into mathematical instructions, program sequencing and control instructions, instructions for accessing memory etc.

String

This feature can be extracted through static analysis. While looking for the presence of a malware, characteristic strings like author name, file names, typical code fragments, etc., are searched in order to identify the footprint.

Network Activity

This feature comes under the category of dynamic features. Network analysis can reveal a lot of important information. Monitoring used protocols, HTTP/HTTPs requests, security firewalls, TCP/UDP ports, etc., can be useful in determining the conditions where the health of a computer network is compromised.

The incoming and outgoing traffic of a sample can be monitored in order to be alerted if suspicious fluctuations are taking place.

API and System Calls

This is one of the few features that can be extracted both through static and dynamic analysis. These can be extracted through disassembling the PE file and obtaining the information about all the calls that are going to be executed once the file is run, or it can be run in a secure, observed environment to get the knowledge of the execution calls. The amount of data that is obtained by extracting this feature is massive, and therefore often, preprocessing techniques are used to break it down to simpler formats that are easy to access and read. One of the more common formats is control flow graph. A control flow graph (CFG) is a directional graph that depicts the flow of calls in a programme. Like a usual graph it uses nodes and edges to convert the list of calls into a graphical format.

CPU Registers

This feature comes under the category of static feature analysis. It can be extracted such that the values stored in a register, the number of registers, the re-assignment of registers, or the presence of a hidden or unwanted register can be recorded.

File Characteristic or System

This can be a static or dynamic feature. It is important to have knowledge about which files are running which operational commands and the interaction of these commands of a particular sample with the environment. The information that can be mined from this data covers a lot of ground. It includes information like how a file is read or modified in the environment, which files belong to which directory or repository, the frequency of presence of a sample file in infected and non-infected systems, how a certain sample is deleted from the environment. This can easily be extracted while a simulated or virtual environment is created using sandbox services and memory analysis toolkits. Using static analysis, the PE files can be examined for sections, imported symbols, or compilers preferred for execution.

In recent developments, another subset of Machine learning - reinforcement learning is becoming popular for feature selection. This is an upgrade from the traditional machine learning techniques that require human input to function. Furthermore, these techniques only help in detecting single view features. With Reinforcement learning, multiview features can be taken into consideration and variants of multiple malware can be detected. (Z. Fang, 2019) proposes a Deep Q-learning based Feature Selection Architecture that trains its model on the basis of its interaction with the feature space.

These are just a few features that can be used for preparing a dataset for the model to train on. Several specific features can also be generated using machine learning techniques that are in relevance to certain objectives. Keep in mind that too many features can overcomplicate things and the model might not fit onto generic data. On the other hand, less features can lead to lack of information for the model to extract patterns. Hence, it is vital for us to select the appropriate number of features to be used. Feature selection techniques like correlation come handy in this scenario.

Model Evaluation

In highly sensitive matters like that of malware detection, it is very important to have a good, appropriate model as even one corrupt file can infect a lot of valuable data. Here are few of the criteria a model should fulfil in order for it to be called good.

It Should be Trained on a Proper Dataset

It is very important for our model to be trained on a large dataset to have high accuracy. If our dataset is not large enough, it might now be able to extract enough information to build a model that does not fit well with the training or testing dataset. Hence, our dataset should be large enough to contain diverse cases that help in not developing a bias towards specific recurring cases. However, our dataset should also not have too many features that may lead to overfitting. In such a case, our model does well with the training dataset but doesn't do good enough with the testing dataset. Hence our dataset on which we train our model should be optimum.

Algorithm and Model Should be Adaptable to the Latest Malware

Since new malwares are being developed by writers everyday, it is important for our model to respond properly to the latest attacks. Not only are there new types of malware, but also companies are producing new benign files to be up-to-date with the latest technology. Hence, it is also important for our model to recognize a new benign sample as much as it is to recognize a malicious one. The algorithms should be adjustable and flexible and our model needs to be adaptable to new changes while retraining. The new datasets must also contain the latest samples so that the model can extract information and learn from them while retraining.

False Positives Rate Must be Low

When a harmless file is labeled as malicious, that outcome is labeled as a false positive. False positives may occur under various circumstances like our model is not trained on a proper dataset, or new types of benign files are being generated and fed to the model that it is unable to recognise and label properly. A false positive may end up being as harmful as a malicious file as a lot of important information may be lost due to one mis-classification. Therefore, It is important for a model to have a low false rate and in an ideal scenario it tends to zero.

CHALLENGES IN MACHINE LEARNING-BASED MALWARE ANALYSIS

Machine learning-based malware analysis has brought a great revolution in detecting malware; however, it is still not fully developed. There are many challenges associated with this approach. Some of them are described below.

Anti-Analyzation Techniques Incorporated by Malware Writers

Since malware authors are aware of malware detection softwares, they are actively using the knowledge to create techniques that help a malware go unnoticed by them (Gibert, 2020). For static analysis, they prefer techniques like obfuscation, packaging or encryption to hide the information regarding the malware. A solution to these techniques is dynamic analysis. During dynamic analysis these files can be de-obfuscated, unpacked or decrypted while being monitored in a controlled environment. A more advanced anti-analyzation technique is environmental awareness. In this technique, the malware is designed such that it knows when the file is being run for inspection. This is most commonly prevalent in an environment that is set up on virtual machines, sandboxes etc. due to the files that are installed for their setup or the mode that they run in. The malware instantly recognizes when it is being run in a monitored environment and stops the execution of malicious payload. An alternative approach can be time-based execution. In this technique the malicious payload is set up such that it only runs on specific dates and time. Another option for malware authors is user interaction based. In this technique, the malicious payload is only run when a user interacts with a file in a previously defined manner. These challenging techniques need to be addressed head on while malware analysis as they are becoming more and more popular among attackers due to their success rate. One counter-technique identified by researchers is by using binary reverse engineering such as function similarity identification to realize the presence of de-obfuscating, unpacking or decrypting techniques.

Operation Set and Feature Selection

Operations such as Opcodes, instructions, APIs and system calls, etc., are valuable features for the prediction of a malicious sample. But by disintegrating raw data into simpler data structures, the outcome may result in a large number of features to be trained on. If the number of features go beyond an optimum number, our model will not turn out to be generalized enough and may suffer from what is called the 'curse of dimensionality'. At the same time, losing some of the features may lead to loss of important information and resulting in error. This challenge can be addressed by using better feature selection techniques or changing the type of algorithm used, but sometimes it is not feasible to change the initial structure of a model. In such cases program analysis advances can be used to improve the accuracy of the disassemblers and decompilers as they have a higher error rate during dynamic analysis than the operations during the static analysis. Hence methods that improve the quality of disassemblers and decompilers can be used. A hybrid of both can also be considered for improving the overall quality.

FUTURE DIRECTION

Automated Generation of Malware

Nowadays malware authors are using auto-generative tools to build out new malware and their variants at a rapid speed (Zarras, 2014). This is quite worrisome for the organizations dealing with critical, sensitive and high frequency data as the frequency of input might not give enough time for a solution to a day zero malware. A proposed solution to this problem can be building models advanced enough to suggest solutions to a given problem. This is a predictive maintenance solution as it allows not only the file to be separated but also a possible method to navigate through a corrupted system. Further, public sandboxes and repositories can be used to keep the dataset updated with the latest malware that has been detected. This solution is the one that can be implemented in the near future as the field of predictive maintenance still needs a lot of development before it can be considered as a reality.

Malware Attribution

Another method that is gaining momentum these days is the method of identifying the malware by the author of the file, i.e., the attribution of a technique to its author (Gupta, 2019). It is quite an unusual method, but researches have shown that the possibilities of the type of malware can be streamlined to a great extent if the author of a malicious code is revealed. The used programming language, IP addresses, and URLs that have been included or the style of the comments and/or code that has been used to develop a malicious payload can be used to identify the author (Gupta, Brij B, 2021). Some authors want to be boastful of their developments and try to leave an encrypted signature behind in their codes. These can be some useful clues to figure out the author or the ATP group that is behind certain malware. However, the dependence of this technique on finding the source code using leaks or public disclosures makes it unreliable, at least in the near future, but once a concrete development is made in this direction, this method can be revolutionary in the field of malware analysis.

Prediction of Future Variants

Generating variants is a simpler task for attackers in comparison to developing a whole new malware as it requires just a few changes to develop a new, stronger variant of a malware (Yamaguchi (2021)). Attackers use this to their advantage as it enables them to continuously attack their target in rapid succession. This may lead to weakening of the strength of the security system of an organization and at the same time corruption of important files. Researchers are developing solutions using machine learning that aim at being effective against all the possible variants of a malware without necessarily being developed first (Gou, Z, 2017).

Prioritizing the Malware

While all malwares have malicious intentions, some are more harmful to others. Hence, it is important to determine the level of urgency for each malware especially when dealing with sensitive data. The level of urgency can be based on several factors like extent of damage, number of days since it was launched or other local factors specific to the data. This can lead to faster results and less computational costs.

Developing a Basic Solution for all Malware

While this is a far-fetched trend, researchers are trying to figure out a solution that helps in preventing any sort of malware from attacking. Discovering a common factor would mean that a common solution for all the malware would be possible (Gou, Z, 2017). Such solutions also have a better chance at being adaptive to new malware. However, this is still far from reality as the types of malware discovered, all of them have quite distinctive footprints and ways of corrupting computer networks. None-the-less, researchers are hopeful regarding this approach.

Application with Latest Techniques

1. Integration of AI and Deep Learning Techniques

A rapidly growing niche of machine learning is deep learning. Deep Learning networks make use of artificial neural networks that are specialized in picking up on complex, non-linear patterns that machine learning algorithms may miss out on. CNN can be used to project the features as an image and predict the outcomes. RNN may be used to suggest the next step in a sequence of attacks by the malware. Furthermore, advanced ML techniques like reinforcement learning are becoming popular as, if successful, they are better at handling sensitive files.

2. Integration of IoT and Cloud Computing

Internet of Things and Cloud Computing have led to a revolutionaliation of data and how it is collected. However, since most of the passage of data in IoT is via the internet, the chances of being attacked by Malware have become higher. In techniques like federated learning, where the updated weights, if corrupted, can ruin the final result of other devices as well. Hence, malware analysis systems that use machine learning should be established along with IoT devices for their protection. Furthermore, the concept of IoT can itself be used to advance the results of malware analysis. Federated learning can be used to collect the information about other attacks as well that will help in building a better, diverse model. (Zekri, 2017) describes in great detail the DDoS or Distributed Denial of Service Attacks that use multiple attackers to attack innocent computers, capture them using bugs and security discrepancies and then use the majority of the victim's cloud bandwidth to send a large amount of packets and data. Though this signature can be detected quite easily using prior knowledge if the malware is present in native form, zero-day malware goes undetected if machine learning is not used instead of conventional detection methods.

CONCLUSION

Since data is becoming such an important commodity, attacks on data are also becoming more severe and destructive. We have learnt about malware, malware detection methods and types of malware. Further we have discussed some feature extraction techniques followed by a brief introduction of some of the important features. Some of the popular machine learning algorithms have been discussed in the further section. It is followed by some pointers that describe the qualities of a good machine learning model that have to be kept in mind while constructing one. It is important to be aware of some of the difficulties one might face while attempting to build a machine learning model for malware analysis, so in the next part the challenges and issues have been described. Lastly, up and coming trends have been featured in the last section to make the readers aware of the latest developments in the field of machine learning and malware analysis. Malware analysis is a relatively new concept and a lot of discoveries are yet to be made in this field and with the help of machine learning we can take this concept one step further.

REFERENCES

Cabău, G., Buhu, M., & Oprişa, C. (2016). Malware classification using filesystem footprints. *2016 IEEE International Conference on Automation, Quality and Testing, Robotics (AQTR)*, 1-6. 10.1109/AQTR.2016.7501294

Choi, S. (2020). Combined kNN Classification and hierarchical similarity hash for fast malware detection. *Applied Sciences*, *10*(15), 5173.

Fang, Z., Wang, J., Geng, J., & Kan, X. (2019). Feature Selection for Malware Detection Based on Reinforcement Learning. *IEEE Access: Practical Innovations, Open Solutions*, *7*, 176177–176187. doi:10.1109/ACCESS.2019.2957429

Feizollah, A. (2014). *Comparative study of k-means and mini batch k-means clustering algorithms in android malware detection using network traffic analysis. In 2014 international symposium on biometrics and security technologies (ISBAST)*. IEEE.

Ganesh, M. (2017). CNN-based android malware detection. In *2017 International Conference on Software Security and Assurance (ICSSA)*. IEEE. 10.1109/ICSSA.2017.18

Gavriluţ, D., Cimpoeşu, M., Anton, D., & Ciortuz, L. (2009). Malware detection using machine learning. *2009 International Multiconference on Computer Science and Information Technology*, 735-741. 10.1109/IMCSIT.2009.5352759

Gibert, D., Mateu, C., & Planes, J. (2020). The rise of machine learning for detection and classification of malware: Research developments, trends and challenges. *Journal of Network and Computer Applications*, *153*, 102526. doi:10.1016/j.jnca.2019.102526

Gou, Z., Yamaguchi, S., & Gupta, B. B. (2017). Analysis of various security issues and challenges in cloud computing environment: a survey. In Identity Theft: Breakthroughs in Research and Practice (pp. 221-247). IGI global. doi:10.4018/978-1-5225-0808-3.ch011

Gupta, B. B., & Sheng, Q. Z. (Eds.). (2019). *Machine learning for computer and cyber security: principle, algorithms, and practices*. CRC Press. doi:10.1201/9780429504044

Gupta, B. B., Yadav, K., Razzak, I., Psannis, K., Castiglione, A., & Chang, X. (2021). A novel approach for phishing URLs detection using lexical based machine learning in a real-time environment. *Computer Communications*, *175*, 47–57. doi:10.1016/j.comcom.2021.04.023

Idika, N., & Mathur, A. P. (2007). A survey of malware detection techniques. Purdue University.

Kaspersky. (2021). *Machine Learning for Malware Detection*. Retrieved from https://media.kaspersky.com/en/enterprise-security/Kaspersky-Lab-Whitepaper-Machine-Learning.pdf

Keyes, L., & Kaur, L. Gagnon, & Massicotte. (2021). EntropLyzer: Android Malware Classification and Characterization Using Entropy Analysis of Dynamic Characteristics. In Reconciling Data Analytics, Automation, Privacy, and Security: A Big Data Challenge (RDAAPS). IEEE.

Kim. (2018). A multimodal deep learning method for android malware detection using various features. *IEEE Transactions on Information Forensics and Security*, *14*(3), 773-788.

Lashkari, A. H. (2018). Toward developing a systematic approach to generate benchmark android malware datasets and classification. In *2018 International Carnahan Conference on Security Technology (ICCST)*. IEEE. 10.1109/CCST.2018.8585560

Liu, L., Wang, B., Yu, B., & Zhong, Q. (2017). Automatic malware classification and new malware detection using machine learning. *Frontiers of Information Technology & Electronic Engineering, 18*(9), 1336–1347. doi:10.1631/FITEE.1601325

Mahdavifar, Fitriah Kadir, Fatemi, Alhadidi, & Ghorbani. (2020). Dynamic Android Malware Category Classification using Semi-Supervised Deep Learning. *The 18th IEEE International Conference on Dependable, Autonomic, and Secure Computing (DASC).*

Pang, Y. (2019). A signature-based assistant random oversampling method for malware detection. In *2019 18th IEEE International conference on trust, security and privacy in computing and communications/13th IEEE international conference on big data science and engineering (TrustCom/BigDataSE)*. IEEE. 10.1109/TrustCom/BigDataSE.2019.00042

Sathyanarayan, V. S., Kohli, P., & Bruhadeshwar, B. (2008). Signature generation and detection of malware families. In *Australasian Conference on Information Security and Privacy*. Springer. 10.1007/978-3-540-70500-0_25

Sharmeen, S., Huda, S., Abawajy, J. H., Ismail, W. N., & Hassan, M. M. (2018). Malware threats and detection for industrial mobile-IoT networks. *IEEE Access: Practical Innovations, Open Solutions, 6,* 15941–15957. doi:10.1109/ACCESS.2018.2815660

Shhadat, I., Hayajneh, A., & Al-Sharif, Z. A. (2020). The use of machine learning techniques to advance the detection and classification of unknown malware. *Procedia Computer Science, 170,* 917–922. doi:10.1016/j.procs.2020.03.110

Siddiqui, M., Wang, M. C., & Lee, J. (2008). A survey of data mining techniques for malware detection using file features. *Proceedings of the 46th annual southeast regional conference.* 10.1145/1593105.1593239

Sihwail, Omar, & Ariffin. (2018). A survey on malware analysis techniques: Static, dynamic, hybrid and memory analysis. *International Journal on Advanced Science, Engineering and Information Technology, 8*(4-2), 1662.

Taheri, A., & Lashkari. (2019). Extensible Android Malware Detection and Family Classification Using Network-Flows and API-Calls. *The IEEE (53rd) International Carnahan Conference on Security Technology.*

Ucci, D., Aniello, L., & Baldoni, R. (2019). Survey of machine learning techniques for malware analysis. *Computers & Security, 81,* 123–147. doi:10.1016/j.cose.2018.11.001

Wroblewski, G. (2013). General method of program code obfuscation. In *The 5th Conference on Information and Knowledge Technology*. IEEE.

Yamaguchi, S., & Gupta, B. (2021). Malware threat in Internet of Things and its mitigation analysis. In *Research Anthology on Combating Denial-of-Service Attacks* (pp. 371–387). IGI Global. doi:10.4018/978-1-7998-5348-0.ch020

Yousefi-Azar, M., Varadharajan, V., Hamey, L., & Tupakula, U. (2017). Autoencoder-based feature learning for cyber security applications. *2017 International Joint Conference on Neural Networks (IJCNN)*, 3854-3861. 10.1109/IJCNN.2017.7966342

Zarras, A. (2014). Automated generation of models for fast and precise detection of HTTP-based malware. In *2014 Twelfth Annual International Conference on Privacy, Security and Trust*. IEEE. 10.1109/PST.2014.6890946

Zekri, El Kafhali, Aboutabit, & Saadi. (2017). *DDoS attack detection using machine learning techniques in cloud computing environments.* . doi:10.1109/CloudTech.2017.8284731

Chapter 2
Research Trends for Malware and Intrusion Detection on Network Systems:
A Topic Modelling Approach

Santosh Kumar Smmarwar

National Institute of Technology, Raipur, India

Govind P. Gupta

(iD) https://orcid.org/0000-0002-0456-1572

National Institute of Technology, Raipur, India

Sanjay Kumar

National Institute of Technology, Raipur, India

ABSTRACT

With more uses of internet-based services, the risk of cyberattacks is growing continuously. To analyze these research trends for malware and intrusion detection, the authors applied the topic modeling approach in the study by using the LDA (latent dirichlet allocation) and calculating the maximum and minimum probability of the words, which appears in the large collection of text. The LDA technique is useful in finding the hidden topics for further research in the areas of network and cybersecurity. In this chapter, they collected the abstract of two thousand papers from the Scopus library from 2014 to 2021. These collected papers are from reputed publications such as Elsevier, Springer, and IEEE Transactions. The main aim of this study is to find research trends based on keywords that are untouched or on which less research work has been done. To the best of the authors' knowledge, this will be the first study done by using the LDA technique for topic modeling in the areas of network security to demonstrate the research gap and trends for malware and intrusion detection systems.

DOI: 10.4018/978-1-7998-7789-9.ch002

Copyright © 2022, IGI Global. Copying or distributing in print or electronic forms without written permission of IGI Global is prohibited.

INTRODUCTION

According to a report of Equinix (Catalin Cimpanu et al. 2020), a 45% rise in cyber-attack may be seen till 2023 on the network communication system domain with the increasing use of computer communication networks and internet-based services. The threat of attack is ever-expanding over network infrastructure as the different techniques of attacks are being used by attackers. The traditional method of detecting new attacks is not effective as of as it should be to detect and respond before misuse of unauthorized users to the computer resources and private information of the organizations. There are various kind of attack exist known as intrusion, anomaly, malware, viruses, ransomware, adware, Trojan horses, DDoS, DoS, and many more. Malware is the malicious code that moves across the computer network to gain unauthorized access into the computer's critical resources, files, root directory, etc. Malware is designed to steal information, provide losses for the computer system, embedded into the user's code to scan sensitive information, and sending data on third parties servers. Different types of Malware has been classified based on their activity into computer systems such as adware, Trojan, bot, worm, virus, spyware, Ransomware, Rootkit, downloader, Launcher, Backdoor, etc. (Gibert et al., 2020), malware analysis follows two approaches for detecting malware as static analysis and dynamic analysis. The static approach follows the finding unwanted pattern without executing the codes, whereas the dynamic approach works on running code and monitoring the behavior of systems activity (Ren et al., 2019).

Intrusion is unauthorized access that tries to intrude into the privacy of a network. There are different types of intruders such as masquerade and clandestine users to detect intruders, an in-network system deploys a smart system known as an intrusion detection system. An intrusion detection system (IDS) is a security model of the network system used to trace the unauthorized activity of the network through the scanning process of traffic analysis of network packets. The intrusion model identifies the system activities behavior whether it is normal or abnormal and responds to it to the network administrator. The IDS works based on predefined records it contains and finds out the intrusion. It is a predictive model used in the cyber and network security domain that consists of various machine learning algorithms in identifying the intrusion very accurately (Belavagi et al., 2016).

There is two class of intrusion detection systems such as network based detection system and host based detection system (Farnaaz et al., 2016). Network-based detection systems work as passive mode means only monitor the activity of network traffic and send it to central authority while in the case of host-based systems, it is capable of detecting the internal activity of the system and also filter the packet data. The IDS can be classified as anomaly-based and misuse-based detection to detect new attacks and unknown patterns as well as known attacks from databases respectively (Stein et al., 2005, Belavagi et al., 2016). There is a lot of work is being done by researchers in the field of intrusion and anomaly detection and proposed various techniques of machine learning, deep learning, and data mining tools in the areas of the internet of things to developed efficient IDS (Da Costa et al., 2019, Hasan et al., 2019), However less work has done to find out research trend in network security. So our contribution in this paper is to find out the research gap from a large collection of abstract papers by using the topic modeling approach and LDA technique of text mining. In this study, the authors have collected the data of 2000 abstract papers from the Scopus library. These collected data having the eight Columns such as Author's name, Title, Year of publication, Links of paper, Abstract, Author Keywords, Indexed keywords, and References. After collecting authors are doing text cleaning process in which removing unnecessary information which has less meaning in deciding the topic to further research gap, then after applying topic modeling approach to generate most frequent word occurring in the corpus of text data and finally showing the data visualization of topics obtained from LDA approach to know the research gap.

Figure 1. Study overview

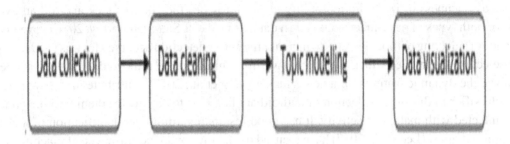

LITERATURE REVIEW

Intrusion in any network is malicious code that moves across the network to monitor the network traffic data over the communication channel among computers. It is an act of illegal activity which violates the policy of digital information and tries to gain access into systems in an unauthorized way. There is various form of malicious activity-travel across the computer network such as anomaly, malware, viruses, worms, Trojan horses, etc. the intensity of damage varies according to the type of attack. there are various areas where the spread of intrusion has been expanded and damages the systems critical resources, steal private information, and violate confidentiality, integrity, and authentication such areas are the internet of things, cloud computing, internet of vehicles, wireless sensor networks, big data systems and many application of latest technology are untouched from various types of new attacks are growing. Therefore, we need to protect the network resources as the utmost requirement of today's time for various business applications by employing different techniques of machine learning, deep learning, as well as data mining tools also (Binbusayyis et al., 2020), brings into intrusion detection systems (IDS). In this paper, we have shown related work of previous year papers of different areas from 2014 to 2021 related to intrusion detection, anomaly, and malware detection. This work is finding the research gap in the literature by using topic modeling and recommended future directions of research in the areas of cybersecurity. (Chhabra et al., 2013) provides the methods to control the DDoS attack in MANET and pointed out the critical challenges of this attack that is difficult to prevent due to its dynamic nature of attacking. (Canfora et al., 2014) discuss the intensity and impact of malware attacks and have proposed a new technique to detect viruses, malicious activity from datasets by doing an in-depth analysis of changing patterns of malicious code. Results of new techniques have shown better precision percentage in the detection of malware code as well as classify their categories also.(R. Ray et al., 2014) have worked on identifying inefficiencies in the areas of IoT that are prone to the security of devices such as privacy concerns and authentication of various devices. In this paper, the author suggested the deployment of RFID in IoT to provide a secure platform as well as the capability of detecting malware attacks. The result of the proposed method achieved good security from the existing protocol and provides scalability to the IoT framework. (Elhag et al., 2015) have proposed a model to improve detection accuracy by incorporating genetic fuzzy techniques inside the pairing-based learning model. This framework is based on two concepts, first is to define the boundary label of sets and make the two classes of data set by using the divide and conquer approach. (Jamali & Jafarjadeh, 2015) worked on the design of an intelligent automatic smart detection system to detect attacks having no predefined structure by using the automatic learning approach. This model provides satisfactory performance on KDD99 datasets from an existing system. (Feizollah et al., 2016) studied the weakness of the Android system through which malware attack is major threat such loopholes as openness of IPC with reusability feature provides the gap to attack and did an extensive analysis of both types of data infected and clean data. (Anusha & Sathiyamoorthy, 2016) have given the importance of selecting optimal features to increase the better detection accuracy for this used the optimal feature selection techniques which is particle swarm optimization to remove the unnecessary features and analyze the dynamic features for a new attack. (Wang et al., 2017) contribute in this work to apply the ML classifier to the large collection of android applications to categorize them into the attack-free app and infected with malicious activity. It has good results regarding the identification of a good and bad category of apps. (Lee et al., 2017) have focused on the improving performance of machine learning classification techniques by selecting the best subset of features of a dataset. For this author used two approaches like sequential forward search to obtain reduced dimension and the second is random forest classifier to achieve better classification accuracy.

(Gupta & Gupta, 2017) have discussed the security challenges, issues attacks, mitigation approaches and various types of loopholes in web application to keep secure web application in era of digital age from various cyber threat. (Zhang et al., 2017) proposed a prototype framework to protect the piracy, copyrights issues in multimedia social networks named CyVOD. This framework prevents the digital contents from transmitting in unauthorized way. (Jerlina & Marimuthu, 2018) explained the issues accompanied in previous work related to malicious activity in network systems such as more detection time and computation time of unwanted activity in the network. It has removed the above concern by applying feature extraction for preprocessing and generating the rule-based system by using the Rete algorithm. (Vijayanand et al., 2018) also discussed factors of intrusion detection systems that may degrade the performance of the models such as irrelevant variables and redundant features for wireless mesh networks. These issues have been overcome in this research work by support vector machines and genetic algorithms. (Hong et al., 2019) has proposed a new concept of smart electronic device enabled with intelligent detection system able to identify the behavior of data such as anomalous data and normal data. This new concept depended on the nearest node to take rightful and accurate decisions in finding the source of the attack on the embedded system. (Dwivedi et al., 2019) proposed a new approach of increasing the security of network domain from various unwanted malicious code. This technique applied the group classifier to select the best attribute from multiple variables. The grasshopper optimizing algorithm selects the best optimal subset of features to improve the detection rate of anomaly. (Hassan et al., 2020) proposed a hybrid model of deep learning to extract hidden features of intrusion details from large volumes of data called big data clouds. This deep learning approach is able to detect the unknown structure of code through the technique of CNN. (Almogren, 2020) has explored the new potential threat in the edge of things via relocation of data storage at edge nodes to efficiently processing of data. This environment of edge nodes also having security issues so it could be overcome by a deep belief network (DBN). It is a very effective and advanced approach to deep learning from the existing method about the performance of intrusion detection systems. (Tewari & Gupta, 2020) have proposed a protocol mutual authentication to safe the RFID tags from cyberattacks for IoT devices. This prevent the attack from using the recurring rotation based approach on the authentication features. (Stergiou et al., 2020) worked on the 6G wireless technology to provide secure and innovative platform based on IoT for communication between smart building and in fog network to handles the big data. This work support the secure browsing and data sharing for organization and users in fog networks. (Guo et al., 2021) worked in the areas of mobile application where authors have shown the concern of event call back issues not paid attention efficiently. This research work has solved the above issue by proposing call back based multilayer embedding method as callback2vec. This new method categorizes the normal API and ordinarily API call-backs. (Li et al., 2021) have pointed out the updating of ML classifiers to new types of attacks on the internet of vehicles (IoV). It proposed a dual model-based updating approach to tackle unlabeled data in the classifier using the transfer learning framework. It is time-efficient as well as achieving a good accuracy level. (Kumar et al., 2021) proposed an intelligent cyber-attack detection system for IoT network using the hybrid feature reduced approach and overcome the curse dimensionality problems. The feature are combined using the AND operation to get the optimize attributes.

APPROACH FOR ANALYSIS OF RESEARCH TRENDS FOR MALWARE AND INTRUSION DETECTION

The figure 1 demonstrates that this work is done in four steps such as data collection, data cleaning, topic modeling, and finally visualization of data. The process is broadly classified into two subparts that are pre-processing of collected data and topic generation. The first part includes removing unnecessary information, converting data into lower case, removing special symbols, punctuations, numbers, comma, spaces, brackets, etc. To obtain a structured store of words (document term matrix) and useful pattern of the word cloud is known as document term matrix for deciding topics frequency and interpretation of topics. In the second stage, the authors would get the topics by applying LDA (latent Dirichlet allocation) to generate the topics (Altaweel et al., 2019), and get important insights about the further research gap.

LATENT DIRICHLET ALLOCATION

An unsupervised machine learning approach known as the Latent Dirichlet allocation (LDA) algorithm is used for topic modeling from text data. It is a statistical probabilistic generative model to extract hidden topics from unobserved documents. In-text data consist of a number of the document in which document each document having the number of topics, further each topic contains the number of words that may be similar or different. The LDA works based on a three-layer Bayesian probability calculation model that provides the relative probability of each word. The Topics are defined as the distribution of words present in the corpus of data. This distribution of topics may be in symmetrical or asymmetrical order in documents. The LDA model is represented through a plate notation, which has some dependencies variables. The LDA model has two boxes called plates as inner plate and outer plate; these plates contained the repeated objects. The outer plates indicate the document and the inner plate contained the repeated words from the available documents (Blei et al., 2003, Gangadharan et al., 2020, Wang et al., 2018). The description of the variable used in the LDA model is defined as follows:

D is the number of documents, E is the number of words where document u has E_U words, α is the parameter of Dirichlet prior on per-document topic distributions, β represents the parameter of Dirichlet prior on the per-topic distribution, θs is the topic distribution for document u, λ is the word distribution for topic T, $Z_{U,V}$ is the topic for a Vth word in document u, $W_{u,v}$ is the specific words (Altaweel et al., 2019).

Figure 2. Graphical depiction of LDA model

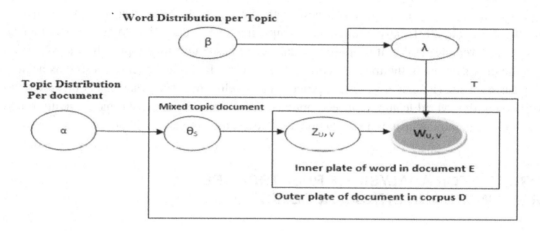

In figure 2, the observable variables are represented in the form of $W_{U,V}$ by shadow circle while another circle indicates that the unstructured and unobservable variables (Altaweel et al., 2019). In this LDA process, the original document is decomposing into the document-word matrix which represents the corpus. The θ entity in the model shows that row having document and columns defined by topics, whereas λ consists of rows described by topics and columns described by words. The general structure of work has shown in figure 3.

DATA GATHERING

The data collection for study is done from the Scopus library which is a citation index database. A total of 2000 research papers abstract have been collected related to network attacks through indexed keyword, author keyword search. These papers are of 2014 to the 2021 year published in a various reputed journals like Elsevier, Springer, IEEE computer society, information sciences, network, and computer application, IEEE Transaction, etc.

PRE-PROCESSING

The author's data is in structure form and having the eight columns like "Author", "Title", "Year", "link", "Abstract", "Author keywords", "Indexed keywords" and "References". The whole study of data collection is based on abstract collection from which find out the hidden topics for topic generation and convert these abstract data into CSV (comma-separated values) file and import it into the R software, which is a statistical programming tool. After converting data into CSV file format we start it's cleaning and before doing cleaning ensures that R software contains the required package such as "tm" and "topic models".

Figure 3. General architecture of study

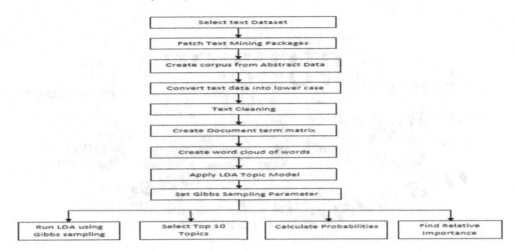

The cleaning process starts with the selection of abstracts from data and converts it into lower case and removes the numbers, full stop, punctuations, and whitespaces and stop words. Stop words are those which do not have any special meaning in deciding topics from the text(e.g., demonstrative pronouns "this", "these", "that", and "those"; indefinite articles "a(n)" and the definite article "the"; verb "to be", which causes changes in grammatical person and tense; and auxiliary verbs, such as "have", "has", "do", and "does", that exist in the grammatical system without specific meanings). Once authors remove these words, white space is created so authors have to remove that also, some of the words which are identical but since their ending is different due to change in tenses and number(singular/plural) software perceive it differently, so to remove it use the "stemming" operation, Where only the roots of words are extracted. The tm package, a natural language (English) processing program within R, provides the stemming function i.e. word "passed" and "passing" are the past and present progressive forms of the verb "pass" so all these words present in the article are converted into its root word "pass" and counted. After doing all of this operation get the collection of 7604 words. These words can be represented in various ways; figure 4 is showing the word cloud which builds with the help of an R software package called "wordcloud2" in this cloud words are shown with respect to their frequency. Basically, the word cloud is used to represent the summary of cleaned data in visualize of various keywords in an oval shape, circle shape, etc. the size of the keyword in the word cloud varies according to the term frequency of word occurrence as demonstrated in figure 5.

TOPIC MODELLING

Topic modelling is an approach of text mining in which text is organize, structured and summarizes in proper way to find out the hidden topics from large collection of data. It is an unsupervised machine learning technique that has the ability to scan set of multiple documents, detect words, and symmetrical expression of words present in corpus of data. Topic modelling can be used to classify the set of text data into a few topics based on the frequency of occurrence of words in data.

Figure 4. Word cloud

Figure 5. Occurrence of term (frequency more than 1000) in corpus

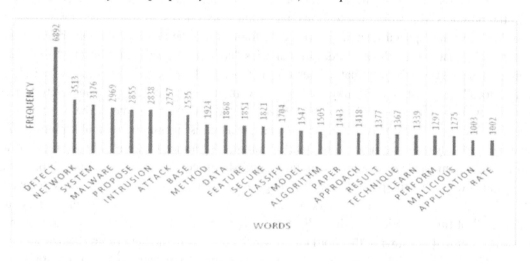

Topic modelling in this study uses a LDA package of R language which is a statistical model to calculate probability (>0.5) of appearance of topics belongs to the particular topics. LDA convert all the word set data into document term matrix then after calculate the sum of each row (document) and eliminate empty documents. After this we need to make sample of whole text data by using Gibbs sampling. Topic modelling on collected sample data, probability of appearance of specific words in each topics, the distribution of topics in each paper by taking K=25(number of topics) initially, but authors see in result that topics has many common words, so authors reduce the number of topics to 20 etc. after many iterations reach a conclusion that 15 topics are appropriate for our study, in figure 6 shown the top 15 words from each topic with their corresponding frequency given. The table 2 shows that the topic with the corresponding maximum and minimum probability of words. Probability of each document corresponding to each topic is calculated and extracted. And the highest probability of each document corresponding to their topic is fall in that topic. Table 2 shows that the range of probability of maximum and minimum of all 15 topics. The topics1 has maximum 0.348008 and minimum 0.145022 probabilities. It means that 14.50% chances that document 7 is related to topic1 and its topic name given "strategies to detect intrusion". The topic 2 has maximum probability of 0.370766 that means there are 37.07% chances that belongs to document 14. Similarly for other remaining 13 topics also belongs to corresponding document number as shown in table 1.

Table 1. Document to Topics

Documents	1	2	3	4	5	6	7	8	9	10	11	12	13	14	15
Topics	7	6	17	13	11	17	1	13	19	18	4	14	4	2	10

This study has been done to extract the topics that have been researched and published in previous work in network security papers abstract. The topic name has been given on basis of search keyword appears frequently in documents. The top 10 most frequent word has been found in each 15 topics as shown in figure.6. These are categorises into fifteen topics named topic 1, topic 2, topic 3 etc. To giving the name for each topic the authors selected the 11-13 an abstract belongs to a specific topic and shown the authors keyword of the abstracts in table 1. For example to name topic 1, following keywords have been taken from some of the abstracts such as Computer crime (Sovilj D et al., 2020), Advanced metering infrastructures (Budnarain P. et al., 200), Anomaly detection (Sanner S. et al., 2020), Optimal strategies (Salmon G., Rao M. et al., 2020). According to this keyword it can be observe that it related to cyber-attacks prevention method, so the topic 1 named as "strategies to detect intrusion".

For topic 2 the indexed keyword such as Artificial intelligence (Zhang Z et al., 2021), Deep learning (Cheng Y. et al., 2021), Signature-based approach (Gao Y et al., 2021), Digital storage (Nepal S et al., 2021), Feature extraction (Zou Y et al., 2021), from these keywords it can be seen that it is about the "AI and ML methods for intrusion detection" as shown in table 3.

Figure 6. Top 10 words of each topic and corresponding frequency

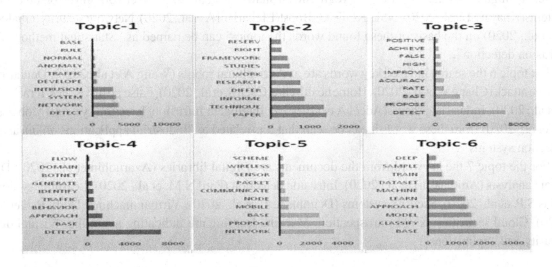

Table 2. Topic with the corresponding maximum and minimum probability of words

Topics	Max Probability	Min Probability
Topic 1	0.348008	0.145022
Topic 2	0.370766	0.043084
Topic 3	0.394062	0.162393
Topic 4	0.488400	0.162835
Topic 5	0.472347	0.135659
Topic 6	0.351085	0.170370
Topic 7	0.445926	0.151986
Topic 8	0.471888	0.156410
Topic 9	0.328070	0.144144
Topic 10	0.543507	0.185185
Topic 11	0.423019	0.155718
Topic 12	0.484496	0.154472
Topic 13	0.475634	0.151515
Topic 14	0.408951	0.195184
Topic 15	0.431159	0.151852

The topic 3 keywords includes Personal computing (Jeon S et al., 2020), Data recovery (Moon J et al., 2020), Bioinformatics, Sequence Covering Similarity, Host-based intrusion detection, System calls (MartÃnez-GarcÃa H.A. et al., 2020) from these words it can be concluded that it is related to "Bio-inspired intrusion detection".

The indexed keyword for topic 4 as follows Future research directions (Khasawneh et al. 2020), Individual classifiers (Ozsoy M et al., 2020), Different attacks (Donovick C et al., 2020), Ensemble learning (Abu-Ghazaleh N et al., 2020), Insider attack (Ponomarev D. et al., 2020) according to it topic 4 named as "Advance methods for intrusion detection".

For the topic 5 the important words are Internet technology(Kaur S. et al., 2020), Intrusion Detection Systems(Singh M et al.,2020), Logistic regressions(Shawly T. et al.,2020), Network intrusion detection systems(Khayat M et al., 2020), NSL-KDD,XGBoost(Elghariani A et al., 2020), Network security(Ghafoor A. et al., 2020) on the basis of these found words the topic 5 can be named as "Statistical methods for intrusion detection".

For topic 6 the search indexed key words are as Agricultural robots (Wang A et al., 2020), Denial-of-service attack(Chang W et al., 2020), Home health care(Chen S. et al., 2020), False positive rates(Ieracitano C et al., 2020), Industrial process(Adeel A et al.,2020), Intelligent Intrusion detection systems(Mohaisen A., et al., 2020) from these words it can be seen that it is related to "Industrial applications on intrusion detection systems" .

For the topic 7 the keyword from the documents are Digital libraries (Azarudhin et al., 2020), Dynamic analysis (Anithaashri et al., 2020), Intrusion detection (Patil N.M. et al., 2020), Learning systems (Dias S.P. et al., 2020), Security systems (Dcunha A.A. et al., 2020), Virtual machine (Dodti R.J. et al., 2020), Cloud securities, KVM introspection, Machine learning are indicating about the "Virtual data security and applications".

The topic named given "Medical applications of Intrusion detection" for topic 8 on the basis of found keywords such as Biochips (Aonzo S. et al., 2020), Diagnosis(Merlo A. et al., 2020), DNA sequences(Migliardi M. et al, 2020), Drug delivery(Oneto L et al.,2020), Gene encoding(Palmieri F. et al., 2020), Malware(Borah S. et al., 2020), Medical applications(Karsligil et al., 2020), Application programs(Sun B et al., 2020), Evolutionary algorithms(Sharma J et al., 2020), Inspection equipment(Yaacoubi O., 2020).

For the topic 9 keywords are includes Hamming distance (Taheri R et al., 2020), Malware (Ghahramani M. et al., 2020), nearest neighbor search (Javidan R. et al., 2020), Static analysis (Shojafar M. et al., 2020), All nearest neighbors (Pooranian Z. et al., 2020), Clustering (Conti M. et al., 2020), K nearest neighbor (Romli R.N. et al., 2020). It is about detection techniques, so it is named as "Unsupervised techniques for intrusion detection".

The topic 10 keywords are Anomaly detection (Patil R. et al., 2020), Computer crime (Dudeja H. et al., 2020), (Modi C. et al., 2020), Gradient methods (Pandey S.K. et al., 2019), Intrusion detection (Modi C. et al., 2020), Momentum (Sekhar R. et al., 2019), Technical vulnerabilities (Krishnan P. et al., 2020). These keywords are describing about cyber threat. So it named as "Security threats due to Intrusions".

For the topic 11 the indexed keywords are Command and control systems (Ganeshan R et al., 2020), Complex networks (Rodrigues P. et al., 2020), Computer crime (Thanudas B et al., 2019), Graphic methods (Sreelal S. et al., 2019), Internet protocols (Cyril Raj V. et al., 2019), Internet service providers (Maji S. et al., 2019), Botnet(Pao H.-K. et al., 2019); DNS, Domain names(Shi Y. et al., 2018), Graph clustering(Chen G et al., 2018). This is explaining about research of network threat. So it is named as "Network research on intrusion detection".

For the topic 12 the keywords are Field programmable gate arrays (Abawajy J.H. et al., 2020), Intrusion detection (Chowdhury M et al., 2020), Learning systems (Kelarev A. et al., 2020), Benchmarking (Mishra P. et al., 2020), Computer crime (Verma I. et al., 2020), Decision trees (Gupta S. et al., 2020) from these words it can be named as "Firmware based intrusion detection systems".

For the topic 13 keywords included are Contamination (Yang K. et al., 2018) Earth (Ren J. et al., 2018), Infrared devices (Zhu Y. et al., 2018), Intrusion detection(Zhang W.,2018), Moon(Yang Y. et al., 2018), Signal detection(Cai Z. et al., 2018), Sounding apparatus(Wang C. et al., 2018), Calibration reference(Zhang J. et al., 2018,), Cross-track infrared sounder(Chen J. et al., 2018). These keywords are showing some relationship towards environmental. So it is named as "Environmental applications on intrusion detection".

For the topic 14 there are some of keywords such as Chemical detection (Sahu S.K. et al., 2019), Computer crime (Katiyar A. et al., 2019), Hidden Markov models (Kumari K.M. et al., 2019), Malware (Kumar G. et al., 2019), Markov processes (Choi W. et al., 2018), Mercury (Joo K. et al., 2018), Commerce (Jo H.J. et al., 2018), Competition(Park M.C. et al., 2018), Computer crime(Lee D.H. et al., 2018). These words are showing relationship about substance related detection. So this topic named as "Intrusion detection systems based on substance identification"

For the last topic 15 the Computation theory (Guo Y. et al., 2019), Computer games(Zhang H. et al., 2019), Game theory(Zhang L. et al., 2019), Trusted computing(Fang L. et al., 2019), Coalitional game(Li F et al., 2109), Cooperative intrusion detection(Bhandari S. et al., 2019), Detection accuracy(Panihar R. et al., 2019), Fairness assurance(Naval S. et al., 2018), Security(Laxmi V. et al., 2018), Stackelberg Games(Zemmari A. et al., 2018). These are the word describing about the games related work. So this is named as "Gaming applications and intrusion detection".

RESULT ANALYSIS

In this section, authors have obtained five tables in this study; table 1 contains the "document to topics" that combines the number of documents into topics on basis of search keywords. The table 2 is created by calculated corresponding maximum and minimum probability of fifteen topics using the LDA technique, each topic showing relative maximum and minimum probability of words for example topic 1 has maximum probability 0.348008 and minimum probability is 0.145022 and likewise for remaining topics, Maximum and minimum words frequency of top 10 words for 15 topics to find out the research trends. Table 3 shows that topic wise some of the major keywords and citations, authors found fifteen topics that get after applying the LDA algorithm, need to determine the name of topics based on words frequency of appearance was considered first. And based on that write the name for each topic in table 3 with citations shows like in topic one has the index keywords "Advanced metering infrastructures, Computer crime, Learning algorithms, Support vector machines, Training and testing, Anomaly detection, Optimal strategies" so authors write it as the "strategies to detect intrusion". For topic 2 the indeed keywords are "Artificial intelligence, Deep learning, Signature-based approach, Digital storage, Data mining, Feature extraction, Pattern mining, Malware". So on the basis of indexed keyword named it as "AI and ML methods for intrusion detection" Similarly for others topic name also.

The table 4 shows that number of articles per topic, after applying the LDA authors get to know that which document fall in which topic, and based on that we classify the entire document corresponding to 15 topics, shown in table 4 it is seen in table that some of the topic has a greater number of document while other are very less. This can be represented in better way by the graphical means shown in figure 7, there is in topic 15 the least no of document (57) are fall, it also mean that the research in this field is not done very frequently as in other topics, so by this authors can conclude that there is a gap in this field and can be explore more for research work. So finally authors came to know to that in field of the network research on intrusion detection (topic11) research has been done least. Topic 2 has less number of documents (76) comes, so in this topic also less research has been done. Similarly for topic 15 come out 84 documents under this topic so authors can say that it is also less research done topic.

Table 5 in this study shows that the year wise article distribution of data of fifteen topics from 2013-2014 up to 2019-2020 which indicates the research done of topics. In topic 1 that is related to "strategies to detect intrusion" the article distribution of research growing up from 2013 to 2016 and from 2016 onwards to 2018 falls down. Again it is seen that a little rise in research from 2018 to 2020 has done. For topic 2 " AI and ML methods for intrusion detection" the article distribution among 2013-2014 and 2019-2020 indicating a continue rise up to 2015-2016, after 2016 has been observed the slowdown in number of article from the graph till 2018 and again rise in article distribution from 2018 to 2020. The article distribution for topic 3 that is related to "bio-inspired intrusion detection" in the year 2013 to 2016 was continuous rise around 35% then after seen constant distribution for bio-inspired intrusion detection. The topic 4 is related to "advances method for intrusion detection" for this around 36% increase in article distribution in the year 2013-2014 to 2015-2016 seen and later on it has been constant contribution of article have seen till 2019-2020. For topic 5 from 2013-2014 to 2015-2016 the statistical methods for intrusion detection has risen around 70% contribution of articles and then after it is seen constant contribution from the curve from 2017-2018 to 2019-2020.

For the topic 6 which is related to "industrial application on intrusion detection system" the curve showing very slowly increase in article distribution for this areas from 2013-2014 to 2019-2020 around 85% articles.

For the topic 7 that is "virtual data security and application" the research trends for this in starting has been growing slowly around 33% contribution of research articles observed.

The topic 8 which is indicating "medical applications of intrusion detection" also showing constant rise of curve from 2013-2014 to 2019-2020 regarding the research trends in this field. The research article trends for topic 9 which is related to "unsupervised techniques for intrusion detection" indicating sudden increase in articles from 2013-2014 to 2015-2016. In between 2016 and 2017 trend has decreased slightly and then after it increases the from 2018 to2020. For the topic 10 that is "security threat due to intrusions" the research has increased from 2013-2014 to 2019-2020 around 51.10%. Topic 11 related to "Network research on intrusion detection" for this the article distribution trend of research has risen from 2013-2014 to 2019-2020 around 32.50% from the graph can be seen.

The topic 12 that is "Firmware based intrusion detection system" involves the around 69% growth over the year from 2013-2014 to 2015-2016, in between it has decreased the growth of articles a little bit again from 2017-2018 to 2019-2020 the increment in research articles can be seen around 80%. For the topic 13 that is "environmental application on intrusion detection" research has done around 25% from the 2013-2014 to 2015-2016 and after that from 2017-2018 to 2019-2020 sudden growth in article distribution up to 70% can be seen from the graph. In the topic 14 the research article distribution was around 40% from 2013-2014 to 2019-2020 in the areas of "Intrusion detection system based on substance identification". For the last topic 15 related to "Gaming application and intrusion detection" showing continuous growth over the years up to 2015-2016 from 2013-2014 of around 20% articles distribution and slightly decrease in growth, again it can be seen rise up to 39% article distribution in this domain.

Table 3. Topic wise some of the major keywords and citations

Sr. No	Topic Name	Indexed Keywords	Citations
1.	Strategies to detect intrusion	Advanced metering infrastructures, Computer crime, Learning algorithms, Support vector machines, Training and testing, Anomaly detection, Optimal strategies	Sovilj D., Budnarain P., Sanner S., Salmon G., Rao M., 2020 Shamshirband S., Fathi M., Chronopoulos A.T., Montieri A., Palumbo F., 2020.
2.	AI and ML methods for intrusion detection	Artificial intelligence, Deep learning, Signature-based approach, Digital storage, Data mining, Feature extraction, Pattern mining, Malware	Zhang Z., Cheng Y., Gao Y., Nepal S., Liu D., Zou Y., 2021. Abdulqadder I.H., Zhou S., Zou D., Aziz I.T., Akber S.M.A. 2020
3.	Bio-inspired intrusion detection	Personal computing, Data recovery, Malware, Bioinformatics, Sequence Covering Similarity, Host-based intrusion detection, System calls	Jeon S., Moon J., 2020, MartÃnez-GarcÃa H.A., 2020
4.	Advance methods for intrusion detection	Future research directions, Individual classifiers, Different attacks, Ensemble learning, Generative methods, Neural networks, Insider attack, Sensitivity values	Khasawneh K.N., Ozsoy M., Donovick C., Abu-Ghazaleh N., Ponomarev D., 2020
5.	Statistical methods for intrusion detection	Internet technology, Intrusion Detection Systems, Logistic regressions, Network intrusion detection systems, NSL-KDD, XGBoost, Network security	Kaur S., Singh M., 2020, Shawly T., Khayat M., Elghariani A., Ghafoor A., 2020
6.	Industrial applications on intrusion detection systems	Agricultural robots, Denial-of-service attack, Home health care, False positive rates, Industrial processes, Intelligent Intrusion detection systems	Wang A., Chang W., Chen S., Mohaisen A., 2020, Ieracitano C., Adeel A., Morabito F.C., Hussain A., 2020

continues on following page

Table 3. Continued

Sr. No	Topic Name	Indexed Keywords	Citations
7.	Virtual data security and applications	Digital libraries, Dynamic analysis, Intrusion detection, Learning systems, Security systems, Virtual machine, Cloud securities, KVM introspection, Machine learning	Azarudhin, Anithaashri T.P., 2020 Patil N.M., Dias S.P., Dcunha A.A., Dodti R.J., 2020
8.	Medical applications of Intrusion detection	Biochips, Diagnosis, DNA sequences, Drug delivery, Gene encoding, Malware, Medical applications, Application programs, Evolutionary algorithms, Inspection equipment	Aonzo S., Merlo A., Migliardi M., Oneto L., Palmieri F., 2020
9.	Unsupervised techniques for intrusion detection	Hamming distance, Malware, Nearest neighbor search, Static analysis, All nearest neighbors, Android, Clustering, Dissimilarity measures, K nearest neighbor (KNN)	Taheri R., Ghahramani M., Javidan R., Shojafar M., Pooranian Z., Conti M., 2020
10.	Security threats due to Intrusions	Anomaly detection, Computer crime, Efficiency, Gradient methods, Intrusion detection, Momentum, Technical vulnerabilities, Vehicle security	Patil R., Dudeja H., Modi C., 2020, Pandey S.K., 2019
11.	Network research on intrusion detection	Command and control systems, Complex networks, Computer crime, Graphic methods, Internet protocols, Internet service providers, Botnet; DNS, Domain names, Graph clustering	Ganeshan R., Rodrigues P., 2020 Thanudas B., Sreelal S., Cyril Raj V., Maji S. Pao H.-K., Lee F.-R., Lee Y.-J., 2019, Shi Y., Chen G., Li J., 2018
12.	Firmware based intrusion detection systems	Field programmable gate arrays (FPGA), Intrusion detection, Learning systems, Benchmarking, Classification (of information), Computer crime, Decision trees; Errors	Abawajy J.H., Chowdhury M., Kelarev A., 2020 Mishra P., Verma I., Gupta S., 2020
13.	Environmental applications on intrusion detection	Contamination; Earth (planet), Infrared devices, Intrusion detection, Moon, Signal detection, Sounding apparatus, Calibration reference, Cross-track infrared sounder	Yang K., Ren J., Zhu Y., Zhang W.,2018 Yang Y., Cai Z., Wang C., Zhang J.,2018, Chen J., Wang C., Zhao Z., Chen K., Du R., Ahn G.-J. 2018
14.	Intrusion detection systems based on substance identification	Chemical detection, Computer crime, Hidden Markov models, Malware, Markov processes, Mercury (metal),Commerce, Competition, Computer crime, Dynamic loads	Sahu S.K., Katiyar A., Kumari K.M., Kumar G., Mohapatra D.P., 2019, Choi W., Joo K., Jo H.J., Park M.C., Lee D.H., 2018
15.	Gaming applications and intrusion detection	Computation theory, Computer games, Game theory, Trusted computing, Coalitional game, Cooperative intrusion detection, Detection accuracy, Fairness assurance, Security, Stackelberg Games	Guo Y., Zhang H., Zhang L., Fang L., Li F. 2019, Bhandari S., Panihar R., Naval S., Laxmi V., Zemmari A., Gaur M.S., 2018

Table 4. Number of articles per topic

Topics	No. of Docs
Strategies to detect intrusion	150
AI and ML methods for intrusion detection	76
Bio-inspired intrusion detection	101
Advance methods for intrusion detection	115
Statistical methods for intrusion detection	180
Industrial applications on intrusion detection systems	145
Virtual data security and applications	85
Medical applications of Intrusion detection	324
Unsupervised techniques for intrusion detection	105
Security threats due to Intrusions	136
Network research on intrusion detection	57
Firmware based intrusion detection systems	205
Environmental applications on intrusion detection	126
Intrusion detection systems based on substance identification	111
Gaming applications and intrusion detection	84
Total	2000

Figure 7. Number of articles per topic

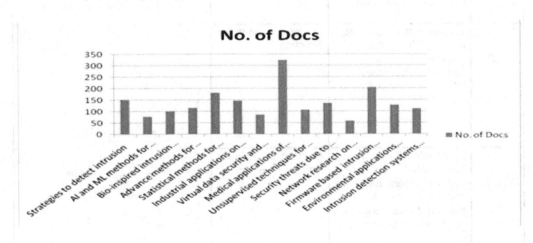

DISCUSSION

In the context of intrusion and malware detection in security domain there are many things to consider, like most important one is the security of users confidential data, integrity, authenticity as well as physical security also necessary to make the network system more trustable and robust from cyber-attacks. Therefore to ensure the security of system model must have some necessary quality like intrusion detection and prevention mechanism. So designing the good security framework model is a very high potential in growth of advancement in technology. Although a lot of intrusion detection and malware detection system have been proposed by previous researchers but as the more use of internet in various fields increase the threat of cyber-attack. so to understand the research trends in the field of cyber and network security we here collect 2000 papers abstracts related to that and analyse through topic modelling to get insights about research gap in this area.

Table 5. Data of year wise research done

Topic No.	Topic Keyword	Topic Name	Year wise article distribution
Topic1	Advanced metering infrastructures, Computer crime, Anomaly detection, Optimal strategies	Strategies to detect intrusion	
Topic2	Artificial intelligence, Deep learning, Signature-based approach, Digital storage, Data mining, Feature extraction, Pattern mining, Malware, Learning algorithms, Support vector machines, Training and testing	AI and ML methods for intrusion detection	
Topic3	Personal computing, Data recovery, Bioinformatics, Sequence Covering Similarity, Host-based intrusion detection, System calls	Bio-inspired intrusion detection	
Topic4	Future research directions, Individual classifiers, Different attacks, Ensemble learning, Generative methods, Neural networks, Insider attack, Sensitivity values	Advance methods for intrusion detection	
Topic5	Internet technology, Intrusion Detection Systems, Logistic regressions, Network intrusion detection systems, NSL-KDD, XGBoost, Network security	Statistical methods for intrusion detection	

continues on following page

Table 3. Continued

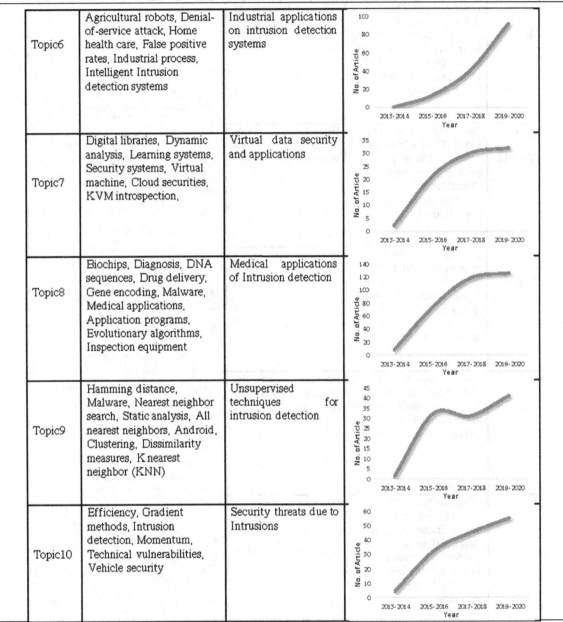

Topic6	Agricultural robots, Denial-of-service attack, Home health care, False positive rates, Industrial process, Intelligent Intrusion detection systems	Industrial applications on intrusion detection systems	
Topic7	Digital libraries, Dynamic analysis, Learning systems, Security systems, Virtual machine, Cloud securities, KVM introspection,	Virtual data security and applications	
Topic8	Biochips, Diagnosis, DNA sequences, Drug delivery, Gene encoding, Malware, Medical applications, Application programs, Evolutionary algorithms, Inspection equipment	Medical applications of Intrusion detection	
Topic9	Hamming distance, Malware, Nearest neighbor search, Static analysis, All nearest neighbors, Android, Clustering, Dissimilarity measures, K nearest neighbor (KNN)	Unsupervised techniques for intrusion detection	
Topic10	Efficiency, Gradient methods, Intrusion detection, Momentum, Technical vulnerabilities, Vehicle security	Security threats due to Intrusions	

continues on following page

In the this study, the 15 topics which we get after multiple iteration regarding the intrusion detection, according to perplexity calculation in topic modelling, the number of appropriate topics amounted to 15, all these 15 topics are related to different areas such as, Agricultural robots, Home health care, Bio-informatics, Computation theory, Computer games, Game theory, Trusted computing, Vehicle security, Graph clustering etc.

Table 3. Continued

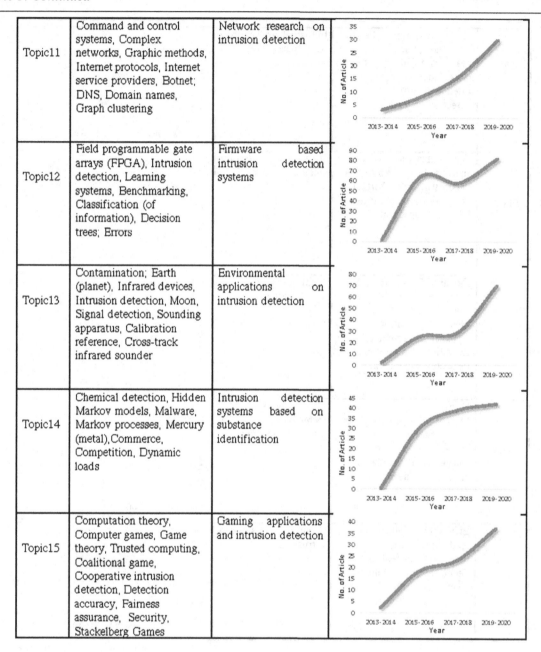

Topic11	Command and control systems, Complex networks, Graphic methods, Internet protocols, Internet service providers, Botnet; DNS, Domain names, Graph clustering	Network research on intrusion detection	
Topic12	Field programmable gate arrays (FPGA), Intrusion detection, Learning systems, Benchmarking, Classification (of information), Decision trees; Errors	Firmware based intrusion detection systems	
Topic13	Contamination; Earth (planet), Infrared devices, Intrusion detection, Moon, Signal detection, Sounding apparatus, Calibration reference, Cross-track infrared sounder	Environmental applications on intrusion detection	
Topic14	Chemical detection, Hidden Markov models, Malware, Markov processes, Mercury (metal),Commerce, Competition, Dynamic loads	Intrusion detection systems based on substance identification	
Topic15	Computation theory, Computer games, Game theory, Trusted computing, Coalitional game, Cooperative intrusion detection, Detection accuracy, Fairness assurance, Security, Stackelberg Games	Gaming applications and intrusion detection	

As all topics shown in the table 5 describes their keyword and topics names related to intrusion detection areas. The topic 1 shows that the strategies to intrusion detection and year wise article distribution from year 2013 to 2020 in which around 52.4% research articles are based on the strategies of intrusion detection. Topic 2 is related to AI and ML methods for intrusion detection which depicted that in year from 2013 to 2016 around 43.30% AI and ML techniques applied and after that suddenly the scope of these machine learning has been gradually increase to 49.6%. Topic 3 is about the Bio-inspired intrusion detection; this shows that around 36.3% research related to these areas. Topic 4 and topic 5 are related to advance and statistical methods for intrusion detection in which around 36.7% and 61.8% respectively work has been done. Topic 6, topic 7, topic 8, topic 13, topic 15 are based on the Industrial applications, Virtual data security and applications, Medical applications of Intrusion detection, Environmental applications on intrusion detection, Gaming applications and intrusion detection respectively. This distribution of articles in these fields is around 82.3%, 31.7% and 89.4, 70.3%, 35.8% research work respectively. The percent wise distribution of remaining topics like topic 9, topic 10, topic 11, topic12, topic 14 research trends is around between 31.4% to 41.8% related to Unsupervised techniques for intrusion detection, Security threats due to Intrusions, Network research on intrusion detection, Firmware based intrusion detection systems, Intrusion detection systems based on substance identification.

CONCLUSION

In the field of intrusion detection although many researches had been done over the years, but these researches are not a very organised in a structured way. so it create a research gap over time, this study aim to find research gaps and try to focus on that and bring it into the light. For execution of such task, we use here a specific technique called topic modelling, in this technique through the function called "LDA". In this work, we got to know that there are some topic which are very less number of document and research done. The graph in table 5, we observe the topic 15 is least no. of doc. So the research in the field of Gaming applications and intrusion detection are not done in frequent ways as in other topics, but analysing only one thing at a time not always give fruitful results. So here also we cannot just relay on topic but also topic ten is important because security threat is one of the pillars of designing the security framework to detect intrusion which lead towards more security parameters, good healthy environment of network communication and lead to more transparent, secure, and reliable. In this study although there are many limitations, some important are discussed in following section, one of them major limitations are this study is based on analysis of the abstract and index keyword collected from limited number of the article (2000). And considering that the sample (Gibbs sampling) which we use for performing the "LDA" is representative of the whole populations. In addition on this study during the topic name selection is based on some of the index keyword among many of there, so here also it assume that these words correctly describe the topic name and the index keyword which taken from some of the documents not from all which fall in that topic through the "LDA" i.e. in (topic 1) we have total of 150 documents but the words chosen for the topic name are only from four documents, so it is also a limitations of this study, it will be our future work to remove this limitations.

REFERENCES

Almogren, A. S. (2020). Intrusion detection in Edge-of-Things computing. *Journal of Parallel and Distributed Computing*, *137*, 259–265. doi:10.1016/j.jpdc.2019.12.008

Altaweel, M., Bone, C., & Abrams, J. (2019). Documents as data: A content analysis and topic modeling approach for analyzing responses to ecological disturbances. *Ecological Informatics*, *51*, 82–95. doi:10.1016/j.ecoinf.2019.02.014

Anusha, K., & Sathiyamoorthy, E. (2016). A decision tree-based rule formation with combined PSO-GA algorithm for intrusion detection system. *International Journal of Internet Technology and Secured Transactions*, *6*(3), 186–202. doi:10.1504/IJITST.2016.080399

Belavagi, M. C., & Muniyal, B. (2016). Performance evaluation of supervised machine learning algorithms for intrusion detection. *Procedia Computer Science*, *89*, 117–123. doi:10.1016/j.procs.2016.06.016

Binbusayyis, A., & Vaiyapuri, T. (2020). Comprehensive analysis and recommendation of feature evaluation measures for intrusion detection. *Heliyon*, *6*(7), e04262. doi:10.1016/j.heliyon.2020.e04262 PMID:32685709

Blei, D. M., Ng, A. Y., & Jordan, M. I. (2003). Latent dirichlet allocation. *The Journal of Machine Learning Research, 3*, 993-1022.

Canfora, G., Mercaldo, F., Visaggio, C. A., & Di Notte, P. (2014). Metamorphic malware detection using code metrics. *Information Security Journal: A Global Perspective, 23*(3), 57-67.

Chhabra, M., Gupta, B., & Almomani, A. (2013). *A novel solution to handle DDOS attack in MANET*. Academic Press.

da Costa, K. A., Papa, J. P., Lisboa, C. O., Munoz, R., & de Albuquerque, V. H. C. (2019). Internet of Things: A survey on machine learning-based intrusion detection approaches. *Computer Networks*, *151*, 147–157. doi:10.1016/j.comnet.2019.01.023

Dwivedi, S., Vardhan, M., Tripathi, S., & Shukla, A. K. (2020). Implementation of adaptive scheme in evolutionary technique for anomaly-based intrusion detection. *Evolutionary Intelligence*, *13*(1), 103–117. doi:10.100712065-019-00293-8

Elhag, S., Fernández, A., Bawakid, A., Alshomrani, S., & Herrera, F. (2015). On the combination of genetic fuzzy systems and pairwise learning for improving detection rates on intrusion detection systems. *Expert Systems with Applications*, *42*(1), 193–202. doi:10.1016/j.eswa.2014.08.002

Farnaaz, N., & Jabbar, M. A. (2016). Random forest modeling for network intrusion detection system. *Procedia Computer Science*, *89*, 213–217. doi:10.1016/j.procs.2016.06.047

Feizollah, A., Anuar, N. B., Salleh, R., Suarez-Tangil, G., & Furnell, S. (2017). Androdialysis: Analysis of android intent effectiveness in malware detection. *Computers & Security, 65*, 121-134.

Gangadharan, V., & Gupta, D. (2020). Recognizing Named Entities in Agriculture Documents using LDA based Topic Modelling Techniques. *Procedia Computer Science*, *171*, 1337–1345. doi:10.1016/j.procs.2020.04.143

Gibert, D., Mateu, C., & Planes, J. (2020). The rise of machine learning for detection and classification of malware: Research developments, trends and challenges. *Journal of Network and Computer Applications*, *153*, 102526. doi:10.1016/j.jnca.2019.102526

Guo, C., Huang, D., Dong, N., Zhang, J., & Xu, J. (2021). Callback2Vec: Callback-aware hierarchical embedding for mobile application. *Information Sciences*, *542*, 131–155. doi:10.1016/j.ins.2020.06.058

Gupta, S., & Gupta, B. B. (2017). Detection, avoidance, and attack pattern mechanisms in modern web application vulnerabilities: Present and future challenges. *International Journal of Cloud Applications and Computing*, *7*(3), 1–43. doi:10.4018/IJCAC.2017070101

Hasan, M., Islam, M. M., Zarif, M. I. I., & Hashem, M. M. A. (2019). Attack and anomaly detection in IoT sensors in IoT sites using machine learning approaches. *Internet of Things*, *7*, 100059. doi:10.1016/j. iot.2019.100059

Hassan, M. M., Gumaei, A., Alsanad, A., Alrubaian, M., & Fortino, G. (2020). A hybrid deep learning model for efficient intrusion detection in big data environment. *Information Sciences*, *513*, 386–396. doi:10.1016/j.ins.2019.10.069

Hong, J., & Liu, C. C. (2017). Intelligent electronic devices with collaborative intrusion detection systems. *IEEE Transactions on Smart Grid*, *10*(1), 271–281. doi:10.1109/TSG.2017.2737826

Jamali, S., & Jafarzadeh, P. (2017). An intelligent intrusion detection system by using hierarchically structured learning automata. *Neural Computing & Applications*, *28*(5), 1001–1008. doi:10.100700521-015-2116-4

Jerlin, M. A., & Marimuthu, K. (2018). A new malware detection system using machine learning techniques for API call sequences. *Journal of Applied Security Research*, *13*(1), 45–62. doi:10.1080/1936 1610.2018.1387734

Kumar, P., Gupta, G. P., & Tripathi, R. (2021). Toward Design of an Intelligent Cyber Attack Detection System using Hybrid Feature Reduced Approach for IoT Networks. *Arabian Journal for Science and Engineering*, *46*(4), 3749–3778. doi:10.100713369-020-05181-3

Lee, J., Park, D., & Lee, C. (2017). Feature selection algorithm for intrusions detection system using sequential forward search and random forest classifier. *Transactions on Internet and Information Systems (Seoul)*, *11*(10), 5132–5148.

Li, X., Hu, Z., Xu, M., Wang, Y., & Ma, J. (2021). Transfer learning based intrusion detection scheme for Internet of vehicles. *Information Sciences*, *547*, 119–135. doi:10.1016/j.ins.2020.05.130

Ray, B. R., Abawajy, J., & Chowdhury, M. (2014). Scalable RFID security framework and protocol supporting Internet of Things. *Computer Networks*, *67*, 89–103. doi:10.1016/j.comnet.2014.03.023

Ren, Z., Chen, G., & Lu, W. (2020). Malware visualization methods based on deep convolution neural networks. *Multimedia Tools and Applications*, *79*(15), 10975–10993. doi:10.100711042-019-08310-9

Stein, G., Chen, B., Wu, A. S., & Hua, K. A. (2005, March). Decision tree classifier for network intrusion detection with GA-based feature selection. In *Proceedings of the 43rd annual Southeast regional conference-Volume 2* (pp. 136-141). 10.1145/1167253.1167288

Stergiou, C. L., Psannis, K. E., & Gupta, B. B. (2020). IoT-based big data secure management in the fog over a 6G wireless network. *IEEE Internet of Things Journal*, *8*(7), 5164–5171. doi:10.1109/ JIOT.2020.3033131

Tewari, A., & Gupta, B. B. (2020). Secure Timestamp-Based Mutual Authentication Protocol for IoT Devices Using RFID Tags. *International Journal on Semantic Web and Information Systems*, *16*(3), 20–34. doi:10.4018/IJSWIS.2020070102

Vijayanand, R., Devaraj, D., & Kannapiran, B. (2018). Intrusion detection system for wireless mesh network using multiple support vector machine classifiers with genetic-algorithm-based feature selection. *Computers & Security*, *77*, 304–314. doi:10.1016/j.cose.2018.04.010

Wang, W., Feng, Y., & Dai, W. (2018). Topic analysis of online reviews for two competitive products using latent Dirichlet allocation. *Electronic Commerce Research and Applications*, *29*, 142–156. doi:10.1016/j.elerap.2018.04.003

Wang, W., Li, Y., Wang, X., Liu, J., & Zhang, X. (2018). Detecting Android malicious apps and categorizing benign apps with ensemble of classifiers. *Future Generation Computer Systems*, *78*, 987–994. doi:10.1016/j.future.2017.01.019

Zhang, Z., Sun, R., Zhao, C., Wang, J., Chang, C. K., & Gupta, B. B. (2017). CyVOD: A novel trinity multimedia social network scheme. *Multimedia Tools and Applications*, *76*(18), 18513–18529. doi:10.100711042-016-4162-z

Chapter 3
Deep–Learning and Machine–Learning–Based Techniques for Malware Detection and Data–Driven Network Security

Praneeth Gunti
National Institute of Technology, Kurukshetra, India

Brij B. Gupta
National Institute of Technology, Kurukshetra, India

Francisco José García Peñalvo
ⓘ https://orcid.org/0000-0001-9987-5584
University of Salamanca, Spain

ABSTRACT

A never-ending fight is taking place among malware creators and security experts as the advances in malware are daunting. The machine learning strategies are indeed the new mode of researching malware. The purpose of this chapter is to explore machine learning methods for malware recognition and in general deep learning methods. The chapter gives complete explanations of the techniques and resources used in a standard machine learning process for detecting malware. It examines the study issues that are posed by existing study methods and introduces the potential avenues of study in future. By administering a study to the participants, scholars have a better knowledge of the malware detections. The authors start by discussing simple dynamic modelling methods, their importance to the data analytics of malware, and their implementations. They use open access resources such as virustotal.com that review sample of dynamic analysis in reality.

DOI: 10.4018/978-1-7998-7789-9.ch003

Copyright © 2022, IGI Global. Copying or distributing in print or electronic forms without written permission of IGI Global is prohibited.

INTRODUCTION

Throughout this section, you will understand the fundamentals of complex malware detection. Unlike static research, which relies on what kind of malware seems like in document format, the dynamic analysis comprises executing malware in a secure, confined area and then determine how it acts. It would be like putting a harmful bacterial strain over to an enclosed area to see the impact against many cells. Utilising dynamic analysis, we may switch through typical static analysis obstacles, like packaging and deception, and also obtain more precise visibility into the intent of a specific malware test. Security and Privacy is needed everywhere like in web applications (Gupta 2016), IoT devices (Tewari, 2017)(Ab Malek, 2016), cloud computing (Al-Qerem, 2020), routing protocols (Jerbi, 2020) in WSN etc., so that our data and the transactions are protected.

Does Dynamic Analysis Needed?

To grasp why dynamic analysis need, remember the topic of packaged malware. Recognise that packaging malware relates to compacting or misrepresenting the x86 base source code of the software to conceal the deceptive existence of the application. The bundled malicious code unwraps its own as it attacks the target computer of that kind by which the program could be executed. We can attempt to dismantle a sealed or abstracted malicious payload utilising static detection methods; however, it is a tedious method. For instance, through static testing, we would first have to identify the position of the ambiguous script within the malicious document. After that, we will need to locate the deception functions that will successfully de-obfuscate this script to be executed. After finding the macros, we would discover why this de-obfuscation technique operates to execute that on the program. And afterwards, will we start the actual method of reversing the malicious script. An easy but intelligent solution to this method is running the malicious program in a secure, enclosed atmosphere termed a sandbox. Testing malicious code in a sandbox helps this one disassembles its own as it does before harming a primary target. By merely executing malware, we will figure out how many servers a certain binary malware binds to, which machine configuration settings it adjusts, as well as which Input/Output interface it is attempting to do.

Resources for Dynamic Malware Identification

Dynamic modelling is valuable for both malware processing and malware reverse engineering. Since dynamic modelling shows how a malicious test performs, we may equate its behaviour with many certain malware mixtures. For instance, since dynamic analysis reveals which documents the malware suspects send to the filesystem, we could use this information to link the malicious documents that write related config files to the disc. These kinds of hints allow one to categorise malicious files focused on general characteristics. It will also support us in recognising malicious files created by similar organisations or are members of common groups. Most notably, dynamic processing is valuable for creating machine-based malware indicators. We may prepare a detector to differentiate between harmful and benevolent clones by analysing their actions through dynamic study. For instance, by analysing millions of complex review reports from either malware or innocuous archives, a machine learning algorithm will understand that if msword.exe executes a program called powershell.exe, this behaviour is harmful; however, while msword.exe runs Browser, it is pretty safe.

All Important Methods for Dynamic Research

You will access various downloadable, accessible, dynamic analysis resources online—this segment reports on virustotal.com and CuckooBox. The virustotal.com platform has a web application that lets anyone apply complex review samples for free. CuckooBox is an application framework that helps you configure your custom dynamic testing system such that you could always test binaries locally. The developers and administrators of virustoral.com even manage CuckooBox under the hood. Therefore, knowing how to interpret the data on virustotal.com would help one analyse the outcomes of CuckooBox.

Malicious Code Actions

Below were the main groups a malware can undertake and the threat forms.

- Editing the file system, for instance, copying a machine driver to memory, updating machine config files, inserting new programmes to the operating system, and adjusting the windows registry to guarantee start-up software.
- Editing a Windows registry for changing the device config. For instance, adjust the firewall configurations.
- Setup application driver, for instance, processing a system driver to monitor consumer keyboard strokes.
- Actions on the network, for instance, resolve web addresses and render HTTP queries.

We would discuss these habits in more depth utilising malicious payload and review the virustotal. com analysis.

Barriers to the Fundamental Dynamic Analysis

Dynamic analysis is an effective technique, but it's not a solution for malware assessment. It has significant restrictions. One drawback is that malware developers are conscious of CuckooBox as well as other hierarchical testing systems and aim to bypass these by having their malware unable to function as it notices that it is operating in CuckooBox. The CuckooBox engineers are conscious that malware writers are attempting to do just that, but they try to get through tries by malware and bypass CuckooBox. This cat and mouse activity is played on an ongoing basis so that some malware tests can eventually recognise that they will be operating in dynamic analysis conditions and would struggle to function as we attempt to execute them. Another drawback is that dynamic detection could not expose critical malware behaviours despite any effort to bypass them. Take the problem of discrete malware which links directly to a remote server while operating and waiting for instructions to be given. For e.g., such instructions can request a malware template to scan for some types of target hosting data, record keyboard strokes, or switch on a camera. Throughout this scenario, if the remote server does not transmit instructions when it is no longer online, neither of such harmful actions can be observed. Owing to these drawbacks, dynamic processing is not a cure for malware analysis. In reality, skilled malware researchers mix dynamic and static research to deliver the optimal results feasibly.

REVIEW OF MALWARE

The method of malware deconstructing to learn how it operates, evaluate its features, root and possible effect is named malware analysis. With millions of new malicious programmes in the wild and mutated copies of previously identified programmes, the cumulative amount of malware identified by protection researchers has increased in recent years. As a consequence, malware detection is essential to any company or network that leads to data breaches.

XSS vulnerabilities can be exploited by adding JavaScript function calls and function description to perform harmful acts. (Gupta, 2016)(Gangwar, 2015)(Gupta, 2015) Address this by implementing server-side XSS attack prevention and detection solutions, called XSS-SAFE, focused on automatic injection information and disinfectant insertion into the JavaScript injection code.

The ad hoc mobile network is a less networked service owing to its operational capacity, without any existing infrastructure being supported. In MANET, safety plays a crucial role because of applications such as battlefield and disaster relief networks. The absence of trustworthy unified authority and scarce infrastructure means that MANETs are more insecure than wired networks. A system for handling DDoS attacks in the mobile ad hoc network is urgently needed. (Chhabra, 2013) addressed the different mechanisms for attacking the threats and the problems caused by DDoS attacks, including how the attacks can influence MANET.

(Zhang, 2017) suggested a comprehensive multimedia networking site trinity method, designed the algorithm for an enhanced hybrid suggestion by combining interactive filters and content-based recommendations and created the CyVOD working prototype. Mobile multimedia DRM modes are added to the network, including offline and online. Managing digital ownership is accomplished by digital content encryption and secured access rights. In addition, security protocols are introduced that validate user identification to prevent unauthorised users from transmitting their digital content maliciously. Compared with the only content-driven approaches, the enhanced hybrid proposed methodology used in CyVOD has upgraded the performance.

In particular, the researchers used the Attack Evaluation Practice, which describes a number of aspects to help estimate the extent of danger related to known vulnerabilities. Ten of the various vulnerabilities protected by (Gupta, 2017) was based on clear vulnerabilities.

There have been two main methods of malware detection: static analysis and dynamic analysis (Gibert, 2020). On the one side, the static analysis requires testing the malware without executing it. The dynamic analysis, on the other hand, includes executing the malware. Segments 2.1 and 1.2 offer a brief overview of all methods.

Static Analysis

The static analysis comprises of analysing the program or configuration of the executable without loading it. This review method will validate if a document is malicious, including usability details and can even be often used to make a clear collection of signatures. For e.g., the most popular technique used to recognise malicious software uniquely is hashing. The hashing software generates a special hash, a kind of fingerprint that distinguishes the programme. The two main standard block ciphers are Message-Digest Algorithm 5 (MD5) and Secure Hash Algorithm 1 (SHA-1). The most popular method to static evaluation is:

- Locate sets of plot lines or strings. Trying to search via the sequences of a programme is the best way to provide clues regarding its features. Binary derived sequences can include connections to document locations of files changed or executed by the application, URLs viewed by the software, domain names, Email addresses, threat instructions, dynamic link libraries (DLLs) identities enabled registry entries, etc. The Strings search method may be used to check for ASCII or Unicode strings that neglect meaning and encoding in the runtime.
- Collecting the related resources and features of an application, and also the documentation regarding the file. These numbers include a census of which code is exchanged among software solutions. The titles of these Windows features help one grasp what they are doing. The Utility Dependency Walker is a free Windows framework that used a list of borrowed and transferred features from an executable.
- PE headers and parts review. The import route headers contain more detail than only the last import file names. The files included metadata on their own, like the parts of the real files. To obtain this knowledge, you must use the PEView method.
- Looking for shrouded or encrypted code. Malware authors utilise packaging and coding techniques to render their data impossible to examine. Programs packaged or encrypted provide shorter and greater entropy than legal programmes. To identify loaded files, PEiD is used.
- Unplugging the programme or interpreting computer code in a programming language, i.e. decompiling the application. Some reverse-engineering methods load executables into disassemblers to explore what the programmes do. In this case, the essential resources for unplugging Windows PE format executable are Ghidra, Radare2 and IDA Pro.

Dynamic Analysis

Runtime Functional Analysis permits the operation of the software and viewing the actions of the programme on the device. This method is usually conducted when dynamic analysis has hit a dead-end or completed static analysis. Dynamic research looks for the individual operations undertaken by a machine. A successful external review must be run in a secure setting where the device is not at risk, and all networked networks are safe. In this way, dedicated utilities are equipped.

The computer must be physically separated from the Internet or some other network to avoid malware from spreading. There are also protection concerns affecting several of the networked physical equipment.

The second possibility is to use "data computers" to do transient analysis. "Virtual system" is like a device with some functionalities. The OS operating on the VM is maintained separated from the host OS, and hence, the malware can't damage the host OS. VMware, Oracle VM and VirtualBox are the virtual device instances implementations that are used. There is a range of methods on the market to do complex research on machine code. The Cuckoo Sandbox is recognised as the best free software malware analysis framework. This method helps researchers to track API calls, evaluate internet traffic, and run storage evaluation. There are different surveillance methods to track illegal acts and seek out fraudulent activity. Process Monitoring or procmon is a software for Windows which monitors machine or process operation. Task Manager shows different details on what processes are installed into the operating system. Regshot is a registry comparison registry that enables registrations to be recorded. NetCat is a network monitoring application. Wireshark is a free software data packets analyser that can be used to maintain track of internet traffic. Besides tech, debuggers are still an important weapon. A debugger may be used to test the routines of other applications. They give an informative description of a strategy and how a programme unfolded. The perfect platform for malware researchers is OllyDbg since it's open and has several modules to expand its capability.

It's a challenge that persists against the usage of virtual machines and sandboxing in virus and malware detection. And if you undertake all care when downloading applications, there will still be a chance of contamination when using them. From period to period, vulnerabilities are discovered in VMware software frameworks that enable a malware threat to be exploited.

Malware Development

The danger faced by malicious apps is tremendous, and there are a number of complex, advanced and easy-to-access malware to screw up critical networks. Malware is often continually changing and forced to keep up with threat defence. Malware campaigns improved following the rise in the polymorphic and metamorphic methods used to track, remove and conceal the existence of the malware. Polymorphic malware transforms the program while retaining untouched features of the malware software. Encryption and packaging are techniques that are used to conceal code. Compression may be used to mask the essence of an application or software. Finally, at runtime, data reconstruction is performed. Malware operators build resources such as crypters to encrypt or modify malware code so that it is more challenging for scholars to analyse it. A crypter helps you to decode malicious data, which means that the code is secure. The malware updates the code on re-distribution or copies itself. Malware writers may employ several transforming strategies including, though not limited to, renaming, permuting, extending, shrinking and inserting garbage code into their malware. Because of the extent of malware, the procedures required to study malware are sometimes lengthy and complex.

Orthodox antivirus approaches, which are signature-based and heuristic, are quite time-consuming. A signature is an attribute that identifies an exe file, equivalent to a fingerprint. Signature-based techniques are unsuitable for identifying unidentified malware variants. We should seek more behavioural research tools that can easily spot ransomware. To solve some of the difficulties of conventional antivirus programs and maintain up with emerging ransomware threats and disruptive behaviour shifts, security researchers built and used machine learning strategies in their approaches.

TYPICAL MACHINE LEARNING ALGORITHMS

During the last decade, there's been a sharp growth in computer educational methods to cope with malware issues. The progress of machine learning would never be feasible without these technological advances. The progress of machine learning would never be feasible without these technological advances.

- The first improvement is the substantial rise in viruses branded and counted that has been published to the security world as well as to the academic circle. The spectrum of these streams varies from small high-quality large-scale samples to massive quantities of malware (Ronen, 2018).
- The second trend is that computing capacity has considerably improved and is getting cheaper. This resulted in speeding up the training phase and adapting more powerful and more sophisticated learning algorithms to the continued rapid growth of data.
- Machine learning has made several advancements over the past decade and has scaled on a wide variety of activities.

A timeline is collecting data in data science, cleaning it, choosing the necessary models, training specific models, and eventually conducting forecasting. See Fig. 1. Rather than handling the malware like a virus on the kernel level, most data preparation methods include pre-processing the exe file to retrieve a series of functions that include an intuitive overview of the programme. The sample data has been utilised to teach a method to optimise a specific problem. It is necessary to identify and discriminate between various forms of malware to identify the threats effectively. The key variation among machine learning systems is the way it recovers security data. A single value $y = f(x)$ is extracted by a malware detection method that ranges from 0 to 1. On another side, a classification method produces the likelihood of a provided executable contributing from each output variable or group.

Figure 1. Workflow of machine learning

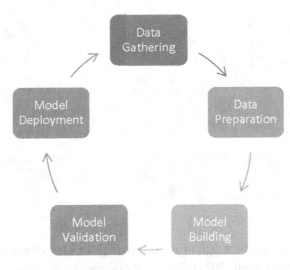

The classification system of the characteristics is given in Fig 2. According to this discourse, the forms of malware detection methods may be classified into two types: static aspects and dynamic aspects.

DEEP LEARNING METHODS

Standard machine learning methods use professional experience because of manual data collection. This offers an analytical perspective of how machine learning tools provide access to knowledge regarding malware-related behaviour. The primary facets of a good machine learning project were feature architecture and function extraction. Along with recent developments in computer vision and natural language processing (NLP) study, there has been an advent of machine learning methods for malware classification. These methods used in combination with ML. have rendered workflows entirely trainable from raw data to the production of known objects. These methods are also used in securing IoT devices and SDN networks (Letteri, 2019), Two-Phase Load Balancing Algorithm for Cloud Environments (Singh, 2021).

Figure 2. Taxonomy of the characteristics used in conventional M.L. methods.

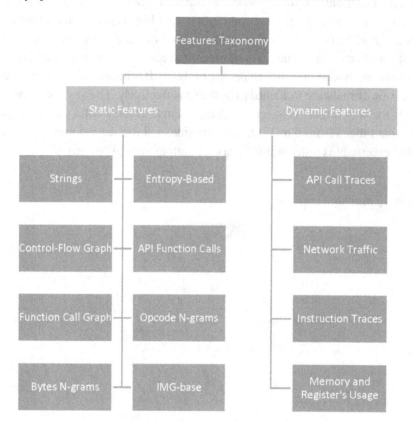

There are several methods in the usage of deep learning for identifying, classifying malicious applications, adversarial attacks (Mani, 2021). The goal audiences and groups concerned are described in depth below.

Tiesquare Matrix Illustration

Machine learning approaches in this segment can deliver a collection of features that are a sequence of code. Then, the function vector is forwarded to a flow forward neural network. The obtained feature vectors can be used in training feed-forward neural networks as well.

(Saxe, 2015) also addressed implementing the neural network malware detection method that consists of three key components. The scheme is constructed of the five components as below: Their method was tested on a dataset of 431926 exe files and obtained a recognition accuracy of 95%.

(Huang and Stoke, 2016) indicated an algorithm for malware identification and recognition focused on deep learning. They derived static and interactive experiments, such as null-terminated cards, activity plus variable, and trigrams. Due to the increased dimensional space of input space, unsupervised dimensionality reduction was made to create descriptive functions to classify each class. After that, the variable of the function was decreased to 5000 characteristics utilising Random Principal Component Analysis (RPCA). Finally, a deep architecture was educated utilising predictive features.

Researchers have pointed out a malware categorisation framework that map a high-dimensional function map into a significantly low dimensional using randomly created vectors. Random forecasts decreased the number of features from 180,000 to 4000 (Dahl, 2013). After the network sort learnt a non-linear paradigm to identify malware, The device was tested on a database of 2.6 million labelled items and an output ratio of 0.49%.

Image-Based Representation

The input for neural network approaches contains picture representations of binary material. Instead of focusing on hand-engineered attribute separators, they tried implementing a fully connected neural network framework for object training and testing for greyscale pictures.

(Gibert, 2019) used a Convolutional Network Design consisting of three convolutional chains and one connected block. Each convolutional chain consisted of ReLU activation, limit and widespread acceptance. The convolutional levels served as attention detectors for the particular attributes or trends throughout the input data and the properly connected layers to integrate the observed functions and calculate a specific output. People's success in grouping was assessed towards handcrafted attribute extraction methods (Nataraj, 2011)(Kancherla, 2013)(Ahmadi, 2016), and they performed well. In this review, (Rezende, 2017) proposed to use the ResNet-50 design and pretrained weights for malware picture classification (Nataraj, 2011).

API Calls Traces

The method used in API function calls is to create an input functionality vector, and the vector's location shows if the application triggered a specific API function. It's doesn't recognise the series in which all the API operations might have been used. Another alternate solution is to record the series of API function calls and use it to construct classifiers.

(Athiwaratkun, 2017) sought to reflect the connection relationships between API behaviour of various sizes. They also worked with Long Short-Term Memory and Gated Recurrent Unit as a paradigm for expression. Their strategy occupies two phases. In the first point, we shall build our function candidates by using LSTM or GRU. Ses attributes are classed with regression analysis then softmax. They also came up with a convolutional neural network (Zhang, 2015). This network takes as input a series of around 1014 chars, each character being an activity. Patterns shorter than 10,000 chars are padded out at the edge of a series with 0 bytes. There are nine layers in the character-level structure, two fully connected layers and seven convolutional layers.

(Kolosnjaji, 2016) examined whether we can use neural networks (NN) to enhance the grouping of freshly obtained malware variants into predetermined malware groups. They tested two forms of neural networks, convolutionary, for modelling request series. They developed a neural network architecture that incorporates the regularisation of n-grams and an entirely sequential model. Also, the API call series of vulnerabilities without API requests replicated greater than two times in a sequence. Each specific call was defined by one-hot encryption to identify variable per each request. It requires a convolution accompanied by combining that serves as the function extractor. Thus, the fingerprints in the convolutional portion of the system rely on the persistent portion of the system. To compute an aggregate average, a pooling method was used. They added dropout to avoid overfitting and a softmax layer for performance probabilities.

Guidance Cases

Software may be modelled as a series of procedures. These guidelines can be derived from static evaluation and dynamic research. On the other side, you may inquire into acquiring them by unplugging the executable code. Security administrators may also track and map the series of orders performed at runtime. These strings of guidelines may be utilised to teach an end-to-end device to learn the required functions without needing to explicate a million examples during preparation.

(Gibert, 2017) proposes a Neural Network that takes an encoding as a function compared to a Convolutional Neural Network. Convolution operation will learn to recognise n-gram-like signs since it recognises subsets of the script. It helps them identify quite long n-grams, which are inefficiently calculated using a clear evaluation of all n-grams. This is done by computing for varying sizes of different variables. For e.g., in their study, the researchers incorporated 64 filters of length h x k per each h Î {2, 3, 4, 5, 6, 7}. The highest amount was selected as the equivalent function of the filter (also known as global max-pooling). By doing this, we will find basic terms from input records. The softmax framework outputs the likelihood over each of the groups.

Another possible way to cope with a hierarchical system of PE exe files is to tackle it with a Hierarchical Convolutional Neural Network (HCNN) (Gibert, 2019). Instead of displaying malware as a linear set of commands, the author described them according to the functions of machine programmes. As a result, assembly language commands were broken into components with the aid of mnemonics. As a result, the hierarchy of convolutional functions grasped both the mnemonic-level and the more realistic function-level of functions.

Digital Representation

A computer programme is also described using sequences of octets. In other terms, each character is a unit of an input string. The most significant benefit of utilising the graph is that it can reflect malware indistinctly if it is a PE file or a non-PE (including an ELF file). This poses a major challenge in portraying an executable as a series of bytes. First, by considering each character as a unit in a series, the series would consist of millions of measures, rendering it one of the most demanding string categorisation tasks. Each byte signifies unique knowledge. Many binary files display varying degrees of spatial similarity. Machines prefer to execute orders close to one another, but this law does not often apply due to system requests and hops, and so commands and operation may be passed to other references in the cache. These differences are held on the differential file and its hexadecimal type, respectively. Such considerations should be addressed when constructing a system of analysis that identifies malware from a series of bytes.

Use Convolutional Neural Network (CNN) to classify object to generate object recognition instead of object category recognition (Raff, 2017). They merged the convolutional triggering with a universal maximal pooling stage before a completely linked layer. Instead of taking raw values as data, they mapped each byte to a fixed-size function vector.

(Krcál, 2018) completed an information-rich design consisting of a hidden layer, accompanied by four convolutions, four max-pooling layers, another four convolutions, preceded by mean international pooling then four completely linked layers. They tested their design towards the MalConv framework and experienced an improvement of the predictive efficiency of about 1%. Besides, they handcrafted functionality to create a better classifier.

Network Traffic

This system was suggested by (Prasse, 2017)(Muna, 2018) to identify malware on user machines. The researchers retrieved separate functionality for client machines and site names from the obtained network streams from the client-side. Then LSTM or recurrent neural network takes streams of inflow as feedback and trains to decide whether the streams derive from malicious programs.

(AL-Hawawreh, 2018) defined intrusion detection techniques focused on deep learning frameworks to identify breaches in Network ICSs. A Deep Autoencoder knows regular network patterns in the unsupervised learning process, and a Deep Neural Network utilises the approximate variables of the Autoencoder to fine-tune its variables and identify connection requests predictions.

MACHINE LEARNING ENABLED MALWARE DETECTORS

A novel, complex image recovery model driven by visual salinity is described by (Wang, 2020). Image forgery detection approaches include certain pattern descriptives to identify the image and run ML algorithms to detect whether or not the image is fabricated. In the method, a noise map with a Wiener-filter-based noise-reducing procedure is retrieved from the picture. The noise map is implemented with an interrelation with both a pixel and the adjacent pixels using a multi-resolution regression filter (Ghoneim, 2018)(Yamaguchi, 2017).

Mostly with Free Software Machine Learning Resources accessible nowadays, you could create customised, machine-based malware identification tools, either as the primary identification mechanism or to support troubleshooting tools, with minimal difficulty. So why develop one's own machine learning software while professional antivirus approaches are always accessible? Once you get access to real-life instance breaches, like ransomware used for a specific community of intruders attacking your system, creating personal new machine learning-based identification technology will provide us with training samples of such vulnerabilities (Saxe, 2018).

On the other hand, commercial virus protection machines can ignore these warnings unless they have malware signatures. Business methodologies are indeed "locked books"—that means we may not recognise how they function and have a local opportunity to adjust it. While we develop our detector systems, we know what they've done, and we can adapt it to the preference so that we minimise false positivity and false negativity. This is useful as in certain implementations, and you may be able to accept more significant false positives in return for fewer false negatives (for instance, while you're scanning the network for malicious items such that you might hand-inspect them to decide whether they were fraudulent). In contrast, you may be prepared to forgive more significant false negatives in certain implementations to return besides less false positives.

Throughout this part, you will explore how to build your custom high-level detecting software. I begin by illustrating the fresh thoughts underlying machine learning, involving storage capabilities, judgement limits, testing set, inadequately and over-fitting. After which, we concentrate on four simple methodologies— random forest, logistic regression, decision tree and nearest neighbours how they could be used to diagnose.

Measures Involved in Developing Machine Learning–Based System

There is indeed a significant differentiation among other programming methods and machine learning. While the standard algorithms instruct the programme what to perform, machine learning programs learn by experience how and when to solve problems. For example, instead of merely taking out a series of preloaded guidelines, machine learning vulnerability monitoring mechanisms could be programmed to decide if a data is harmful or safe through analysing through observations of safe and dangerous data.

The expectation of information protection machine learning techniques was how they could robotise generating signatures and then have the competence to accomplish better reliably than signature-based malware analysis strategies, particularly on modern, previously undiscovered malware. Primarily, the procedure we adopt to create every machine-based detector, such as a decision tree, comes out to the following points:

- Set of malicious and benignware cases. We can use such scenarios (named learning scenarios) to teach the framework of machine learning to recognise vulnerabilities.
- Remove the characteristics within each learning scenario to display the method as a numerical series. This move also involves analysis into creating better functionality that can allow the machine learning system to develop correct inferences.
- Teach the machine learning algorithm to identify malware by utilising the functionality we've collected.
- Test the solution to such data not used in the practice scenarios to determine how effectively our recognition method performs.

Let us address all of these measures in further depth in the subsequent pages.

Collecting Training Instances

Machine learning indicators succeed or fail based on the testing data given. The capacity of the malicious detector to identify malicious binaries strongly relies on the amount and consistency of the testing instances you include. Be interested in consuming a lot of time collecting training data while developing machine learning detection systems, so the more samples you provide to the device, the more effective it will be. The consistency of the teaching samples is, therefore, quite critical. The vulnerabilities and benignware that you are accumulating could represent the variety of vulnerabilities and benignware that you anticipate your scanner to recognise whenever you request to determine if recent documents are harmful or benign.

For e.g., if you'd like to identify vulnerabilities from either a particular potential risk community, you need to gather quite so many malicious files as practicable from a certain community for use in your device training. If you aim to identify a large group of malware (like ransomware), it is crucial to gather many more qualitative data of such a category as practicable.

Simultaneously, the harmless practice sets that you supply to the device must represent the sort of benign documents that you would expect your detection system to examine until it is deployed. For example, when you focus on malware detection on a network connection, you can train your machine with extensive testing of benignware that graduates and college staff are using to prevent false positives.

These benign instances could involve video games, text editors, personalised applications created by the institution IT unit, and other safety programmes.

Extraction Features

To differentiate data as safe or unsafe, we prepare machine learning models by presenting the characteristics of application binaries; these were all file characteristics that will allow the machine to differentiate between safe and unsafe data. For e.g., below are a few characteristics that may be used to decide if a document is safe or unsafe:

- If it is electronically signed
- Existence of deformed headers
- The existence of encrypted information
- If the programme has also been presented on over 100 machines.

To achieve this environment, the files must be taken out. For, e.g., we could build programmes to decide if a document is electronically signed, has incorrect information, is compressed etc. In defence data science, we also use many functionalities in machine learning detection systems. For, e.g., we could build functionality for any API request throughout the Win32 API so that a binary will include that functionality and possess the specific API call.

Building Strong Functionality

Our aim should be to pick the characteristics that produce the best reliable outcomes. This segment points forth several of the general principles to be observed.

First, when choosing characteristics, pick those that reflect your most robust assumption about what would allow a machine learning program to differentiate unsafe files against safe ones. For e.g., the "includes encrypted information" function may be a nice malware flag since we recognise that malware always includes encrypted information, and we are assuming that benignware would have encrypted information more seldom. The advantage of machine learning is that when this theory is incorrect and benignware includes encrypted information as much as malware would, the program can indeed disregard this function. If the idea is correct, the device can know how to utilise the "includes encrypted information" function to identify malware.

Second, don't include too many functions further that range of options will get so huge, especially compared to the amount of practice set for the detection technique. That's what machine learning researchers term the "Dimensionality Curse." For e.g., when you have 1,000 characteristics and just 1,000 samples of training, the odds are that you may not have good examples of coaching to tell your machine learning model how each function means to a provided binary. Stats informs us that this is necessary to offer the device a few characteristics compared to the number of practice samples you have accessible, and just let it shape possibly the best assumptions regarding which functionality really imply malware. Ultimately, make sure that the applications reflect various possibilities on what comprises vulnerability or benignware. For e.g., you can want to create encrypted communication characteristics, like when a document uses encrypted communication API calls or a Public Key Infrastructure (PKI), but ensure you can use non-encryption-related characteristics to protect your decisions. That means, if the code is unable to identify malware depending on one form of function, it may still identify it by utilising other functions.

Education of Machine Learning Applications

After taking out functions from the testing binaries, it's essential to teach your machine learning models. Because this appears like, computationally, it relies mainly on the machine learning method you use. For e.g., teaching the decision tree method requires a separate learning algorithm than practising the logistic regression methodology. Luckily, both machine learning detection systems have the same general design. You supply them with learning data that includes functionalities from the test binaries and related identifiers that say the program which repositories are vulnerabilities and what are benignware. The methods then train to assess whether or not fresh, prior unknown binaries are harmful or benevolent. The teaching is addressed in more depth further in this chapter

This textbook focuses on the category of machine learning techniques defined as controlled machine learning techniques. To use machine learning models for malware detection, we prepare models by telling them which instances are harmful and harmless. Another type of machine learning techniques, unsupervised methods, doesn't enable us to recognise which instances are harmful or benevolent in our practice collection. Malware detection algorithms are far less successful at identifying harmful malware, and we would not include them in the textbook.

Testing artificial intelligence frameworks and models. After you have learned the machine learning method, you have to verify how reliable it is. You achieve it by executing a professional data system that you've not learned and seeing how well it decides if or not their samples are harmful or benevolent. In defence, we usually teach our machines examples that we've collected until that moment in time. Afterwards, we evaluate samples that we've encountered after the last moment in time, calculate how our programs can identify new malware, and assess how well our machines can prevent generating false positivity on a recent dataset. Many machine learning analysis requires lots of experiments like result shows: we build a machine learning framework, evaluate it, and then modify it, improve it once again, and evaluate it once more, perform the process until we are glad by the performance.

Let's explore how some machine learning algorithms operate. This is the most challenging part of the chapter but satisfying if you interpret it correctly. Throughout this discussion, we discuss the coherent principles that encompass these frameworks; then we will move through each method in depth.

Analyzing Function Spaces and Judgement Limits

Two basic geometric concepts will allow you to recognise all machine learning-based identification techniques: the concept of a geometrical space function as well as the concept of Judgement limits. You identify malware binaries on one side of the judgement border and benignware binaries on the other side. As we use a machine learning method to find data as harmful or harmless, we automatically extract functions which we can put tests in a function room, and afterwards, we test what side of the judgement limit the tests are using to decide if the samples are harmful or harmless.

This geometry of knowing the spaces and the limits of options is valid for structures running in one, two, or 3-dimensional structures (characteristics), but it often encompasses function environments with billions of dimensions. In contrast, billion-plus dimensional spaces cannot be visualised or conceived. We'll stick to two-dimensional illustrations in this section to keep them more accessible to visualise.

Still, please note that real security machine learning applications almost all use thousands, millions, or billions of dimensions, as well as the core principles we present in a two-dimensional setting are for practical cases of more than two dimensions.

Build a toy malware detection issue to explain the concept of a judgement limit in a function space. Assume we have such a classification model of malicious and harmless tests. Now suppose we derive the below two attributes within each binary: the amount of the document which tends to be compressed, as well as the number of questionable operations within each binary source.

CONCLUSION

This chapter provides a comprehensive analysis of the literature relating to machine learning methods used for malware identification and categorisation. The end of this article concerns a total of 67 academic papers on malware identification on Windows platforms. These experiments are evaluated using different critical variables such as the attributes of the databases, classification algorithms, properties of the studies and the analytical tasks. Our analysis made four significant contributors to this report. The process of feature extraction, selection and reduction to match model is defined. In this sense, there are three critical types: (1) static approaches, (2) dynamic approaches, and (3) hybrid approaches.

State-of-the-art information extraction techniques utilise a static-based methodology where no coding is executed. In addition, dynamic-based approaches provide certain methods that target runtime features of malware operation. This hybrid method incorporates both static and dynamic elements of the system. This chapter adds to the research on malware identification by deep learning by presenting a comprehensive overview of the different methods focused on the network design and how its input data are structured. Deep neural network methods are classified according to the form of the input.

- Computer programme strategies that conduct software engineering to retrieve a functionality vector
- Computer programme techniques that take the greyscale expression of an exe file as input
- Software programme techniques that are fed the series of API feature requests
- Computer programme techniques that design a programme as a set of commands
- Computer programme techniques that depict a computer programme as a stream of bytes
- Computer programme techniques that seek to define a programme with its internet traffic.

This chapter discusses approaches that utilise upwards of one modality of the input to identify malware in an automated manner. Hybrid approaches include both early and late fusion systems. We will address the idea drift problem and adversarial learning. In addition, we would address the state of the measurements being used by the research community to test their processes and the question of classification imbalance. You have already heard about the benefits and disadvantages of dynamic analysis. Now that you've studied how to do simple dynamic research, you're able to look deeper into the data science of malware. The majority of this textbook reflects on the performance of malware data science on dynamic malware data processing.

REFERENCES

Ab Malek, M. S. B., Ahmadon, M. A. B., Yamaguchi, S., & Gupta, B. B. (2016, October). On privacy verification in the IoT service based on PN 2. In *2016 IEEE 5th Global Conference on Consumer Electronics* (pp. 1-4). IEEE.

Ahmadi, M., Ulyanov, D., Semenov, S., Trofimov, M., & Giacinto, G. (2016, March). Novel feature extraction, selection and fusion for effective malware family classification. In *Proceedings of the sixth ACM conference on data and application security and privacy* (pp. 183-194). ACM.

Al-Qerem, A., Alauthman, M., Almomani, A., & Gupta, B. B. (2020). IoT transaction processing through cooperative concurrency control on fog–cloud computing environment. *Soft Computing, 24*(8), 5695–5711.

Athiwaratkun, B., & Stokes, J. W. (2017, March). Malware classification with LSTM and GRU language models and a character-level CNN. In *2017 IEEE International Conference on Acoustics, Speech and Signal Processing (ICASSP)* (pp. 2482-2486). IEEE.

Chhabra, M., Gupta, B., & Almomani, A. (2013). A novel solution to handle DDOS attack in MANET. *Journal of Information Security, 4*(3), 34631. Advance online publication. doi:10.4236/jis.2013.43019

Dahl, G. E., Stokes, J. W., Deng, L., & Yu, D. (2013, May). Large-scale malware classification using random projections and neural networks. In *2013 IEEE International Conference on Acoustics, Speech and Signal Processing* (pp. 3422-3426). IEEE.

Ghoneim, A., Muhammad, G., Amin, S. U., & Gupta, B. (2018). Medical image forgery detection for smart healthcare. *IEEE Communications Magazine, 56*(4), 33–37.

Gibert, D., Mateu, C., & Planes, J. (2019, July). A hierarchical convolutional neural network for malware classification. In *2019 International Joint Conference on Neural Networks (IJCNN)* (pp. 1-8). IEEE.

Gibert, D., Mateu, C., & Planes, J. (2020). The rise of machine learning for detection and classification of malware: Research developments, trends and challenges. *Journal of Network and Computer Applications, 153*, 102526.

Gibert, D., Mateu, C., Planes, J., & Vicens, R. (2019). Using convolutional neural networks for classification of malware represented as images. *Journal of Computer Virology and Hacking Techniques, 15*(1), 15–28.

Gou, Z., & Yamaguchi, S. (2017). Analysis of various security issues and challenges in cloud computing environment: a survey. In Identity Theft: Breakthroughs in Research and Practice (pp. 221-247). IGI Global.

Gupta, B. B., Gupta, S., Gangwar, S., Kumar, M., & Meena, P. K. (2015). Cross-site scripting (XSS) abuse and defense: Exploitation on several testing bed environments and its defense. *Journal of Information Privacy and Security, 11*(2), 118–136.

Gupta, S., & Gupta, B. B. (2015, May). PHP-sensor: a prototype method to discover workflow violation and XSS vulnerabilities in PHP web applications. In *Proceedings of the 12th ACM International Conference on Computing Frontiers* (pp. 1-8). ACM.

Gupta, S., & Gupta, B. B. (2016). XSS-SAFE: A server-side approach to detect and mitigate cross-site scripting (XSS) attacks in JavaScript code. *Arabian Journal for Science and Engineering, 41*(3), 897–920.

Gupta, S., & Gupta, B. B. (2016). JS-SAN: Defense mechanism for HTML5-based web applications against javascript code injection vulnerabilities. *Security and Communication Networks, 9*(11), 1477–1495.

Gupta, S., & Gupta, B. B. (2017). Detection, avoidance, and attack pattern mechanisms in modern web application vulnerabilities: Present and future challenges. *International Journal of Cloud Applications and Computing, 7*(3), 1–43.

Huang, W., & Stokes, J. W. (2016, July). MtNet: a multi-task neural network for dynamic malware classification. In *International conference on detection of intrusions and malware, and vulnerability assessment* (pp. 399-418). Springer. 10.1007/978-3-319-40667-1_20

Jerbi, W., Guermazi, A., & Trabelsi, H. (2020). A novel secure routing protocol of generation and management cryptographic keys for wireless sensor networks deployed in internet of things. *International Journal of High Performance Computing and Networking, 16*(2-3), 87–94.

Kancherla, K., & Mukkamala, S. (2013, April). Image visualization based malware detection. In *2013 IEEE Symposium on Computational Intelligence in Cyber Security (CICS)* (pp. 40-44). IEEE.

Kolosnjaji, B., Zarras, A., Webster, G., & Eckert, C. (2016, December). Deep learning for classification of malware system call sequences. In *Australasian Joint Conference on Artificial Intelligence* (pp. 137-149). Springer. 10.1007/978-3-319-50127-7_11

Krčál, M., Švec, O., Bálek, M., & Jašek, O. (2018). *Deep convolutional malware classifiers can learn from raw executables and labels only*. Academic Press.

Letteri, I., Penna, G. D., & Gasperis, G. D. (2019). Security in the internet of things: Botnet detection in software-defined networks by deep learning techniques. *International Journal of High Performance Computing and Networking, 15*(3-4), 170–182.

Mani, N., Moh, M., & Moh, T. S. (2021). Defending deep learning models against adversarial attacks. *International Journal of Software Science and Computational Intelligence, 13*(1), 72–89.

Muna, A. H., Moustafa, N., & Sitnikova, E. (2018). Identification of malicious activities in industrial internet of things based on deep learning models. *Journal of Information Security and Applications, 41*, 1-11.

Nataraj, L., Karthikeyan, S., Jacob, G., & Manjunath, B. S. (2011, July). Malware images: visualization and automatic classification. In *Proceedings of the 8th international symposium on visualization for cyber security* (pp. 1-7). Academic Press.

Prasse, P., Machlica, L., Pevný, T., Havelka, J., & Scheffer, T. (2017, September). Malware detection by analysing encrypted network traffic with neural networks. In *Joint European Conference on Machine Learning and Knowledge Discovery in Databases* (pp. 73-88). Springer. 10.1007/978-3-319-71246-8_5

Raff, E., Barker, J., Sylvester, J., Brandon, R., Catanzaro, B., & Nicholas, C. (2017). *Malware detection by eating a whole exe*. arXiv preprint arXiv:1710.09435.

Rezende, E., Ruppert, G., Carvalho, T., Ramos, F., & De Geus, P. (2017, December). Malicious software classification using transfer learning of resnet-50 deep neural network. In *2017 16th IEEE International Conference on Machine Learning and Applications (ICMLA)* (pp. 1011-1014). IEEE.

Ronen, R., Radu, M., Feuerstein, C., Yom-Tov, E., & Ahmadi, M. (2018). *Microsoft malware classification challenge*. arXiv preprint arXiv:1802.10135.

Saxe, J., & Berlin, K. (2015, October). Deep neural network based malware detection using two dimensional binary program features. In *2015 10th International Conference on Malicious and Unwanted Software (MALWARE)* (pp. 11-20). IEEE. 10.1109/MALWARE.2015.7413680

Saxe, J., & Sanders, H. (2018). *Malware Data Science: Attack Detection and Attribution*. No Starch Press.

Singh, A., & Kumar, R. (2021). A Two-Phase Load Balancing Algorithm for Cloud Environment. *International Journal of Software Science and Computational Intelligence*, *13*(1), 38–55.

Solis, D., & Vicens, R. (2017, October). Convolutional neural networks for classification of malware assembly code. In *Recent Advances in Artificial Intelligence Research and Development: Proceedings of the 20th International Conference of the Catalan Association for Artificial Intelligence, Deltebre, Terres de L'Ebre, Spain, October 25-27, 2017 (Vol. 300*, p. 221). IOS Press.

Tewari, A., & Gupta, B. B. (2017). A lightweight mutual authentication protocol based on elliptic curve cryptography for IoT devices. *International Journal of Advanced Intelligence Paradigms*, *9*(2-3), 111–121.

Wang, H., Li, Z., Li, Y., Gupta, B. B., & Choi, C. (2020). Visual saliency guided complex image retrieval. *Pattern Recognition Letters*, *130*, 64–72.

Zhang, X., Zhao, J., & LeCun, Y. (2015). *Character-level convolutional networks for text classification*. arXiv preprint arXiv:1509.01626.

Zhang, Z., Sun, R., Zhao, C., Wang, J., Chang, C. K., & Gupta, B. B. (2017). CyVOD: A novel trinity multimedia social network scheme. *Multimedia Tools and Applications*, *76*(18), 18513–18529.

Chapter 4
The Era of Advanced Machine Learning and Deep Learning Algorithms for Malware Detection

Kwok Tai Chui
Hong Kong Metropolitan University, Hong Kong

Patricia Ordóñez de Pablos
The University of Oviedo, Spain

Miltiadis D. Lytras
Deree College — The American College of Greece, Greece

Ryan Wen Liu
ⓘD https://orcid.org/0000-0002-1591-5583
Wuhan University of Technology, China

Chien-wen Shen
National Central University, Taiwan

ABSTRACT

Software has been the essential element to computers in today's digital era. Unfortunately, it has experienced challenges from various types of malware, which are designed for sabotage, criminal money-making, and information theft. To protect the gadgets from malware, numerous malware detection algorithms have been proposed. In the olden days there were shallow learning algorithms, and in recent years there are deep learning algorithms. With the availability of big data for training of model and affordable and high-performance computing services, deep learning has demonstrated its superiority in many smart city applications, in terms of accuracy, error rate, etc. This chapter intends to conduct a systematic review on the latest development of deep learning algorithms for malware detection. Some future research directions are suggested for further exploration.

DOI: 10.4018/978-1-7998-7789-9.ch004

Copyright © 2022, IGI Global. Copying or distributing in print or electronic forms without written permission of IGI Global is prohibited.

INTRODUCTION

Computing tools and smartphones have played an impactful role towards smart city vision in recent decades (Ficco, Esposito, Xiang, & Palmieri, 2017; Rose, Raghuram, Watson, & Wigley, 2021). According to the Statista (Technology Markets: Software, 2021), as shown in Figure 1, there is a steady growth rate of around 7.1-7.7% in the revenue of software development from 2017 to 2025, except the historical low 2.6% in 2020 and bounced back to 9% in 2021 during pandemic. The projection could be altered depending on the deployment of 5G and development of 6G (Stergiou, Psannis, & Gupta, 2020).

Intuitively, the more the number of software linking to gadgets, the more the number of malware attacks. Yet, numerous types of malware have been developed such as scareware, wiper, rogue software, adware, spyware, ransomware, Trojan horses, worms, and computer viruses (Kumar, 2020; Rendell, 2019). Surprisingly, the global yearly malware attacks (SonicWall, 2021) does not follow an increasing trend, as shown in Figure 2. From 2015 to 2017, the percentage changes in the number of malware attacks are -3.7% and 8.9%, respectively. There was a notably increment by 22.1% from 2017 to 2018 and slightly decrement by 5.7% from 2018 to 2019. Compared the last two recorded periods from 2019 to 2020, a significant drop (43.4%) in the number of malware attacks was observed. The key explanation to the drop of the malware attacks is malware detection algorithms which can detect malware and thus avoid the damage of gadgets.

A lot of traditional machine learning algorithms was employed for malware detection in literature, including decision tree, Naïve Bayes, support vector machine, K-nearest neighbour, Bayseian network, multi-layer perception, J48, and random forest, (Jerlin, & Marimuthu, 2018; Li et al., 2018; Narudin, Feizollah, Anuar, & Gani, 2016). There is room for improvement in terms of accuracy. Owning to the fact that a large amount of data is available as training dataset, attention is drawn into deep learning which can further enhance the accuracy of the detection model.

Figure 1. The worldwide statistics on the revenue of software development (by segment).

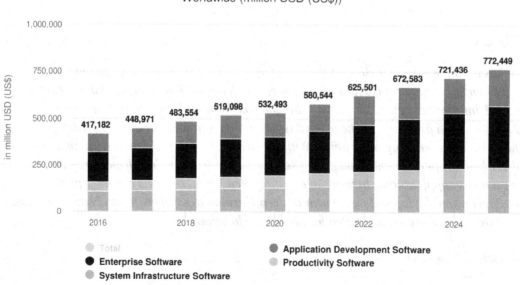

Figure 2. The global yearly number of malware attacks between 2015 and 2020.

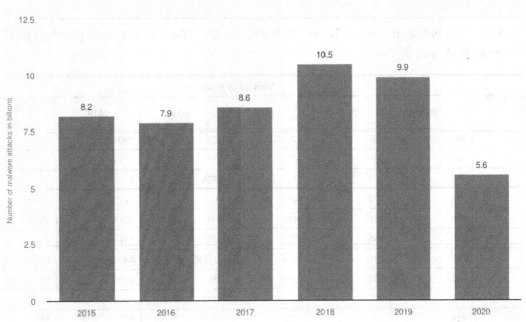

The research contributions are two-fold (i) a systematic review has been conducted to review the latest development of deep learning-based malware detection; and (ii) Future research directions on the enhancement of detection models.

This chapter is structured as follows. Section 2 introduces typical deep learning algorithms. This is followed by the systematic review in the deep learning algorithms for malware detection. At last, a conclusion is drawn.

TYPICAL DEEP LEARNING ALGORITHMS

Ten typical deep learning algorithms namely convolutional neural network (CNN), restricted Boltzmann machine (RBM), deep belief network (DBN), autoencoders (ATE), self organizing map (SOM), multilayer perceptron (MLP), generative adversarial network (GAN), recurrent neural network (RNN), gated recurrent unit (GRU), and long short-term memory network (LSTM), are briefly introduced with background information and their variants proposed in recent years. Table 1 summarizes the number of publications related to each deep learning algorithms in 2016-2021 (up to 10 August 2021) using the document search (TITLE-ABS-KEY) in Scopus. The Year 2021 is for reference only because there are four more months before the end of 2021.

All deep learning algorithms (except RBM) receive increasing attention based on the increasing number of publications from 2016 to 2020. The average annual growth in the nine algorithms are 222%, 31%, 113%, 4%, 54%, 4560%, 99%, 538%, and 160% for CNN, DBN, ATE, SOM, MLP, GAN, RNN, GRU, and LSTM, respectively. The remarkable change in the adoption of GAN is because of the effectiveness in generating new and synthetic training data for model enhancement (Chui, Liu, Zhao, & De Pablos, 2020; Zhang, Sindagi, & Patel, 2019).

Table 1. Number of publications with Scopus indexing in selected deep learning algorithms from 2016 to 2021 (up to 10 August 2021).

Deep learning algorithm	Number of publications					
	2016	2017	2018	2019	2020	2021 (up to 10 Aug.)
CNN	2934	6607	13159	22776	29010	17503
RBM	301	331	324	355	329	171
DBN	357	489	585	726	800	449
ATE	216	378	625	973	1192	683
SOM	872	881	960	925	1012	555
MLP	798	896	1229	1794	2513	1684
GAN	24	291	1360	3158	4402	2640
RNN	1424	2345	3909	5988	7076	3895
GRU	46	126	323	720	1036	681
LSTM	1192	1907	3865	6953	8838	5475

Convolutional Neural Network (CNN)

Many review articles have summarized the performance of CNN models for computer vision (Dhillon, & Verma, 2020), natural language processing (Wu et al., 2020), and remote sensing (Ma et al., 2019), which revealed the superiority of CNN in these domains. The applications align with the biological process (Vardhana, Arunkumar, Lasrado, Abdulhay, & Ramirez-Gonzalez, 2018).

Taking classification problem as example, which is comprised of feature learning and model construction. For feature learning, there are three major components namely convolution filter/kernel, activation function, and pooling. For readers who are expertise in mathematics or digital signal processing, the convolution of matrix is equivalent to the concept of cross-correlation. When it comes to the model construction, flattening, fully-connected layer, and softmax function are major components.

Restricted Boltzmann Machine (RBM)

As a form of generative stochastic artificial neural network, RBM restricts the connections between hidden units so that the training time can be reduced. The most basic architecture is a two-layered neural networks with one input layer followed by one hidden layer. In recent years, researchers prefer the selections of other deep learning algorithms instead of RBM owning to the high performance requirement in today's complex research topics (Larochelle, Mandel, Pascanu, & Bengio, 2012).

Some improved variants of RBM have been proposed in recent years. To improve the accuracy and training time, fuzzy logic was introduced to eliminate the redundancy of data (Lü, Meng, Chen, &

Wang, 2019). Another work suggested the adoption of AdaBoost backward propagation to enhance the optimization process (Liu, Sun, Kornhauser, Sun, & Sangwa, 2019).

Deep Belief Network (DBN)

DBN is usually formulated with multiple RBMs. The architecture is structured as directed acyclic graph, containing a list of stochastic and weighted variables. The training of model can be simplified by introducing unbiased sampling where there is no interaction between neurons (Movahedi, Coyle, & Sejdić, 2017). However, the type of DBN is defined as generative probabilistic model. With strong relation to RBMs, DBN is considered as one of the early deep learning-based model. Likewise, DBN receives relatively less attention compared with other deep learning algorithms.

To improve the generalization, robustness, and accuracy of the model, a compensation of time varying delay was added to the input layer of DBN (Hao, Wang, Shan, & Zhao, 2019). When it comes to large-scale datasets, traditional computing framework may not be feasible to manage the training of model in a reasonable timeframe. A distributed parallel approach was introduced to allocate the computational load with high-performance clusters (Shi, Zhang, Zhang, & Hu, 2020).

Autoencoders (ATE)

ATE is comprised of three components, encoding algorithm, decoding algorithm, and loss function. It is usually adopted to reduce the dimensionality of features. Therefore, many previous works incorporated ATE with deep learning algorithms, for instance, CNN (Toğaçar, Ergen, & Cömert, 2020), MLP (Ahmadlou et al., 2021), GAN (Wang, Sun, & Jin, 2020), and LSTM (Wang et al., 2021). ATE can be easily transformed into deep learning by the extension of single layer to multi-layer ATE.

There are other variants of ATE include variational ATE (Zavrak, & Iskefiyeli, 2020), concrete ATE (Chow et al., 2020), contractive ATE (Diallo et al., 2021), denoising ATE (Ashfahani, Pratama, Lughofer, & Ong, 2020), and sparse ATE (Mienye, Sun, & Wang, 2020).

Self Organizing Map (SOM)

SOM reduces the complexity of model by representing higher dimensional data to lower dimensional data (named map) with a formulation of unsupervised learning. In addition, the topological properties of the data have been preserved due to neighbourhood function. The idea of SOM ensures various modules of the network gives comparable reaction to inputs. This can be correlated to eyes, ears, skin, etc. of human beings. The weights of the nodes are defined by best matching unit (Bernard, Hueber, & Girau, September 2020).

In general, there are two types of SOMs, growing hierarchical SOM (GH-SOM) and hierarchical SOM (H-SOM) (Qu et al., 2021). GH-SOM takes the advantages in self-learning, dynamic self-adaptability, and low computing latency (Vasighi, & Amini, 2017) whereas H-SOM represents hierarchical data effectively with low computational overhead (Aghajari, & Chandrashekhar, 2017).

Multilayer Perceptron (MLP)

It is often confused by mixing the technique of feedforward artificial neural network with MLP. However, the multiple layers of perceptron are crucial for MLP where the feature vector is attached to weight vector. Fundamentally, MLP is comprised of three types of layers namely input, hidden, and output layers.

Updating the weights has become important to control the error of model. Learning rate can limit and relieve the adjustment of weights between epochs (Takase, Oyama, & Kurihara, 2018). A latest work has suggested the addition of weight decay or L2-regularization (Richemond, & Guo, 2019).

Generative Adversarial Network (GAN)

Although we are living in a big data era where tremendous amount of data is generating by humans, sensors, devices, or generally speaking internet-of-things network, data collection of some groups of samples is challenging attributable to limited budget and rare cases in nature. A typical example is fault samples of machines that suffers from downtime during data collection and requires maintenance afterwards (Lei et al., 2020).

Some variants of GANs have been proposed to improve the robustness in noise and repentance of generated data. Examples are conditional GAN, cGAN (Liao, Lin, Zhao, & Gabbouj, 2019), information maximized generative adversarial networks, infoGAN (Gong, Xu, & Lei, 2020), and auxiliary classifier GAN, acGAN (Wang et al., 2019).

Recurrent Neural Network (RNN)

The inputs and outputs in traditional neural network do not depend on each other and one input maps to one output. In contrast, the outputs of RNN depend on previous input sequences and there is no restriction on the mapping between inputs and outputs. However, RNN suffers from the challenges of gradient explosion and vanishing gradient (Yue, Fu, & Liang, 2018).

In general, there are four classes of RNN namely one-to-one (Xiang et al., 2018), one-to-many (Yang, Liu, Qu, Sang, & Lv, 2021), many-to-one (Dadoun, & Troncy, 2020), and many-to-many (Das, Koperski, Bremond, & Francesca, November 2018).

Gated Recurrent Unit (GRU)

GRU is a RNN variant that improves the performance of short-term memory. The regulation of information is managed by hidden state. The update and reset gates help to resolve the issue of vanishing gradient. The former is related to the information from the past moving forward to the future whereas the latter is related to the information from the past being ignored.

There are two types of architectures namely minimal gated unit (Dong, Du, & Yan, 2019) and fully gated unit (Khan, Wang, & Ngueilbaye, 2021). Some research studies suggested GRU outperforms RNN and LSTM in small-scale datasets (Gruber, & Jockisch, 2020).

Long Short-Term Memory (LSTM) Network

Both GRU and LSTM can manage the issue of vanishing gradient. The complexity of LSTM is higher with three gates namely input, forget, and output gates, and thus requiring more computing power. Based on Table 1, LSTM is more famous compared with RNN and GRU. One of the reasons could be due to the performance in general applications (Fischer, & Krauss, 2018; Yuan, Li, & Wang, 2019).

SYSTEMATIC REVIEW IN THE DEEP LEARNING ALGORITHMS FOR MALWARE DETECTION

Popularity of Typical Deep Learning Algorithms for Malware Detection

We use Scopus to examine the number of publications of the abovementioned 10 deep learning algorithms for malware detection which is summarized in Table 2. The ranking is similar to the results in Table 1 for general applications.

Table 2. Number of publications of typical deep learning algorithms for malware detection using Scopus.

Deep learning algorithms for malware detection	Number of publications
CNN	485
RBM	16
DBN	33
ATE	91
SOM	36
MLP	76
GAN	73
RNN	168
GRU	30
LSTM	196

Shortlisted Research Articles

The articles with top number of citations in each of the deep learning algorithms are selected for in-depth discussion. Table 3 summarizes the brief information of the shortlisted articles.

In the field of anomaly detection for computer network, traffic classification is important to manage the network security. In (Wang, Zhu, Zeng, Ye, & Sheng, 2017, January), a CNN-based traffic classification model was implemented. The key steps are (i) generating session and flow of the network traffic; (ii) removing emptied or duplicated files; (iii) sanitizing the trace; (iv) trimming to obtain uniform length; (v) generating images; (vi) generating IDX files; and (vii) implementing CNN models with IDX files. Performance evaluation showed an average accuracy of 99.4%.

Table 3. Summary of the shortlisted articles.

Deep learning algorithms	Title of article	Number of citations
CNN	Malware traffic classification using convolutional neural network for representation learning	235
RBM	A survey of deep learning methods for cyber security	100
DBN	DeepSign: Deep learning for automatic malware signature generation and classification	111
ATE	Autoencoder-based feature learning for cyber security applications	114
SOM	Malware classification using self organising feature maps and machine activity data	54
MLP	Analysis of machine learning techniques used in behavior-based malware detection	151
GAN	A survey of deep learning methods for cyber security	100
RNN	Malware classification with recurrent networks	175
GRU	Malware classification with LSTM and GRU language models and a character-level CNN	91
LSTM	A deep Recurrent Neural Network based approach for Internet of Things malware threat hunting	112

A review article (Berman, Buczak, Chavis, & Corbett, 2019) has summarized the results of nine articles using RBM for malware detection with nine benchmark datasets. Many of the works achieved accuracy over 95%. The extensive review for other deep learning algorithms such as ATE, CNN, and RNN are included in the article.

A DBN-based approach was proposed to generate and classify malware signature (David, & Netanyahu, 2015, July). The sandbox contains the characteristics of the programs which serve as binary vector. Six types of malware were selected for performance evaluation of the classifier namely DarkComet, Andromeda, Cidox, SpyEye, Carberp, and Zeus. The analysis revealed that the malware classification accuracy was over 98%.

A generic ATE-approach was presented for malware and intrusion detection (Yousefi-Azar, Varadharajan, Hamey, & Tupakula, 2017, May). It takes three major advantages (i) unique pre-training; (ii) minimal dimensions of feature vector; and (iii) unique fine-tuning phase. It was tested with four classifiers, XGBoost, SVM, k-NN, and naïve Bayes, where accuracy was in descending order.

Differed from the work (Wang, Zhu, Zeng, Ye, & Sheng, 2017, January), the SOM-based approach captured the fuzzy boundary of the machine activity data, including malicious and normal samples (Burnap, French, Turner, & Jones, 2018). Besides, various types of cross-validation were evaluated which influenced the performance of the classification accuracy. The proposed approach outperformed SVM, MLP, Bayesian network, and random forest by 8.4-37.7%.

Four algorithms namely SVM, decision tree, naïve Bayes, and k-NN were compared with MLP for malware detection (Firdausi, Erwin, & Nugroho, 2010, December). Decision tree with J48 setting achieved the highest accuracy of about 97% as it performed better in feature extraction.

The work (Pascanu, Stokes, Sanossian, Marinescu, & Thomas, 2015, April) combined echo state network, RNN, and logistic regression for malware classification. The true positive rate improvement was 98% compared with traditional event model. RNN, GRU, and LSTM were used for malware detection (Athiwaratkun, & Stokes, 2017, March). Results showed that LSTM achieved the highest accuracy and improved the true positive rate by 31%. A deep RNN was proposed for malware detection in an internet of things network and reached an accuracy of 98% (HaddadPajouh, Dehghantanha, Khayami, & Choo, 2018).

Table 4. Performance comparison between existing works for malware detection.

Works	Methods	Datasets	Results
(Wang, Zhu, Zeng, Ye, & Sheng, 2017, January)	CNN	10 types of malware traffic and 5 types of normal traffic	Average accuracy = 99.4%
(Berman, Buczak, Chavis, & Corbett, 2019)	RBM	9 benchmark datasets	Accuracy > 95%
(David, & Netanyahu, 2015, July)	DBN	6 types of malware	Accuracy > 98%
(Yousefi-Azar, Varadharajan, Hamey, & Tupakula, 2017, May)	ATE	9 types of malware with 10868 labled samples	Accuracy = 98.2%
(Burnap, French, Turner, & Jones, 2018)	SOM	594 malicious files	Accuracy = 93.8%
(Firdausi, Erwin, & Nugroho, 2010, December)	MLP	220 malware	Accuracy = 91%
(HaddadPajouh, Dehghantanha, Khayami, & Choo, 2018)	RNN	280 malware	Accuracy = 98%

Further Recommended Readings

Authors would like to suggest some more articles as future research directions, including cross-site scripting detection (Chaudhary, Gupta, Chang, Nedjah, & Chui, 2021), cloud security (Gou, Yamaguchi, & Gupta, 2017), attack pattern recognition (Gupta, & Gupta, 2017), surveillance system (Chui, Vasant, & Liu, 2019), distributed denial-of-service attack (Chhabra, Gupta, & Almomani, 2013; Gaurav, Gupta, Hsu, Yamaguchi, & Chui, 2021, January), fog computing (Hallappanavar, & Birje, 2021), multimedia social network (Zhang, Sun, Zhao, Wang, Chang, & Gupta, 2017), mutual authentication protocol (Tewari, & Gupta, 2020), and IT threats (Ordóñez de Pablos, Almunawar, Chui, & Kaliannan, 2021).

Challenges

Various issues are summarized as challenges in malware detection.

- Limited evaluation of malware detection models using small-scale datasets. In Table 4, the sample sizes of the datasets are not large-scale to reflect the practicality in real-world application
- It is desired to implement an algorithm fits the malware detection of all types of malware. This is to ensure a light hardware requirement to perform the computational tasks
- Malware attack can lead to the lost of huge amounts of money. The ultimate goal of the detection accuracy is 100%. Ensemble learning and boosting algorithm are potential approaches to further enhance the performance of the model.

CONCLUSION

In this chapter, we have studied ten typical deep learning algorithms in all disciplines and concluded that CNN, GAN, RNN, and LSTM are the most widely used algorithms. Attention is drawn into malware detection in which articles of each of the deep learning algorithm with highest number of citations are shortlisted for further discussion. Although various existing works have resulted a high accuracy, true positive rate, and true negative rate of the malware detection models, there is room for improvement because the experiments were under some constraints that may not be fully applied to generic and real-world scenarios. Several future recommendation readings are suggested as future research directions.

REFERENCES

Aghajari, E., & Chandrashekhar, G. D. (2017). Self-organizing map based extended fuzzy C-means (SEEFC) algorithm for image segmentation. *Applied Soft Computing*, *54*, 347–363. doi:10.1016/j.asoc.2017.01.003

Ahmadlou, M., Al-Fugara, A. K., Al-Shabeeb, A. R., Arora, A., Al-Adamat, R., Pham, Q. B., Al-Ansari, N., Linh, N. T. T., & Sajedi, H. (2021). Flood susceptibility mapping and assessment using a novel deep learning model combining multilayer perceptron and autoencoder neural networks. *Journal of Flood Risk Management*, *14*(1), e12683. doi:10.1111/jfr3.12683

Ashfahani, A., Pratama, M., Lughofer, E., & Ong, Y. S. (2020). DEVDAN: Deep evolving denoising autoencoder. *Neurocomputing*, *390*, 297–314. doi:10.1016/j.neucom.2019.07.106

Athiwaratkun, B., & Stokes, J. W. (2017, March). Malware classification with LSTM and GRU language models and a character-level CNN. In *2017 IEEE International Conference on Acoustics, Speech and Signal Processing (ICASSP)* (pp. 2482-2486). IEEE. 10.1109/ICASSP.2017.7952603

Berman, D. S., Buczak, A. L., Chavis, J. S., & Corbett, C. L. (2019). A survey of deep learning methods for cyber security. *Information (Basel)*, *10*(4), 122. doi:10.3390/info10040122

Bernard, Y., Hueber, N., & Girau, B. (2020, September). A fast algorithm to find Best Matching Units in Self-Organizing Maps. In *International Conference on Artificial Neural Networks* (pp. 825-837). Springer.

Burnap, P., French, R., Turner, F., & Jones, K. (2018). Malware classification using self organising feature maps and machine activity data. *Computers & Security*, *73*, 399–410. doi:10.1016/j.cose.2017.11.016

Chaudhary, P., Gupta, B. B., Chang, X., Nedjah, N., & Chui, K. T. (2021). Enhancing big data security through integrating XSS scanner into fog nodes for SMEs gain. *Technological Forecasting and Social Change*, *168*, 120754. doi:10.1016/j.techfore.2021.120754

Chhabra, M., Gupta, B., & Almomani, A. (2013). A novel solution to handle DDOS attack in MANET. *Journal of Information Security*, *4*(3), 34631. doi:10.4236/jis.2013.43019

Chow, J. K., Su, Z., Wu, J., Tan, P. S., Mao, X., & Wang, Y. H. (2020). Anomaly detection of defects on concrete structures with the convolutional autoencoder. *Advanced Engineering Informatics*, *45*, 101105. doi:10.1016/j.aei.2020.101105

Chui, K. T., Liu, R. W., Zhao, M., & De Pablos, P. O. (2020). Predicting students' performance with school and family tutoring using generative adversarial network-based deep support vector machine. *IEEE Access: Practical Innovations, Open Solutions*, *8*, 86745–86752. doi:10.1109/ACCESS.2020.2992869

Chui, K. T., Vasant, P., & Liu, R. W. (2019). Smart city is a safe city: information and communication technology–enhanced urban space monitoring and surveillance systems: the promise and limitations. In *Smart Cities: Issues and Challenges* (pp. 111-124). Elsevier. doi:10.1016/B978-0-12-816639-0.00007-7

Dadoun, A., & Troncy, R. (2020). *Many-to-one Recurrent Neural Network for Session-based Recommendation.* arXiv preprint arXiv:2008.11136.

Das, S., Koperski, M., Bremond, F., & Francesca, G. (2018, November). Deep-temporal lstm for daily living action recognition. In *2018 15th IEEE International Conference on Advanced Video and Signal Based Surveillance (AVSS)* (pp. 1-6). IEEE. 10.1109/AVSS.2018.8639122

David, O. E., & Netanyahu, N. S. (2015, July). Deepsign: Deep learning for automatic malware signature generation and classification. In *2015 International Joint Conference on Neural Networks (IJCNN)* (pp. 1-8). IEEE. 10.1109/IJCNN.2015.7280815

Dhillon, A., & Verma, G. K. (2020). Convolutional neural network: A review of models, methodologies and applications to object detection. *Progress in Artificial Intelligence, 9*(2), 85–112. doi:10.100713748-019-00203-0

Diallo, B., Hu, J., Li, T., Khan, G. A., Liang, X., & Zhao, Y. (2021). Deep embedding clustering based on contractive autoencoder. *Neurocomputing, 433*, 96–107. doi:10.1016/j.neucom.2020.12.094

Dong, A., Du, Z., & Yan, Z. (2019). Round trip time prediction using recurrent neural networks with minimal gated unit. *IEEE Communications Letters, 23*(4), 584–587. doi:10.1109/LCOMM.2019.2899603

Ficco, M., Esposito, C., Xiang, Y., & Palmieri, F. (2017). Pseudo-dynamic testing of realistic edge-fog cloud ecosystems. *IEEE Communications Magazine, 55*(11), 98–104. doi:10.1109/MCOM.2017.1700328

Firdausi, I., Erwin, A., & Nugroho, A. S. (2010, December). Analysis of machine learning techniques used in behavior-based malware detection. In *2010 second international conference on advances in computing, control, and telecommunication technologies* (pp. 201-203). IEEE. 10.1109/ACT.2010.33

Fischer, T., & Krauss, C. (2018). Deep learning with long short-term memory networks for financial market predictions. *European Journal of Operational Research, 270*(2), 654–669. doi:10.1016/j.ejor.2017.11.054

Gaurav, A., Gupta, B. B., Hsu, C. H., Yamaguchi, S., & Chui, K. T. (2021, January). Fog Layer-based DDoS attack Detection Approach for Internet-of-Things (IoTs) devices. In *2021 IEEE International Conference on Consumer Electronics (ICCE)* (pp. 1-5). IEEE.

Gong, J., Xu, X., & Lei, Y. (2020). Unsupervised specific emitter identification method using radio-frequency fingerprint embedded InfoGAN. *IEEE Transactions on Information Forensics and Security, 15*, 2898–2913. doi:10.1109/TIFS.2020.2978620

Gou, Z., Yamaguchi, S., & Gupta, B. B. (2017). Analysis of various security issues and challenges in cloud computing environment: a survey. In Identity Theft: Breakthroughs in Research and Practice (pp. 221-247). IGI Global. doi:10.4018/978-1-5225-0808-3.ch011

Gruber, N., & Jockisch, A. (2020). Are GRU cells more specific and LSTM cells more sensitive in motive classification of text? *Frontiers in Artificial Intelligence, 3*, 40. doi:10.3389/frai.2020.00040 PMID:33733157

Gupta, S., & Gupta, B. B. (2017). Detection, avoidance, and attack pattern mechanisms in modern web application vulnerabilities: Present and future challenges. *International Journal of Cloud Applications and Computing*, *7*(3), 1–43. doi:10.4018/IJCAC.2017070101

HaddadPajouh, H., Dehghantanha, A., Khayami, R., & Choo, K.-K. R. (2018). A deep recurrent neural network based approach for internet of things malware threat hunting. *Future Generation Computer Systems*, *85*, 88–96. doi:10.1016/j.future.2018.03.007

Hallappanavar, V. L., & Birje, M. N. (2021). A reliable trust computing mechanism in fog computing. *International Journal of Cloud Applications and Computing*, *11*(1), 1–20. doi:10.4018/IJCAC.2021010101

Hao, X., Wang, Z., Shan, Z., & Zhao, Y. (2019). Prediction of electricity consumption in cement production: A time-varying delay deep belief network prediction method. *Neural Computing & Applications*, *31*(11), 7165–7179. doi:10.100700521-018-3540-z

Jerlin, M. A., & Marimuthu, K. (2018). A new malware detection system using machine learning techniques for API call sequences. *Journal of Applied Security Research*, *13*(1), 45–62. doi:10.1080/1936 1610.2018.1387734

Khan, M., Wang, H., & Ngueilbaye, A. (2021). Attention-Based Deep Gated Fully Convolutional End-to-End Architectures for Time Series Classification. *Neural Processing Letters*, 1–34.

Kumar, S. (2020). An emerging threat Fileless malware: A survey and research challenges. *Cybersecurity*, *3*(1), 1–12. doi:10.118642400-019-0043-x

Larochelle, H., Mandel, M., Pascanu, R., & Bengio, Y. (2012). Learning algorithms for the classification restricted boltzmann machine. *Journal of Machine Learning Research*, *13*(1), 643–669.

Lei, Y., Yang, B., Jiang, X., Jia, F., Li, N., & Nandi, A. K. (2020). Applications of machine learning to machine fault diagnosis: A review and roadmap. *Mechanical Systems and Signal Processing*, *138*, 106587. doi:10.1016/j.ymssp.2019.106587

Li, J., Sun, L., Yan, Q., Li, Z., Srisa-An, W., & Ye, H. (2018). Significant permission identification for machine-learning-based android malware detection. *IEEE Transactions on Industrial Informatics*, *14*(7), 3216–3225. doi:10.1109/TII.2017.2789219

Liao, K., Lin, C., Zhao, Y., & Gabbouj, M. (2019). DR-GAN: Automatic radial distortion rectification using conditional GAN in real-time. *IEEE Transactions on Circuits and Systems for Video Technology*, *30*(3), 725–733. doi:10.1109/TCSVT.2019.2897984

Liu, Q., Sun, L., Kornhauser, A., Sun, J., & Sangwa, N. (2019). Road roughness acquisition and classification using improved restricted Boltzmann machine deep learning algorithm. *Sensor Review*, *39*(6), 733–742. doi:10.1108/SR-05-2018-0132

Lü, X., Meng, L., Chen, C., & Wang, P. (2019). Fuzzy removing redundancy restricted boltzmann machine: Improving learning speed and classification accuracy. *IEEE Transactions on Fuzzy Systems*, *28*(10), 2495–2509. doi:10.1109/TFUZZ.2019.2940415

Ma, L., Liu, Y., Zhang, X., Ye, Y., Yin, G., & Johnson, B. A. (2019). Deep learning in remote sensing applications: A meta-analysis and review. *ISPRS Journal of Photogrammetry and Remote Sensing*, *152*, 166–177. doi:10.1016/j.isprsjprs.2019.04.015

Mienye, I. D., Sun, Y., & Wang, Z. (2020). Improved sparse autoencoder based artificial neural network approach for prediction of heart disease. *Informatics in Medicine Unlocked*, *18*, 100307. doi:10.1016/j.imu.2020.100307

Movahedi, F., Coyle, J. L., & Sejdić, E. (2017). Deep belief networks for electroencephalography: A review of recent contributions and future outlooks. *IEEE Journal of Biomedical and Health Informatics*, *22*(3), 642–652. doi:10.1109/JBHI.2017.2727218 PMID:28715343

Narudin, F. A., Feizollah, A., Anuar, N. B., & Gani, A. (2016). Evaluation of machine learning classifiers for mobile malware detection. *Soft Computing*, *20*(1), 343–357. doi:10.100700500-014-1511-6

Ordóñez de Pablos, P., Almunawar, M. N., Chui, K. T., & Kaliannan, M. (Eds.). (2021). *Handbook of Research on Analyzing IT Opportunities for Inclusive Digital Learning*. IGI Global. doi:10.4018/978-1-7998-7184-2

Pascanu, R., Stokes, J. W., Sanossian, H., Marinescu, M., & Thomas, A. (2015, April). Malware classification with recurrent networks. In *2015 IEEE International Conference on Acoustics, Speech and Signal Processing (ICASSP)* (pp. 1916-1920). IEEE. 10.1109/ICASSP.2015.7178304

Qu, X., Yang, L., Guo, K., Ma, L., Sun, M., Ke, M., & Li, M. (2021). A survey on the development of self-organizing maps for unsupervised intrusion detection. *Mobile Networks and Applications*, *26*(2), 808–829. doi:10.100711036-019-01353-0

Rendell, D. (2019). Understanding the evolution of malware. *Computer Fraud & Security*, *2019*(1), 17–19. doi:10.1016/S1361-3723(19)30010-7

Richemond, P. H., & Guo, Y. (2019). *Combining learning rate decay and weight decay with complexity gradient descent-Part I*. arXiv preprint arXiv:1902.02881.

Rose, G., Raghuram, P., Watson, S., & Wigley, E. (2021). Platform urbanism, smartphone applications and valuing data in a smart city. *Transactions of the Institute of British Geographers*, *46*(1), 59–72. doi:10.1111/tran.12400

Shi, G., Zhang, J., Zhang, C., & Hu, J. (2020). A distributed parallel training method of deep belief networks. *Soft Computing*, *24*(17), 1–12. doi:10.100700500-020-04754-6

SonicWall. (2021). Annual number of malware attacks worldwide from 2015 to 2020 (in billions). In *Statista*. Retrieved 9 August 2021, from https://www.statista.com/statistics/873097/malware-attacks-per-year-worldwide/

Stergiou, C. L., Psannis, K. E., & Gupta, B. B. (2020). IoT-based big data secure management in the fog over a 6G wireless network. *IEEE Internet of Things Journal*, *8*(7), 5164–5171. doi:10.1109/JIOT.2020.3033131

Takase, T., Oyama, S., & Kurihara, M. (2018). Effective neural network training with adaptive learning rate based on training loss. *Neural Networks*, *101*, 68–78. doi:10.1016/j.neunet.2018.01.016 PMID:29494873

Technology markets: Software, Revenue by segment. (2021). In *Statista*. Retrieved 9 August 2021, from https://www.statista.com/statistics/873097/malware-attacks-per-year-worldwide/

Tewari, A., & Gupta, B. B. (2020). Secure Timestamp-Based Mutual Authentication Protocol for IoT Devices Using RFID Tags. *International Journal on Semantic Web and Information Systems*, *16*(3), 20–34. doi:10.4018/IJSWIS.2020070102

Vardhana, M., Arunkumar, N., Lasrado, S., Abdulhay, E., & Ramirez-Gonzalez, G. (2018). Convolutional neural network for bio-medical image segmentation with hardware acceleration. *Cognitive Systems Research*, *50*, 10–14. doi:10.1016/j.cogsys.2018.03.005

Vasighi, M., & Amini, H. (2017). A directed batch growing approach to enhance the topology preservation of self-organizing map. *Applied Soft Computing*, *55*, 424–435. doi:10.1016/j.asoc.2017.02.015

Wang, D., Vinson, R., Holmes, M., Seibel, G., Bechar, A., Nof, S., & Tao, Y. (2019). Early detection of tomato spotted wilt virus by hyperspectral imaging and outlier removal auxiliary classifier generative adversarial nets (OR-AC-GAN). *Scientific Reports*, *9*(1), 1–14. doi:10.103841598-019-40066-y PMID:30867450

Wang, H., Peng, M. J., Miao, Z., Liu, Y. K., Ayodeji, A., & Hao, C. (2021). Remaining useful life prediction techniques for electric valves based on convolution auto encoder and long short term memory. *ISA Transactions*, *108*, 333–342. doi:10.1016/j.isatra.2020.08.031 PMID:32891421

Wang, W., Zhu, M., Zeng, X., Ye, X., & Sheng, Y. (2017, January). Malware traffic classification using convolutional neural network for representation learning. In *2017 International Conference on Information Networking (ICOIN)* (pp. 712-717). IEEE. 10.1109/ICOIN.2017.7899588

Wang, Y. R., Sun, G. D., & Jin, Q. (2020). Imbalanced sample fault diagnosis of rotating machinery using conditional variational auto-encoder generative adversarial network. *Applied Soft Computing*, *92*, 106333. doi:10.1016/j.asoc.2020.106333

Wu, S., Roberts, K., Datta, S., Du, J., Ji, Z., Si, Y., Soni, S., Wang, Q., Wei, Q., Xiang, Y., Zhao, B., & Xu, H. (2020). Deep learning in clinical natural language processing: A methodical review. *Journal of the American Medical Informatics Association: JAMIA*, *27*(3), 457–470. doi:10.1093/jamia/ocz200 PMID:31794016

Xiang, W., Zhang, H., Cui, R., Chu, X., Li, K., & Zhou, W. (2018). Pavo: A rnn-based learned inverted index, supervised or unsupervised? *IEEE Access: Practical Innovations, Open Solutions*, *7*, 293–303. doi:10.1109/ACCESS.2018.2885350

Yang, K., Liu, D., Qu, Q., Sang, Y., & Lv, J. (2021). An automatic evaluation metric for Ancient-Modern Chinese translation. *Neural Computing & Applications*, *33*(8), 3855–3867. doi:10.100700521-020-05216-8

Yousefi-Azar, M., Varadharajan, V., Hamey, L., & Tupakula, U. (2017, May). Autoencoder-based feature learning for cyber security applications. In *2017 International joint conference on neural networks (IJCNN)* (pp. 3854-3861). IEEE. 10.1109/IJCNN.2017.7966342

Yuan, X., Li, L., & Wang, Y. (2019). Nonlinear dynamic soft sensor modeling with supervised long short-term memory network. *IEEE Transactions on Industrial Informatics*, *16*(5), 3168–3176. doi:10.1109/TII.2019.2902129

Yue, B., Fu, J., & Liang, J. (2018). Residual recurrent neural networks for learning sequential representations. *Information (Basel)*, *9*(3), 56. doi:10.3390/info9030056

Zavrak, S., & Iskefiyeli, M. (2020). Anomaly-based intrusion detection from network flow features using variational autoencoder. *IEEE Access: Practical Innovations, Open Solutions*, *8*, 108346–108358. doi:10.1109/ACCESS.2020.3001350

Zhang, H., Sindagi, V., & Patel, V. M. (2019). Image de-raining using a conditional generative adversarial network. *IEEE Transactions on Circuits and Systems for Video Technology*, *30*(11), 3943–3956. doi:10.1109/TCSVT.2019.2920407

Zhang, Z., Sun, R., Zhao, C., Wang, J., Chang, C. K., & Gupta, B. B. (2017). CyVOD: A novel trinity multimedia social network scheme. *Multimedia Tools and Applications*, *76*(18), 18513–18529. doi:10.100711042-016-4162-z

Chapter 5
Malware Detection in Industrial Scenarios Using Machine Learning and Deep Learning Techniques

Ángel Luis Perales Gómez
University of Murcia, Spain

Lorenzo Fernández Maimó
iD https://orcid.org/0000-0003-2027-4239
University of Murcia, Spain

Alberto Huertas Celdrán
University of Zurich, Switzerland

Félix Jesús García Clemente
iD https://orcid.org/0000-0001-6181-5033
University of Murcia, Spain

ABSTRACT

In the last decades, factories have suffered a significant change in automation, evolving from isolated towards interconnected systems. However, the adoption of open standards and the opening to the internet have caused an increment in the number of attacks. In addition, traditional intrusion detection systems relying on a signature database, where malware patterns are stored, are failing due to the high specialization of industrial cyberattacks. For this reason, the research community is moving towards the anomaly detection paradigm. This paradigm is showing great results when it is implemented using machine learning and deep learning techniques. This chapter surveys several incidents caused by cyberattacks targeting industrial scenarios. Next, to understand the current status of anomaly detection solutions, it analyses the current industrial datasets and anomaly detection systems in the industrial field. In addition, the chapter shows an example of malware attacking a manufacturing plant, resulting in a safety threat. Finally, cybersecurity and safety solutions are reviewed.

DOI: 10.4018/978-1-7998-7789-9.ch005

Copyright © 2022, IGI Global. Copying or distributing in print or electronic forms without written permission of IGI Global is prohibited.

INTRODUCTION

Nowadays, industry plays a fundamental role in our society since an essential part of the economy is based on this sector. Therefore, any advance that involves a significant increase in the industrial production of factories is associated with an improvement in the economy and, consequently, with the growth of countries. In this context, industrial processes automation has been the way followed by factories to increase production without increasing cost.

Decades ago, automation in factories consisted of small isolated elements capable of making measurements and, based on these measurements, performing certain types of actions. However, new technologies are being introduced progressively in the industrial ecosystem, facilitating the automation of processes. In recent years, new terms, such as Industry 4.0 (Lasi et al., 2014), Industrial Internet of Things (IIoT) (Boyes et al., 2018), and recently, Industry 5.0 and Society 5.0 (Perakovic et al., 2020), have emerged strongly. In general, these terms are related to each other and refer to introducing new smart devices in industrial factories. These devices use typical technologies of communication networks, such as Ethernet or WiFi, to exchange information between them. In addition, more and more factories are being connected to the Internet (Mirian et al., 2016) to provide new functions such as remote control or information sharing between factories in different geographical areas. In addition, and based on the Industry 5.0 paradigm, Artificial Intelligence (AI) techniques are being introduced in industrial scenarios (Skovelev et al., 2017).

Although Industry 4.0/5.0 comprises many different elements and the identification of its parameters is crucial (Perakovic et al., 2020), the core part of the factory automation are the Industrial Control Systems (ICS) that encompass a large number of heterogeneous devices whose goal is to control and supervise industrial processes. To achieve this goal, ICS comprise devices that operate in both the logical and physical layers of industrial processes. This is the reason why ICS are also known as Cyber-Physical Systems (CPS). Devices in the logical layer govern the system behavior, while devices in the physical layer, such as controllers and sensors, interact with the physical world.

ICS control and supervise the industrial processes from manufacturing industries to critical infrastructures such as power-grids or gas pipelines. They are placed from the second level to below in the automation pyramid, as shown in Figure 1. In the zero level of the pyramid, we found low-level devices nearest to the controlled process; in other words, the physical layer. Among these devices, actuators and sensors are responsible for getting information from the environment and making actions over the physical world. In the upper level, the Programmable Logic Controllers (PLC) are located. PLC serve as intermediaries between the lower level (sensors and actuators) and the next upper level. To be specific, PLC receive commands from the upper level that are transmitted to actuators/sensors. Sensors and actuators execute the commands received and send back the result to the PLC, which transmits it to the upper level. In the second level of the automation pyramid, we find the Supervisory Control And Data Acquisition (SCADA) systems (Boyer, 2019). These systems are responsible for monitoring and controlling all the devices in the ICS. At this level, we see devices and software closer to traditional networks than control networks are. For example, devices that incorporate web, database, and historian servers are located at this level. SCADA collect the information from different PLC and store it in databases. Most SCADA can manage alarms and display trend graphics and other useful information shown in Human-Machine Interface (HMI) devices. Operators use these devices to monitor the correct operation of the processes. If a process malfunction is detected, operators can interact with the process through the HMI. The last two levels of the automation pyramid are more related to business tasks than factory processes. Specifically, the third level is in charge of tracking and gathering accurate, real-time data about the complete production lifecycle through the Management Execution System (MES). This level groups all tasks between order release and completion of the product for distribution. Finally, the fourth level is in charge of production planning and order management through Enterprise Resource Planning (ERP), a suite of different software that monitors all business levels, including manufacturing, orders, sales, finances, payroll, among others. Figure 2 illustrates a general ICS architecture and how the monitoring level is connected with the lower levels.

Figure 1. Automation pyramid

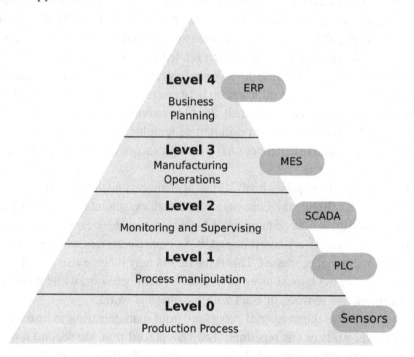

Since ICS supervise and control the factory production, they need to be available as long as possible. Otherwise, factory production may be affected, producing economic losses. This need forces many ICS around the world to remain outdated because updating an ICS component involves halting the process and replacing the component, thus stopping production. Moreover, this situation causes a large number of ICS to be made up of obsolete devices that potentially have critical vulnerabilities. In the past, since factories were isolated environments, this circumstance was not a critical issue. However, in recent years, the adoption of open standards and the opening to the Internet have exposed these vulnerabilities, causing an increment in the number of attacks affecting ICS (Miller et al., 2012; Nicholson et al., 2012; Repository of Industrial Security Incidents).

Most of the cyberattacks are carried out by means of malware that is introduced in the control network. The most notorious incident was carried out in 2010 by Stuxnet malware, which goal was to sabotage uranium enrichment plants of Iran. Another important incident dates from 2017 when Wannacry spread around the world. Wannacry is a type of malware called ransomware that encrypts files in the computer hard drive and asks for a ransom in bitcoin. Although Wannacry was not aimed to attack ICS, it reached many critical infrastructure systems such as hospitals and manufacturer factories.

Figure 2. Organization of the different devices within an ICS

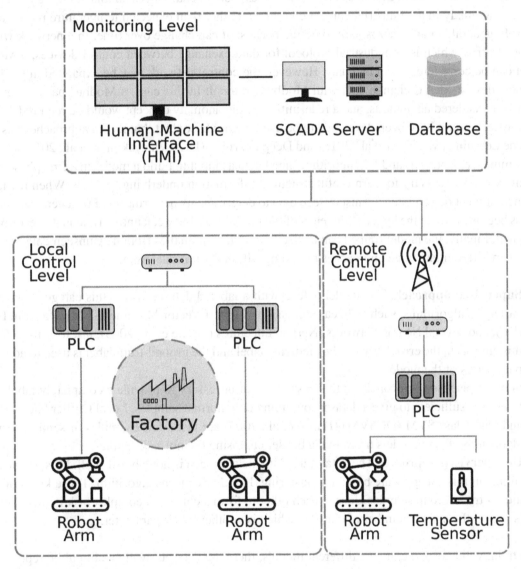

Due to the attention that industrial scenarios are receiving by attackers, there is also a growing interest in introducing cybersecurity mechanisms to protect them. One of the most powerful mechanisms to secure them is called Intrusion Detection Systems (IDS), which are in charge of analyzing the network (NIDS) or the host (HIDS) to detect cyberattacks. If the IDS detects any unusual activity, it triggers an alarm to inform the administrators, who will take the appropriate actions to respond to the detected activity.

Due to the specialized attacks that suffer control networks, traditional IDS fail to detect attacks in the control network context. These IDS are signature-based; in other words, they compare the pattern obtained with those stored in their databases (Wu et al., 2008). If the pattern match, it is considered an attack. For this reason, the research community is now moving towards IDS based on the anomaly detection (AD) paradigm (Liao et al., 2013) instead of signature-based IDS. AD systems try to find the boundary between normal and abnormal behaviors.

An anomaly is a pattern that does not match the expected behavior (Chandola et al., 2009). For example, an anomaly in an industrial context could be a higher than expected temperature received by a sensor. In general, an anomaly is hard to define because it can change over time. In a network without Modbus traffic, which is an industrial protocol for data exchange between control devices, a Modbus packet can be considered as an anomaly. However, the control network may be expanded in the future with new devices that exchange data with Modbus protocol. In this case, a Modbus packet would no longer be considered anomalous, and a redefinition of the anomaly concept would be required.

Many techniques have been developed to be used in an AD context, but recent approaches based on Machine Learning (ML) (Xin et al., 2018) and Deep Learning (DL) (Vinayakumar et al., 2019) are gaining prominence. Both ML and DL algorithms need data as input to build a model in a first phase called training, where models try to learn useful structural information underlying the data. When the model is trained, it must be validated against unseen data to determine its performance. From here, an iterative process begins in which the hyper-parameters of the model must be tweak until an adequate performance is reached. Finally, the model trained can be used to predict anomalies from new unseen data.

We can differentiate three approaches regarding ML and DL model training.

- **Supervised approach**. The model is feed with a labeled dataset. Inside this category, we find a variety of algorithms, such as linear regression, Support Vector Machine (SVM), Random Forest (RF), and several Neural Networks (NN) architectures (Hastie et al., 2005), just to name a few. In this approach, the error between the predicted label and the ground-truth label is used to adjust the parameters of the model.
- **Semi-supervised approach**. In this case, it is not necessary to provide a completely labeled dataset. It is sufficient to give a dataset containing only normal samples. Local Outlier Factor (LOF) and One-Class SVM (OCSVM) (Hastie et al., 2005) are just a few examples of semi-supervised algorithms. These models try to find a border enclosing the normal samples.
- **Unsupervised approach**. The dataset used in this approach is not labeled at all. Most of the algorithms in this category are based on clustering, like the K-means algorithm. These kinds of techniques try to group samples close to each other to form a cluster. A complex task in this approach is to find the correct number of clusters, which is another hyper-parameter.

To train, validate, and compare different models, there are datasets available in public repositories. Even though many of them are available in the context of corporate networks (despite its drawbacks (Tavallaee et al., 2009), in control networks, it is less frequent to find datasets ready to be used in model training and validation. The lack of these datasets is motivated by the fact that control network traffic manages confidential data about the processes carried out in the factory (e.g., the temperature that a tank must maintain or the speed at which an engine must turn). This secrecy in the industry hinders the capture of network traffic and, therefore, restricts the availability of industrial datasets.

Although cybersecurity in industrial scenarios has been improved in recent years, we have identified a series of open challenges that affect to Industry 4.0/5.0 scenarios that need to be solved to secure the industrial devices on which automation is based. The first open challenge is related to the lack of industrial-oriented datasets that hinder the training of ML/DL models to be used in AD-based IDS. Moreover, many of the available industrial datasets are collected from a synthetic scenario instead of a real one, resulting in not representative datasets. Likewise, the high specialization of ICS makes impossible the dataset exchange between different scenarios. As a result, a dataset obtained from a water management ICS is not appropriate for smart grids. The second open challenge is the lack of a standard methodology to develop AD models to detect cyberattacks specialized in ICS scenarios. The existing solutions apply different steps without standard criteria. The lack of this common methodology may even render the researchers' results invalid because wrong steps are performed. Finally, the third challenge is related to the lack of systems capable of managing cybersecurity and safety in a unified way to protect both assets and workers. These two concepts are closely related to each other, and cybersecurity threats can potentially cause safety threats, as we see in a later section. Until now, the management of cybersecurity and safety has been carried out in a separate way, causing an increase in both the cost and the complexity of having two different systems. In addition, current safety management systems cannot correctly evaluate threats caused by a cyberattack, making detection and mitigation difficult.

This chapter presents a review of works in different fields needed to implement automation in a secure way. In particular, a review of industrial-oriented datasets to train AD-based IDS in industrial scenarios is performed. Besides, different works and methodologies that used those datasets to train AD-based IDS in an industrial context are presented. Finally, we review the different solutions in order to manage cybersecurity and safety in an industrial context.

The chapter is organized as follows. In Section 2, we survey different incidents in ICS produced by cyberattacks over the years. In Section 3, we discuss the different industrial-oriented datasets available in order to train AD-based IDS. In Section 4, we present different solutions that are trained using industrial datasets to detect cyberattacks in industrial scenarios. In Section 5, we present an example where a botnet controls an industrial device and how it can cause a safety threat. In Section 6, we discuss solutions that consider both cybersecurity and safety and, specifically, we review SafeMan, which is a framework that manages cybersecurity and safety in a unified way. Finally, in Section 7, we present the conclusion of this chapter.

INCIDENTS IN INDUSTRIAL CONTROL SYSTEMS

The actors involved in attacks targeting ICS can be of different kinds, from national governments to disgruntled employees. Their motivations are also wide and different. For example, national governments might be interested in spying on another nation, while disgruntled employees only look for revenge due to a dismissal or a reprimand suffered previously. Table 1 summarizes the different actors involved in attacks on industrial systems.

In the following paragraphs, we discuss several cyberattacks targeting ICS over the years (Miller et al., 2012; Nicholson et al., 2012; Repository of Industrial Security Incidents). Some of them are collateral damages caused by worms that hit the Internet and penetrated into the ICS. Others are attacks focused on the corporate network that directly impact ICS. However, the most damaging attacks are targeted against devices that control and supervise the factory processes.

Siberian Gas Pipeline Incident. In 1982, the Siberian gas pipeline suffered an explosion caused by pipeline control software. The reason was that trojan malware was included with the software. The blast was caused during a pressure test on the pipeline due to an increase in the normal pressure. Russian newspaper recognized the explosion, but they denied that it was caused by software. Mainly, the attack had two effects. On the one hand, it affected the USSR economy during a crucial event, the cold war, interrupting the gas supply in the USSR. On the other hand, it had a psychological impact giving an advantage to the USA in the cold war.

Table 1. Different actors involved in industrial attacks (Pillitteri et al., 2014)

Adversary	Description
Nation States	State-run, well organized, and financed. Use foreign service agents to gather classified or critical information from countries viewed as hostile or as having an economic, military, or political advantage.
Hackers	A group of individuals who attack networks and systems seeking to exploit the vulnerabilities in operating systems or other flaws.
Terrorists/Cyberterrorists	Individuals or groups operating domestically or internationally who represent various terrorist or extremist groups that use violence or the threat of violence to incite fear to coerce or intimidate governments or societies into succumbing to their demands.
Organized Crime	Coordinated criminal activities, including gambling, racketeering, narcotics trafficking, and many others. An organized and well-financed criminal organization.
Other Criminal Elements	Another facet of the criminal community, which is usually not well organized or financed. Consists typically of few individuals or of one individual acting alone.
Industrial Competitors	Foreign and domestic corporations operating in a competitive market and often engaged in the illegal gathering of information from competitors or foreign governments in the form of corporate espionage.
Disgruntled Employees	Angry, dissatisfied individuals with the potential to inflict harm on the smart grid network or related systems. This can represent an insider threat depending on the current state of the individual's employment and access to the systems.
Careless or Poorly Trained Employees	Those users who, either through lack of training, lack of concern, or lack of attentiveness, pose a threat to smart grid systems. This is another example of an insider threat or adversary.

Nuclear Power Plant Incident. In 1992, a computer programmer in the Ignalia Power Reactor Station (Lithuania) introduced a computer virus in one station to sabotage the reactor, causing the station to shut down. It is speculated that the virus affects the cooling system causing it to break.

Salt River Project Incident. In 1994, between July 8th and August 31st, Lane Jarret Davis accessed a computer belonging to the Salt River Project through a dial-up modem. Lane was able to access and delete data from systems responsible for the monitoring and delivery of water and power customers as well as personnel and financial data. Salt River Project estimated the loss in $40,000 without regarding the loss due to productivity.

Omega Engineering Incident. On July 31st, 1994, a worker from the manufacturing plant of Omega Engineering in Bridgeport, N.J., found malware on his computer after login. The malware removed all the programs that ran the manufacturing operations of the company. After the incident, the CFO of Omega declared that the malware removed the software that controlled the production of 25,000 different products and customized those products with 500,000 different designs. Omega loss is quantified as 12 million in damages that breaks down into 10 million in sales and other costs, and 2 million to reprogram the system, apart from losing its competitive position in the market for high-tech instruments and measurements.

SQL Slammer (Moore et al., 2003). In 2003, a new cyber threat was discovered by Michael Bacarella. SQL Slammer was a tiny worm (just 376 bytes) that exploited a SQL Server buffer overflow vulnerability. The worm used the UDP protocol and the port associated with Microsoft SQL Server (1434). This worm not only affected IT devices and data networks but also control devices and control networks. The worm replicated and sent itself to a large number of devices. This caused Denial-of-Service (DoS) attacks in a significant number of networks around the world.

SQL Slammer entered the automation network segment in a drilling company and caused a DoS attack. The attack caused intermittent network traffic between operator terminals and SCADA servers. Unfortunately, the attack also affected a PLC and Distributed Control System (DCS) connected to the SCADA.

In the power industry, there have been several incidents where SQL Slammer blocked the communications between SCADA and PLC, but the most important one was on January 25th, in the Davis-Besse nuclear power plant. The infection caused data overload in the network, causing the communication between computers were blocked.

At first, the plant was safe from the SQL Slammer worm because it was connected to the Internet via a firewall. The firewall was setup to blocking UDP connection on port 1434 (Microsoft SQL Server). However, the entry point of the SQL Slammer worm was a T1 line behind the firewall that provided a path to enter the system. This path bypasses all access control securities applied by the firewall. Once the worm entered to the internal network, it randomly spread to other hosts whose port 1434 was open.

Another impact of SQL Slammer was in an automotive manufacturer. On June 25th, the worm affected 17 plants, including around 1000 computers. The estimated cost to the company was 150 million dollars.

CSX Train Signalling System Incident. In 2003, another worm spread over the Internet; this time, it was Sobig. It entered into the CSX network affecting the train signaling system. Around 1:15 a.m., Sobig shut down signaling, dispatching, and other systems. As a result, passenger and freight train traffic was stopped as soon as possible, and some trains suffered delays between 15 and 30 minutes.

Sasser (Li et al., 2008). In 2004 a worm named Sasser spread over the Internet. The worm exploited a buffer overflow vulnerability in a Microsoft Windows component called Local Security Authority Subsystem Service (LSASS). Like the previous worms, Sasser affected not only corporate networks but also control networks, which it reached because they were connected to the Internet. One case was a chemical plant in the USA, where Sasser infected the DCS, causing problems in the HMI and losing control of the plant for 5 hours. Another case, this time in the U.K., was an oil company, where Sasser infected several HMI in the control network due to non-updated antivirus.

Steel Plant infection with Ahack Worm (Ahmadian et al., 2020). In 2008, a worm infected a steel plant in Brazil. An employed used a G3 modem to connect to the Internet from the plant. This action infected the employed computer and the power and blast furnace plants with the Ahack worm, which started sending data packets over the network at high speed, flooding the network. This caused a loss of communication between PLC and SCADA and, therefore, problems in several HMI. The worm caused a loss of production due to many SCADA servers being rebooted, which subsequently caused financial loss.

Stuxnet (Lagner, 2011). In 2010, a new malware was discovered in a uranium enrichment plant of Iran, marking a turning point. The malware was known as Stuxnet. The main Stuxnet feature was its sophistication. It used up to five zero-day exploits to attack ICS. The main goal of Stuxnet was to reprogram PLC in the centrifuges to change its speed. The Stuxnet attack consisted of four steps. The first step was the intrusion inside the Natanz nuclear plants. The intrusion is believed to have been caused by an infected USB drive. Someone plugged an infected USB drive into a computer inside the internal network, and the worm started to replicate itself. The second step was the spread through the network, looking for computers that control centrifuges. The goal of centrifuges is to spin material at high speed to separate their components. In the Natanz nuclear plants, the centrifuges tried to separate the uranium types to isolate the type used for both nuclear power and weapons. The final step of Stuxnet was to reprogram the PLC that control the centrifuges to modify their speeds. This was accomplished in two ways. First, it made the centrifuges spin at a higher rate than the normal state for 15 minutes. After 15 minutes, Stuxnet reprograms the PLC again to back it to normal speed. The second way to modify the centrifuges speed rate was to slow down for 50 minutes. These two ways were repeated for months until Stuxnet was discovered.

Over time, the exceeded speed of centrifuges caused that many of them broke. It was reported that around 20% of centrifuges in the Natanz plants were decommissioned.

Considering the strong interest that many counties have in nuclear power and weapons, Stuxnet was considered the first weapon in cyber warfare. Although nobody knows the authorship of Stuxnet, it is believed that State intelligence services are behind the attack. Authorship by groups of hackers without connection to the government was ruled out due to the complexity of the malware. Furthermore, Stuxnet targeted particular devices and software, such as PLC Siemens and WinCC SCADA software, that are prohibitively expensive for an ordinary hacker group.

Flame (Munro, 2012). In 2012 a new malware was discovered in the middle east. It is considered a cyber-espionage weapon like Stuxnet. After infecting a device, Flame spied on the activity of the machine and stole data from it with keystroke monitoring and packet sniffing functionality. In addition, the malware has backdoor capabilities that enable cyber attackers to update the malware and erase it as desired. Flame was a modular malware, and it consisted of more than 20 different modules. Although the first contagion was in 2010, two years passed until it was discovered.

Shamoon attacks Saudi Arabian Oil Company (Zhioua, 2013). In 2012, the Shamoon virus reached the national oil company of Saudi Arabia, Aramco. This time, the attack had political intentions and was launched by a hacker group called *Cutting Sword of Justice*. The virus reached the internal corporate network and erased the hard drive of about 30,000 computers. To clean up the malware, Aramco was forced to disconnect its internal network for more than a week.

Dragonfly targets their attacks to Energy Industry (Kshetri et al., 2017). Dragonfly is a hacker group whose activity dates back to 2011. After a period of inactivity, they returned to activity in 2014, targeting their attacks on the energy industry. From 2014 to nowadays, they have been the authors of several cyberattacks, such as those targeting Ukraine's power system in 2015 and 2016. Dragonfly uses different vectors of attack to access the network victim. Among them, we can find malicious emails, watering hole attacks, and Trojanized software.

Wannacry (Ehrenfeld, 2017). In 2017, Wannacry infected near 300,000 computers around the world. Although Wannacry was not aimed to attack ICS, it reached many critical infrastructure systems such as hospitals and manufacturer factories. Wannacry is a ransomware that encrypts files in the computer hard drive and asks for a ransom in bitcoins. It is based on an exploit called EternalBlue, stolen by The Shadow Brokers hacker group from the U.S. National Security Agency (NSA). EternalBlue exploits a vulnerability in Microsoft Samba protocol, allowing the ransomware to spread itself across the network.

EKANS, a ransomware specially designed to attack ICS (Rege et al., 2020). It can force computers to stop specific processes. This is performed by killing the applications that control the processes. It is accomplished by a static kill list stored in the EKANS source code. Once the processes are stopped, and the hard drive encryption is finished, a ransom note is stored in the root of the system drive and on the user's desktop.

Figure 3 summarizes the most important cyberattacks over the years.

Figure 3. Timeline of cyberattacks targeting ICS

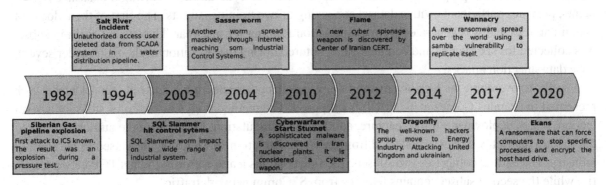

INDUSTRIAL-ORIENTED DATASETS FOR ANOMALY DETECTION

There are several datasets focused on traditional networks to test the performance of ML/DL models objectively. The most well-known dataset is called KDDCup99 (KDD Cup 99 Dataset), which is an evolution of the Darpa98 dataset (DARPA 98 Dataset). Although KDDcup99 has several deficiencies (Tavallaee et al., 2009), it is still widely used in research work in the field of AD in traditional networks. To solve these deficiencies, a new dataset called NSL-KDD (NSL-KDD Dataset) was developed. Another widely used dataset is CTU-13 (Garcia et al., 2014), which is a botnet-oriented dataset, and it was collected from real network traffic at the Czech Technical University. CTU-13 includes malicious traffic from different bots combined with normal and background network traffic. In contrast, CICIDS 2017 (Sharafaldin et al., 2018) is a dataset collected from a simulated scenario that contains traffic from two different networks: the outside and inside network. To carry out the network traffic capture, 4 computers were infected, launching cyberattacks against 14 victim computers.

Unlike traditional networks, the number of industrial-oriented datasets is quite limited. In the following lines, we summarize the most relevant works found in the literature concerning industrial datasets.

In (Industrial Control System (ICS) Cyber Attack Datasets), there are three available industrial datasets. The Power System Dataset (Pan et al., 2015) was collected from a power system, while several false data injection attacks were executed. It includes logs from the Snort IDS and measurements from Synchrophasor. The Gas Pipeline Dataset (Beaver et al., 2013) was collected from a gas pipeline while both false data injection and Denial-of-Service (DoS) attacks were executed. The dataset includes different features from the PLC that controls the process. Finally, Water Storage Dataset (Morris et al., 2011) was collected from a water tank on which three different attacks were launched: reconnaissance, false data injection, and DoS attacks (Morris et al., 2011).

Another set of industrial-oriented datasets were developed by the Center for Cybersecurity Research, iTrust (Centre for Research in Cyber Security, iTrust). All the datasets developed were collected from real testbeds in their facilities, while false data injection attacks were executed. In particular, we highlight the following datasets: Secure Water Treatment (SwaT) (Mathur et al., 2016), Water Distribution (WADI) (Water Distribution (WADI) Dataset), and Electric Power and Intelligent Control (EPIC) (Adepu, 2018). The three datasets contain normal and malicious samples from false injection attacks. All of them are available upon prior request.

The BATADAL (Taormina et al., 2018) (BATtle of the Attack Detection ALgorithms) competition, which is carried out to propose algorithms for the detection of cyberattacks affecting industrial environments, provides participants with a dataset consisting of two training subsets. The first of them does not contain attacks and was generated from a simulation running for one year. The second training subset was collected for six months and contains data captured during the operation of the plant under several false data injection attacks.

Finally, to overcome the lack of a methodology to collect datasets from industrial scenarios, the work presented in (Perales Gómez et al., 2019) is proposed. The methodology consists of 4 steps: attack selection, attack deployment, traffic capture, and feature computation. In addition, the authors presented the Electra dataset, which was collected from an electric traction substation widely used in the railway industry. The dataset comprises two subsets: the first contains features from Modbus TCP network traffic, while the second subset contains features from S7Comm network traffic.

MACHINE LEARNING AND DEEP LEARNING SOLUTIONS TO DETECT CYBERATTACKS IN INDUSTRIAL SCENARIOS

The usage of ML and DL techniques has been widely studied both on traditional networks and IoT scenarios. For example, the authors of (Cvitić et al., 2020) propose an ensemble ML approach to classify IoT devices in smart homes regardless of their purpose or functionality. The results showed that this approach can classify IoT devices into four previously defined classes with an accuracy of 99.79%. Another example is proposed in (Yin et al., 2020), where authors presented an integrated solution that uses Convolutional Neural Networks (CNN) and recurrent autoencoder to detect anomalies in IoT devices. In addition, the authors used a two-stage sliding window in the data preprocessing step to extract high-order features.

Since data from sensors and actuators follow a temporal pattern, anomaly detection in industrial scenarios is frequently treated as a time series classification problem. Therefore, many authors developed techniques to deal with time, especially 1-Dimensional Convolutional Neural Networks (1D CNN) and Long-Short Term Memory (LSTM) neural networks. For example, in (Kravchik et al., 2018), the authors analyzed an LSTM and 1D CNN to detect anomalies. The authors also proposed a method to compute high-order features based on calculating the difference between the current and the past value with a given lag. The authors of (Shalyga et al., 2018) tested Dense Neural Networks (DNN), 1D CNN, and LSTM networks as core models of an automatic architecture optimization based on Genetic Algorithms (GAs). The architecture proposed used the Numenta Anomaly Benchmark (NAB) metric (Lavin et al., 2015) instead of the widely extended F1-score. The authors of (Zizzo et al., 2019) presented an IDS based on an LSTM model where Cumulative Sum (CUSUM) was proposed as a method to compute the threshold to trigger an anomaly. A novel Generative Adversarial Network-based Anomaly Detection (GAN-AD) method based on LSTM models was presented in (Li et al., 2018).

Other ML/DL models than CNN and LSTM networks have also been proposed in the literature. For example, the authors of (Inoue et al., 2017) evaluated DNN and SVM to detect anomalies in Cyber-

Physical Systems (CPS). The test dataset used in the evaluation phase was scaled with its own mean and standard deviation. The usage of AutoEncoders (AE) was explored in (Kravchik et al., 2019). The authors suggested carrying out both filtering and extraction feature steps. The filtering step was intended to select those features most suitable to model an anomaly detection task. In comparison, the extraction process computes features in the frequency domain. However, feature extraction creates features based on the most energetic bands, removing important information from the remaining signal. In addition, the threshold function used to determine the presence of an anomaly is defined as a function of the mean and standard deviation of the test dataset.

Regarding the semi-supervised approach, the authors of (Elnour et al., 2020) proposed a novel method named Dual Isolation Forest (DIF), where two Isolation Forests (IF) were trained. The original scaled training data was used to train the first IF. While the second IF was trained with a new training dataset resulting from applying the Principal Component Analysis (PCA) to the original training dataset. The training dataset to train both IF contained normal data from normal and test datasets. While the test dataset only contained data from cyberattacks.

Concerning methodology to train AD-based IDS in industrial scenarios, (Pinelli et al., 2003; Fabio et al., 2018) presented one of the most prominent works. The authors proposed two methodologies for gas turbines. The first one presented the k-σ methodology, whereas the second presented an optimization over the k-σ methodology. A significant limitation of these methodologies is that they are based on the mean and the standard deviation of the data, detecting only a limited type of cyberattacks.

To solve the lack of an AD-based methodology using ML and DL techniques, the authors of (Perales Gómez et al., 2020) presented MADICS, a methodology for anomaly detection in industrial scenarios. The methodology consists of five steps: dataset preprocessing, feature filtering, feature extraction, anomaly detection, and validation. In addition, the authors implemented MADICS in the SWaT testbed, which is a scaled-down but fully operational raw water purification plant. The authors achieved a state-of-the-art precision score (0.984), while both the recall (0.750) and the F1-score (0.851) metrics were above the average of relevant works in the literature. Table 2 shows a comparative analysis of the different ML/DL techniques examined.

However, it is worth mentioning the vulnerability of ML and DL models to evasion attacks (Perales Gómez et al., 2021). These attacks consist in generating adversarial samples in the IDS inference phase which will be misclassified by the IDS, eventually reaching the target industrial device and, therefore, impacting the physical world, potentially damaging workers and assets.

AN EXAMPLE OF A CYBERATTACK CAUSING A SAFETY THREAT

The solutions presented in Section 4 only consider the cybersecurity aspect, but attacks shown in Section 2 not only impacted the cyber layer but also on the physical layer causing the degradation of services and potentially injuring citizens and workers. As an example, we show a specific attack detailed graphically in Figure 4. This attack is carried out in a factory with a production line composed of a pool of conveyor belts that transport raw products. In addition, several six-axis robotic arms perform specific actions on those raw products. Each of the conveyor belts is controlled by a PLC that receives commands from the SCADA server following a Master/Slave architecture. That is, the SCADA initiates the communication, whereas the PLC can only respond to the SCADA. In addition, the SCADA server has an HMI where the status of the controlled process is shown.

Table 2. Comparative analysis of different ML/DL techniques in industrial scenarios.

Work	ML/DL Method	Precision	Recall	F1-score	Year
(Inoue et al., 2017)	DNN	0.982	0.678	0.802	2017
(Inoue et al., 2017)	SVM	0.925	0.699	0.796	2017
(Kravchik et al., 2018)	1D CNN	0.968	0.791	0.871	2018
(Shalyga et al., 2018)	DNN	0.967	0.696	0.812	2018
(Shalyga et al., 2018)	1D CNN	0.952	0.702	0.808	2018
(Shalyga et al., 2018)	RNN	0.936	0.692	0.796	2018
(Li et al., 2018)	GAN	0.984	0.750	0.851	2018
(Zizzo et al., 2019)	LSTM	N/A	N/A	0.817	2019
(Kravchik et al., 2019)	Autoencoder	0.924	0.827	0.873	2019
(Elnour et al., 2020)	DIF	0.935	0.835	0.882	2020
(Perales Gómez et al., 2020)	LSTM	0.984	0.750	0.851	2020

Due to a vulnerability in a computer of the corporate network, a bot is introduced. From the corporate network, the bot compromises several legacy devices in the control network forming a botnet. Each of the infected devices is capable of capturing and modifying the traffic network. First, the operator requests that the arm robot base be rotated by 15 degrees (Step 1). This action is sent to the SCADA server that is in charge of controlling and supervising the process. In turn, the SCADA server sends the control command to the PLC in charge of controlling the specific arm robot. However, a device controlled by the bot intercepts the command (Step 2) and modifies it to change the rotation angle to 180 degrees (Step 3). Then, the PLC receives the command and rotates the base motor of the robot arm by 180 degrees (Step 4). Currently, the base motor is already rotated by 180 degrees and may injure workers who share space with the robot. Although the cyberattack that puts at risk the safety of workers is already carried out, the bot can modify the response from the arm robot to the HMI to hide its presence. In this case, the response is sent from the arm robot to the PLC (step 5), and the PLC transmits the response to the SCADA server (Step 6). At this moment, the device controlled by the bot intercepts the response and changes the rotation to 15 degrees (Step 7). Finally, the response arrives at the SCADA server, shown in the HMI (Step 8). Since the bot modified the response of the robot arm, the HMI shows that the action performed was to rotate the base motor by 15 degrees instead of 180 degrees.

Figure 4. Safety threat generated by a cyberattack

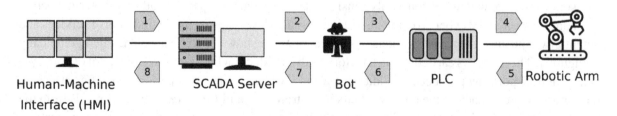

CYBERSECURITY AND SAFETY MANAGEMENT

Until now, cybersecurity and safety management in industrial scenarios have been usually carried out by different and isolated systems. In this context, there are many works focused on safety or cybersecurity. Cybersecurity solutions have been reviewed in the previous section. Regarding the existence of systems to improve safety in the industry, the authors of (Vignali et al., 2019) presented a software based on augmented reality and IIoT intending to increase workers' safety. The software took data from the server and sent it to the operators' mobile devices to report anomalies, allowing rapid response. In addition, the authors of (Lien et al., 2017) proposed the usage of robots to monitor the environments and detect obstacles. These robots were equipped with small and low-cost radars. The information collected by the robots was sent to a safety controller to be studied and the operation state inferred.

However, after studying the works related to cybersecurity and safety integration, we determined that they are quite limited. To put it in context, the authors of (Lyu et al., 2019) presented a review of existing works related to risk assessment and management from the cybersecurity and safety perspective and their integration. In addition, the authors of (Khan et al., 2018) pointed out the importance of managing cybersecurity and safety in an integrated way in future food manufacturing systems. Among the limited work available, we highlight the paper presented in (Riel et al., 2017), where authors proposed a method to deal with major challenges of design for safety and cybersecurity in the automotive context. Similarly, the authors of (Khalid et al., 2017) presented a solution based on addressing issues in the systematic development of safe and secure human-robot collaboration.

The authors of (Khalid et al., 2018) presented a framework to improve security in spaces where humans co-work with robots. The proposed solution was based on a strategy form of two components. The first component allows deploying secure adaptors using cybersecurity methods. The second component provides calibration support and comparison in real-time from the reference sensor library through an independent and intelligent module.

Special mention deserves SafeMan, a framework capable of managing cybersecurity and safety in a unified way (Perales Gómez et al., 2020). SafeMan was proposed as an extensible and flexible framework made up of different modules and applications deployed as needed. The modules of SafeMan are four, and each one has a specific responsibility. The Operation Support System (OSS) is in charge of storing the required policies by other modules and specify their behavior. The Risk Assessment App Manager (RAAM) deploys the monitoring applications at the edge of the network. Integrated Risk Assessment System (IRAS) is in charge of analyzing the output of the applications deployed by RAAM to evaluate the risk. Finally, Action Decision System (ADS) is responsible for carrying out the decision determined by IRAS.

In addition, SafeMan defines three applications that the RAAM subsystem can deploy. The Cyber Threat Detection (CTD) application is in charge of analyzing the network traffic to detect cyberattacks. To this end, ML/DL algorithms for AD to model the regular traffic and detect anomalous activity are proposed. The Indoor Localization and Activity Recognition (ILAR) application is in charge of tracking workers' position and their activities to detect safety threats. To work properly, this application requires a sensorized environment based on both radio-frequency and computer vision technologies. Finally, the Safety in Shared-Workspace (SSW) application was proposed to monitor the workspace where human employees co-work with robots to detect safety threats. As a result, using these applications, SafeMan can detect potentially dangerous situations, such as the presence of workers in restricted areas, the presence of objects that pose an obstacle in the path of robots, or the detection of robot malfunctions, to name a few.

CONCLUSION AND FUTURE WORK

Our factories have changed from an isolated to an interconnected approach. This has caused that many factories have been the target of cyberattacks over the years. Most of these cyberattacks have been carried out by malware, and to put in context the increment of these cyberattacks, the chapter reviewed different incidents caused by cyberattacks in industrial scenarios.

In addition, in the chapter, we also reviewed the three most important challenges that need to be solved to implement secure automation in the industry. The first of them states the need for a framework capable of managing cybersecurity and safety in a unified way. In Section 5, we introduced an example of a cyberattack causing a safety threat to illustrate this need. This highlights the need to consider cyberattacks as a source of a safety threat. Therefore, they need to be managed in a unified way.

The second challenge states the lack of industrial-oriented datasets needed to train an AD system in an industrial scenario. In Section 3, we have reviewed the most prominent industrial datasets. However, we highlighted the need for a methodology to generate such datasets because an industrial dataset collected from a water distribution factory cannot be used to train AD systems in power generation factories.

The final challenge states the need for a methodology to train AD systems in industrial scenarios. In Section 4, we reviewed the current solutions using ML/DL in the industrial context to highlight this point. Most of these works use ML/DL models capable of working with time-series to detect anomalies. However, each author applies different steps without standard criteria. This can lead to cause methodological errors in their solutions.

Finally, we showed three solutions that solve the aforementioned challenges. Electra dataset and its associate methodology to generate industrial-oriented datasets overcome the first challenge. MADICS, which is a methodology for AD in industrial scenarios, solves the second challenge. Finally, the Safe-Man framework, which manages cybersecurity and safety in a unified way, solves the third challenge discussed in the chapter since it considers cyberattacks as a source of a safety threat.

As future work, we plan several lines of work. One of them is applying MADICS methodology to different industrial scenarios that follow the Industry 4.0 paradigm. Another line is the implementation of SafeMan on a real manufacturing plant to manage cybersecurity and safety. In this way, we expect to detect harmful situations that put at risk the workers' safety and, therefore, reduce the accidents in the factory.

ACKNOWLEDGMENT

This work has been funded by Spanish Ministry of Science, Innovation and Universities, State Research Agency, FEDER funds, under Grant RTI2018-095855-B-I00, and the Swiss Federal Office for Defence Procurement (armasuisse) (project code and CYD-C-2020003).

REFERENCES

Adepu, S., Kandasamy, N. K., & Mathur, A. (2018). Epic: An electric power testbed for research and training in cyber physical systems security. In *Computer Security* (pp. 37–52). Springer.

Ahmadian, M. M., Shajari, M., & Shafiee, M. A. (2020). Industrial control system security taxonomic framework with application to a comprehensive incidents survey. *International Journal of Critical Infrastructure Protection*, *29*, 100356. doi:10.1016/j.ijcip.2020.100356

Beaver, J. M., Borges-Hink, R. C., & Buckner, M. A. (2013, December). An evaluation of machine learning methods to detect malicious SCADA communications. In *2013 12th international conference on machine learning and applications* (Vol. 2, pp. 54-59). IEEE. 10.1109/ICMLA.2013.105

Boyer, S. A. (1999). *SCADA: Supervisory control and data acquisition* (Vol. 3). ISA.

Boyes, H., Hallaq, B., Cunningham, J., & Watson, T. (2018). The industrial internet of things (IIoT): An analysis framework. *Computers in Industry*, *101*, 1–12. doi:10.1016/j.compind.2018.04.015

Centre for Research in Cyber Security. (n.d.). *iTrust*. https://itrust.sutd.edu.sg/

Chandola, V., Banerjee, A., & Kumar, V. (2009). Anomaly detection: A survey. *ACM computing surveys (CSUR), 41*(3), 1-58.

Cvitić, I., Peraković, D., Periša, M., & Gupta, B. (2021). Ensemble machine learning approach for classification of IoT devices in smart home. *International Journal of Machine Learning and Cybernetics*, 1-24. https://www.ll.mit.edu/r-d/datasets/1998-darpa-intrusion-detection-evaluation-dataset

DatasetN. S. L.-K. D. D. (n.d.). https://www.unb.ca/cic/datasets/nsl.html

Ehrenfeld, J. M. (2017). Wannacry, cybersecurity and health information technology: A time to act. *Journal of Medical Systems*, *41*(7), 104. doi:10.100710916-017-0752-1 PMID:28540616

Elnour, M., Meskin, N., Khan, K., & Jain, R. (2020). A dual-isolation-forests-based attack detection framework for industrial control systems. *IEEE Access: Practical Innovations, Open Solutions*, *8*, 36639–36651. doi:10.1109/ACCESS.2020.2975066

Fabio Ceschini, G., Gatta, N., Venturini, M., Hubauer, T., & Murarasu, A. (2018). Optimization of statistical methodologies for anomaly detection in gas turbine dynamic time series. *Journal of Engineering for Gas Turbines and Power*, *140*(3), 032401. doi:10.1115/1.4037963

Garcia, S., Grill, M., Stiborek, J., & Zunino, A. (2014). An empirical comparison of botnet detection methods. *Computers & Security, 45*, 100-123.

Hastie, T., Tibshirani, R., & Friedman, J. (2009). *The elements of statistical learning: data mining, inference, and prediction*. Springer Science & Business Media. Industrial Control System (ICS) Cyber Attack Datasets. https://sites.google.com/a/uah.edu/tommy-morris-uah/ics-data-sets

Inoue, J., Yamagata, Y., Chen, Y., Poskitt, C. M., & Sun, J. (2017, November). Anomaly detection for a water treatment system using unsupervised machine learning. In *2017 IEEE International Conference on Data Mining Workshops (ICDMW)* (pp. 1058-1065). IEEE. http://kdd.ics.uci.edu/databases/kddcup99/kddcup99.html

Khalid, A., Kirisci, P., Ghrairi, Z., Thoben, K. D., & Pannek, J. (2017, July). Towards implementing safety and security concepts for human-robot collaboration in the context of Industry 4.0. In *39th International MATADOR Conference on Advanced Manufacturing (Manchester, UK)*.

Khalid, A., Kirisci, P., Khan, Z. H., Ghrairi, Z., Thoben, K. D., & Pannek, J. (2018). Security framework for industrial collaborative robotic cyber-physical systems. *Computers in Industry*, *97*, 132–145. doi:10.1016/j.compind.2018.02.009

Khan, Z. H., Khalid, A., & Iqbal, J. (2018). Towards realizing robotic potential in future intelligent food manufacturing systems. *Innovative Food Science & Emerging Technologies*, *48*, 11–24. doi:10.1016/j.ifset.2018.05.011

Kravchik, M., & Shabtai, A. (2018, January). Detecting cyber attacks in industrial control systems using convolutional neural networks. In *Proceedings of the 2018 Workshop on Cyber-Physical Systems Security and PrivaCy* (pp. 72-83). 10.1145/3264888.3264896

Kravchik, M., & Shabtai, A. (2021). Efficient cyber attack detection in industrial control systems using lightweight neural networks and PCA. *IEEE Transactions on Dependable and Secure Computing*, 1. doi:10.1109/TDSC.2021.3050101

Kshetri, N., & Voas, J. (2017). Hacking power grids: A current problem. *Computer*, *50*(12), 91–95. doi:10.1109/MC.2017.4451203

Langner, R. (2011). Stuxnet: Dissecting a cyberwarfare weapon. *IEEE Security and Privacy*, *9*(3), 49–51. doi:10.1109/MSP.2011.67

Lasi, H., Fettke, P., Kemper, H. G., Feld, T., & Hoffmann, M. (2014). Industry 4.0. *Business & Information Systems Engineering*, *6*(4), 239–242. doi:10.100712599-014-0334-4

Lavin, A., & Ahmad, S. (2015, December). Evaluating Real-Time anomaly detection algorithms--The Numenta anomaly benchmark. In *2015 IEEE 14th International Conference on Machine Learning and Applications (ICMLA)* (pp. 38-44). IEEE.

Li, D., Chen, D., Jin, B., Shi, L., Goh, J., & Ng, S. K. (2019, September). MAD-GAN: Multivariate anomaly detection for time series data with generative adversarial networks. In *International Conference on Artificial Neural Networks* (pp. 703-716). Springer. 10.1007/978-3-030-30490-4_56

Li, P., Salour, M., & Su, X. (2008). A survey of internet worm detection and containment. *IEEE Communications Surveys and Tutorials*, *10*(1), 20–35. doi:10.1109/COMST.2008.4483668

Liao, H. J., Lin, C. H. R., Lin, Y. C., & Tung, K. Y. (2013). Intrusion detection system: A comprehensive review. *Journal of Network and Computer Applications*, *36*(1), 16–24. doi:10.1016/j.jnca.2012.09.004

Lien, J., Amihood, P. M., Javidan, A. J., Karagozler, M. E., Olson, E. M., & Poupyrev, I. (2017). *Embedding Radars in Robots for Safety and Obstacle Detection*. Academic Press.

Lyu, X., Ding, Y., & Yang, S. H. (2019). Safety and security risk assessment in cyber-physical systems. *IET Cyber-Physical Systems. Theory & Applications*, *4*(3), 221–232.

Mathur, A. P., & Tippenhauer, N. O. (2016, April). SWaT: a water treatment testbed for research and training on ICS security. In *2016 international workshop on cyber-physical systems for smart water networks (CySWater)* (pp. 31-36). IEEE.

Miller, B., & Rowe, D. (2012, October). A survey SCADA of and critical infrastructure incidents. In *Proceedings of the 1st Annual conference on Research in information technology* (pp. 51-56). 10.1145/2380790.2380805

Mirian, A., Ma, Z., Adrian, D., Tischer, M., Chuenchujit, T., & Yardley, T. (2016, December). An internet-wide view of ICS devices. In *2016 14th Annual Conference on Privacy, Security and Trust (PST)* (pp. 96-103). IEEE. 10.1109/PST.2016.7906943

Moore, D., Paxson, V., Savage, S., Shannon, C., Staniford, S., & Weaver, N. (2003). *The spread of the sapphire/slammer worm*. CAIDA, ICSI, Silicon Defense, UC Berkeley EECS and UC San Diego CSE.

Morris, T., & Gao, W. (2014, March). Industrial control system traffic data sets for intrusion detection research. In *International Conference on Critical Infrastructure Protection* (pp. 65-78). Springer. 10.1007/978-3-662-45355-1_5

Morris, T., Srivastava, A., Reaves, B., Gao, W., Pavurapu, K., & Reddi, R. (2011). A control system testbed to validate critical infrastructure protection concepts. *International Journal of Critical Infrastructure Protection, 4*(2), 88–103. doi:10.1016/j.ijcip.2011.06.005

Munro, K. (2012). Deconstructing flame: The limitations of traditional defences. *Computer Fraud & Security, 2012*(10), 8–11. doi:10.1016/S1361-3723(12)70102-1

Nicholson, A., Webber, S., Dyer, S., Patel, T., & Janicke, H. (2012). SCADA security in the light of Cyber-Warfare. *Computers & Security, 31*(4), 418–436. doi:10.1016/j.cose.2012.02.009

Pan, S., Morris, T., & Adhikari, U. (2015). Developing a hybrid intrusion detection system using data mining for power systems. *IEEE Transactions on Smart Grid, 6*(6), 3104–3113. doi:10.1109/TSG.2015.2409775

Perakovic, D., Perisa, M., Cvitic, I., & Zoric, P. (2020). Identification of the relevant parameters for modeling the ecosystem elements in Industry 4.0. In *4th EAI International Conference on Management of Manufacturing Systems* (pp. 111-123). Springer. 10.1007/978-3-030-34272-2_11

Peraković, D., Periša, M., Cvitić, I., & Zorić, P. (n.d.). *Information and communication technologies for the society 5.0 environment*. Academic Press.

Perales Gómez, Á. L., Fernández Maimó, L., Huertas Celdrán, A., & García Clemente, F. J. (2020). MADICS: A Methodology for Anomaly Detection in Industrial Control Systems. *Symmetry, 12*(10), 1583. doi:10.3390ym12101583

Perales Gómez, Á. L., Fernández Maimó, L., Huertas Celdran, A., García Clemente, F. J., Cadenas Sarmiento, C., Del Canto Masa, C. J., & Méndez Nistal, R. (2019). On the generation of anomaly detection datasets in industrial control systems. *IEEE Access: Practical Innovations, Open Solutions, 7*, 177460–177473. doi:10.1109/ACCESS.2019.2958284

Perales Gómez, Á. L., Fernández Maimó, L., Huertas Celdrán, A., García Clemente, F. J., & Cleary, F. (2021). Crafting Adversarial Samples for Anomaly Detectors in Industrial Control Systems. In *The 4th International Conference on Emerging Data and Industry 4.0 (EDI40)*.

Perales Gómez, Á. L., Fernández Maimó, L., Huertas Celdrán, A., García Clemente, F. J., Gil Pérez, M., & Martínez Pérez, G. (2020). SafeMan: A unified framework to manage cybersecurity and safety in manufacturing industry. *Software, Practice & Experience.*

Pillitteri, V. Y., & Brewer, T. L. (2014). *Guidelines for smart grid cybersecurity.* Academic Press.

Pinelli, M., Venturini, M., & Burgio, M. (2003, January). Statistical methodologies for reliability assessment of gas turbine measurements. In *Turbo Expo: Power for Land, Sea, and Air* (Vol. 36851, pp. 787-793). 10.1115/GT2003-38407

Rege, A., & Bleiman, R. (2020, June). Ransomware Attacks Against Critical Infrastructure. In *ECCWS 2020 20th European Conference on Cyber Warfare and Security* (p. 324). Academic Conferences and Publishing Limited. https://www.risidata.com/

Riel, A., Kreiner, C., Macher, G., & Messnarz, R. (2017). Integrated design for tackling safety and security challenges of smart products and digital manufacturing. *CIRP Annals, 66*(1), 177–180. doi:10.1016/j.cirp.2017.04.037

Shalyga, D., Filonov, P., & Lavrentyev, A. (2018). *Anomaly detection for water treatment system based on neural network with automatic architecture optimization.* arXiv preprint arXiv:1807.07282.

Sharafaldin, I., Lashkari, A. H., & Ghorbani, A. A. (2018, January). Toward generating a new intrusion detection dataset and intrusion traffic characterization. In ICISSp (pp. 108-116). doi:10.5220/0006639801080116

Skobelev, P. O., & Borovik, S. Y. (2017). On the way from Industry 4.0 to Industry 5.0: from digital manufacturing to digital society. *Industry 4.0, 2*(6), 307-311.

Taormina, R., Galelli, S., Tippenhauer, N. O., Salomons, E., Ostfeld, A., Eliades, D. G., Aghashahi, M., Sundararajan, R., Pourahmadi, M., Banks, M. K., Brentan, B. M., Campbell, E., Lima, G., Manzi, D., Ayala-Cabrera, D., Herrera, M., Montalvo, I., Izquierdo, J., Luvizotto, E. Jr, ... Ohar, Z. (2018). Battle of the attack detection algorithms: Disclosing cyber attacks on water distribution networks. *Journal of Water Resources Planning and Management, 144*(8), 04018048. doi:10.1061/(ASCE)WR.1943-5452.0000969

Tavallaee, M., Bagheri, E., Lu, W., & Ghorbani, A. A. (2009, July). A detailed analysis of the KDD CUP 99 data set. In *2009 IEEE symposium on computational intelligence for security and defense applications* (pp. 1-6). IEEE.

Vignali, G., Bottani, E., Guareschi, N., Di Donato, L., Ferraro, A., & Pirozzi, M. (2019, June). Development of a 4.0 industry application for increasing occupational safety: guidelines for a correct approach. In *2019 IEEE International Conference on Engineering, Technology and Innovation (ICE/ITMC)* (pp. 1-6). IEEE. 10.1109/ICE.2019.8792814

Vinayakumar, R., Alazab, M., Soman, K. P., Poornachandran, P., Al-Nemrat, A., & Venkatraman, S. (2019). Deep learning approach for intelligent intrusion detection system. *IEEE Access: Practical Innovations, Open Solutions, 7*, 41525–41550. doi:10.1109/ACCESS.2019.2895334

Water Distribution (WADI) Dataset. (n.d.). https://itrust.sutd.edu.sg/testbeds/water-distribution-wadi/

Wu, H., Schwab, S., & Peckham, R. L. (2008). *U.S. Patent No. 7,424,744.* Washington, DC: U.S. Patent and Trademark Office.

Xin, Y., Kong, L., Liu, Z., Chen, Y., Li, Y., Zhu, H., Gao, M., Hou, H., & Wang, C. (2018). Machine learning and deep learning methods for cybersecurity. *IEEE Access: Practical Innovations, Open Solutions*, *6*, 35365–35381. doi:10.1109/ACCESS.2018.2836950

Yin, C., Zhang, S., Wang, J., & Xiong, N. N. (2020). Anomaly detection based on convolutional recurrent autoencoder for IoT time series. *IEEE Transactions on Systems, Man, and Cybernetics. Systems*, 1–11. doi:10.1109/TSMC.2020.2968516

Zhioua, S. (2013, July). The middle east under malware attack dissecting cyber weapons. In *2013 IEEE 33rd International Conference on Distributed Computing Systems Workshops* (pp. 11-16). IEEE. 10.1109/ICDCSW.2013.30

Zizzo, G., Hankin, C., Maffeis, S., & Jones, K. (2019). *Intrusion detection for industrial control systems: Evaluation analysis and adversarial attacks*. arXiv preprint arXiv:1911.04278.

KEY TERMS AND DEFINITIONS

Actuator: A device responsible for moving a physical mechanism.

Botnet: A network of internet-connected devices infected by a bot, generally used to perform Distributed Denial-of-Service (DDoS) attacks and send spam.

Human Machine Interface: A device that shows information about the process status and where an operator can interact with the process.

Industrial Control System: A set of heterogeneous devices and networks in charge of controlling industrial devices. industrial control systems includes supervisory control and data acquisition systems, programmable logic controllers, sensors, and actuators.

Intrusion Detection System: A system that analyzes networks or hosts in order to detect anomalous activities.

Malware: A software specially designed to cause damage to the user computer.

Programmable Logic Controller: A industrial device to control industrial processes. It serves as an intermediary between SCADA and sensors/actuators.

Ransomware: A type of malware that blocks access to computer data, generally using a cipher algorithm, and ask for a ransom.

Sensor: A device capable of performing measures and send the information to a computer.

Supervisory Control and Data Acquisition: A system used in industrial scenarios to supervise and control processes.

Chapter 6
Malicious Node Detection Using Convolution Technique:
Authentication in Wireless Sensor Networks (WSN)

Priyanka Ahlawat

National Institute of Technology, Kurukshetra, India

Pranjil Singhal

National Institute of Technology, Kurukshetra, India

Khushi Goyal

National Institute of Technology, Kurukshetra, India

Kanak Yadav

National Institute of Technology, Kurukshetra, India

Rohit Bathla

National Institute of Technology, Kurukshetra, India

ABSTRACT

Considering the situation when the node which is entering in the network is a malicious node, it can check and record the various operations of the network which could be responsible for some serious security issues. In order to safeguard the network, the author propose an approach which is in view of the advanced encoding strategy, termed as convolution coding approach. According to the requirement of network, the initial bits are assigned, and by applying the convolution technique, the final code is generated for each and every node. Considering the fact that it is a digital method, the codes can be represented by using the binary number system. All the nodes that are a part of the network will be having their corresponding final binary code, say C. The verification of each node is carried out by matching the generated code C with the security code within a particular time period before transmitting the data. This process enables the detection of malicious or attacker node. Furthermore, to enhance the versatility and execution, the system is organized into clusters.

DOI: 10.4018/978-1-7998-7789-9.ch006

Copyright © 2022, IGI Global. Copying or distributing in print or electronic forms without written permission of IGI Global is prohibited.

INTRODUCTION

Wireless sensor networks (WSNs) are basically described in the form of a collection of sensor hubs or nodes which are spread in a region and utilized for checking and recording various observations, perceptions and states of being of a specific domain and conditions of any particular surrounding. Because of the autonomous structures of Sensors networks, the nodes are having the permission to enter or then leave the system or formed network at any instant of time. It makes the system vulnerable and prone to attacks. The main characteristics of WSNs are their infrastructure-less nature and the ability that they can be self-configured without the need of any predefined structure or configuration. WSNs comprises of a set of a number of small senor nodes. The communication carried out in such network is wireless. Primarily, WSNs were developed for some complex military communications in certain areas where it was not feasible to establish wired networks. Nowadays wireless sensors are useful in numerous other applications, considering few as, industrial modelling, logistics, defence and security, forest fire monitoring, monitoring of poisonous gases etc. The key features of a WSN are that they are spatially distributed, infrastructure less, self organized, do not require any predefined structure. Generally, the sensor nodes are having very low storage capacity, low computational capabilities and limited supply of energy. Sensor nodes are allowed to be a part or leave the system at any given moment. This autonomous behaviour of the network which allows node mobility is solely responsible for some serious security concerns. Any malicious or attacker node can enter into the legitimate network and cause some serious damage. The secrecy and integrity of the information transferred within the network could be tampered or lost, threatening the entire sensor network.

Hence, there is a serious need of some security mechanism in order to keep the authenticity, integrity and confidentiality of the data which is being monitored, collected by sensor nodes and further transferred in the network for the purpose of its storage, processing and analysis. As these networks could be easily compromised due to its limitations, it is really critical to complete the task of detection and isolation of the malicious nodes for avoiding any chance of some further damage (Perrig A.,2002)

Till now a number of approaches are proposed and implemented in order to fulfil the objective of providing security standards to the network. One of approach among them is cryptography, which basically executes the task of securing the original data by the use of a key. Encryption could be done by two methods: symmetric cryptography and asymmetric cryptography. In the case of symmetric cryptography, we can use the same key for both of the operations .While with later cryptographic technique; we need to use unique keys for encryption and decryption. As there is a need of keys for encryption and decryption, each node in the network is to be provided with unique keys. Due to limited supply of energy and storage space in WSNs it becomes difficult to perform cryptography. Therefore, for the systems having bigger sets of sensor hubs or nodes, the process of generation of keys becomes cumbersome and more complex .Later some hybrid cryptographic techniques were also suggested such as a combination which make use of both type of cryptographic techniques and digital signature. However, the efficiency of these techniques was also not sufficient enough because the complexity used to increase with the networks having bigger sets of nodes, we are considering.

While with the implementation of this technique, we are considering to obtain a binary code word for security purpose, which need to be matched by all the nodes before accessing the information. The process of generation of code word is to be done into two steps.

Initially we the security bits are assigned according to the network requirement depending upon its size, which is directly proportional to the number of sensor nodes present in the system. After that by implementing the convolution code generation technique the final security binary code is obtained (Alghamdi,2019) . Before accessing the network there is a need of matching the code word with the generated code for each node within a given time period. As the malicious nodes will not be able to perform this task .Furthermore in order to get better performance and improve the results of Convolution technique the system will be arranged in the form of clusters. Here, clustering proves to be a significant improvement. As the process of matching the code word becomes easy and the scalability of the network also improves. Hence malicious nodes will be detected before they could tamper the network by using convolution technique.

Overview

As the nodes of a wireless sensor network (WSN) are equipped in remote areas and vulnerable environment. The network could be easily compromised by some attackers due to the constraints of a WSN such as autonomous nature, limited battery lifetime, memory space and computing capability. This could lead to the reduction in reliability of the data which is to be retrieved and transferred causing some serious damage. In order to prevent the network from some serious security issues and information breaches there is a critical need of some effective security measures for our network.

Challenges and Issues

- Isolation of the malicious nodes for avoiding any chance of some further damage
- Mechanism in order to keep the authenticity, integrity and confidentiality of the data which is being monitored, collected by sensor nodes
- Transferred in the network for the purpose of its storage, processing and analysis.
- Nodes will be detected before they could tamper the network

Organization

The techniques which were proposed earlier were not efficient enough to perform the desired task .Whereas the convolution technique is really effective enough in fulfilling the security requirements considering various storage and energy constraints of a wireless network. There is a restriction for all the nodes to match the code word with the generated code before accessing the network .So that we can prevent the network and the information being transferred from being compromised. The detection and elimination of malicious node could be successfully executed.

Hence, the network will be secured from vulnerable attacks and security threats and the information will be reliable as it will be prevented from various attacks including eavesdropping and cannot be tampered.

LITERATURE SURVEY

Mostly wireless sensor networks are worked without any human supervision and it can easily lead to the compromise of an individual node. Many approaches have been proposed regarding the security of these networks considering different aspects of WSN like limited memory, battery lifetime and computational capacity. Here are some works closely related to identification and isolation of t he malicious node in the system of sensor nodes.

The combination of two security protocols has been proposed by (Perrig A.,2002) to enhance the security standards of the system of sensor networks & improve the performance of overall wireless network but it came up with the obvious effects of merging the demerits of both the combined protocols.

The proposed work of Necla and Ismail, 2012reports the use of algorithms of Encryption which is Scalable enough and another one which is Cipher Block Chaining- Message Authentication Code so that the security can be ensured in the network on a dynamic level of system. The problem faced with this approach was that with the increment in the amount of bits to be transmitted, there is a clear increment in the consumption of power in the network. For the security of mobile ad-hoc networks, a zone routing model has been proposed by Ranjeetha et al.,2017which uses key distribution. But because of lack of the central authority, key distribution can be a complex task in such networks.

The approach by Zang et al., 2013 proposes that keys should be maintained in hierarchical networks which can be done by giving unique keys to the base stations, heads of clusters instead of providing the same key to all. Zheng et al.,2017gave the method where dynamic trust can be used to provide security. With the help of direct and indirect trust, dynamic trust can be found and a sliding window is used to improve flexibility. But, regular update of parameters can be problematic. Noor et al., 2012used the secondary routing and secondary gateway in cluster network to develop a method which is efficient in terms of power consumption to provide security to the system. But in autonomous structure of networks, clustering might be bit difficult. An energy efficient optimized algorithm which improve performance, improve the reliability of the system and safeguard the network from various forms of attack.,2018

Using node to node interactions, Kaur et al.,2016 proposed a key distribution method which was secured enough and differentiated attacking node so that a safe routing is mapped is from one initiating node for communication to the destination. But this method tend to fail in the condition where at any time interval, a group of malicious nodes enter the network and tends to present themselves as active nodes. Imad et al.,2016 presented a method in which on considering the value of trust factor of nodes, trust among the nodes establishes in the system. This trust is maintained in the observations of the nodes and this trust is responsible for the successful transmission of information. However, each time during the process of transferring information with trust participating as router, node energy is reduced.

Chan et al.,2003 introduced a technique which used pair-wise key distribution of random key within the nodes of the system so that reliability in communications can be maintained. But the process of distribution of the keys needed prior the validation of trust to which node that particular key has been given. Regarding the topology of the network, a hierarchical network is proposed in as WSN is an energy sensitive network and this approach can help in energy saving. MECH (maximum energy cluster head) protocol is a LEACH (low energy adaptive clustering hierarchy) like method where network is divided into various groups of clusters where every cluster is having a unique cluster head.

Various existing methods use the technique of key distribution, as it consumes more energy, hence these methods are not efficient enough and needs more storage to obtain and store the encryption and decryption pin. For more complex and large systems, it becomes difficult to provide pin to each node when they enter the network. More space for storage is to be provided for that which is generally less. In the proposed method, an encoding approach is implemented which is already present in the systems for digital communication. Different code word is obtained at different hop without the help of any additional hardware. Key distribution complexity is removed and because of the use of ex-or gates, power consumption is also low. Thus, the proposed work is suitable for heterogeneous multi-hop networks.

PROPOSED WORK

Network Model

WSN is an energy sensitive model. Thus, we use the MECH (Maximum Energy Cluster Head) protocol to build the network. It is same as a protocol such LEACH where the network is divided in clusters.

The below Figure 1 shows the architecture of MECH protocol where sensor nodes play two roles: member node and cluster head. Sensors organize themselves into clusters and one cluster head node is associated with each cluster, which manages the data between the base station and member nodes and it also manages the cluster. The main aim of the network model is to enhance the execution of Convolution Technique. Clustering basically helps for improving the scalability of the network. It makes the network less complex and more organized easing the process of validation of nodes by matching their respective code words

Figure 1. The key architecture

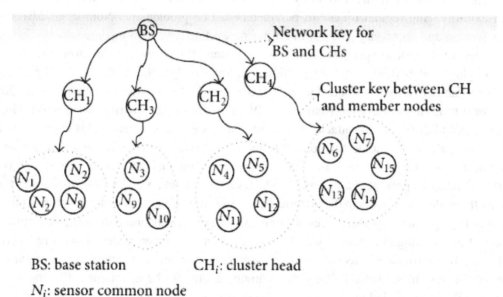

BS: base station   CH_i: cluster head

N_i: sensor common node

Code Generation

In this approach, Convolution Coding Approach (a digital encoding technique) creates the security code. Initially, on the basis of network requirement, security bits can be selected and then in order to make a security code, convolutional technique is applied on the ISB (Initial Security Bits) and modulo 2 operation is used for that.

All the data, including the security information is broadcasted by the source node to all of its neighbouring nodes, and the node can access the data if it is a legitimate node and then it keeps on broadcasting the data to its neighbours. And it continues till the information reaches the destination node. If it is not legitimate, it cannot retrieve the data as it does not have any information about the security operation and thus cannot produce a security code (CB) in a limited time. In this manner we will be able to identify and isolate the malicious nodes present in our legitimate network before it can access to the data which is being shared and transferred in the network.

DATA FLOW DIAGRAMS

We propose an approach of Malicious Node Detection using Convolution Technique based on a system-wide quantitative data flow model. The basic model of our data flows analysis on this incremental and aggregated approach towards the quantitative data flow graphs. These basic graphs describe the interaction among various system entities such as methods, support, data, or system registries. We demonstrate the feasibility of our approach through these data flow diagrams.

Level 0 DFD

It's designed such as abstraction design, explaining the operation as a separate rule with its connection to outside entities. It describes the whole system as private, including information and output data indicated by arrows. Our basic approach considering the input to the network that the situation when the node which is entering in the network is an a malicious node then it can check and record the various operations.

Figure 2. Level 0 DFD

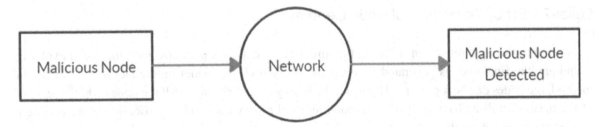

Level 1 DFD

The structure consists of a collection of sensor nodes that will be transmitting the information. This access point will regularly receive sensor nodes' information to collect data sent by sensor nodes. There are two sorts of attackers, static one and dynamic one. Static, which regularly transfers false information to other node & reverse the data whenever is demanded. The dynamic which conveys both accurate data and wrong data to nodes. Hence the arrangement becomes unclear whether it is a real sensor or an invalid sensor. Ultimately, we suggest how malicious node can be identified by using convolutional code generator. In order to safeguard the network we are hereby proposing an approach which is in view of the advanced encoding strategy, termed as Convolution coding approach.

Figure 3. Level-1 DFD

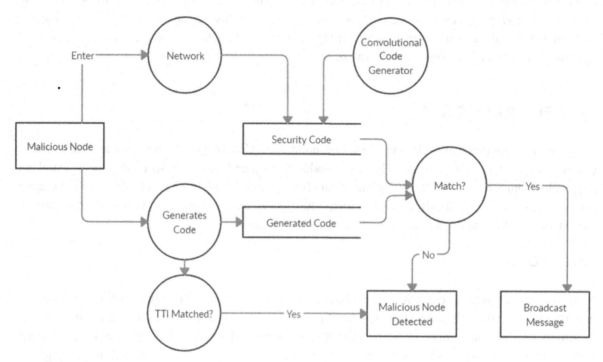

Level 2 DFD

Level-2 DFD of Convolutional Code Generator

According to the requirement of network, the initial bits are assigned and by applying the convolution technique, the final code is generated for each and every node. Considering the fact that it is a digital method, the codes can be represented by using the binary number system. All the nodes which are a part of the network will be having their corresponding final binary code. The verification of each node is carried out by matching the generated code with the security code within a particular time period before transmitting the data. This process enables the detection of malicious or attacker node. Furthermore to enhance the versatility and execution, the system is organised into clusters.

Figure 4. Level-2 DFD of convolutional code generator

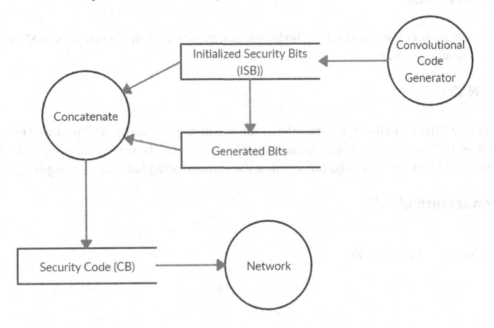

Level-2 DFD of Network

Figure 5. Level-2 DFD of network

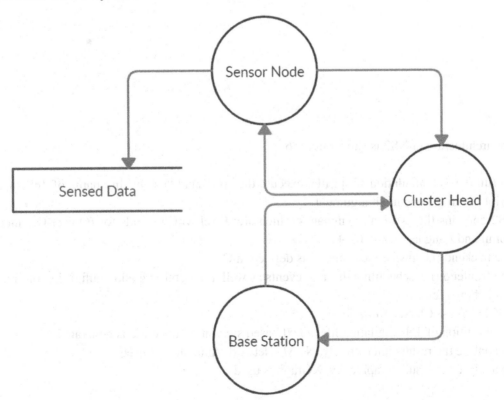

IMPLEMENTATION

The implementation of the Convolution Technique for malicious node detection is WSN is done in Network Simulator 2 (NS2).

What is NS2?

NS2 is an event-driven simulator. To study the dynamic nature of networks, NS2 is proved to be useful. The various simulations on wired & wireless network protocols can be performed using ns2. The users can define the network protocols and can simulate the corresponding behaviours using NS2.

The Architecture of NS2

Figure 6. Core architecture of NS2

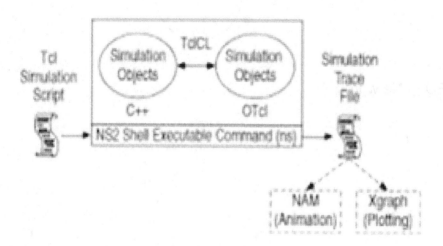

The core architecture of NS2 is shown in fig.6

- To run the Tcl simulation script file, execute the command "ns" having name of Tcl simulation script file in the one input argument.
- NS2 contains the two main languages which are: OTcl which stands for (Object-Oriented Tool Command Language). and C++.
- The backend (i.e. inside mechanism) is defined in C++.
- The frontend (i.e. scheduling discrete events as well as assembling and configuring of objects) is defined in OTcl.
- TclCl = Tcl + Classes Libraries.
- On execution of Tcl simulation file, a text based simulation trace file is generated.
- To analyse the results interactively, NAM (Network Animator) is used.
- To analyse the results graphically, XGraph is used.

Implementing Hierarchical Network

- The hierarchical network is implemented MECH protocol. The basic structure is as follows:
- Each node is provided with a different ID.
- Every sensor node is known and have a fixed position.
- Base station consists of infinite energy.
- All the sensors are fixed in the transmission area of base station.
- The sensor nodes are able to adjust the transmit power.

Cluster Formation

- Base station construct the remaining energy matrix and distance matrix.
- Each and every sensor node sends its location and energy to their base station.
- A network is divided by the base station in k number of clusters as follows:
- Base station construct the remaining energy matrix and distance matrix.
- The matrices are broadcasted to each node by the base station.
- The sensor node having maximum energy in each subdivision is chosen to be a cluster head (CH) and if the two sensor nodes have same energy, the the node having smallest ID is chosen to be the cluster head.
- The sink node broadcasts the Cluster Head's ID to the sensor nodes.
- By using distance matrix, all the sensor nodes associate themselves to the closest Cluster Head.

Re-Clustering

- The Cluster Heads are chosen again if the energy of a Cluster Head becomes less than its threshold energy.
- Then, the base station updates the energy matrix when the cluster head is changed.

Implementing Convolution Technique

In this approach, we used manageable dispersed data convolution solutions that can quickly adjust to changeable environmental and thus cognitive performance of malicious nodes.

The following advantages are:

- It can be easily applied to large-size systems.
- The network includes a considerable area; we distribute this area into smaller sections.
- Scalability and Efficiency inside wireless sensor network for huge size networks.

The Convolution technique is implemented in the following steps:

Step 1: Based on the requirement of the network, the initial security bits are selected at each hop. It is expressed as I_{sb}.

$$I_{SB} = Hc - 1 \tag{1}$$

where Hc is the hop count.

    Example, if the hop count is 1, then,

$$I_{S1} = 1 - 1 = 0$$

If hop count is 2, then

$$I_{S2} = 2 - 1 = 1$$

If hop count is 3, then

$$I_{S3} = 3 - 1 = 2$$

Step 2: The I_{SB} is represented in 3-bits using 3-bit convolutional code generator. It is expressed as:

$$I_{SB} = S_{1B}S_{2B}S_{3B} \tag{2}$$

Example, for hop count 1, IS1 = 0 i.e.

$$I_{S1} = S_{11}S_{21}S_{31} \tag{3}$$

$$I_{S1} = 0\ 0\ 0$$

For hop count 2, $I_{S2} = 1$, i.e.

$$I_{S2} = S_{12}S_{22}S_{32} \tag{4}$$

$$I_{S2} = 0\ 0\ 1$$

For hop count 3, $I_{S3} = 2$, i.e.

$$I_{S3} = S_{13}S_{23}S_{33} \tag{5}$$

$$I_{S3} = 0\ 1\ 0$$

Step 3: Calculate the bits G_{1B}, G_{2B}, G_{3B} using modulo 2 addition of the I_{SB} (initial security bits) as follows:

$$G_{1B} = (S_{1B} + S_{2B})\ \%\ 2 \tag{6}$$

$$G_{2B} = S_{1B} \tag{7}$$

$$G_{3B} = (S_{3B})\ \%\ 2 \tag{8}$$

For example, at hop count 1, i.e. $I_{S1} = 0\ 0\ 0$, then

$G_{11} = (0 + 0) \% 2 = 0$

$G_{21} = 0$

$G_{31} = 0 \% 2 = 0$

At hop count 2, i.e. $I_{S2} = 0\ 0\ 1$, then

$G_{12} = (0 + 0) \% 2 = 0$

$G_{22} = 0$

$G_{32} = 1$

At hop count 3, i.e. $I_{S3} = 0\ 1\ 0$, then

$G_{13} = (0 + 1) \% 2 = 1$

$G_{23} = 0$

$G_{33} = 0 \% 2 = 0$

Step 4: To analyse the trust of the node, obtain the security code (CB) by concatenating the initial security bits (I_{SB}) with the generated bits (G_{1B}, G_{2B}, G_{3B}) as follows:

$$C_B = \prod_{i=1}^{N} S_{iB} G_{iB}$$

where SiBGiB are put in sequence series and N represents total number of considered initial bits.
For example, At hop 1, i.e. $I_{S1} = 0\ 0\ 0$, $G_{11} = 0$, $G_{21} = 0$, $G_{31} = 0$, then

$$CB = S_{11} S_{21} S_{31} G_{11} G_{21} G_{31} \tag{9}$$

$CB = 0\ 0\ 0\ 0\ 0\ 0$

At hop 2, i.e. $I_{S2} = 0\ 0\ 1$, $G_{12} = 0$, $G_{22} = 0$, $G_{32} = 1$, then

$$CB = S_{12} S_{22} S_{32} G_{12} G_{22} G_{32} \tag{10}$$

$CB = 0\ 0\ 1\ 0\ 0\ 1$

At hop count 3, i.e. $I_{S3} = 0\ 1\ 0$, $G_{13} = 1$, $G_{23} = 0$, $G_{33} = 0$, then

$$CB = S_{13} S_{23} S_{33} G_{13} G_{23} G_{33} \tag{11}$$

CB= 0 1 0 1 0 0

Step 5: Verify the CB of every node in the routing process. If the security code is matched in the defined time, then the node will be considered to be legitimate and can transmit the data otherwise, the node is considered to be malicious.

Since, the malicious node does not know the security operation, so it takes enough time to generate the security code, if length of security code is 8 so it generate 2^8 combinations which is difficult to guess in the defined TTL.

The proposed approach is applied in simple wireless network as well as hierarchical network to test the performance of convolution technique.

RESULT

Simulation in NS2

For getting better insights of the performance of the convolution technique, we simulated it using NS2. The Simulation Parameters are listed below:

Time of simulation: 30 s
Nodes count considered: 3 – 10
Link layer: Logical link
Size of packet: 500 bytes
Propagation model: Two-ray ground
Type of MAC used: 802.11
Network area: 500 m×500 m
Type of queue: Drop-tail
Type of Routing: AODV
Speed of node: 5, 15, 25 m/s.

Initially we just implemented the convolution technique which provided significant simulation results. Then to improve the performance of this technique, cluster based network architecture is implemented.

The cluster based architecture helped to improve upon the time constraint. For the particular network, there is an improvement of approximately 4 seconds.

The results of the simulation clearly indicate that the convolution is successful in detection of the malicious node. It also keeps on focus the energy and storage constraints of the wireless sensor network. Less computational work is performed as compared to other key distribution mechanism. The performance is further improved by forming various cluster within the network as it eases the process of validating legitimate nodes and identification & isolation of malicious nodes present in the network.

Figure 7. Communication before node detection.

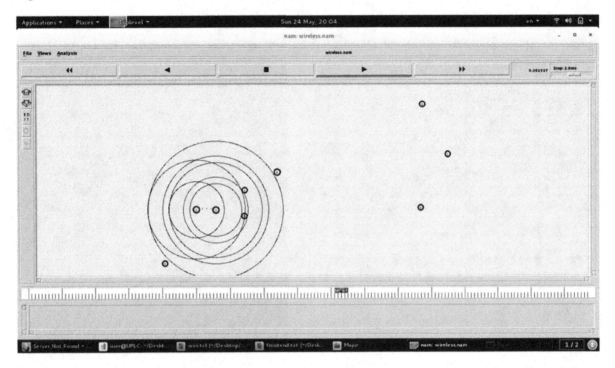

Figure 8. Simulation after detection of malicious node.

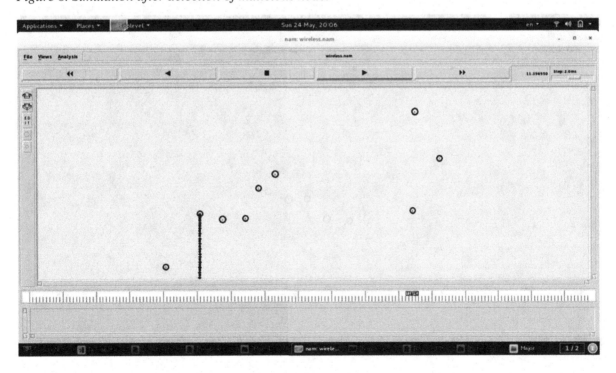

Figure 9. Packet drop values for malicious node.

Figure 10. Clustered based network architecture.

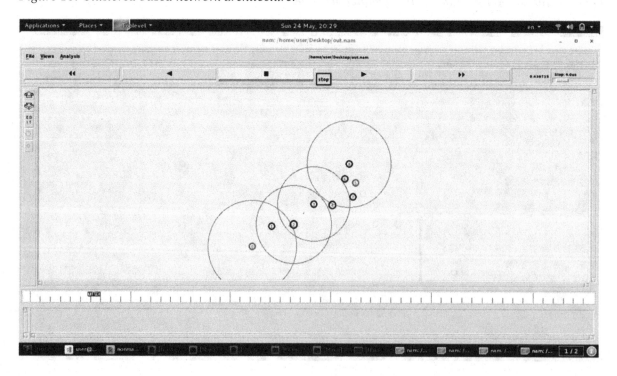

Figure 11. Packet drop values for malicious nodes and improved time constraint.

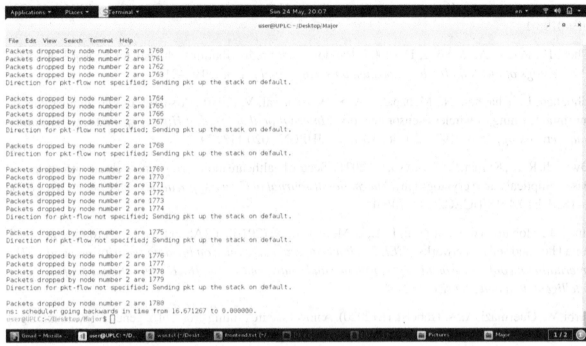

CONCLUSION AND FUTURE SCOPE

WSNs are having a vast application domain nowadays. They are really compact and efficient in transfer of data in various physical environments. The approach proposed, through convolutional codes provides security to wireless networks without using some sort of key distribution, which is not effective because it consumes more storage space and power. The proposed technique is efficient as we are using simple mathematical equations for the generation of security code, it thus reduce computational power .Easy detection of the malicious nodes is possible for secured transmission of information from the source node to the destination node.

Furthermore, to improve its performance cluster based network architecture was implemented. It resulted in improved value for time constraints. It also increases the scalability of the network. The results of simulation show that the proposed approach gives quite decent results, and it is easy and helpful to provide the security to WSN.

REFERENCES

Al-Qerem, A., Alauthman, M., Almomani, A., & Gupta, B. B. (2020). IoT transaction processing through cooperative concurrency control on fog–cloud computing environment. *Soft Computing*, *24*(8), 5695–5711. doi:10.100700500-019-04220-y

Alghamdi, T. A. (2019). Convolutional technique for enhancing security in wireless sensor networks against malicious nodes. *Human-centric Computing and Information Sciences, 9*(1), 38. doi:10.118613673-019-0198-1

Chen, H., Perrig, A., & Song, D. (2003) Random Key Predistribution Schemes for Sensor Networks. *Proceedings of the 2003 IEEE symposium on security and privacy*, 197–213.

Chouhan, L., Chauhan, N., Mahapatra, A. S., & Agarwal, V. (2020). A survey on the applications of machine learning in wireless sensor networks. *International Journal of High Performance Computing and Networking, 16*(4), 197–220. doi:10.1504/IJHPCN.2020.113779

Dwivedi, R. K., Kumar, R., & Buyya, R. (2021). Secure healthcare monitoring sensor cloud with attribute-based elliptical curve cryptography. *International Journal of Cloud Applications and Computing, 11*(3), 1–18. doi:10.4018/IJCAC.2021070101

Imad, J., Mohammed, F., Jaroodi, J. A., & Mohamed, N. (2016). TRAS: a trust-based routing protocol for ad hoc and sensor networks. *IEEE 2nd international conference on big data security on cloud, IEEE international conference on high performance and smart computing, IEEE international conference on intelligent data and security*, 382–387.

Jerbi, W., Guermazi, A., & Trabelsi, H. (2020). A novel secure routing protocol of generation and management cryptographic keys for wireless sensor networks deployed in internet of things. *International Journal of High Performance Computing and Networking, 16*(2-3), 87–94. doi:10.1504/IJHPCN.2020.112693

Kaur, J., Gill, S. S., & Dhaliwal, B. S. (2016). Secure trust based key management routing framework for wireless sensor networks. *Journal of Engineering (Stevenage, England), 2016*, 1–9.

Learning-Based Security Technique for Selective Forwarding Attack in Clustered WSN. (n.d.). *Applied Soft Computing, 108*, 107473. doi:10.1016/j.asoc.2021.107473

Necla, B., & Ismail, E. (2012). WSNSec: A scalable data link layer security protocol forWSNs. *Ad Hoc Networks, 10*(1), 37–45. doi:10.1016/j.adhoc.2011.04.013

Noor, Z., Jung, L., Alsaadi, F., & Alghamdi, T. (2012). Wireless sensor network (WSN) routing security, reliability and energy efficiency. *J Appl Sci, 12*(6), 593–59. doi:10.3923/jas.2012.593.597

Perrig, A., Szewczyk, R., Wen, V., Cullar, D., & Tygar, J. D. (2002). SPINS: Security protocols for sensor networks. *Int J Commun Comput Inform, 8*(5), 521–534.

Ranjeetha, S., Renuga, N., & Sharmila, R. (2017) Secure zone routing protocol for MANET. *International conference on emerging trends in engineering, science and sustainable technology (ICETSST-2017)*, 67–76.

Salhi, D. E., Tari, A., & Kechadi, M. T. (2021). Using Clustering for Forensics Analysis on Internet of Things. *International Journal of Software Science and Computational Intelligence, 13*(1), 56–71. doi:10.4018/IJSSCI.2021010104

Stergiou, C. L., Psannis, K. E., & Gupta, B. B. (2020). IoT-based big data secure management in the fog over a 6G wireless network. *IEEE Internet of Things Journal, 8*(7), 5164–5171. doi:10.1109/JIOT.2020.3033131

Tao, Y., Xiangyang, X., Tonghui, L., & Leina, P. (2018). A secure routing of wireless sensor networks based on trust evaluation model. *Procedia Computer Science*, *131*, 1156–1163. doi:10.1016/j.procs.2018.04.289

Zhang, Y., Wu, C., Cao, J., & Li, X. (2013). A secret sharing-based key management in a hierarchical wireless sensor network. *International Journal of Distributed Sensor Networks*, *2013*(6), 1–7. doi:10.1155/2013/406061

Zhang, Wu, & Cao. (2008). A Secret Sharing-Based Key Management in Hierarchical Wireless Sensor Network. In *Securing wireless sensor networks: A survey*. IEEE Communications Surveys and Tutorials.

Zhengwang, Y., Wen, T., Song, X., Liu, Z., & Fu, C. (2017). An efficient dynamic trust evaluation model for wireless sensor networks. *Journal of Sensors*, *2017*, 1–16.

Chapter 7
Scalable Rekeying Using Linked LKH Algorithm for Secure Multicast Communication

Priyanka Ahlawat

National Institute of Technology, Kurukshetra, India

Kanishka Tyagi

National Institute of Technology, Kurukshetra, India

ABSTRACT

In the real scenario, there is a large multicast group where nodes leave and join frequently, and also the number of nodes leaving and joining is also not proportionate. Hence, scalable rekeying process is an important issue that needs to be concerned for the secured group communication for dynamic groups. In basic rekeying scheme, which is based on the logical key hierarchy, the rekeying cost depends on the logarithm of the size of group for a join or depart request by the user. However, the memory efficiency of this group rekeying protocol (GREP) is a huge storage overhead over the system. The authors aim to provide a survey of various group key management schemes and then propose an efficient scalable solution based on linked LKH and the linked list data structure. Results have shown that the Linked LKH algorithm has a very low effective cost for rekeying the LKH as compared to the basic LKH algorithm (i.e., based on the number of new joined and departure requests).

INTRODUCTION

Group Communication among valid users is a powerful Message exchange Model. Group communication applications include content distribution over large-scale networks, smart wireless networks, software updates, Video Conferencing, and many more (He Niedermeier & Meer 2013). **Key** management security should have basic requirements like authenticity, integrity, **and** confidentiality. The factors that affect any group key management process's performance are scalability, 1 affects n problem, delays bandwidth for efficient group key distribution. Scalability refers to the network's ability to handle large

DOI: 10.4018/978-1-7998-7789-9.ch007

Copyright © 2022, IGI Global. Copying or distributing in print or electronic forms without written permission of IGI Global is prohibited.

dynamic groups, i.e., if the number of users becomes large, the key management scheme should handle without degrading its performance. 1-affects n problem relates with new key generation after a leave or joins processes during a rekeying. Quality of service should also be maintained during a rekeying process, such as control packets, storing keys, and delay induced during encryption and decryption. Key management is very important in group communication restricting access control (Duma, Shahmehri, lambrix 2003). Key management establishes and maintains the secret keying relationships between valid parties according to a policy. It includes member identification and authentication. in this regard, authentication plays a significant role. Once a new member joins, it has to be validated (Zhu, Jajodia 2003). It is also **essential** to change or update the group key at regular intervals to effectively maintain a communicated message's security. Also, key independence has to be properly maintained in which each key is independent of another key. It means the method of generating a new group key should be independent of the previous key generation. It also enhances the security of the overall system. Combinatorial optimization of group key is given in (Eltoweissy, Heydari, Morales, Sudborough, 2004). Any Participant can become a part of Group Communication by becoming a group member explicitly. A group member holds a secretly shared cryptographic Group key and used the same for exchanging the messages. When a participant becomes a group member, it is required to maintain backward secrecy, i.e., the participant cannot decipher the messages exchanged before it's joined.

Similarly, whenever the group member leaves the group, Group communication must maintain the forward secrecy. After the group leaves, it must prevent the node from accessing the messages. To achieve the forward secrecy and backward secrecy, group rekeying is performed, which ensures a new and different key among the group members when a node leaves or joins the group. However, group rekeying doesn't play an effective role if we could ensure the group's structure by defining the members through the pre-registration of members (Panda, Thool 2016). Group key management can be classified into three classes: centralized, decentralized, and distributed key management. In centralized schemes, a single entity generates, distributes, and management of the group key.

Hence a single entity controls **the** entire group. Minimization of storage, computational power, and bandwidth are the key challenges in this scheme. In decentralized schemes, the process of management of group keys is divided among different group members. Hence a single point of failure is not a problem in this scheme.

In distributed group key management, No key server is explicitly declared. In this scheme, group members perform the key generation function. It can be contributory or done by individual members. Maintaining security in every group communication protocol is a critical issue.

The safety goal in a group communication process is to guarantee access only to valid group members. The entry and leave of the group members or users are the main reason for modifying the group key and giving them greater confidence in secure communication, known as re-keying. Since it is a frequently performed activity during group communication, it is necessary to do the group key update in a scalable and efficient way. Previously, the client-server paradigm is the most commonly used technique for conferencing, chat groups, immersive video games, etc., that use the principle of unicast for data transmission. Present-day developments in Internet technology, with the increase in bandwidth, are encouraging new developments in the environment. Unlike the old network communication models, where packets are to be delivered in a unicast model, the multicasting technique provides an effective delivery service to a larger user community with efficient and effective network resources (Xu, Y., & Sun, Y 2005). The key tree approach is efficiency depends crucially on whether the key tree stays balanced. Rebalancing with fixed time intervals is used to balance the key tree if it becomes unbalanced.

This increases the network overhead. With the advancement of many group-oriented applications like pay-per-view, group-oriented mobile commerce, and military applications, security service models are required to support group-oriented privacy and data integrity in communication. One realistic solution is to use a standard group key to encrypt the transmitted messages that can only be accessible to approved or valid members. As group membership may be dynamic, this group key needs to be securely updated and redistributed to all authorized or valid group members if there is a change in group membership. It is used to provide secrecy in the forward direction and backward direction. Forward secrecy means a member leaving or departing a group may get details about future group messages, and backward secrecy means a valid group member entering can get information about past group communication. The primary update method is called the rekeying and rekeying expense, which denotes the number of messages that need to be disseminated to the members during rekeying. A variety of scalable approaches have been proposed, and this chapter analyzes the tree approach in detail. In short, the key tree method uses a key hierarchy, where each member is allocated a set of keys based on their position in the key tree. The key tree method is rekeying cost increases linearly with the group size logarithm for a request to join or depart.

However, the effectiveness of the key tree approach depends on whether the key tree is balanced or not. The key tree is balanced if the distance from the root to any two leaf nodes differs by no more than one. The height from the root to any of the leaf **nodes** is log k (N) for a balanced key tree with N group members. **K** is the out-degree of the key tree, but if the key tree is unbalanced, the distance (length) from the root to a leaf node is N. In other words, this means a member or user might need to perform N-1 decryptions before the valid user gets the group key and store log k (N). Some members may need to hold the number of keys in an unbalanced key tree, N keys, while others might need to store just two keys. Individual rekeying, **i.e.,** rekeying for any request to join or leave, has two disadvantages. First, it is inefficient in terms of computation and communication overhead as rekeying messages have to perform authentication; a high rate of join/departure requests will lead to the degradation of performance as the signing process may sometimes get computationally costly. Second, suppose there is a high delay in rekeying message transmission and regular join /departure request rates. In that case, a participant can need a large amount of memory space to store rekeying and data messages that can not decrypt. Batch rekeying has been proposed to mitigate these problems by commercializing between performance and safety. Under this scheme, participants join and leave over a period of time before rekeying is conducted are consolidated. We intend to apply the algorithms that are appropriate for a batch join event within the proposed work. The algorithms balance the main tree and reduce its rekeying costs, which lead to savings in bandwidth relative to the existing algorithms. Having a balanced key tree for each batch greatly benefits mobile devices since they usually have restricted storage and processing power. The ever-increasing number of Internet applications, such as software and content distribution, pay-per-view, video conferencing, real-time information services, requires effective and reliable communication platforms with multicast. There are many security technologies designed for unicast communication,they are not feasible multicast behaviour. Alternatively, frameworks are adopted which use a secure model of group communication. Under such a model, the multicast group members share an asymmetric key, here called the session key, used to encrypt traffic in the multicast group. If group membership changes during the departure of any valid user, the group needs to be rekeyed accordingly, and the new members should not be given access to previous **sessions or** group keys (backward secrecy). The members left should not be given access to a future session or group keys (forward secrecy). The rekeying caused by leaving the members can be very costly linear to the group size in static key management. Therefore, scalable key management is a significant problem that needs to be considered to facilitate safe multicasting for large and diverse groups. Yet reliability, achieving scalability, and pulling the security specifications in various directions, and balancing them to suit the application needs is still an open problem. Several approaches were proposed for the scalable multicast key management schemes based on the Logical Key Hierarchy (LKH) and its variants. The schemes are effective in rekeying costs and key storage requirements for each group member. The storage requirements are still high for the group controller and individual members, rising linearly with the number of users. Individual rekeying, i.e., rekeying after every request to enter or leave, has two disadvantages. The problem of delay and requirement of signed authentication leads to batch rekeying with hybrid rekeying in Logical Key Hierarchy (LKH). Logical key hierarchy and its variants are analyzed with a centralized or distributed approach; each method's work is presented along with its properties. Compared with the unicast-based approach, the hierarchical key distribution approach, LKH, is scalable and efficient group rekeying compared with the unicast-based approach. OFT is effective on bandwidth compared to LKH. OFC, IHC, and SDLKH reduce overhead communication than LKH, mainly in the operation of leave users. Distributed LKH and LKH Diffie-Hellman every the number of keys each user holds. We classify them as Pair-wise schemes and Group-wise schemes based on whether the key is generated for pair-wise nodes or group members. The key management is classified as centralized and distributed based on whether the generation, maitainence of the cryptographic group key have been allocated to a single node or multiple nodes. In centralized schemes, a single entity generates the group key. That entity also performs access control and key distribution.

The main drawback is that the central server becomes a single point of failure. If the key server fails, the complete group will be affected. The group becomes vulnerable if key servers get compromised. **Also,** if a group becomes large, then scalability will also become an issue. The performance of the centralized system depends on storage requirements, size of messages. The size of messages is characterized by the number of bytes in a rekey process for the join and leave operation. Secondly, backward and forward secrecy is also to be maintained. Collusion should also be maintained. Expelled members should not be able to regenerate the group key by sharing keying information, among others. Based on whether node keys are updated or not during the whole lifetime, we classify the schemes as static and dynamic schemes. Based on whether location or deployment knowledge is considered a parameter during the key pre-distribution process, we classify the Location-dependent and Location-independent schemes. Authors classified key management schemes for WSNs mainly based on the storage overhead per sensor node (Dave, 2016). They are classified into three categories based on the storage incompetent, storage competent, and highly storage competent key management schemes. Some of the schemes have focused on diminishing storage space requirements. The authors give a probabilistic key distribution scheme that launches pair wise keys between neighbouring sensor nodes. The random key pre-distribution rule (RKP), it is mainly classified into three-level known as key pre-distribution, discovering shared key, and path key formation. In the key pre-distribution phase, each sensor node randomly chose m keys from a key pool S. Each sensor node **discovers** the keys shared with its neighbours in the shared key discovery phase (Eschenauer and Gligor, 2002). If two neighbouring sensor nodes have no shared key identifiers during the shared key discovery process, they will form a shared key via two or more hops during the path key formation phase. The authors proposed a secured broadcast/multicast scheme for ranked sensor networks. The scheme can guard against the common node capture attacks of wireless networks. Altering the session key every time can also attain flawless forward secrecy in this scheme (Chen, Huang, Lin 2012). Lightweight key management based on initial trust is given in (Dutertre Cheung, & Levy 2004). A survey-based on dynamic key management is given in (Eltoweissy, Moharrum & Mukkamala 2006). Location-based key management-based pairwise keys are given by (Liu & Ning 2003).

Key management based on deployment knowledge is given by (Du, Deng, Han, Chen & Varshney 2004). In group key management, a trusted server generates the group key whenever a new member enters into a system. **It** will send that key to new members using the unicast method and other members using multicast manner using group key. Forward and backward secrecy is the most important aspect to be maintained in group key management. thus, changing the group key requires changing and informing all members. If a new member joins, he should not receive old messages; thus, to maintain backward secrecy, the group key is changed. When a member leaves, he should not be able to decrypt old messages; thus, forward secrecy has to be maintained. The old group key is to be cannot be used in a multicast manner to obtain a new key during leave. Thus, leave operation is more complex than the join process.

It leads to more communication and computation overhead. Thus, if a system is dynamic, scalability becomes a very important issue in group key management. Tree-based key management is given in (Messai, Aliouat,& Seba 2010).

Figure 1. Classification of centralized group key management schemes

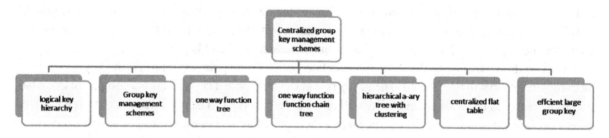

This chapter focuses on a comprehensive overview of different group key management schemes along with key management solutions. This chapter is organized as follows: We give an overview of different group key management schemes. Section 2 presents various schemes for secure multicast. In section 3, we present our proposed scheme based on a simple logical key hierarchy (LKH). Section 4 gives a result analysis of the proposed scheme. Section 5 presents the conclusion along with the future scope.

BACKGROUND

In group key communication, communication within a group is visible and accessible to its group members only. It is done by generating a cryptographic key generated by the group manager, which is distributed to all valid members of the group. Whenever a node joins the group, the node is given a group key. It is also ensured that it should be able to decipher the backward messages among the group. This is backward secrecy. When a node leaves the group, the also group key has to be renewed. It will prevent the new node from getting future messages.

This is called forward secrecy. This requires that group key management should be scalable, dynamic, and efficient. In paper (Duma et al., 2003), secure multicast communication is presented for pay per view and secure video conferencing. A tree-based approach is used to derive a group key that cost scales with the group size logarithm. In the proposed scheme, two merging algorithms are used. To increase efficiency, batch rekeying is used. This results in a balanced key with reduced rekeying cost. In paper (Pande & Thool, 2016), efficient group management with efficient rekeying is given. The GREP algorithm is presented that leverages the history of joins to make the scheme more efficient and scalable. The overhead is also independent of group size. It also has the advantage it easily recovers from collusion attacks. It is implemented in Contiki OS. It is shown that GREP is efficient, good scalability, and deployable on the resource-constrained nodes (Tiloca, Dini, Rizki, Raza 2019). A group key management scheme for encrypted multicast traffic is transmitted for satellite communication. In the proposed scheme, a Logical key hierarchy is used for member registration and periodic admission (Howarath, Iyengar, Sun, Cruickshank 2004). It results in reduced cost and optimum out-degree. It also increases network utilization. But In a real-scenario, we have a large multicast group where node leaves and joins occur frequently, and also the number of nodes leaving and joining is also not proportionate.

Hence Scalable rekeying is an important issue that needs to be concerned for the Secured Group communication for dynamic groups.. Applications such as teleconferences, information services, distributed interactive simulations use group communications. Hence, providing confidentiality, authenticity, and integrity of messages becomes an important factor in determining the group model's performance.

A novel solution to scalability is provided where the secure group is presented as a triple (U, K, R) where U is a set of users, K is the set of keys, and R stands for user key relationships. Key graphs are used to denote secure groups. Three strategies are presented to secure distributed rekey messages (Wong, Gouda, Lam 2000).

In secure group communication, members share a unique cryptographic key. Rekeying process is frequently invoked in dynamic groups that require an efficient group key generation. A group key agreement is proposed that exploits the state vectors of group members. State vectors is defined as a set of randomly generated nonces representing a logical link between group members. It enables group members to generate multiple cryptographic keys independently. Thus, with local knowledge of a secret once, each member can generate and share a number of secure keys, which makes it more secure and efficient in computation and communication (Mohammad & Shin 2017).

A logical key hierarchy is used to generate the group key in multicast group rekeying. However, it does not consider the changing behavior or probabilities of leave and joining different group members. It makes a basic scheme unsuitable for dynamic groups. Based on the basic behaviour of different users, the active members and inactive members are partitioned. They are set on different locations on a key hierarchy. it leads to a decrease in the number of encryptions in the group manager and ultimately leads to reduced communication overhead (Yong & Sun 2005).

A survey on LKH is presented with performance evaluation for LKH and its variant key management methods. Among LKH and its variant key management methods in (Wong et al., 2000), hierarchical methods are presented, which work with a centralized or distributed approach and are close to LKH results. Each form of Hierarchical Key Distribution works differently (Ng, W. H. D., Howarth, M., Sun, Z., & Cruickshank 2007). The difference is studied and discussed in maintaining the Hierarchical Key Tree. LKH and its variants are studied to know each method's functioning, its core purpose, computation, and communication method, and its differences from each other, know which method is appropriate for an application, and summarize the comparison of these variants with LKH. The author proposes a two-level Hybrid Key Tree multicast key management scheme. The entire multicast group of users is partitioned into clusters of similar size. Global level controls cluster membership in the multicast community, and cluster-level controls user membership in clusters. The various mapping of encrypted group keys to nodes in the key tree and the different key management algorithms used for global and cluster level controlling allow the two levels in HKT to have efficient security and performance characteristics (Ng, W. H. D., Cruickshank, H., & Sun, Z. 2006).

Table 1. Comparison of centralized group key management schemes on different parameter

Group key management scheme	Communication cost of server	Join rekeying cost	Leave rekeying cost
LKH	O(logN)	d+1	2d
OFT	O(logN)/2	d+1	d+1
OFC	O(logN)	logdN +1	(d − 1)logdN
IHC/ SD-LKH	O(logN)	1+logdN	(d − 1)logdN
Distributed LKH	log2Nd	-	-
Diffie–Hellman LKH	log2N+1	-	-

Table 2. Comparison of centralized group key management schemes on different parameter

Group key management scheme	Server cost	Join	Leave	1-affects n problem
LKH	O(logN)	d+1	2d	yes
OFT	O(logN)/2	d+1	d+1	yes
OFC	O(logN)	logdN +1	(d − 1)logdN	yes
IHC/ SD-LKH	O(logN)	1+logdN	(d − 1)logdN	yes
Distributed LKH	log2Nd	-	-	yes
Diffie–Hellman LKH	log2N+1	-	-	yes

REVIEW OF LITERATURE

A centralized approach that is Logical key hierarchy is a key management and distribution scheme where a key is obtained at three different levels: individual, intermediate, and group level. Probably, it can apply to all hierarchical tree structures. The number of messages expected for the process of rekeying is decreased related to GKMP(Pande & Thool, 2016)

In OFT, for the key generation, the bottom-up approach is used. It is a tree-based structure to overcome rekeying costs. For every single operation, each time key is determined at the leave node and broadcast to the root, minimizing the storage and computation cost. This algorithm key is communicated to the root level(Sherman & McGrew, 2003)

NSGC shares keys within nodes and provides security with very little cost. Each node's own individual key or unique key is used to calculate the group communication's static group key.(Kumar & Lavanya, 2015)KMSGC is an improved protocol based on a grouping system inside the cluster moreover gives an explanation for various problems, e.g., reduced scalability, delivery time, and low operating frequency. (Bao et al., 2014)

To ensure effective delivery of group key within the structure, an advanced protocol is used that depends on an enhanced key distribution algorithm. Limiting the time and storage requirements statically generates variable-length UID using one-way hash function (Kumar et al., 2013).

For ensures key communication during rekeying, a probabilistic security-based scheme is used between any set of two nodes or nodes with base station taking the constraints of cost (Albakri et al., 2019).

Dynamically symmetrical and balanced tree approaches are now used to save and manipulate the keys. The balancing of the tree remains the same in any member who joins/leaves in the group. Two merging algorithms are used for the design of this protocol: merging algorithms and batch balanced Algorithm (Ng et al., 2007).

The ternary tree-based protocol always handles the issues that appear in secure multicast communication and highlights the adoption of reasonable procedures to solve those issues (Vijayakumar et al., 2013).

PROPOSED WORK

In this section, we proposed a new algorithm for rekeying. Logical Key Hierarchy works quite optimal for small group communication. But when considering Large scalable groups, Logical Key Hierarchy performance degrades as the number of members increases beyond a particular height. Taking advantage of the Logical Key Hierarchy efficiency over small groups, we have consolidated the Logical Key Hierarchy and the Linked List concept. We maintained a Logical Key Hierarchy up to an optimum height and kept the pointer to the Logical Key Hierarchy's root in a Linked List. Let say 'k' be the optimum height of the Logical Key Hierarchy for which LKH rekeying based algorithms works in an optimum manner. Now for the height 'k' we can have the maximum number of members in a group = 2k. Hence, a new LinkedIn node is created for the rest members, and a new LKH is constructed. Forward and Backward secrecy is maintained in the same way as in the normal LKH. It can be seen that the number of group members is significantly less affected as compared to normal LKH as we have restricted the height of the tree. The algorithm works in three phases Initialization, Joining, and Leaving the Group. In the Initialization phase, we construct the LKH tree based on the static number of Group members. Joining and Leaving phase are used for the Dynamic working of Linked LKH. In the Joining phase, the New joining members request the GC, and in the Leaving Phase, the Group members who wished to leave the Group are processed. It can be noted that If the Leave and Join phase can occur simultaneously, then the Leave process is given priority first to work.

Table 3. Symbol table

Symbol	Meaning
N	Total number of group members.
J	Total number of joining members.
D	Total number of departing members.
K	Optimal Height of LKH tree

Pseudo Code for Proposed Algorithm

Initialization

1. Initialize the LKH root and Linked List node.
2. Store the address of the LKH root in the formed Linked list node.
3. Create an LKH node and place it as a leaf node.
4. Balance the LKH tree if required.
5. Generate a Unique key for the formed LKH node using the KeyGenerator (called by Group Controller).
6. Assign a Unique Member ID using a Member (Called by Group Controller).
7. Now make an entry in the Members_Available Hash-set of the Linked List node corresponding to the Key and MemberId of the LKH node formed.
8. Continue the steps 3) - 7) until the $N <= 2^k$
9. If $N > 2^k$, then repeat the steps from 1) - 8) and initialize the next pointer of the current Linked List node to the new Linked List node formed.

Joining

1. Scan the Linked List and compare the space available in the corresponding LKH.
2. If space is found then we simply insert the joining members.
3. Recursively update the keys from new Joined node members up to root using the keygenerator.
4. Balance the LKH tree if necessary.
5. Update the Member_Available Hash-set with the new joining members.
6. If no space is found during Step 1) then, we extend the Linked List and insert the new joining members as in the Initialization phase.

Leaving

1. The Members who are to leave, sent the leave request to the Group Controller.
2. Find the Linked List node by using the Member_Identify Hash-map (called by GC).
3. Remove the member node from the corresponding LKH tree.
4. Update the MemberId and key used by the removed node.
5. Backtrack the path from the removed node to the root and update the keys using the KeyGenerator (called by GC)
6. Update the Member_available Hash set for the Linked list node.
7. Repeat the above procedure until all the request removed nodes are processed.

Figure 2. Represents a linked logical key hierarchical for 12 group members represented by U1 –U12.

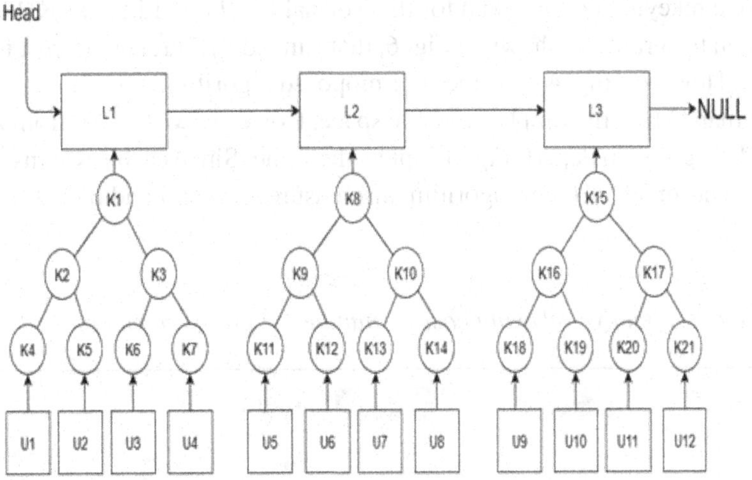

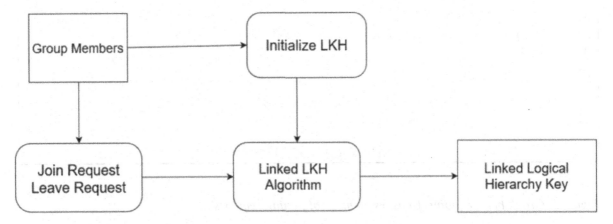

Figure 3. Represents the data flow diagram (DFD) for linked logical key hierarchy algorithm

RESULT ANALYSIS

A Logical Key Hierarchy is proved to be a Memory Efficient approach than Group Rekeying Protocol. However, the Normal LKH approach still suffers an overhead of rekeying the LKH tree for a large group. We can find that Logical Key Hierarchy rekeying depends on the tree's height and thus indirectly over the number of Group members. Effective rekeying cost for a Normal LKH = log(N) where 'N' is the Group members' number. Our Proposed Linked LKH algorithm performs rekeying efficiently than the normal LKH algorithm, taking the Optimal Height 'K' and making this height as a constraint over the maximum height results in less rekeying update messages traversal within the tree. Considering the Hash-set working complexity as Constant 'C' for finding the LKH corresponding to a new joined or leaving the node.

Effective rekeying cost for Linked LKH = log(K) + C = Constant O   (1)

As shown in Figure 4, the graph represents the relation between the number of nodes in the tree (x-axis) and the effective rekeying cost (y-axis) for the Normal LKH and Linked LKH algorithm.

It is observed from the graph, as shown in Fig. 6, that Linked LKH rekeying cost is much lesser than the traditional LKH. However, Fig. 4 describes our proposed algorithm's linear complexity, as we need to traverse the Hashmap to find the Empty available space. However, we benefit from limiting the height of LKH when a node is going to depart. Fig. 6 depicts the same. Since each LKH inside the Linked List node is similar to the normal LKH, our algorithm also ensures forward and backward secrecy.

Figure 4. Graph between effective rekeying cost vs. number of group members

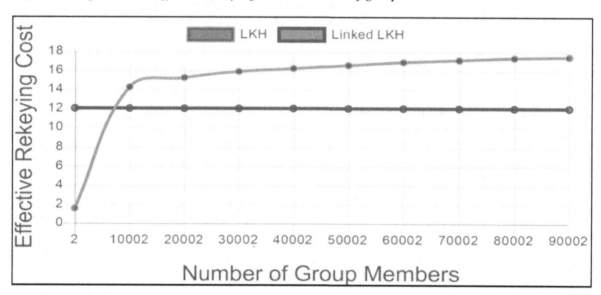

Figure 5. Graph between joining cost vs. number of joining requests

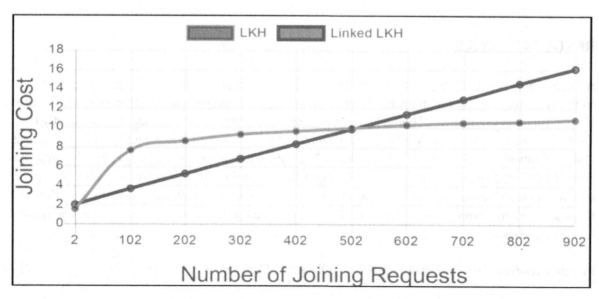

Figure 6. Graph between leaving cost vs. number of departure requests

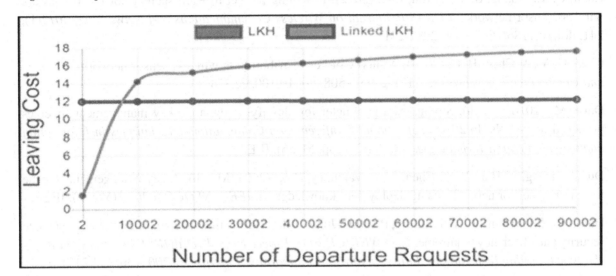

CONCLUSION

This paper has proposed a new LinkedIn LKH algorithm that is more efficient than the existing traditional LKH algorithm. Since the proposed Linked LKH algorithm is based on the LKH, it has less storage overhead than the GREP. The effective rekeying cost of the Linked LKH algorithm is Constant, which is better than the traditional LKH, which depends on the number of Group members' logarithmic factor. We have also graphically observed our algorithm and the LKH algorithm by considering the effective rekeying cost. However, there is still Initialization complexity overhead for the Linked LKH, which increments directly with Group members. The Initialization complexity is not so important if we have already constructed a tree by using the method like Pre-registration of the Group Members. As a Future work, the Initialization phase complexity can be made to be concerned, which will lead to an overall less effective cost for constructing and maintaining the LKH.

REFERENCES

Albakri, A., Harn, L., & Song, S. (2019). Hierarchical key manage- ment scheme with probabilistic security in a wireless sensor network (WSN). *Security and Communication Networks*, 2019.

Bao, X., Liu, J., She, L., & Zhang, S. (2014, June). A key management scheme based on grouping within cluster. In *Proceeding of the 11th World Congress on Intelligent Control and Automation* (pp. 3455- 3460). IEEE.

Barskar, R., & Chawla, M. (2016). A survey on efficient group key management schemes in wireless networks. *Indian Journal of Science and Technology*, 9(14), 1–16. doi:10.17485/ijst/2016/v9i14/87972

Bilal, M., & Kang, S. G. (2017). A secure key agreement protocol for dynamic group. *Cluster Computing*, 20(3), 2779–2792. doi:10.100710586-017-0853-0

Chen, C. T., Huang, S. Y., & Lin, I. C. (2012). Providing perfect forward secrecy for location-aware wireless sensor networks. *EURASIP Journal on Wireless Communications and Networking, 2012*(1), 241. doi:10.1186/1687-1499-2012-241

Chen, C. Y., & Chao, H. C. (2014). A survey of key distribution in wireless sensor networks. *Security and Communication Networks, 7*(12), 2495–2508. doi:10.1002ec.354

Dave, M. (2016, March). Storage as a parameter for classifying dynamic key management schemes proposed for WSNs. In *2016 International Conference on Computational Techniques in Information and Communication Technologies (ICCTICT)* (pp. 51-56). IEEE.

Du, W., Deng, J., Han, Y. S., Chen, S., & Varshney, P. K. (2004, March). A key management scheme for wireless sensor networks using deployment knowledge. In *IEEE INFOCOM 2004* (Vol. 1). IEEE.

Duma, C., Shahmehri, N., & Lambrix, P. (2003, June). A hybrid key tree scheme for multicast to balance security and efficiency requirements. In *WET ICE 2003. Proceedings. Twelfth IEEE International Workshops on Enabling Technologies: Infrastructure for Collaborative Enterprises, 2003* (pp. 208-213). IEEE.

Dutertre, B., Cheung, S., & Levy, J. (2004). *Lightweight key management in wireless sensor networks by leveraging initial trust*. Technical Report SRI-SDL-04-02, SRI International.

Eltoweissy, M., Heydari, M. H., Morales, L., & Sudborough, I. H. (2004). Combinatorial optimization of group key management. *Journal of Network and Systems Management, 12*(1), 33–50. doi:10.1023/B:JONS.0000015697.38671.ec

Eltoweissy, M., Moharrum, M., & Mukkamala, R. (2006). Dynamic key management in sensor networks. *IEEE Communications Magazine, 44*(4), 122–130. doi:10.1109/MCOM.2006.1632659

Eschenauer, L., & Gligor, V. D. (2002). A key-management scheme for distributed sensor networks. *Proceedings of the 9th ACM Conference on Computer and Communication Security*, 41–47. 10.1145/586110.586117

He, X., Niedermeier, M., & De Meer, H. (2013). Dynamic key management in wireless sensor networks: A survey. *Journal of Network and Computer Applications, 36*(2), 611–622. doi:10.1016/j.jnca.2012.12.010

Howarth, M. P., Iyengar, S., Sun, Z., & Cruickshank, H. (2004). Dynamics of key management in secure satellite multicast. *IEEE Journal on Selected Areas in Communications, 22*(2), 308–319. doi:10.1109/JSAC.2003.819978

Jain, A. K., & Gupta, B. B. (2019). A machine learning based approach for phishing detection using hyperlinks information. *Journal of Ambient Intelligence and Humanized Computing, 10*(5), 2015–2028. doi:10.100712652-018-0798-z

Kumar, N. S., & Lavanya, S. (2015). A novel scheme for secure group communication in multicast network. *International Journal of Security and Networks, 10*(2), 65–75. doi:10.1504/IJSN.2015.070409

Kumar, S., Purusothaman, T. N. M., & Lavanya, S. (2013). Design and performance analysis of scalable and efficient group key Manage- ment scheme [SEGKMS] for group communication in multicast net- works. *Life Science Journal, 10*(2).

Liu, D., & Ning, P. (2003, October). Location-based pairwise key establishments for static sensor networks. In *Proceedings of the 1st ACM workshop on Security of ad hoc and sensor networks* (pp. 72-82). 10.1145/986858.986869

Messai, M. L., Aliouat, M., & Seba, H. (2010). Tree based scheme for key Management in wireless sensor networks. *EURASIP Journal on Wireless Communications and Networking, 2010*(1), 1–10. doi:10.1155/2010/910695

Ng, W. H. D., Cruickshank, H., & Sun, Z. ((2006) Scalable balanced batch rekeying for secure group communication. *Computers & Security, 25*(4), 265-273.

Ng, W. H. D., Howarth, M., Sun, Z., & Cruickshank, H. (2007). Dynamic balanced key tree management for secure multicast communications. *IEEE Transactions on Computers, 56*(5), 590–605. doi:10.1109/TC.2007.1022

Ouaguid, A., Abghour, N., & Ouzzif, M. (2018). A novel security framework for managing android permissions using blockchain technology. *International Journal of Cloud Applications and Computing, 8*(1), 55–79. doi:10.4018/IJCAC.2018010103

Pande, A. S., & Thool, R. C. (2016, September). Survey on logical key hierarchy for secure group communication. *2016 International.*

Rafaeli, S., & Hutchison, D. (2003). A survey of key management for secure group communication. *ACM Computing Surveys, 35*(3), 309–329. doi:10.1145/937503.937506

Rahman, M., & Sampalli, S. (2015). An efficient pairwise and group key management protocol for wireless sensor network. *Wireless Personal Communications, 84*(3), 2035–2053. doi:10.100711277-015-2546-4

Seetha, R., & Saravanan, R. (2015). A survey on group key management schemes. *Cybernetics and Information Technologies, 15*(3), 3–25. doi:10.1515/cait-2015-0038

Sherman, A. T., & McGrew, D. A. (2003). Key establishment in large dynamic groups using one-way function trees. *IEEE Transactions on Software Engineering, 29*(5), 444–458. doi:10.1109/TSE.2003.1199073

Stergiou, C., Psannis, K. E., Gupta, B. B., & Ishibashi, Y. (2018). Security, privacy & efficiency of sustainable cloud computing for big data & IoT. *Sustainable Computing: Informatics and Systems, 19*, 174–184. doi:10.1016/j.suscom.2018.06.003

Tiloca, M., Dini, G., Rizki, K., & Raza, S. (2019). Group rekeying based on member join history. *International Journal of Information Security*, 1–39. doi:10.100710207-019-00451-0

Vijayakumar, P., Bose, S., Kannan, A., & Jegatha Deborah, L. (2013). *Computation and Communication Efficient Key Distribution.* Academic Press.

Wallner, D., Harder, E., & Agee, R. (1999). *Key management for multicast: Issues and architectures.* RFC 2627.

Wong, C. K., Gouda, M., & Lam, S. S. (2000). Secure group communications using key graphs. *IEEE/ACM Transactions on Networking, 8*(1), 16–30. doi:10.1109/90.836475

Xu, Y., & Sun, Y. (2005, December). A new group rekeying method in secure multicast. In *International Conference on Computational and Information Science* (pp. 155-160). Springer. 10.1007/11596981_23

Yousefpoor, M. S., & Barati, H. (2019). Dynamic key management algorithms in wireless sensor networks: A survey. *Computer Communications, 134*, 52–69. doi:10.1016/j.comcom.2018.11.005

Zheng, Q., Wang, X., Khan, M. K., Zhang, W., Gupta, B. B., & Guo, W. (2017). A lightweight authenticated encryption scheme based on chaotic scml for railway cloud service. *IEEE Access: Practical Innovations, Open Solutions, 6*, 711–722. doi:10.1109/ACCESS.2017.2775038

Zhu, S., & Jajodia, S. (2003, December). Scalable group rekeying for secure multicast: A survey. In *International Workshop on Distributed Computing* (pp. 1-10). Springer. 10.1007/978-3-540-24604-6_1

KEY TERMS AND DEFINITIONS

Backward Secrecy: It is characteristic of a rekeying process in a group communication where after joining a group, a new group key is generated and given to users of a group and to new user in order to prevent the new member to read old messages.

Forward Secrecy: It is the characteristic of a rekeying process during a group communication where after leaving the group, the user must be prevented from accessing the future messages.

Key Independence: The new group key generated by the key server should be completely independent of the previous old group key during a rekeying process in a group communication.

Key Management: It is collection of different processes required to generate the cryptographic keys, distribution, and setup between the communicating nodes to carry out a secure information exchange.

Key Predistribution: It is one of the phases of key management where keys are generated either in centralized manner or distributed manner and distributed to valid nodes of the network.

Chapter 8
Botnet Defense System and White–Hat Worm Launch Strategy in IoT Network

Shingo Yamaguchi
Yamaguchi University, Japan

Brij Gupta
National Institute of Technology, Kurukshetra, India

ABSTRACT

This chapter introduces a new kind of cybersecurity system named botnet defense system (BDS) that defends an IoT system against malicious botnets. This chapter consists of two parts. The former part describes the concept and design of the BDS. The concept is "fight fire with fire." To realize the concept, the BDS uses bot technology. The BDS builds a white-hat botnet on the IoT system by itself and uses it to exterminate the malicious botnets. The white-hat botnet autonomously spreads over the IoT system and thus drastically increases the defense ability. The latter part explains the strategy of the BDS. The white-hat botnet is a so-called double-edged sword. It defends the IoT system against malicious botnet but wastes the system's resources. Therefore, the BDS should strategically use the white-hat botnet. Some strategies have been proposed. Their characteristics are discussed through the simulation with the agent-oriented petri nets.

INTRODUCTION

Internet of Things (IoT) aims everything including humans to interact and to create new values from sharing information. IoT has enriched our lives while gives rise to a new risk on cybersecurity. IoT devices are explosively increasing, and the number is predicted to reach 30 billion by 2023 (Cisco, 2020). The problem is that most of them are vulnerable. This is because they do not have resources to run security functions and their vendors may sacrifice security in the price competition and/or their rush to market. In September 2016, that risk became reality. IoT was used as a springboard of giant distributed denial-

DOI: 10.4018/978-1-7998-7789-9.ch008

Copyright © 2022, IGI Global. Copying or distributing in print or electronic forms without written permission of IGI Global is prohibited.

of-service (DDoS) attacks, which struck many of the world's biggest sites such as Netflix and Twitter (O'Brien, S.A.,2016). These attacks were brought about by malware called Mirai. Mirai infects IoT devices and turns them into bots. Those bots form a network (botnet) that can be used for DDoS attacks. For the detail of Mirai, refer to (Sinaović, H., & Mrdovic, S., 2017) and (Yamaguchi, S. & Gupta, B., 2019). Mirai's DDoS attacks have a tendency to be large-scale and disruptive. This is because IoT devices are characterized by large-volume, pervasiveness, and high vulnerability (Kolias, C., Kambourakis, G., Stavrou, A., & Voas, J., 2017). Mirai has spread to emerging markets and developing countries (Nakao, K., 2018). In early October 2016, Mirai infected over 300,000 IoT devices in 164 countries (Devry, J., 2016). To make matters worse, Mirai's authors published the source code (Bonderud, D., 2016). It gave rise to many variants of Mirai such as Satori (360 netlab., 2017) and Okiru (Arzamendi, P., Bing, M. & Soluk, K., 2018). Even now after five years since Mirai appeared, Mirai and variants continue to rage all over the world (Milić, J., 2019).

Some techniques have been proposed against Mirai's threat. The United States Computer Emergency Readiness Team (US-CERT) showed rebooting the infected device can clear Mirai (US-CERT, 2016). This is because Mirai penetrates only to the dynamic memory of the device. However, Moffitt, T. (2016) reported that Mirai can reinfect the device within minutes unless the vulnerability is patched. The other techniques can be roughly divided into three categories: detection, mitigation, and spread prevention. The following are typical examples.

Detection Techniques: Bezerra, V.H., da Costa, V.G.T., Barbon, J., Miani, R.S., & Zarpelão, B.B. (2019) have proposed a host-based approach to detect IoT botnets called IoTDS (Internet of Things Detection System). IoTDS monitors a device and collects its CPU use and temperature, memory consumption, and the number of processes. If the device detects any anomaly from the data, an alert of botnet detection is sent to the central server.

Meidan, Y., Bohadana, M., Mathov, Y., Mirsky, Y., Shabtai, A., Breitenbacher, D., & Elovici, Y. (2018) have proposed a network-based anomaly detection method for the IoT called N-BaIoT. N-BaIoT extracts behavior snapshots of the network and uses deep autoencoders to detect anomalous network traffic from compromised IoT devices.

Mitigation Techniques: Some of this category include both detection and mitigation (Jaramillo, L.E.S., 2018) and (Alomari, E., Manickam, S., Gupta, B. B., Anbar, M., Saad, R. M., & Alsaleem, S., 2016). Manso, P., Moura, J., & Serrão, C. (2019) have proposed a Software-Defined Intrusion Detection System. This system can automatically detect several DDoS attacks. Once the IDS detects an attack, it notifies a software-defined networking controller to control devices. Therefore, it timely enables to detect a botnet exploitation, to mitigate malicious network traffic, and to protect normal network traffic.

Ceron, J.M., Steding-Jessen, K., Hoepers, C., Granville, L.Z., & Margi, C.B. (2019) have proposed a network layer that adapts itself to mitigate the network traffic generated by malware. It can modify the traffic at the network layer based on the actions performed by the malware.

Spread Prevention Techniques: Gopal, T.S., Meerolla, M., Jyostna, G., Eswari, L., Reddy, P., & Magesh, E. (2018) have proposed a whitelisting based solution to prevent Mirai from spreading. They showed the successful blocking of Mirai malware through the experiment.

Frank, C., Nance, C., Jarocki, S., & Pauli, W. E. (2018) have proposed two scripts executable on actual devices to protect devices from becoming Mirai bots. They show that the hardening script was shown to be successful in preventing the initial Mirai infection on the device and the detection script was successful in recognizing and stopping an already existing infection in a controlled test environment.

These techniques are useful to detect Mirai bots and to mitigate their threat. However, they are not radically something to exterminate Mirai bots. As described before, the simplest solution is rebooting the infected device and patching its vulnerability. However, patching by manpower tactics is unrealistic because IoT devices are explosively increasing. Thus, an innovative approach is needed to drastically increase the defense ability against Mirai.

This chapter introduces a new kind of cybersecurity system named Botnet Defense System (BDS) that exterminates malicious botnets (Yamaguchi, S., 2020a). After the introduction in Section 1, Section 2 describes the concept and design of BDS. The BDS adopts the concept of "fight fire with fire" and makes use of botnet technology for defense. The BDS builds a white-hat botnet on the IoT system by itself and uses it to exterminate the malicious botnets. The white-hat botnet autonomously spreads over the IoT system and thus drastically increases the defense ability. Section 3 explains the strategy of the BDS. The white-hat botnet is a so-called double-edge sword. It defends the IoT system against malicious botnet but wastes the system's resources. Therefore, the BDS should strategically use the white-hat botnet. Some strategies have been proposed. Their characteristics are discussed through the simulation with the agent-oriented Petri nets. Section 5 summarizes key points and gives future research directions.

Figure 1. System configuration and an operation of the BDS.

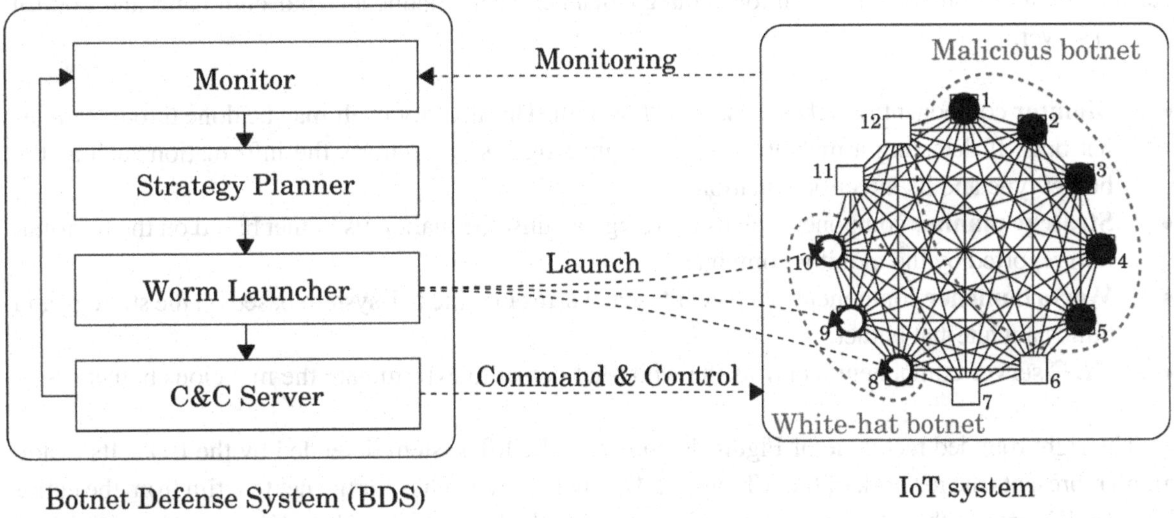

Botnet Defense System (BDS)   IoT system

BOTNET DEFENSE SYSTEM (BDS)

This section describes the concept and design of the BDS and the white-hat worm used in the BDS.

Concept

Botnet technology (Bailey, M., Cooke, E., Jahanian, F., Xu, Y., Karir, M., 2009) has been widely used to conduct malicious activities like DDoS attacks. Ironically, since Mirai's source leaked, this technology has been more accelerating evolution and has produced various variants. The purpose of the variants is no longer limited to DDoS attacks but extends to cryptocurrency mining (Arghire, I., 2017) and proxy function (Cimpanu, C., 2018). In October 2016, a new type of worm called Hajime was found (Edwards, S.,& Profetis, I, 2016). Like Mirai, Hajime infects IoT devices and turns them into bots. Hajime bots block the ports that Mirai uses to infect and prevent Mirai from spreading. These prior cases suggest a new possibility of the botnet technology. That is, the botnet technology could become an innovative solution to defend an IoT system against malicious botnets.

The concept of the BDS is "fight fire with fire". This means to use the same weapon that attackers use. The BDS realizes this concept and fights malicious botnets with a botnet. Concretely, it builds a botnet on the IoT system by itself and uses it to exterminate the malicious botnets. The botnet built by the BDS is used for well-intentioned purposes and thus is called a white-hat botnet. The white-hat botnet autonomously spreads over the IoT system and thus drastically increases the defense ability.

Design

The BDS adopts component-based architecture. This enables us to research and develop the functionalities using components as a unit and further to realize a required instance quickly and flexibly by combining components.

Figure 1 shows the system configuration. The left rounded rectangle represents the BDS. The BDS consists of four components: monitor, strategy planner, worm launcher, and command and control (C&C) server.

- **Monitor** component: watches over the IoT system. This activity itself may be done through white-hat bots. If detecting a malicious botnet, it investigates and reports the information such as the botnet type and its infection situation.
- **Strategy planner** component: plans a strategy against the malicious botnet based on the information reported by the monitor component.
- **Worm launcher** component: sends white-hat worms into the IoT system based on the strategy and builds a white-hat botnet.
- **C&C server** component: controls the white-hat botnet to exterminate the malicious botnet.

The right rounded rectangle of Figure 1 represents the IoT system defended by the BDS. Its inside graph represents the network of the IoT system. Bot malware searches for the next victim from the entire Internet. We project the relationship between victims on the IoT system and consider it as the network of the system. This network consists of 12 nodes and has full mesh topology. The concept of observability and controllability is introduced to the network (Yamaguchi, S., 2021). For simplicity, assume in this chapter that every node is observable and controllable. That is, the BDS can check whether each node has a bot, and can send a white-hat worm to any node without a malicious bot.

Let us illustrate an operation of the BDS with the example of Figure 1.

1. **Monitoring**: The BDS checks whether each node has a bot. As a result, the BDS found out five malicious bots in total at the 1st, 2nd, 3rd, 4th, and 5th nodes. The black circles (●) of Figure 1 represent malicious bots.
2. **Strategy Planning**: The BDS plans a strategy to launch white-hat worms. Based on the IoT system's status, the BDS adopted the Few-Elite strategy described later.

3. **Worm Launching**: Based on the strategy, the BDS sends white-hat worms and builds a white-hat botnet. It sent three white-hat worms in total to the 8th, 9th, and 10th nodes. The white circles (◯) of Figure 1 represent white-hat bots produced by those worms.
4. **C&C**: The BDS controls the white-hat botnet to exterminates the malicious bots. The BDS will finally exterminate the malicious botnet.

White-Hat Worms and Botnets

The distinctive feature of the BDS is to use white-hat worms and their botnets to fight against malicious botnets.

Some worms are not used for malicious activities, but attempt to protect the device from other malware instead. Such worms are called white-hat. An early example of white-hat worms is Linux.Wifatch. It infects a device and disables Telnet to keep other malware out (Ballano, M., 2015). Another representative example is Hajime. It turns devices into bots but possesses no capability for DDoS attacks. It blocks the ports that Mirai uses to infect and protects them against Mirai. However, because not systematically controlled, Hajime botnet continues to spread even after completing the defense against Mirai.

Molesky, M.J., & Cameron, E.A. (2019) have proposed not only the manufacturers but also governments to use white-hat worms to fix critical vulnerabilities of IoT devices. They state that this could be enacted by including explicit terms within the Terms and Conditions agreement at the time of purchase and creates a contract with the consumer allowing for these actions to occur legally and without liability to the company. This suggests white-hat worms are applicable in practice.

The white-hat worm used in the BDS aims to build a time-limited white-hat botnet to exterminate malicious botnets (Yamaguchi, S., 2020b). The worm's capabilities are represented by two attributes.

- **Secondary infection possibility**: The worm infects even the device infected by bot malware, i.e. it infects the botized device, and then removes the malicious bot from the device. Secondary infection possibility is the probability that the worm infects the botized device.
- **Lifespan**: The worm has a lifespan, i.e. it removes itself when exhausting the lifespan. Even after removing the worm, the infected device still is a white-hat bot. It exhibits an immune effect against malware until reboot.

A Mirai variant called OMG possesses proxy functions (ASERT Team., 2018). The white-hat bots used in the BDS also incorporate the proxy functions. They enable the BDS to indirectly access unobservable and uncontrollable nodes, e.g. inside private networks (Yamaguchi, S., 2021).

STRATEGY

This section describes the strategies used in the BDS. Once the BDS detects a malicious botnet, it plans a strategy for exterminating the botnet. A good strategy results in successful extermination, vice versa. Therefore, strategy studies are essential to produce intended results. Strategies can be roughly divided into two categories.

- **Worm launch strategies**: specify how to send white-hat worms to build its botnet.

- **C&C strategies**: specify how to command and control the botnet to exterminate the malicious botnet.

This chapter focuses on the worm launch strategies. For those who are interested in the C&C strategies, refer to Reference (Yamaguchi, S., 2021).

Formal Definition of Worm Launch Strategy

A worm launch strategy L is formalized as a mapping from a monitoring information $(R_{Mirai}, \delta, (\#_{nodes}, N_{topology}, N_{density}), (\ell, \rho))$ to the number $\#_{White}$ of the white-hat worms to launch, i.e.

$$\mathcal{L} : \left(R_{Mirai}, \delta, \left(\#_{nodes}, N_{topology}, N_{density} \right), \left(\ell, \rho \right) \right) \mapsto \#_{White} \qquad (1)$$

where

- Malware is Mirai.
- R_{Mirai} is a Mirai's infection rate and is given as $R_{Mirai} = \#_{Mirai}/\#_{nodes}$, where $\#_{Mirai}$ is the number of Mirai bots, $\#_{nodes}$ is the number of network nodes, and each node has one device.
- δ is the delay time until an infected device is rebooted.
- $(\#_{nodes}, N_{topology}, N_{density})$ is the IoT system's specification. $N_{topology}$ is the network topology such as mesh and tree. $N_{density}$ is the network density and is given as

$$N_{density} = \frac{2 \#_{AC}}{\#_{nodes} \left(\#_{nodes} - 1 \right)} \qquad (2)$$

where $\#_{AC}$ is the number of actual connections between nodes.

- (ℓ, ρ) is the white-hat worm's capability, where ℓ is the lifespan and ρ is the secondary infection possibility.

All-Out Strategy

The All-Out strategy $\mathcal{L}_{All-Out}$ is to launch as many white-hat worms as possible. It is defined as a mapping such that

When adopting this strategy, the BDS sends white-hat worms to all nodes that do not have Mirai bots regardless of the information $(R_{Mirai}, \delta, (\#_{nodes}, N_{topology}, N_{density}), (\ell, \rho))$.

Figure 2 shows an application example of the All-Out strategy to the IoT system of Figure 1. This system has a network composed of 12 nodes, i.e. $\#_{nodes}=12$. Figure 2a shows the state when the BDS detected the Mirai botnet composed of five Mirai bots, i.e. $\#_{Mirai}=5$. Figure 2b shows the state after the BDS sent seven $(=\#_{nodes} - \#_{Mirai})$ white-hat worms to all the nodes that do not have Mirai bots, i.e. the 6th, 7th, …, 12th nodes.

Figure 2. An application example of the all-out strategy. (a) State when the BDS detected a Mirai botnet. (b) State after the BDS sent white-hat worms.

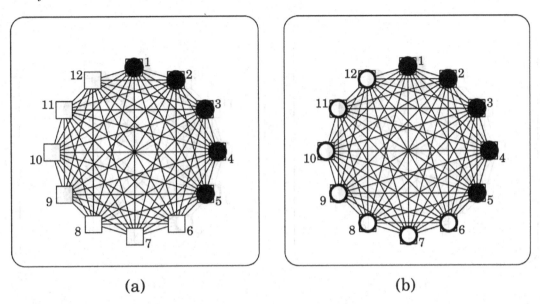

(a)   (b)

When the BDS adopts the All-Out strategy, the built white-hat botnet is the largest and shows the maximum effect against the Mirai botnet. Therefore, the All-Out strategy becomes a baseline in strategy studies. The effect of the All-Out strategy means the upper limit. The other strategies can be evaluated depending on how close their effect is to that of the All-Out strategy.

w-Elite Strategy

The white-hat worms autonomously spread to fight against Mirai. This spread mainly depends on the white-hat worms' capability. If the capability is weak, the worms would die out. If the capability is too strong, the worms would continue to stay on the system even after exterminating Mirai and waste the resources. That is, the white-hat worms are a so-called double-edged sword.

The Few-Elite strategy $\mathcal{L}_{Few-Elite}$ is to launch the minimum necessary number of white-hat worms considering the worms' capability. It is defined as a mapping such that

$$\mathcal{L}_{Few-Elite} : \left(R_{Mirai}, \delta, \left(\#_{nodes}, N_{topology}, N_{density} \right), \left(\ell, \rho \right) \right) \mapsto \#_{elite} \qquad if \ \ell + \alpha\rho \geq \theta \qquad (3)$$

where $\#_{elite}$ is the number of the white-hat worms to launch when the worms' capability is sufficient, α is a weight coefficient and θ is a threshold.

Figure 3 shows an application example of the Few-Elite strategy to the IoT system of Figure 1. Let us assume in this example that $\#_{elite}$=3, α=4, and θ=6. Assume that the BDS possesses two types of white-hat worms. Type A has a capability (Lifespan ℓ_A=1 step, secondary infection possibility ρ_A=75%). Type B has a different capability (ℓ_B=5 steps, ρ_B=50%). Let us first consider Type A. Its capability does not satisfy the precondition of the strategy because $\ell_A+\alpha\rho_A$= 1+4×0.75= 4 $\ngeq$ θ=6. Consequently, the BDS will adopts not the Few-Elite strategy but the other strategies like the All-Out strategy.

Figure 3. An application example of the few-elite strategy. (a) State when the BDS detected a Mirai botnet. (b) State when the BDS possesses a white-hat worm with sufficient capability and sent only three.

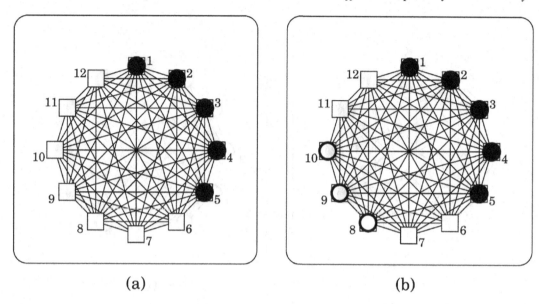

(a)   (b)

Next, let us consider Type B. Its capability satisfies the precondition of the strategy because $\ell_B + \alpha \rho_B = 5 + 4 \times 0.5 = 7 \geq \theta = 6$. As a result, the BDS will adopt the Few-Elite strategy and can reduce the number of worms to launch. What is important here, the precondition of this strategy must be designed to balance between the worms' capability and the effect. Only then, it can become a baseline to identify whether an available worm has sufficient capability.

Environment-Adaptive Strategy

Bots spread through the network. This spread is affected by the network's properties such as topology and density. Such properties may be derived from not only physical but also virtual structures like VPN. If a network has full mesh topology, i.e. the highest network density, the bots can access all the other nodes to infect. In contrast, if a network has tree topology, i.e. the lowest network density, the bots can access only at most two nodes on average. Therefore, in the lower density network, the BDS should launch more white-hat worms even if the worms' capability is high.

The Environment-Adaptive strategy $\mathcal{L}_{Env-Adaptive}$ is to launch as many white-hat worms as possible if the network density is low. It is defined as a mapping such that

$$
\mathcal{L}_{Env-Adaptive} : \left(R_{Mirai}, \delta, \left(\#_{nodes}, N_{topology}, N_{density} \right), \left(\ell, \rho \right) \right)
$$

$$
\mapsto \#_{nodes} - \#_{Mirai} \qquad if \; N_{density} < \frac{2\beta}{\#_{nodes}}
\tag{4}
$$

where $2\beta / \#_{nodes}$ is the lowest density of connected networks composed of $\#_{nodes}$ nodes and β is a weight coefficient.

Figure 4. An application example of the environment-adaptive strategy. The network has tree topology. (a) State when the BDS detected a Mirai botnet. (b) State after the BDS sent white-hat worms. They are sent to all the non-bot nodes because the low-density network limits spread.

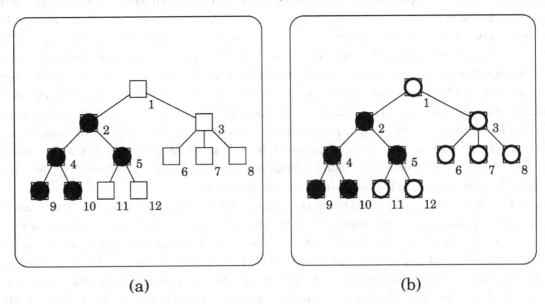

(a)   (b)

Figure 2 An application example of the All-Out strategy. (a) State when the BDS detected a Mirai botnet. (b) State after the BDS sent white-hat worms.Figure 4 shows an application example of the Environment Adaptive strategy to the IoT system whose network is not full mesh but tree topology. In this example, let us assume $\beta=1.2$. In this network, the number $\#_{AC}$ of actual connections between nodes is 11 ($=\#_{nodes}-1=12-1$). We have

$$N_{density} = \frac{2\#_{AC}}{\#_{nodes}\left(\#_{nodes}-1\right)} = \frac{2\times11}{12\left(12-1\right)} \simeq 0.17.$$

This value satisfies the precondition of the Environment-Adaptive strategy because $N_{density}=0.17<2\beta/\#_{nodes}= 2\times1.2/12= 0.2$. Therefore, the BDS will adopt this strategy and send the white-hat worms to all the non-bot nodes.

As another example, let us apply the Environment-Adaptive strategy to the IoT system of Figure 1. In this network, the number $\#_{AC}$ of actual connections between nodes is 66 ($=\#_{nodes}(\#_{nodes}-1)/2$). We have $N_{density}= (2\times66)/(12\times(12-1))=1$. This value does not satisfy the precondition of the Environment-Adaptive strategy because $N_{density}=1 \nless 2\beta/\#_{nodes}=0.2$. Consequently, the BDS will adopts not the Environment-Adaptive strategy but the other strategies like the Few-Elite strategy.

SIMULATION EVALUATION

This section describes the evaluation of the BDS and the proposed launch strategies. The evaluation has done through simulation of the model.

Modeling With Agent-Oriented Petri Net

Yamaguchi, S. (2020b) has proposed to regard a battle between Mirai and white-hat worms as a multi-agent system and to express it with agent-oriented Petri net called Petri nets in a Petri net (PN^2). A PN^2 is intuitively a two-layers Petri net. The lower layer Petri nets (called agent nets) represent agents. The upper layer Petri net (called environment net) represents the environment on which the agents interact with each other. What is important here, each token of the environment net one-to-one corresponds to one of the agent nets. Each token can move over the environment net. It can make its copy or disappear. We assume here that the reader is familiar with Petri nets and PN^2. For more information on Petri nets, refer to (Murata, T., 1989) and (Yamaguchi, S., Bin Ahmadon, M.A., & Ge, Q.W., 2016). For more information on PN^2, refer to (Hiraishi, K., 2001) and (Yamaguchi, S., Tanaka, H., & Bin Ahmadon, M. A., 2020).

Figure 6 shows a PN^2 model representing a battle between Mirai and the white-hat worms. Figure 6a-e show the agent nets while Figure 6f shows the environment net.

Figure 6a-e respectively correspond to the 1st device, the 3rd device, Mirai, the 2nd device, and the white-hat worm. Each agent net represents the state-transition of the corresponding agent. Let us see Figure 6a. It describes the state-transition of the 1st device. Transition t1 (drawn as ÿ) represents an infection action. Its input places p1 (drawn as ○) and output place p2 respectively represent the state before and after the infection. p2 has a token (drawn as •). This means that this device is in the state immediately after the infection. Transition t2 represents a delay. Enabled transitions are highlighted in red. Place p3 has three output transitions. The upper cycle p1t1p2t2p3t3p4t4p5t5p1 represents the behavior as a Mirai bot, where p1 means a non-botized state while p2, p3, p4, and p5 mean botized states. Transitions t3 and t4 represent delays. Transition t5 represents a reboot action. To sum up, the infected device has a delay time of three steps by the reboot. The reboot clears the Mirai bot and makes the device normal (p1). The lower cycle p1t1p2t2p3t6p6t7p7t8p1 represents the behavior of a white-hat bot. Transition t6 represents a self-destruction action for the infected white-hat worm. Therefore, P6 and p7 mean botized states without the presence of the worm, i.e., an immune period. The middle cycle p2t2p3t9p2 represents a behavior by secondary infection. Transition t9 represents a secondary infection action and moves from a Mirai's infected state (p3) to the white-hat worm infected initial state (p2). In this example, the Mirai bot has four states p2, p3, p4, and p5. Only in p3 of them, a white-hat worm may secondarily infect it. Therefore, the secondary infection possibility is 25%.

Next, let us see Figure 6e. It describes the state-transition of a white-hat worm. Transition t1 represents an infection action. Place p1 forms a self-loop with t1 and possesses a token. This means that the worm can repeatedly infect a device. Transitions t2, t3, and t4 respectively represent a reboot action, a self-destruction action, and a secondary infection action.

The environment net of Figure 6f represents the IoT system defended by the BDS. Each place (drawn as ○) represents a network node. This IoT system's network has line topology and consists of three nodes. Every place has a token (drawn as ○) representing a device. It means that each node possesses one device. Furthermore, place P1 has a token representing Mirai, and place P3 has a token representing a white-hat worm. This means that the device at place P1 is infected by Mirai, the device at place P2 is normal, and the device at place P3 is infected by the white-hat worm. Each transition (drawn as ÿ) represents an action of one agent or interaction among agents. Enabled transitions are highlighted in red. Let us consider transition T113. It means that Mirai at P1 infects the device at P2. It is enabled because

- Agent net representing Mirai at P1 has the enabled transition t1 labeled as m_infect; and
- Agent net representing the device at P2 has the enabled transition t1 labeled as infect.

In the same way, transition T214 is enabled. It means that the white-hat worm at P3 infects the device at P2. Let us consider the case of firing T214. This results in a new state shown in Figure 5. P2 has a new token representing a white-hat worm. This worm is the copy of the worm at P3 and infects the device at place P2. In this state, T113 is no longer enabled. This means that the white-hat worm protects the device at P2 from Mirai at P1.

Figure 5. A PN² model representing a battle between Mirai and the white-hat worms on an IoT system defended by the BDS.

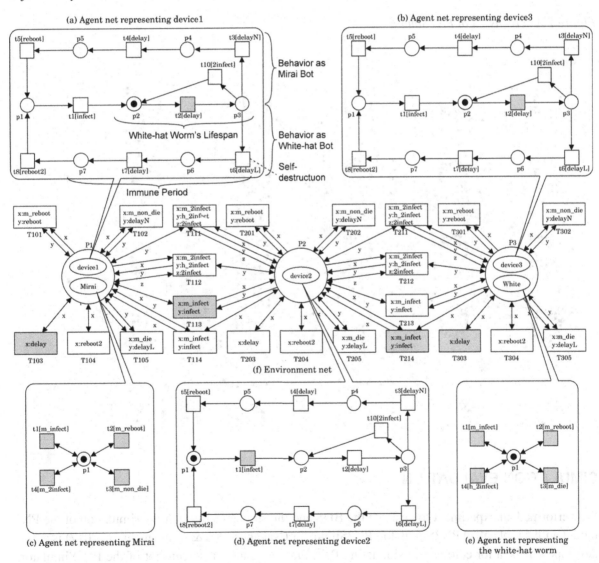

Figure 6. The state just after transition T214 fired, i.e., the white-hat worm infected the device at P2. T113 is no longer enabled. This means that the worm protects the device at P2 from Mirai.

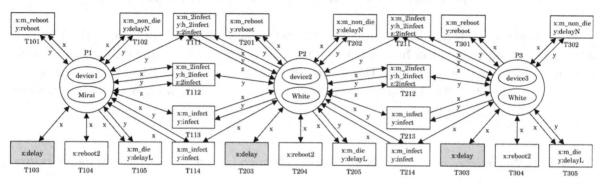

Figure 7 A screenshot of PN2Simulator.

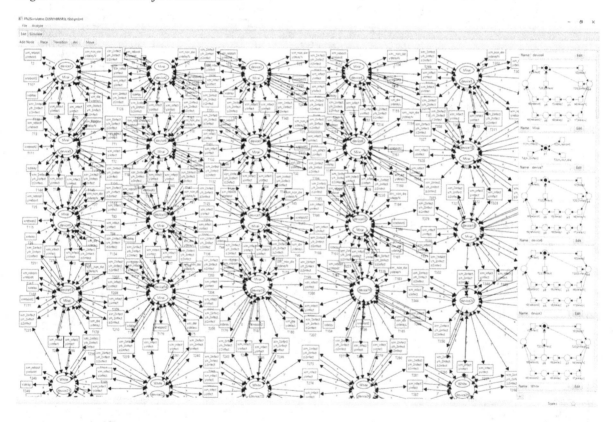

SIMULATION EVALUATION

We performed an experiment to evaluate the BDS and the strategies through the simulation of the PN^2 model with a tool called PN2Simulator. PN2Simulator (Nakahori, K., & Yamaguchi, S., 2017) is a tool developed in Java for editing and simulating PN^2. Figure 7 shows a screenshot of the PN2Simulator. The left-side of the screen shows an environment net, while the right-side shows agent nets. A user can edit those nets through direct manipulation and can execute them by playing a token game interactively.

Figure 8. Illustration of translating a network to a PN² model.

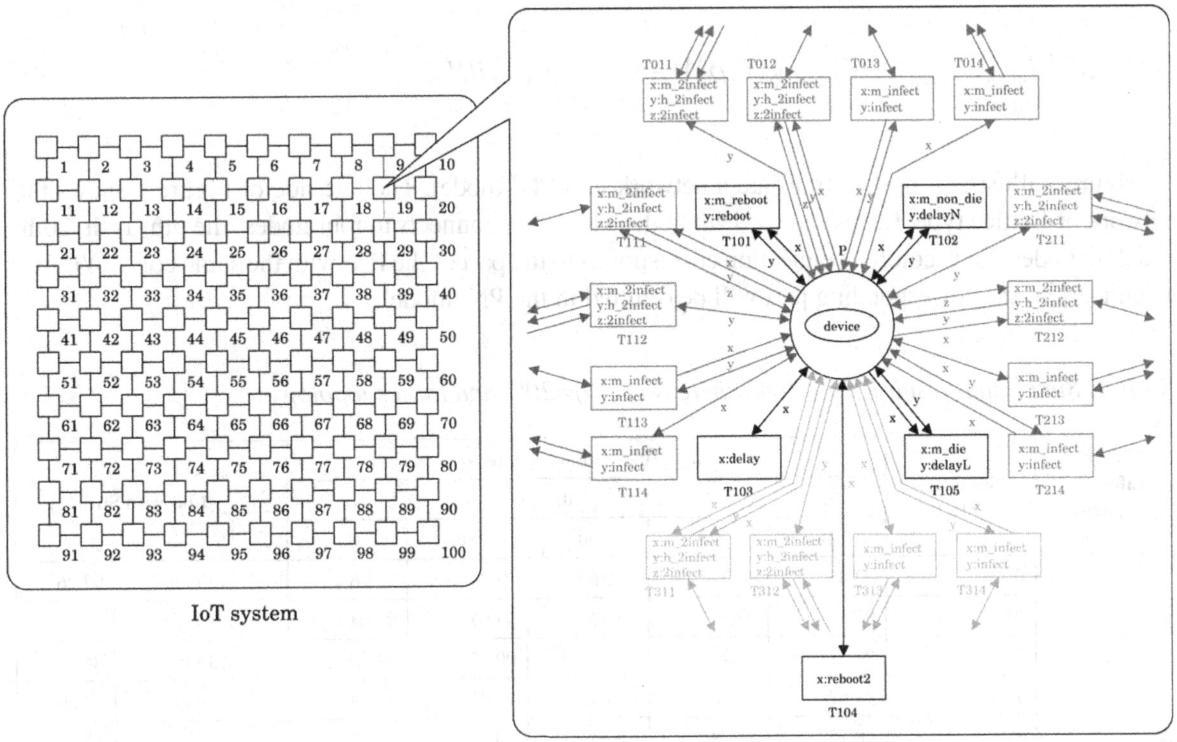

IoT system

We used R_{Mirai} as the evaluation index. The value of R_{Mirai} varies with the progress of the simulation. Therefore, it is written as a function $R_{Mirai}(t)$ of step number t, and set $t=0$ when the BDS detects a Mirai botnet and launches the white-hat worms. $R_{Mirai}(0)$ denotes Mirai's infection rate when the BDS detects the Mirai botnet. $R_{Mirai}(10k)$ denotes Mirai's infection rate after 10000 steps. In the same way, we define $\#_{Mirai}(t)$, $R_{White}(t)$, and $\#_{White}(t)$, where R_{White} and $\#_{White}$ respectively are the white-hat worm's infection rate and the number of the white-hat worms.

We measured $R_{Mirai}(10k)$ by changing the following parameters.

- $\#_{Mirai}(0)=20$, i.e. $R_{Mirai}(0)=20\%$
- $\#_{White}(0)= 10, 20, 30, 50, \text{or } 80$, i.e. $R_{White}(0)= 10\%, 20\%, 30\%, 50\%, \text{or } 80\%$
- The positions of Mirai and white-hat worms at step 0 were decided at random
- The IoT system's specification: Two types: Lattice (square) type ($\#_{nodes}$, $N_{topology}$, $N_{density}$)= (100, *Lattice*, 3.6%) and Tree type (100, *Tree*, 2.0%).
- The white-hat worm's capability:
  ○ Lifespan $\ell= 1,2,3,4$ or 5 steps, where the delay time δ until rebooting =11 steps
  ○ Secondary infection possibility $\rho= 0, 25, 50, 75$ or 100%
- The Few-Elite strategy $\mathcal{L}_{Few-Elite}$:

$$\left(R_{Mirai}, \delta, \left(\#_{nodes}, N_{topology}, N_{density}\right), (\ell, \rho)\right) \mapsto \#_{elite} = 10 \qquad if \ \ell + 4\rho \geq 6 \tag{5}$$

- The Environment-Adaptive $\mathcal{L}_{Env-Adaptive}$:

$$\left(R_{Mirai}, \delta, \left(\#_{nodes}, N_{topology}, N_{density}\right), (\ell, \rho)\right) \mapsto \#_{nodes} - \#_{Mirai} \; if N_{density} < \frac{2 \times 1.2}{\#_{nodes}} \qquad (6)$$

Figure 8 illustrates how to translate a network to a PN^2 model. The left side of Figure 8 shows the network of Lattice type. Let us see the 19th node. This node connects to four nodes: the 9th, 18th, 20th, and 29th nodes. Each colored connection corresponds to the part of the PN^2 with the same color. Without a connection, the corresponding part will be omitted in the PN^2 model.

Table 1. Simulation result R_{Mirai} (10k), where R_{Mirai} (0)=20% and lattice topology.

Lifespan ℓ [step]	Sec.infec. ρ [%]	R_{Mirai}(10k) without Strategy					R_{Mirai}(10k) with Strategy	
		$\#_{White}(0)$						
		10	20	30	50	80		
1	0	97.48	97.32	97.56	97.39	97.26	All-Out	97.26
	25	97.31	97.54	97.50	97.67	97.63	All-Out	97.63
	50	97.51	97.44	93.55	90.66	84.92	All-Out	84.92
	75	94.67	88.82	85.04	72.01	53.59	All-Out	53.59
	100	40.75	42.99	25.38	20.56	12.67	All-Out	12.67
2	0	97.42	97.47	97.46	97.42	97.72	All-Out	97.72
	25	97.60	97.45	97.44	97.64	97.51	All-Out	97.51
	50	79.70	77.45	77.94	74.60	56.79	All-Out	56.79
	75	36.98	28.26	27.33	21.63	24.35	All-Out	24.35
	100	2.94	3.92	2.91	1.97	2.97	Few-Elite	2.94
3	0	97.53	97.59	97.34	97.85	97.72	All-Out	97.72
	25	81.98	78.66	82.62	77.69	76.78	All-Out	76.78
	50	6.33	6.60	13.76	8.41	8.89	All-Out	8.89
	75	1.97	3.90	0.98	2.92	1.95	Few-Elite	1.97
	100	0.00	0.00	0.00	0.97	0.00	Few-Elite	0.00
4	0	97.59	97.32	97.64	97.49	97.40	All-Out	97.40
	25	11.42	13.22	12.41	10.40	11.01	All-Out	11.01
	50	0.00	0.97	0.00	0.00	0.00	Few-Elite	0.00
	75	0.00	0.00	0.00	0.00	0.00	Few-Elite	0.00
	100	0.00	0.00	0.00	0.00	0.00	Few-Elite	0.00
5	0	97.66	97.47	97.47	97.74	97.26	All-Out	97.26
	25	0.51	0.46	0.06	0.04	0.15	Few-Elite	0.51
	50	0.00	0.00	0.00	0.00	0.00	Few-Elite	0.00
	75	0.00	0.00	0.00	0.00	0.00	Few-Elite	0.00
	100	0.00	0.00	0.00	0.00	0.00	Few-Elite	0.00

Figure 9. Influence of white-hat worm's capability on Mira's infection rate in the IoT system with the lattice topology.

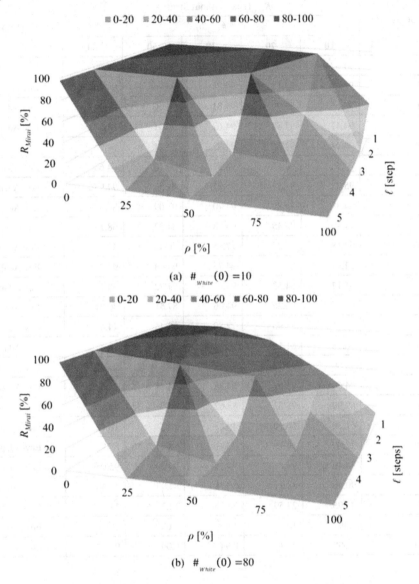

(a) $\#_{White}(0) = 10$

(b) $\#_{White}(0) = 80$

The simulation result is shown in Table 1 and Table 2. They respectively show the results for the Lattice topology network and the Tree topology network. Each cell shows the mean of $R_{Mirai}(10k)$ for 100 trials.

First, let us discuss the case of the Lattice topology. Let us see Table 1. $R_{Mirai}(10k)$ decreased with the increase of the white-hat worm's lifespan ℓ or secondary infection possibility ρ. Figure 9 shows the infulence of (ℓ,ρ) on $R_{Mirai}(10k)$. The X, Y, Z-axes respectively indicate ρ, ℓ, and $R_{Mirai}(10k)$. Regardless of $\#_{White}(0)$, $R_{Mirai}(10k)$ almost monotonously decreased with the increase of $\#_{White}(0)$. This result backs up the All-Out strategy's validity.

Table 2. Simulation result $R_{Mirai}(10k)$, where $R_{Mirai}(0)=20\%$ and tree topology.

Lifespan ℓ [step]	Sec.infec. ρ [%]	$R_{Mirai}(10k)$ without Strategy					$R_{Mirai}(10k)$ with Strategy	
		$\#_{White}(0)$						
		10	20	30	50	80		
1	0	94.82	94.69	94.65	94.32	95.09	Env-Adapt	95.09
	25	94.71	94.73	94.74	94.76	94.45	Env-Adapt	94.45
	50	94.65	94.99	94.81	94.66	91.94	Env-Adapt	91.94
	75	94.47	94.88	94.67	90.91	84.24	Env-Adapt	84.24
	100	94.94	94.66	94.92	87.21	64.96	Env-Adapt	64.96
2	0	94.56	94.65	94.87	94.73	94.63	Env-Adapt	94.63
	25	95.02	94.59	95.02	94.31	94.97	Env-Adapt	94.97
	50	94.88	94.29	94.70	93.09	88.21	Env-Adapt	88.21
	75	94.78	93.45	94.78	84.32	68.13	Env-Adapt	68.13
	100	92.18	86.25	77.85	66.43	42.61	Env-Adapt	42.61
3	0	94.84	94.66	94.75	94.64	94.86	Env-Adapt	94.86
	25	95.17	94.53	94.90	94.72	95.11	Env-Adapt	95.11
	50	94.17	94.26	94.06	87.51	80.35	Env-Adapt	80.35
	75	93.21	83.96	72.80	62.45	44.41	Env-Adapt	44.41
	100	70.98	61.16	42.64	31.31	19.87	Env-Adapt	19.87
4	0	95.09	94.52	94.67	94.73	94.90	Env-Adapt	94.90
	25	94.66	95.01	94.88	94.81	94.63	Env-Adapt	94.63
	50	89.90	93.32	83.62	65.96	49.90	Env-Adapt	49.90
	75	61.26	50.10	49.88	29.34	16.72	Env-Adapt	16.72
	100	22.00	18.79	10.41	8.65	8.49	Env-Adapt	8.49
5	0	94.40	94.47	94.79	94.58	95.05	Env-Adapt	95.05
	25	90.46	88.21	84.38	84.93	75.40	Env-Adapt	75.40
	50	40.95	27.59	29.06	12.33	11.50	Env-Adapt	11.50
	75	2.69	1.84	1.45	0.00	1.91	Env-Adapt	1.91
	100	0.00	2.91	0.94	0.00	0.98	Env-Adapt	0.98

When $\ell=1$, the worm's capability does not satisfy the precondition of the Few-Elite strategy (See Equation 5) because $1+4\rho \ngeq , =6$ for any ρ. Consequently, the BDS adopted not the Few-Elite strategy but the All-Out strategy. In contrast, when $\ell=5$, the worm's capability satisfies the precondition except for $\rho=0\%$. As a result, the BDS adopted the Few-Elite strategy and can reduce $\#_{White}$ to 10 by only increasing $R_{Mirai}(10k)$ at most 0.36%. From the above, we can say that the Few-Elite strategy is effective for the Lattice topology.

Next, let us consider the case of the Tree topology. Let us see Table 2. As with the case of the Lattice topology, $R_{Mirai}(10k)$ decreased with the increase of ℓ, ρ, or $\#_{White}(0)$. Figure 10 shows the infulence of ℓ, ρ, and $\#_{White}(0)$ on $R_{Mirai}(10k)$. The trend is simliar but the reduction rate of $R_{Mirai}(10k)$ siginificantly reduced in comparison with the result of Figure 9. This is because a low-density network restrains the white-hat worm's spread. This network satisfies the precondition of the Environment-Adaptive strategy (See Equation 6) because $N_{density} = 2.0\% < 2 \times 1.2 / \#_{nodes} = 2.4\%$. As a result, the BDS adopted the Environment-Adaptive strategy and did not reduce $\#_{White}(0)$. If reducing $\#_{White}(0)$ to 10, the BDS will not exterminate Mirai well. From the above, we can say that the Enviroment-Adaptive strategy is reasonable for the Tree topology.

Figure 10. Influence of white-hat worm's capability on Mira's infection rate in the IoT system with the tree topology.

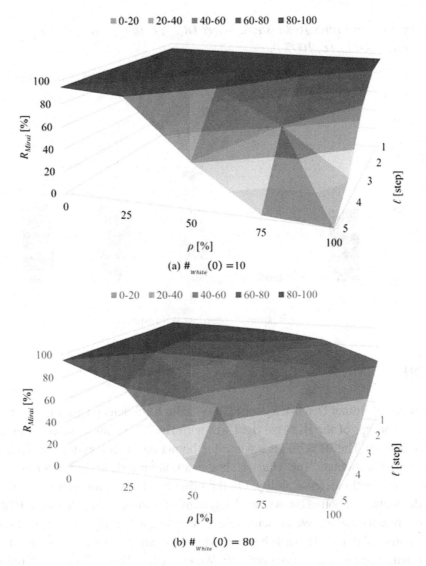

(a) $\#_{White}(0) = 10$

(b) $\#_{White}(0) = 80$

Figure 11 shows the Lattice topology IoT system's state after 10000 steps, where $(R_{Mirai}, \delta, (\#_{nodes}, N_{topology}, N_{density}), (\ell, \rho)) = (20\%, 11 \text{ steps}, (100, \text{Lattice}, 3.6\%), (\ell, 100\%))$. The horizontal axis shows ℓ. The vertical axis shows the mean of infection rate. A stacked colored bar represents different node's state: red for Mirai bot, dark blue for the white-hat bot together with the worm, and light blue for only the white-hat bot without the worm. When ℓ=1, only Mirai bots were left because the white-hat worms were too weak to exterminate Mirai bots. When ℓ=2, the BDS successfully reduced Mirai bots, and the white-hat worms and bots almost disappeared. This is a desirable result. When $\ell \geq 3$, Mirai bots were exterminated but the white-hat worms and bots remained instead. In general, it is not easy to exterminate Mirai and further delete the white-hat worms with the worm launch strategies only. To achieve this, we should use them with C&C strategies. Yamaguchi, S. (2021) has proposed a basic C&C strategy called Pull-Out. As to the Pull-Out strategy, refer to (Yamaguchi, S. (2021)).

Figure 11. IoT system's state after 10000 steps, where $(R_{Mirai}, \delta, (\#n_{odes}, Nt_{opology}, Nd_{ensity}), (\ell, \rho)) = (20\%,$ 11 steps, (100, Lattice, 3.6%), (ℓ, 100%)).

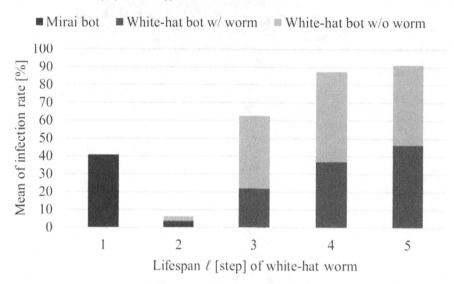

CONCLUSION

This chapter introduced Botnet Defense System (BDS). The BDS defends an IoT system against malicious botnets. The concept of the BDS is "fight fire with fire". To realize the concept, the BDS uses white-hat bot technology. The BDS builds a white-hat botnet on the IoT system by itself and uses it to exterminate the malicious botnets. The white-hat botnet autonomously spreads over the IoT system and thus drastically increases the defense ability. On the other hand, the white-hat worm defends the IoT system against the malicious botnet but wastes the system's resources. Therefore, the BDS should strategically use the white-hat botnet. We presented three worm launch strategies, All-Out, Few-Elite, and Environment-Adaptive. We regard a battle between Mirai and white-hat worms as a multi-agent system and to express it with agent-oriented Petri net PN[2]. We evaluated the BDS and the proposed strategies through simulation of the model. According to the results. the Few-Elite strategy is effective for the Lattice topology, and the Environment-Adaptive strategy is reasonable for the Tree topology. This chapter should become a trigger to interest researchers and engineers in this domain.

ACKNOWLEDGMENT

This work was supported by JSPS KAKENHI Grant Number JP19K11965.

REFERENCES

Alomari, E., Manickam, S., Gupta, B. B., Anbar, M., Saad, R. M., & Alsaleem, S. (2016). A survey of botnet-based ddos flooding attacks of application layer: Detection and mitigation approaches. In *Handbook of research on modern cryptographic solutions for computer and cyber security* (pp. 52–79). IGI Global.

Arghire, I. (2017). *Mirai Variant Has Bitcoin Mining Capabilities*. Retrieved from https://www.securityweek.com/mirai-variant-has-bitcoin-mining-capabilities

Arzamendi, P., Bing, M., & Soluk, K. (2018). *The ARC of Satori*. Retrieved from https://www.netscout.com/blog/asert/arc-satori

ASERT Team. (2018). *OMG - Mirai Minions are Wicked*. Retrieved from https://www.netscout.com/blog/asert/omg-mirai-minions-are-wicked

Bailey, M., Cooke, E., Jahanian, F., Xu, Y., & Karir, M. (2009). A Survey of Botnet Technology and Defenses. In Proc. of the 2009 Cybersecurity Applications & Technology Conference for Homeland Security (pp.299-304). Academic Press.

Ballano, M. (2015). *Is there an Internet-of-Things vigilante out there?* Retrieved from https://www.symantec.com/connect/blogs/there-internet-things-vigilante-out-there

Bezerra, V. H., da Costa, V. G. T., Barbon, J., Miani, R. S., & Zarpelão, B. B. (2019). IoTDS: A One-Class Classification Approach to Detect Botnets in Internet of Things Devices. *Sensors (Basel)*, *19*(14), 3188.

Bonderud, D. (2016). *Leaked Mirai Malware Boosts IoT Insecurity Threat Level*. Retrieved from https://securityintelligence.com/news/leaked-mirai-malware-boosts-iot-insecurity-threat-level/

Ceron, J. M., Steding-Jessen, K., Hoepers, C., Granville, L. Z., & Margi, C. B. (2019). Improving IoT Botnet Investigation Using an Adaptive Network Layer. *Sensors (Basel)*, *19*(3), 727.

Cimpanu, C. (2018). *New Mirai Variant Focuses on Turning IoT Devices into Proxy Servers*. Retrieved from https://www.bleepingcomputer.com/news/security/new-mirai-variant-focuses-on-turning-iot-devices-into-proxy-servers/

Cisco. (2020). *Cisco Annual Internet Report (2018–2023) White Paper*. Retrieved from https://www.cisco.com/c/en/us/solutions/collateral/executive-perspectives/annual-internet-report/white-paper-c11-741490.html

Devry, J. (2016). *Mirai Botnet Infects Devices in 164 Countries*. Retrieved from https://www.cybersecurity-insiders.com/mirai-botnet-infects-devices-in-164-countries/

Edwards, S., & Profetis, I. (2016). *Hajime: Analysis of a Decentralized Internet Worm for IoT Devices*. http://security.rapiditynetworks.com/publications/2016-10-16/Hajime.pdf

Frank, C., Nance, C., Jarocki, S., & Pauli, W. E. (2018). Protecting IoT from Mirai botnets; IoT device hardening. *Journal of Information Systems Applied Research*, *11*(2), 33–44.

Gopal, T. S., Meerolla, M., Jyostna, G., Eswari, L., Reddy, P., & Magesh, E. (2018). Mitigating Mirai Malware Spreading in IoT Environment. In *Proc. of ICACCI 2018* (pp.2226-2230). Academic Press.

Hiraishi, K. (2001). A Petri-net-based model for the mathematical analysis of multi-agent systems. *IEICE Trans. on Fundamentals*, *E84-A*(11), 2829–2837.

Jaramillo, L. E. S. (2018). Malware Detection and Mitigation Techniques: Lessons Learned from Mirai DDOS Attack. *Journal of Information Systems Engineering & Management*, *3*(3), 19.

Kolias, C., Kambourakis, G., Stavrou, A., & Voas, J. (2017). DDoS in the IoT: Mirai and other botnets. *IEEE Computer*, *50*(7), 80–84. doi:10.1109/MC.2017.201

Manso, P., Moura, J., & Serrão, C. (2019). SDN-Based Intrusion Detection System for Early Detection and Mitigation of DDoS Attacks. *Information*, *10*, 106.

Meidan, Y., Bohadana, M., Mathov, Y., Mirsky, Y., Shabtai, A., Breitenbacher, D., & Elovici, Y. (2018). N-BaIoT - Network-Based Detection of IoT Botnet Attacks Using Deep Autoencoders. *IEEE Pervasive Computing*, *17*(3), 12–22.

Milić, J. (2019). *Mirai Botnet Continues to Plague IoT Space*. Retrieved from https://blog.reversinglabs.com/blog/mirai-botnet-continues-to-plague-iot-space

Moffitt, T. (2016). *Source Code for Mirai IoT Malware Released*. Retrieved from https://www.webroot.com/blog/2016/10/10/source-code-Mirai-iot-malware-released/

Molesky, M. J., & Cameron, E. A. (2019). Internet of Things: An Analysis and Proposal of White Worm Technology. In *Proc. of IEEE ICCE 2019*. Academic Press.

Murata, T. (1989). Petri nets: Properties, analysis and applications. *Proceedings of the IEEE*, *77*(4), 541–580.

Nakahori, K., & Yamaguchi, S. (2017). A support tool to design IoT services with NuSMV. In *Proc. of IEEE ICCE 2017* (pp.84–87). IEEE.

Nakao, K. (2018). Proactive cyber security response by utilizing passive monitoring technologies. In *Proc. of IEEE ICCE 2018* (p. 1). 10.1109/ICCE.2018.8326061

netlab. (2017). *Warning: Satori, a Mirai Branch Is Spreading in Worm Style on Port 37215 and 52869*. Retrieved from https://blog.netlab.360.com/warning-satori-a-new-mirai-variant-is-spreading-in-worm-style-on-port-37215-and-52869-en/

O'Brien, S. A. (2016). *Widespread cyberattack takes down sites world wide*. Retrieved from https://money.cnn.com/2016/10/21/technology/ddos-attack-popular-sites/index.html

Sinaović, H., & Mrdovic, S. (2017). Analysis of Mirai malicious software. In *Proc. of SoftCOM 2017* (pp. 1-5). HR.

US-CERT. (2016). *Heightened DDoS threat posed by Mirai and other botnets*. Retrieved from https://www.us-cert.gov/ncas/alerts/TA16-288A

Yamaguchi, S. (2020a). Botnet Defense System: Concept, Design, and Basic Strategy. *Information, 11*, 516.

Yamaguchi, S. (2020b). White-Hat Worm to Fight Malware and Its Evaluation by Agent-Oriented Petri Nets. *Sensors (Basel), 20*, 556.

Yamaguchi, S. (2021). A Basic Command and Control Strategy in Botnet Defense System. In *Proc. of IEEE ICCE 2021*. Academic Press.

Yamaguchi, S., Bin Ahmadon, M. A., & Ge, Q. W. (2016). Introduction of Petri Nets: Its Applications and Security Challenges. In B. Gupta, D. P. Agrawal, & S. Yamaguchi (Eds.), *Handbook of Research on Modern Cryptographic Solutions for Computer and Cyber Security* (pp. 145–179). IGI Publishing.

Yamaguchi, S., & Gupta, B. (2019). Malware Threat in Internet of Things and Its Mitigation Analysis. In R. C. Joshi, B. Gupta, D. P. Agrawal, & S. Yamaguchi (Eds.), *Security, Privacy, and Forensics Issues in Big Data* (pp. 363–379). IGI Publishing.

Yamaguchi, S., Tanaka, H., & Bin Ahmadon, M. A. (2020). Modeling and Evaluation of Mitigation Methods against IoT Malware Mirai with Agent-Oriented Petri Net PN^2. *International Journal of Internet of Things and Cyber-Assurance, 1*(3/4), 195–213.

Chapter 9

A Survey on Emerging Security Issues, Challenges, and Solutions for Internet of Things (IoTs)

Anish Khan

UIET, Kurukshetra University, Kurukshetra, India

Dragan Peraković

ⓘ https://orcid.org/0000-0002-0476-9373

University of Zagreb, Croatia

ABSTRACT

The internet of things is a cutting-edge technology that is vulnerable to all sorts of fictitious solutions. As a new phase of computing emerges in the digital world, it intends to produce a huge number of smart gadgets that can host a wide range of applications and operations. IoT gadgets are a perfect target for cyber assaults because of their wide dispersion, availability/accessibility, and top-notch computing power. Furthermore, as numerous IoT devices gather and investigate private data, they become a gold mine for hostile actors. Hence, the matter of fact is that security, particularly the potential to diagnose compromised nodes, as well as the collection and preservation of testimony of an attack or illegal activity, have become top priorities. This chapter delves into the timeline and the most challenging security and privacy issues that exist in the present scenario. In addition to this, some open issues and future research directions are also discussed.

INTRODUCTION

Since from the beginning till the present day there are numerous definitions coined by different authors and researchers. The term "Internet of Things" refers to a network of physical devices or embedded devices which are capable of sending and receiving information or data via internet know as "Internet of Things (IoT)" (Oracevic et al., 2017, Adat et al., 2018, Lv, Z., 2020, Liu et al., 2017), Khattak et al.,

DOI: 10.4018/978-1-7998-7789-9.ch009

Copyright © 2022, IGI Global. Copying or distributing in print or electronic forms without written permission of IGI Global is prohibited.

2019). A technology that combines real-world with virtual world offers a rich ground for imagination and innovative ideas. The IoT is next phase in evolution of communication technologies. We caught a glimpse in the manner of utilization of technologies is an eye catching transformation that moulds the world from off the beaten track systems to ubiquitous Internet-enabled "things" (Sain et al., 2017).

For trouble free identification and communication purposes, digital identities are issued to every smart object that will help in sharing data and opportunity to use various services. A unique detection-system-radio frequency identification (RFID) has been developed using the concept of digitally identifying many gadgets (Aldowah et al., 2018, Aly et al., 2019, Sahmim & Gharsellaoui, 2017, Arıs et al., 2018). Wireless sensor networks are crucial in the execution of cutting-edge technologies because they are resource constrained. The use of cloud computing results in the creation of a virtual platform for integrating storage devices, development and research tools, and so on (Jose, D. V., & Vijyalakshmi, A., 2018). Users can access applications on demand without considering their physical location. As IoT is a vast area and offers number of applications in every possible way in routine life. For example, health care monitoring systems, smart transportation systems, retail, surveillance, wearable gadgets and many more (Jose, D. V., & Vijyalakshmi, A., 2018, Alaba et al., 2017, Bhattarai, S., & Wang, Y., 2018). Figure 1: Illustrate some of the common applications of Internet of things.

As far as IoT becomes burning matters nowadays, in contrast with this many security and privacy challenges have pop-up and become the bottle neck issues for IoT as the number of edge devices has increased dramatically (Yousefi, A., & Jameii, S. M., 2017). Various real-time attacks, such as zero-day attacks, ransomware, phishing attacks, and DDoS attacks (Sadeeq et al., 2018, Chahid et al., 2017, Hassan, W. H., 2019), have been introduced in recent years. The motive of this paper is to highlight various attacks that make edge devices vulnerable.

The road map of this paper contains eight sections. Section I gives a short and crisp introduction to IoT. Section II tells us about history and growth of IoT. Section III highlights the main elements of IoT. Section IV illustrates the three layer architecture of Internet of Things. Section V gives brief introduction of taxonomy of attacks. Section VI gives bird eye view of security challenges to each layer of IoT and Section VII illustrates some counter measures of various threats. Section VIII tells some future research directions and some open challenges to IoT. Finally, Section VIII concludes this paper.

TIMELINE OF IoT

The "Internet" is a worldwide group of combined servers, PCs, tablets and mobiles that are administered by standard protocols for combined frameworks. This enables users to send, receive and communicate the information (Sfar et al, 2018, Ande et al., 2020, Conti et al., 2018, Maple et al., 2017). The word "Things" has many meanings in English dictionary. The word thing refers to an object, action and situation. For example, a mobile is referred to an object, 'those kinds of things are expected from her'- here things are referred as action (Li, S., & Da Xu, L., 2017).

With the combination of above mentioned terms, a new term originates called "Internet of Things" that means a network of physical devices or embedded devices which are capable of sending and receiving information or data with the help of internet know as "Internet of Things" (Madakam et al., 2015). Vision of Internet of Things is to make things (tube-light, AC, fan, door bell, table etc) smart and to act like living entities by using internet. Internet becomes ubiquitous and spread almost in every part of the world and human life is directly influenced by internet.

Figure 1. Applications of IoT

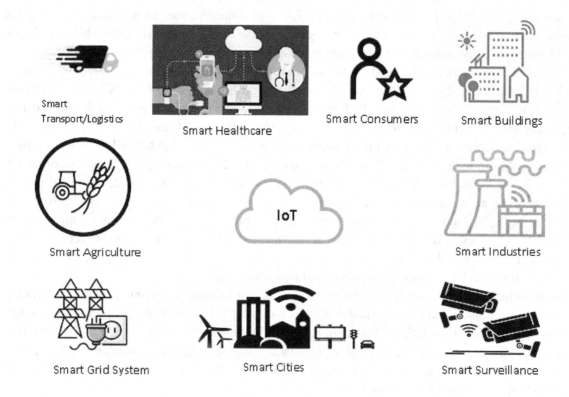

Moreover Internet of Things has no fixed definition; many definitions are available in the literature. Let's have a brief view of some definitions that are available in the literature, Mark-Weiser gave a central statement in seminal paper "The most profound technologies are those that disappear. They weave themselves into the fabric of everyday life until they are indistinguishable from it" at Scientific American in 1991 (Mattern et al., 2010). An expert on digital innovation named Kevin Ashton stated "An open and comprehensive network of intelligent objects that have the capacity to auto-organize, share information, data and resources, reacting and acting in face of situations and changes in the environment" in 1998 (Mattern et al., 2015).

In layman's terms, the IoT is a framework of interconnected gadgets. It leverages the Internet to transfer information and practically any gadget we may think about can be attached to it. In reality, the factors that fueled the rise of smart consumer electronics, such as ubiquitous wireless communication, cloud computing, low-cost sensors, and improved AI, are now being utilized in tandem with big data to strength the next age of industry (Sun et al,2018, Hou et al., 2019, Lin et al., 2017). With the passage of time much advancement are being done in the field of embedded systems and nano-electronics devices that makes possible in the reduction of size and dramatic improvements in computational process. These nano-electro devices are now available with global positioning systems (GPS), attached with the things to make them visible and provide a real time monitoring system (Grammatikis et al., 2019, Al-Garadi et al., 2020). Figure 2 give us a crisp overview of timeline of IoT.

In the month of March 2020, Cisco Annual Internet Report was published that analysis various segments like, small scale business, private sector, enterprises etc. The report envelopes quantitative predictions and calculations in respect to expansion of internet users, devices and network execution and capabilities.

Figure 2. Timeline of Internet of Things

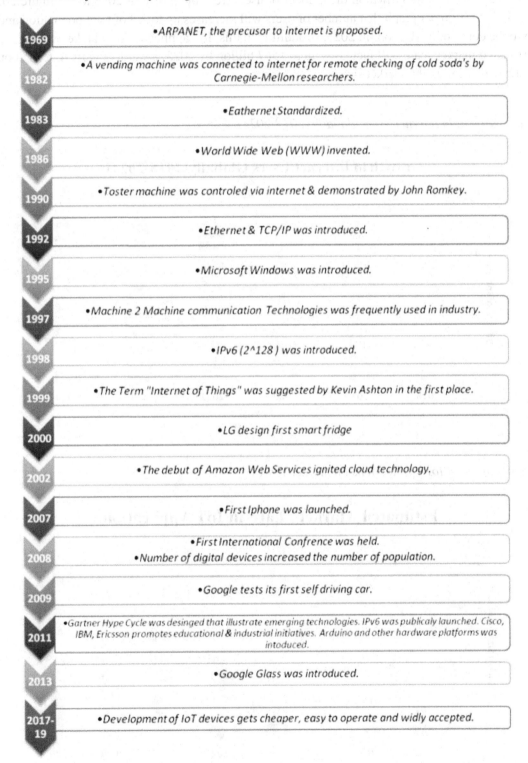

Figure 3 is illustrating growth in the number of users from the past year 2018 to the future 2023. It can be derived from bar graph that number of users will increases up to 2/3 of total population and will reach to the count of 5.3 billion till 2023. In addition to this, IoT applications will take over the market, the estimated market share will increases up to 1567 billion by 2025 onwards. Figure 4. tells about the dramatic expansion in the market size.

Figure 3. Growth in internet users globally (2018-2023)

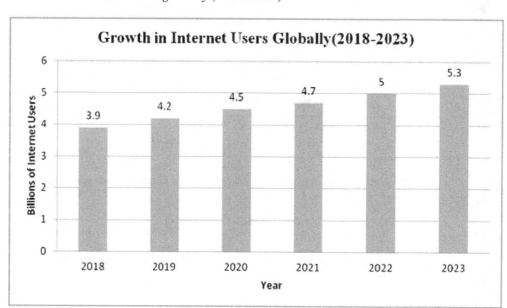

Figure 4. Impact of IoT applications on market shares

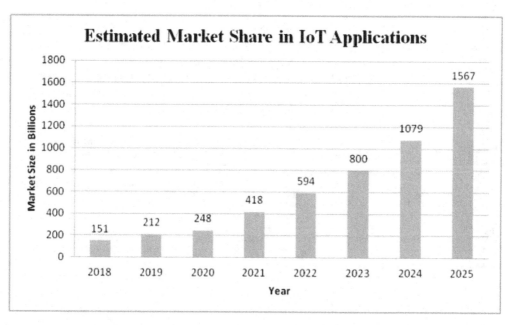

However, with the rapid growth in IoT technology approximately 66% of total population will have access to the internet. There is an unbelievable growth in market shares. The broadband speed will boost up to 110.4 Mbps, WiFi will gain momentum and reaches at a peak of 628 million hotspots. But the fact to be considered is that the risk of security will remain increased with the improvement in the technology. The number of attacks on the machine will almost double as compared to the present scenario. In the year 2018, the number of DDoS attacks was 7.9 million but it can be seen clearly that in the coming years (2023) it will reach at 15.4 millions. Figure 5: gives a bird eye view of expansion in number of DDoS attacks.

Figure 5. Growth in DDoS attacks

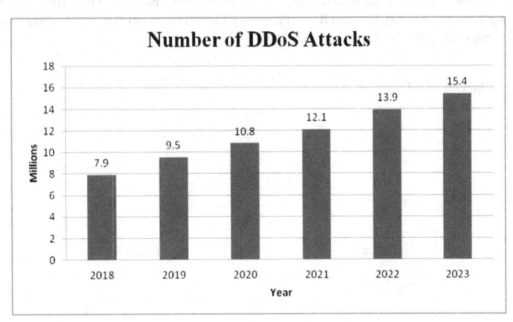

IoT ELEMENTS

Users can take advantage of a variety of advantages and features provided by the Internet of Things. As a result, specific elements are required in order to use them properly. The components required to provide IoT functionalities (Mendez Mena et al., 2018, Samaila et al., 2017, Sha et al., 2018, Misra et al., 2017, Ge et al., 2017, Razzaq et al., 2017, Bertino & Islam, 2017, Dabbagh, & Rayes, 2019, Butun et al. (2019), HaddadPajouh et al., 2019, Gulzar & Abbas, 2019, Yousuf & Mir, 2019). These elements' names and descriptions are as follows:

1. **Identification:** Identification provides each device in a network with a distinct recognition. Identification is divided into two steps: labelling and addressing. The label of the item is referred to as labelling, and the individual address of a certain device is referred to as addressing (Mendez Mena et al., 2018). These two expressions are extremely distinct because two or more devices might have the same name, but their addresses are always uniquely different. There are a variety of ways

for naming network devices, including electron product codes (EPC) and ubiquitous codes. IPv6 is used to provide each object a unique address. Initially, IPv4 was utilized to allocate addresses, but owing to the rising number of IoT devices, it was unable to meet the demand for addressing (Samaila et al., 2017, Misra et al., 2017).

2. **Sensing:** The sensing is the process of gathering information from objects. The information gathered is transmitted to the depository. Actuators, RFID tags, sensor technologies, wearable sensing devices, and other sensing devices are used to gather data from surroundings and devices (Sha et al., 2018, Ge et al., 2017).

3. **Communication:** The principal objective of the Internet is to connect and impart amongst several gadgets. Devices can transmit and accept delivery of information, files, and other data during communication. Many technologies, including as Near Field Communication (NFC), Bluetooth, Wi-Fi, Long Term Evolution (LTE), and Radio Frequency Identification (RFID), enable communication (Razzaq et al., 2017, Bertino, & Islam, 2017).

Figure 6. Elements of IoT

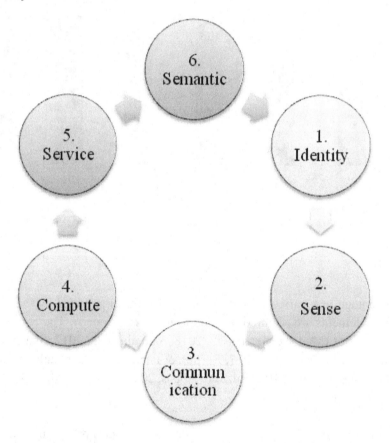

4. **Computation:** Computing performs on the information collected from devices by means of sensors. Numerous hardware and software frameworks have been created to handle computation in IoT applications. Audrino, Raspberry Pi, are utilised for hardware platforms, while the OS is used

for software platforms to execute the processing. Tiny OS, Lite OS, Android, and other operating systems are among the options (Dabbagh, & Rayes, 2019, HaddadPajouh et al., 2019, Gulzar & Abbas, 2019).

5. **Service:** There are four sort of assistance provided by Internet of Things applications. The first is an identity management service. It is in the process of examined which devices made a call. Another service that collects whole information from devices is data gathering. The second last service makes judgments based on the data obtained and responds appropriately to the gadgets. Fourth and final service is universal service, which is utilised to reply to devices instantly, regardless of time or location (Butun et al., 2019, HaddadPajouh et al., 2019).

6. **Semantic:** It is the primary duty of the Internet of Things (IoT) to assist people by completing their duties. To fulfil its obligations, it is the most crucial aspect of IoT. It functions as the IoT's brain. It gathers all relevant data and put together a favourable judgment about how to respond to the devices (Gulzar et al., 2019, Yousuf, & Mir, 2019).

Table 2, tells us about the elements of technology.

IoT ARCHITECTURE

IOT is not an individual technology; it is a cluster of different technologies. Hence, to implement this technology, various IOT architectures are available in literature proposed by different researchers. Here we only discuss the three layered architecture for IoT applications. The layers are "Perception layer", "Network Layer" and "Application layer" (Das et al., 2018, Virat et al., 2018, Yang et al., 2017, Salam, 2020, Husamuddin & Qayyum, 2017, Vashi et al., 2017, Chen et al., 2018, Ammar et al., 2018, Liu et al., 2017, Yaqoob et al., 2017, Mendez et al., 2017, Hameed et al., 2019, Rizvi et al., 2018, Gaurav et al., 2021) as illustrated in Table 1.

1. **Perception Layer:** This layer is often called "Device Layer". The IoT architecture's lowest layer is referred to as "Sensory Layer" or "Recognition Layer", which comprise of sensors that are responsible for the sensing and collecting data from sensors (Das et al., 2018, Virat et al., 2018, Yang et al., 2017). It involves sensing (gathering information from the environment and delivering it to database servers, or the cloud), and recognition methods (recognize devices on the basis of unique identity assigned to them), with minimal human engagement, actuation (taking a mechanical action based on sensed data) and communication (creating connectivity among heterogeneous smart devices) are possible (Singh & Vardhan, 2019). It is distinguished by the ability to capture data from the actual environment and display it in a digital representation. This perception layer can be sub categorised into two categories i.e. Perception Nodes and Perception Network. Perception Nodes contains the Sensors which are utilized to perform an action of information gathering from their respective surroundings. Sensors can be Radio Frequency Identification tag (RFID tags), Barcodes, Temperature sensors, humidity sensors, Near Field Communication sensors etc (Salam, 2020). After gathering information from sensors, it is forwarded to the next layer i.e. Network Layer. The modem through which gathered information is transferred to the next layer is Perception Network (Das et al., 2018, Husamuddin & Qayyum, 2017), which is responsible for the transferring data with wired or wireless communication modems.

Table 1. IoT architecture

Layers↓	Sub Layers↓	Key Features↓	Technology Used↓
Application Layer	Application Support Layer	Portable Devices, User Interface	M2M, Cloud Computing
	IoT Applications		
Network Layer	Access Layer	Information, Connectivity and Transmission	WiFi, Internet, GPRS
	Core Network		
	LAN & WAN		
Perception Layer	Perception Network	Identification, Sensors and Communication	RFID, WSN, GPS
	Perception Node		

Table 2. Elements using technologies

Elements	Technologies
Identification	IPv4, IPv6, Product Code
Sensing	Sensors, Wearable Devices, Actuators
Communication	RFID, WSN, NFC, WiFi
Computation	Arduino, Raspberry Pi, Windows OS
Service	Identity Based, Data Aggregation, Shared Service and Universal Services
Semantic	RDF, OWL, EXI

2. **Network Layer:** The "Network Layer" is often called as "Transportation Layer" and "Transmission Layer". It is found in between perception layer and application layer. This layer is the integration of the various heterogeneous networks and protocols that are responsible for the transmission of the gathered data from the perception layer. Its aim is to convey data collected via wired or wireless communication medium for the processing, data extraction, data assembling and encryption of perception nodes to the information processing unit (Yang et al., 2017, Husamuddin & Qayyum, 2017, Vashi et al., 2017, Hossain et al., 2019). This layer is further divided into three categories i.e. Access, Core and Local/Wide Area Network.

    a.   Access Layer: It is a sort of telecommunications network that acts like a link between subscribers and service providers. It develops communication and infrastructure abilities for target users, such as mobile communication, satellite communication, and wireless communication.

ZigBee, 2G and 3G, Adhoc, GPRS, Wi-Fi, Low Energy Bluetooth networks are examples of access networks that IoT can use. 4G-LTE/5G are a sophisticated telecom technology that allows mobile devices to connect to the Internet at high speeds (Das et al., 2018, Virat et al., 2018, Husamuddin & Qayyum, 2017).

    b.   Core Network: The Internet serves as the IoT's Core Network, providing the necessary infrastructure. It is responsible for pass on information among connected clients via network access. Moreover it serves as backbone of every communications system and functioning as a gateway for data exchange. It facilitates resource pooling communication among restricted gadgets. It allows us to monitor and control physical items from a distance (Vashi et al., 2017, Chen et al., 2018, Ammar et al., 2018).

    c.   LAN/WAN Networks: A local area network associate gadgets in a very restricted area. LAN devices may interact directly with one other and can use gateways to communicate with distant devices. Similarly, Wide Area Networks (WANs) are considered to distribute devices over wider regions. Low-power WAN's is capturing popularity for the reason that they allow low-power gadgets to communicate with each other (Chen et al., 2018, Liu et al, 2017).

3.   **Application Layer:** Application Layer is uppermost layer in three layered architecture that is perceivable to users. The application layer's objective is to supervise and attire applications worldwide using data gathered from the perception layer, which is analyzed by the IT unit. It offers access by using various portable and terminal devices to the end users across the network according to their needs. Application Support Layer and IoT Applications are the two sub layers that make up this layer (Yaqoob et al. 2017, Mendez et al. 2017).

    a.   Application Support Layer: It supports a wide range of corporate services and is in charge of conducting intelligent calculations and data processing. It is in charge of executing smart calculations and data processing and supports a diverse variety of company services. It utilizes middleware, which comprises of workstations for software installment on many devices and applications and is accountable for sophisticated operations. Machine-to-machine applications allow systems to communicate directly with one another via wired or wireless connections (Hameed et al. 2019, Rizvi et al. 2018, Sial et al. 2018).

    b.   IoT Applications: Internet of things is now an important part of our life. Every day we are familiar with many smart device moreover we are using many smart devices in our daily routine. Internet has made everything easy and information is available on our figure tips (Makhdoom et al. 2018, Nurse et al. 2017, Miloslavskaya & Tolstoy 2019). As assumed in late 1990's that till 2020, billions of users will be connected to the internet and this assumptions came true. Internet of things offers number of applications to make life much easier and hassle free like smart home, smart city, smart transport system and many more as illustrated in figure 1.

TAXONOMY OF ISSUES RELATED TO EACH LAYER

With IoT's economic, social and technological importance increasing every day, IoT not only attracts investment, user and scientist but also malicious users who work hard and find a way to make linked devices cyber attack weapons or to steal data. Although it is apparent that linking a huge number of non-conventional equipment via the Internet, including water supply pumps and intelligent appliances, is a scary idea behind the establishment of IoT, and will bring about drastic changes to security and privacy for people and businesses. For example, Proof point security investigators have uncovered cyber assaults that could be the first IoT Botnet attack to exploit around one lakh intelligent domestic appliances like Smart Televisions, smart lighting, Smart Drainage systems, and other appliances. Between the time periods 23rd Dec 2013 till 6th Jan 2014, Around 750,000 malicious spam emails were sent to a range of enterprises and people around the world by attackers (Tzafestas, 2018, Jindal et al. 2018, Sial et al. 2019, Van Oorschot & Smith, 2019).

Although the issues related to security and privacy are not new. Because of the increased IoT popularity more and more devices are deployed or integrated into different systems, organizations, houses, etc. that collect all types of information. The majority of these devices include a variety of security flaws that might be used by hostile actors to damage authorized customers. Various consumers may be unaware that they are being filmed or monitored due to the abilities of several smart gadgets.

The way that information is quickly accessible by means of the Internet and may conceivably be gotten to through ineffectively ensured keen gadgets with practically no safety efforts is one empowering angle that will make IoT information a really engaging objective for criminal clients. As a result, it's critical to make sure that each device is adequately protected. By addressing these issues and guaranteeing IoT security, attackers will be prevented from exploiting vulnerabilities that might lead to the compromising of confidential information and sensitive data. The concept of "one-size-fits-all" criteria cannot be efficiently employed with every specific application inside the IoT environment. The following core security properties can be used to classify security threats: "confidentiality", "integrity", "availability" (CIA), "authentication", "access control", "non-repudiation", "secure booting", and "device tampering" detection (Salman & Jain, 2019, Alrawais et al. 2017, Saha et al. 2017, Mastorakis et al. 2017, Mavropoulos et al. 2019). Table 3 shows various kinds of attacks present in the current scenario.

Table 3. Nature of attacks in current scenario

Nature Of Attack	Explanation	Categorization
Active Attacks	These are typically used to take out hostile activities in opposition to the system, damaging or interrupting legitimate users' services. They threaten the system's secrecy and integrity.	Denial-of-Service (Dos), Distributed Denial of Service (DDOS), Man-in-the-Middle (MitM), Interruption, Alteration
Passive Attacks	These are mostly used to collect relevant information without being detected, i.e., they do not interfere with conversation.	Monitoring, Traffic Analysis, Eavesdropping, Node destruction/malfunction
Network Layer Attacks	By tampering with packets, these attacks attempt to interrupt information exchange between the transmitter and the receiver.	Sybil Attack, Black-hole, spoofing,.
Physical Layer Attacks	These threats are aimed at tampering and exploiting devices, creating them the most sensitive IoT terminal.	Node tampering, Jamming, Replication
Software-Based Attacks	Third-party software's are used in these assaults to obtain access to the system and inflict destruction.	Virus, Trojan horse, Worms
Hardware Based Attacks	These are attacks that reveal sensitive information, such as cryptographic keys, in order to get access to the device.	Timing Analysis, Power Analysis
Privacy Threats	The features of the Internet of Things allow it to conduct targeted attacks on users' privacy.	Identification, profiling, tracking, linkage, inventory
Protocol-Based Attacks	The attacks target Internet of Things (IoT) connection standards.	RFID-based, Bluetooth based, Zigbee Based
Botnet Attacks	Infected gadgets (zombies) such as printers, cameras, sensors, and other smart devices execute large-scale DDOS assaults in order to corrupt other smart equipment. The command and control servers, as well as the bots, are the most important components.	Mirai, Hydra, Bashlite, lua-bot, Aidra

ATTACKS ON DIFFERENT LAYERS

As illustrated in Table 4, different security concerns that compromise anonymity on each layer that have recently been presented are briefly reviewed in this section.

1. **Perception Layer:** The physical layer is made up of numerous enabling sensor technologies including Bluetooth, GPS, and Zigbee, all of which are vulnerable to various sorts of intrusions. These sensors may capture data regarding location, air quality, surroundings, activity, and vibration etc. The main aim of the attacker is to exploit those sensors and to replace those with its own malicious sensors. The attacks listed below are carried out on the hardware components of the IoT network, and the attacker must be proximate to the IoT systems (Bhatt & Ragiri, 2021, Lee & Kim, 2017, Yu et al. 2018, Tewari & Gupta, 2020, Patwary et al. 2020). Conventional security dangers and issues to perception layers are:

    a. Eavesdropping: Eavesdropping is an illegal real-time attack in which an attacker intercepts confidential conversations such as telephone conversations, text messages, fax transfers, or video chat. It aims to retrieve information that is being sent via a network (Lee & Kim, 2017). It utilizes insecure communication to gain access to the data being delivered and processed.

    b. Node Capture: It is among the most dangerous assaults in the IoT's perception layer. A critical node, such as a gateway node, is taken over by an attacker. It has the potential to leak any data, including conversation between sender and recipient, a key utilized for secure connection, and data kept in storage (Yu et al. 2018).

Table 4. Security challenges to each layer

Layer	Technology	Security Challenges
Perception Layer	*WSN*	*Sybil attack, message corruption, False node, Tampering, DoS*
	GPS	*Black hole attack, Loss of event tracing, Spamming, Broadcast tampering, DoS*
	RFID	*Device tracking, Eavesdropping, Spoofing, Unauthorized access*
Network Layer	*Wireless*	*Signal Loss, DDoS, Phishing*
	Wired	*Malicious attacks, Data manipulation, Equipment hijacking*
Application Layer	*Intelligent transport*	*Customer Privacy, Manipulation of sensors, broadcasting manipulated traffic information,*
	Smart grid	*Physical meter tampering, Replay attacks, stealing data from server, false energy consumption data*
	Smart health	*Unintentional actions, Information disclose, Sybil attack*
	Smart Home	*Eavesdropping of Personal information, DoS attack, Replay attack*

c. Malicious Node: In this kind of attack, an assailant installs a malicious node and misrepresents the information. Its primary aim is to halt the channeling of accurate data (Tewari & Gupta, 2020). A hacker inserts a node to devour precious energy from genuine nodes and successfully govern to damage the network.

d. Replay Attack: A playback attacks is another name for it. It is an assault by an intruder that transmits and receives legitimate information on the conservation of the sender (Ali et al.

2019). By demonstrating evidence of his identity and authenticity, an intruder provides the identical verified data to the target that was already received in his conversation. Because the communication is encrypted, the recipient might consider it as a legitimate request and take the attacker's specific behavior (Gupta & Quamara, 2020).

e. Timing Attack: This attack often seen in gadgets with restricted computational capability. It is nothing but an aggressor to discover defects in a framework's uprightness and recover mysteries by observing what amount of time it will require for the framework to answer to different solicitations, input, or cryptographic techniques (Gubbi et al. 2013).

2. **Network Layer:** It is also known as "Transportation Layer". It is found in between perception layer and application layer. It also sets out the framework for interconnecting smart gadgets with network infrastructure. It poses serious security concerns with the integrity and authenticity of data being transmitted across the network Conventional security dangers and issues to network layer are (Ren et al. 2017, Chegini & Mahanti, 2019):

a. Denial of Services (DoS) Attack: A denial-of-service attack (DoS) is a type of cyber-attack that prevents legitimate users from retrieving gadgets or other network resources (Al-Garadi et al. 2020). It's usually done by sending repeated requests to the targeted devices or network resources, making it extremely difficult or inconvenient for some or all legitimate users to utilize them.

b. Man-in-the-Middle Attack (MitM): A MiTM attack occurs when an attacker privately encrypts and changes information between a transmitter and a recipient who believe they are speaking directly with each other (Kouicem et al. 2018, Ogonji et al. 2020, Madakam et al. 2015, Mattern, F., & Floerkemeier, C. 2010, u Farooq et al. 2015). Because the intruders have authority over the communication, he or she may modify messages to suit their purposes. It poses a significant danger to internet security since it allows an attacker to capture and alter data in real time (Roman et al. 2011).

c. Storage Attack: Users private data is saved on storage devices or on the cloud. The attacker can attack both storage devices and the cloud and user details may be altered (Ray, 2018). The duplication by various sorts of individuals of information connected with access gives more opportunities for exploitation (Stankovic, 2014).

d. Exploit Attack: Any unethical or unlawful assault as programming, bits of information, or a string of instructions is referred to as exploitation. In an application framework or equipment, it uses the security vulnerabilities (McEwen & Cassimally, 2013, Madakam et al. 2015, Chen, 2012, Al-Qerem et al. 2020). This is generally used to manipulate the system and capture data stored on a network.

3. **Application Layer:** All applications that employ IoT technology or IoT have been implemented are defined by the application layer. "Smart homes, smart cities, smart health, animal tracking", and other IoT applications becoming feasible (Stergiou et al. 2020, Tewari & Gupta 2017, Cvitić et al. 2021, Masud et al. 2020, Salhi et al. 2021). It is responsible for providing services to the apps.

a. Phishing attack: It's a delicate social engineering tactic that involves impersonating a trusted entity in order to get access to user credentials such as passwords and credit card numbers (Masud et al. 2020, Salhi et al. 2021, Hallappanavar, V. L., & Birje, M. N., 2021, Mishra et al.,2021, Dahiya & Gupta, 2021, Bhushan & Gupta, 2019).

b. Session hijacking attack: The hacker takes advantage of the user's online session to obtain access to the user's sensitive data (Chhabra et al. 2013, Mirsadeghi et al. 2020, Gou, Yamaguchi & Gupta, 2017, Tewari & Gupta, 2020, Gupta & Quamara, 2020).

c. Cross Site Scripting: It's a kind of code infusion assault (Stergiou et al. 2020, Wei et al. 2016, Arias et al.,2015), Harbi et al. 2019). It's nothing but an assailant to infuse a customer side content, for example, java script, onto a confided in site that different clients are visiting. An assailant can altogether change the design and usefulness of the program to suit his requests and use unique information in an unlawful way along these lines (Khattak et al. 2019, Nandy et al. 2019).

d. Malicious Code Attack: It's a piece of programming code that is intended to have potentially negative results and obliterate the framework (Tahsien et al. 2020, Elhoseny et al. 2020). It is a sort of a kind of malware that anti-virus will not have the option to stop or oversee. It can either fire up all alone or work as a program that involves the user's observations to complete a task (Aldowah et al. 2018, Aly et al. 2019, Arıs et al. 2018).

TAXONOMY OF VARIOUS COUNTER MEASURES TO VARIOUS ATTACKS

Although with the rapid increase in cyber attacks many mechanisms are designed and proposed to tackle with disastrous attacks. Taxonomy of some of the counter measures are illustrated below in figure 7:

Figure 7. Counter-measures to various IoT attacks w.r.t. Layers.

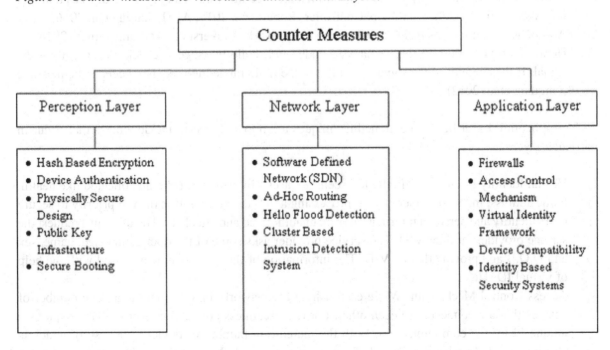

In Perception layer below mentioned techniques are implemented to tackle attacks that occur in particular layer:

1. Hash Based Encryption: To assure users information to be secure, hash based encryption technique is came into existence, it converts the information into unknown form called "Cipher Text". When information is shared among authentic user sender encrypt the data with a key and only authorized receiver can access the information with the decryption key (Li & Xiong, 2013, Sundaram et al. 2015).
2. Public Key Infrastructure: The concept of public key and private key are implemented here. The public key is stored at the base station and the private is distributed among all the nodes that are present in the IoT network. Shared message is encrypted and decrypted with the help of private key at receivers end (Weber, 2010, Li et al. 2013).
3. Device Authentication: Without any authentication the device cannot enters or connect with other nodes in the IoT network (Airehrour et al. 2017).
4. Physically Secure Design: Designing of physically secure devices should be of high quality (Suto, 2010).

In Network Layer below mentioned techniques are implemented to tackle attacks that occur in particular layer:

1. SDN: It stands for Software Defined Network; it provides better results and performance at low cost and uses less network resources. The integration of SDN architecture and IoT architecture are utilized for better security purposes. Combined architecture contains only three devices that are: IoT Agent, IoT Controller and SDN Controller (Robertazzi, 2017, Al Shuhaimi et al. 2016).
2. Ad-hoc Routing: It stops inside attacks from the network (Brakerski & Vaikuntanathan, 2014).
3. Hello Flood Detection: In this scenario, a node sends hello message to check the strength of the signal. If the strength of the signal is similar to the radio range then receiver accepts the message (Ongtang et al. 2012).

In Application Layer below mentioned techniques are implemented to tackle attacks that occur in particular layer:

1. Virtual Identity Framework: In the IoT scenario, user's information is being collected like health, home address, mobile number etc, for processing and transmission. It is the top priority to secure users identity and personal information from unauthorized and attackers. The users just request the service provider for their VID. The service provider asks some of the queries like age, name, sex and D.O.B and provide them a VID. The information of the users is now accessed with the help of virtual ID (Hu et al. 2011).
2. Access Control Mechanism: While establishing the network for IoT, there is a huge number of devices that are connected to each other. For their seamless connection every device requires a unique Id for the communication. With the increase in number of devices, the risk of attack is also increased. Attacks like, Denial of Service (DoS) attack, Man-in-the-middle attack came into existence, to overcome these issues the role of authorization and access control techniques are implemented (Bormann et al. 201, Gupta, K & Shukla, 2016).

3. Identity Based Security Systems: These kinds of systems are very crucial for the detection of user's location in emergencies. Only the authorized person can have access to the live location. The system contains 4 subsystems named as, Client subsystem, Registration subsystem, Users Policy subsystem and User Authentication subsystem (Hu et al. 2011, Sarma et al. 2008).

OPEN CHALLENGES AND FUTURE RESEARCH DIRECTIONS

Let us discuss some open challenges and future research directions:

1. Standardization: Considering most of the studies conducted so far, there's been no universal standardization for the IoT anatomy (Jose & Vijyalakshmi, 2018, Alaba et al. 2017, Florea et al. 2017, Obaidat et al. 2019, Li et al. 2019, Yousefi & Jameii, 2017) [110-115]. The evolution of complex ideas has been sparked by various security challenges and application requirements (Sklavos & Zaharakis, 2016, Gelenbe et al. 2018, Kalyani & Chaudhari 2020, Narendrakumar et al. 2018). However, it has become an epic match to integrate the objectives and features with one full-fledged model for multiple applications.
2. Security and Privacy: An enormous security and privacy threats will appear when IoT networks are deployed on a massive scale. Smart gadgets are inadequate to prop up with extremely secure protocols and algorithms due to resource limitations (Li et al. 2016, Wang et al. 2017, Hassan, 2019, Hossain et al. 2015, Andrea et al. 2015). Clients must always be informed of who will be acquiring their private data, how it is being gathered, and how it will be implemented in order to maintain their virtual privacy (Krichen et al. 2017, Sfar et al. 2018, Kolias et al. 201).
3. Power and Energy Efficient: Using various heterogeneous gadgets for sensing information from real world, bandwidth congestion across communication channels, data computation, storage exhaustion and energy depletion of devices are directly affected. To overcome these issues, energy harvesting systems (Mahmoud et al. 2015, Kouicem et al. 2018, Li et al. 2015, Maple, C. 2017, Li et al. 2017, Granjal et al. 2015, Sun et al. (2018)[128-134].
4. Data Mining/ Big Data: Building connectivity between millions of devices via the Internet will produce enormous amounts of data, so termed as big data. There is inadequacy in dealing with operational network architectures and software applications (Hou et al, 2019, Lin et al. 2017, Vasilomanolakis et al. 2015). For the storage, fetching and refining of the bulk data, appropriate techniques are necessary like, data mining techniques, supervised, unsupervised and deep learning techniques (Chasaki & Mansour, 2015, Grammatikis et al. 2019, Wortmann & Flüchter, 2015, Sicari et al. 2015).
5. Cloud Computing: Merging cloud computing with Internet of Things will accelerate the growth of intelligent apps that can handle thousands of users and a huge number of devices (Al-Garadi et al. 2020, Samaila et al. 2017). Applications must run in both wired and wireless environment. Moreover, real time apps should be worked in parallel so that if any miss happening occurs there will be no compromise with the processing (Ge et al. 2017).
6. Denial of Services (DoS) attacks: Smart devices are resource constrained that only focus on execution of the functioning rather than building a secure environment. This is the main cause behind smart gadgets becoming vulnerable and acting like gold mines for attackers (Madakam et al. 2015, Razzaq et al. 2017, Sadeghi et al. 2015, Tankard, C. 2015). Various newly introduced variants of

DoS attacks have come into existence that will come into consideration when the whole network shuts down. Some well-known DoS attacks in the scenario include Mirai, Hajime, and BrickerBot [150].

CONCLUSION

The Internet of Things is an emerging paradigm which helps us to communicate with non living objects or things with the integration of internet. By considering the capabilities of IoT and smart gadgets that boosts the growth in this field. Millions and billions of devices are connected with each other for the improvement of our lifestyle. In addition to this, many malicious activities are going on that violate our security and privacy. Here in this paper, we briefly go through trending technology and then security challenges related to each layer of the framework. Never the less, taxonomy of various counters measures and some security issues are discussed for the future perspective.

REFERENCES

Adat, V., & Gupta, B. B. (2018). Security in Internet of Things: Issues, challenges, taxonomy, and architecture. *Telecommunication Systems*, *67*(3), 423–441. doi:10.100711235-017-0345-9

Airehrour, D., Gutierrez, J., & Ray, S. K. (2017). A trust-aware RPL routing protocol to detect blackhole and selective forwarding attacks. *Journal of Telecommunications and the Digital Economy*, *5*(1), 50–69.

Al-Garadi, M. A., Mohamed, A., Al-Ali, A. K., Du, X., Ali, I., & Guizani, M. (2020). A survey of machine and deep learning methods for internet of things (IoT) security. *IEEE Communications Surveys and Tutorials*, *22*(3), 1646–1685.

Al-Garadi, M. A., Mohamed, A., Al-Ali, A. K., Du, X., Ali, I., & Guizani, M. (2020). A survey of machine and deep learning methods for internet of things (IoT) security. *IEEE Communications Surveys and Tutorials*, *22*(3), 1646–1685.

Al-Garadi, M. A., Mohamed, A., Al-Ali, A. K., Du, X., Ali, I., & Guizani, M. (2020). A survey of machine and deep learning methods for internet of things (IoT) security. *IEEE Communications Surveys and Tutorials*, *22*(3), 1646–1685.

Al-Qerem, A., Alauthman, M., Almomani, A., & Gupta, B. B. (2020). IoT transaction processing through cooperative concurrency control on fog–cloud computing environment. *Soft Computing*, *24*(8), 5695–5711.

Al Shuhaimi, F., Jose, M., & Singh, A. V. (2016, September). Software defined network as solution to overcome security challenges in IoT. In *2016 5th International Conference on Reliability, Infocom Technologies and Optimization (Trends and Future Directions)(ICRITO)* (pp. 491-496). IEEE.

Alaba, F. A., Othman, M., Hashem, I. A. T., & Alotaibi, F. (2017). Internet of Things security: A survey. *Journal of Network and Computer Applications*, *88*, 10–28. doi:10.1016/j.jnca.2017.04.002

Alaba, F. A., Othman, M., Hashem, I. A. T., & Alotaibi, F. (2017). Internet of Things security: A survey. *Journal of Network and Computer Applications, 88*, 10–28.

Aldowah, H., Rehman, S. U., & Umar, I. (2018, June). Security in internet of things: issues, challenges and solutions. In *International Conference of Reliable Information and Communication Technology* (pp. 396-405). Springer.

Aldowah, H., Rehman, S. U., & Umar, I. (2018, June). Security in internet of things: issues, challenges and solutions. In *International Conference of Reliable Information and Communication Technology* (pp. 396-405). Springer.

Ali, I., Sabir, S., & Ullah, Z. (2019). *Internet of things security, device authentication and access control: a review.* arXiv preprint arXiv:1901.07309.

Alrawais, A., Alhothaily, A., Hu, C., & Cheng, X. (2017). Fog computing for the internet of things: Security and privacy issues. *IEEE Internet Computing, 21*(2), 34–42.

Aly, M., Khomh, F., Haoues, M., Quintero, A., & Yacout, S. (2019). Enforcing security in Internet of Things frameworks: A systematic literature review. *Internet of Things, 6*, 100050. doi:10.1016/j.iot.2019.100050

Aly, M., Khomh, F., Haoues, M., Quintero, A., & Yacout, S. (2019). Enforcing security in Internet of Things frameworks: A systematic literature review. *Internet of Things, 6*, 100050.

Ammar, M., Russello, G., & Crispo, B. (2018). Internet of Things: A survey on the security of IoT frameworks. *Journal of Information Security and Applications, 38*, 8–27.

Ande, R., Adebisi, B., Hammoudeh, M., & Saleem, J. (2020). Internet of Things: Evolution and technologies from a security perspective. *Sustainable Cities and Society, 54*, 101728.

Andrea, I., Chrysostomou, C., & Hadjichristofi, G. (2015, July). Internet of Things: Security vulnerabilities and challenges. In *2015 IEEE symposium on computers and communication (ISCC)* (pp. 180-187). IEEE.

Arias, O., Wurm, J., Hoang, K., & Jin, Y. (2015). Privacy and security in internet of things and wearable devices. *IEEE Transactions on Multi-Scale Computing Systems, 1*(2), 99–109.

Arıs, A., Oktug, S. F., & Voigt, T. (2018). *Security of internet of things for a reliable internet of services.* Academic Press.

Arıs, A., Oktug, S. F., & Voigt, T. (2018). *Security of internet of things for a reliable internet of services.* Academic Press.

Bertino, E., & Islam, N. (2017). Botnets and internet of things security. *Computer, 50*(2), 76–79.

Bhatt, S., & Ragiri, P. R. (2021). Security trends in Internet of Things: A survey. *SN Applied Sciences, 3*(1), 1–14.

Bhattarai, S., & Wang, Y. (2018). End-to-end trust and security for Internet of Things applications. *Computer, 51*(4), 20–27. doi:10.1109/MC.2018.2141038

Bhushan, K., & Gupta, B. B. (2019). Distributed denial of service (DDoS) attack mitigation in software defined network (SDN)-based cloud computing environment. *Journal of Ambient Intelligence and Humanized Computing, 10*(5), 1985–1997.

Bormann, C., Castellani, A. P., & Shelby, Z. (2012). Coap: An application protocol for billions of tiny internet nodes. *IEEE Internet Computing, 16*(2), 62–67.

Brakerski, Z., & Vaikuntanathan, V. (2014). Efficient fully homomorphic encryption from (standard) LWE. *SIAM Journal on Computing, 43*(2), 831–871.

Butun, I., Österberg, P., & Song, H. (2019). Security of the Internet of Things: Vulnerabilities, attacks, and countermeasures. *IEEE Communications Surveys and Tutorials, 22*(1), 616–644.

Chahid, Y., Benabdellah, M., & Azizi, A. (2017, April). Internet of things security. In *2017 International Conference on Wireless Technologies, Embedded and Intelligent Systems (WITS)* (pp. 1-6). IEEE. doi:10.1109/ICOASE.2018.8548785

Chasaki, D., & Mansour, C. (2015). Security challenges in the internet of things. *International Journal of Space-Based and Situated Computing, 5*(3), 141–149.

Chegini, H., & Mahanti, A. (2019, December). A Framework of Automation on Context-Aware Internet of Things (IoT) Systems. In *Proceedings of the 12th IEEE/ACM International Conference on Utility and Cloud Computing Companion* (pp. 157-162). IEEE.

Chen, K., Zhang, S., Li, Z., Zhang, Y., Deng, Q., Ray, S., & Jin, Y. (2018). Internet-of-things security and vulnerabilities: Taxonomy, challenges, and practice. *Journal of Hardware and Systems Security, 2*(2), 97–110.

Chen, Y. K. (2012, January). Challenges and opportunities of internet of things. In *17th Asia and South Pacific design automation conference* (pp. 383-388). IEEE.

Chhabra, M., Gupta, B., & Almomani, A. (2013). A novel solution to handle DDOS attack in MANET. *Journal of Information Security, 4*(3). DOI: doi:10.4236/jis.2013.43019

Conti, M., Dehghantanha, A., Franke, K., & Watson, S. (2018). *Internet of Things security and forensics: Challenges and opportunities*. Academic Press.

Cvitić, I., Peraković, D., Periša, M., & Gupta, B. (2021). Ensemble machine learning approach for classification of IoT devices in smart home. *International Journal of Machine Learning and Cybernetics*, 1–24.

Dabbagh, M., & Rayes, A. (2019). Internet of things security and privacy. In *Internet of Things from hype to reality* (pp. 211–238). Springer.

Dahiya, A., & Gupta, B. B. (2021). A reputation score policy and Bayesian game theory based incentivized mechanism for DDoS attacks mitigation and cyber defense. *Future Generation Computer Systems, 117*, 193–204.

Das, A. K., Zeadally, S., & He, D. (2018). Taxonomy and analysis of security protocols for Internet of Things. *Future Generation Computer Systems, 89*, 110–125.

Elhoseny, M., Shankar, K., Lakshmanaprabu, S. K., Maseleno, A., & Arunkumar, N. (2020). Hybrid optimization with cryptography encryption for medical image security in Internet of Things. *Neural Computing & Applications*, *32*(15), 10979–10993.

Farooq, M., Waseem, M., Mazhar, S., Khairi, A., & Kamal, T. (2015). A Review on Internet of Things (IoT). *International Journal of Computers and Applications*, *113*(1), 1–7.

Florea, I., Ruse, L. C., & Rughinis, R. (2017, September). Challenges in security in Internet of Things. In *2017 16th RoEduNet Conference: Networking in Education and Research (RoEduNet)* (pp. 1-5). IEEE.

Gaurav, A., Gupta, B. B., Hsu, C. H., Yamaguchi, S., & Chui, K. T. (2021, January). Fog Layer-based DDoS attack Detection Approach for Internet-of-Things (IoTs) devices. In *2021 IEEE International Conference on Consumer Electronics (ICCE)* (pp. 1-5). IEEE.

Ge, M., Hong, J. B., Guttmann, W., & Kim, D. S. (2017). A framework for automating security analysis of the internet of things. *Journal of Network and Computer Applications*, *83*, 12–27.

Ge, M., Hong, J. B., Guttmann, W., & Kim, D. S. (2017). A framework for automating security analysis of the internet of things. *Journal of Network and Computer Applications*, *83*, 12–27.

Gelenbe, E., Domanska, J., Czàchorski, T., Drosou, A., & Tzovaras, D. (2018, June). Security for internet of things: The seriot project. In *2018 International Symposium on Networks, Computers and Communications (ISNCC)* (pp. 1-5). IEEE.

Gou, Z., Yamaguchi, S., & Gupta, B. B. (2017). Analysis of various security issues and challenges in cloud computing environment: a survey. In Identity Theft: Breakthroughs in Research and Practice (pp. 221-247). IGI Global.

Grammatikis, P. I. R., Sarigiannidis, P. G., & Moscholios, I. D. (2019). Securing the Internet of Things: Challenges, threats and solutions. *Internet of Things*, *5*, 41–70.

Grammatikis, P. I. R., Sarigiannidis, P. G., & Moscholios, I. D. (2019). Securing the Internet of Things: Challenges, threats and solutions. *Internet of Things*, *5*, 41–70.

Granjal, J., Monteiro, E., & Silva, J. S. (2015). Security for the internet of things: A survey of existing protocols and open research issues. *IEEE Communications Surveys and Tutorials*, *17*(3), 1294–1312.

Gubbi, J., Buyya, R., Marusic, S., & Palaniswami, M. (2013). Internet of things (IoT): A vision, architectural elements, and future directions. *Future Generation Computer Systems*, *29*(7), 1645–1660.

Gulzar, M., & Abbas, G. (2019, February). Internet of things security: a survey and taxonomy. In *2019 International Conference on Engineering and Emerging Technologies (ICEET)* (pp. 1-6). IEEE.

Gupta, B. B., & Quamara, M. (2020). An overview of Internet of Things (IoT): Architectural aspects, challenges, and protocols. *Concurrency and Computation*, *32*(21), e4946.

Gupta, B. B., & Quamara, M. (2020). An overview of Internet of Things (IoT): Architectural aspects, challenges, and protocols. *Concurrency and Computation*, *32*(21), e4946.

Gupta, K., & Shukla, S. (2016, February). Internet of Things: Security challenges for next generation networks. In *2016 International Conference on Innovation and Challenges in Cyber Security (ICICCS-INBUSH)* (pp. 315-318). IEEE.

Hallappanavar, V. L., & Birje, M. N. (2021). A reliable trust computing mechanism in fog computing. *International Journal of Cloud Applications and Computing, 11*(1), 1–20.

Hameed, S., Khan, F. I., & Hameed, B. (2019). Understanding security requirements and challenges in Internet of Things (IoT): A review. *Journal of Computer Networks and Communications.*

Harbi, Y., Aliouat, Z., Harous, S., Bentaleb, A., & Refoufi, A. (2019). A review of security in internet of things. *Wireless Personal Communications, 108*(1), 325–344.

Hassan, W. H. (2019). Current research on Internet of Things (IoT) security: A survey. *Computer Networks, 148*, 283–294. doi:10.1016/j.comnet.2018.11.025

Hassan, W. H. (2019). Current research on Internet of Things (IoT) security: A survey. *Computer Networks, 148*, 283–294.

Hossain, K., Rahman, M., & Roy, S. (2019). Iot data compression and optimization techniques in cloud storage: Current prospects and future directions. *International Journal of Cloud Applications and Computing, 9*(2), 43–59.

Hossain, M. M., Fotouhi, M., & Hasan, R. (2015, June). *Towards an analysis of security issues, challenges, and open problems in the internet of things. In 2015 IEEE world congress on services.* IEEE.

Hou, J., Qu, L., & Shi, W. (2019). A survey on internet of things security from data perspectives. *Computer Networks, 148*, 295–306.

Hou, J., Qu, L., & Shi, W. (2019). A survey on internet of things security from data perspectives. *Computer Networks, 148*, 295–306.

Hu, C., Zhang, J., & Wen, Q. (2011, October). An identity-based personal location system with protected privacy in IoT. In *2011 4th IEEE International Conference on Broadband Network and Multimedia Technology* (pp. 192-195). IEEE.

Husamuddin, M., & Qayyum, M. (2017, March). Internet of Things: A study on security and privacy threats. In *2017 2nd International Conference on Anti-Cyber Crimes (ICACC)* (pp. 93-97). IEEE.

Jindal, F., Jamar, R., & Churi, P. (2018). Future and challenges of internet of things. *International Journal of Computer Science & Information Technology, 10*(2), 13–25.

Jose, D. V., & Vijyalakshmi, A. (2018). An overview of security in Internet of Things. *Procedia Computer Science, 143*, 744–748. doi:10.1016/j.procs.2018.10.439

Jose, D. V., & Vijyalakshmi, A. (2018). An overview of security in Internet of Things. *Procedia Computer Science, 143*, 744–748.

Kalyani, G., & Chaudhari, S. (2020). An efficient approach for enhancing security in Internet of Things using the optimum authentication key. *International Journal of Computers and Applications*, *42*(3), 306–314.

Khattak, H. A., Shah, M. A., Khan, S., Ali, I., & Imran, M. (2019). Perception layer security in Internet of Things. *Future Generation Computer Systems*, *100*, 144–164. doi:10.1016/j.future.2019.04.038

Khattak, H. A., Shah, M. A., Khan, S., Ali, I., & Imran, M. (2019). Perception layer security in Internet of Things. *Future Generation Computer Systems*, *100*, 144–164.

Kolias, C., Stavrou, A., Voas, J., Bojanova, I., & Kuhn, R. (2016). Learning Internet-of-Things security" hands-on. *IEEE Security and Privacy*, *14*(1), 37–46.

Kouicem, D. E., Bouabdallah, A., & Lakhlef, H. (2018). Internet of things security: A top-down survey. *Computer Networks*, *141*, 199–221.

Kouicem, D. E., Bouabdallah, A., & Lakhlef, H. (2018). Internet of things security: A top-down survey. *Computer Networks*, *141*, 199–221.

Krichen, M., Cheikhrouhou, O., Lahami, M., Alroobaea, R., & Maâlej, A. J. (2017, November). Towards a model-based testing framework for the security of internet of things for smart city applications. In *International Conference on Smart Cities, Infrastructure, Technologies and Applications* (pp. 360-365). Springer.

Lee, J. H., & Kim, H. (2017). Security and privacy challenges in the internet of things [security and privacy matters]. *IEEE Consumer Electronics Magazine*, *6*(3), 134–136.

Li, F., Shi, Y., Shinde, A., Ye, J., & Song, W. (2019). Enhanced cyber-physical security in internet of things through energy auditing. *IEEE Internet of Things Journal*, *6*(3), 5224–5231.

Li, F., & Xiong, P. (2013). Practical secure communication for integrating wireless sensor networks into the internet of things. *IEEE Sensors Journal*, *13*(10), 3677–3684.

Li, S., & Da Xu, L. (2017). *Securing the internet of things*. Syngress.

Li, S., & Da Xu, L. (2017). *Securing the internet of things*. Syngress.

Li, S., Da Xu, L., & Zhao, S. (2015). The internet of things: A survey. *Information Systems Frontiers*, *17*(2), 243–259.

Li, S., Tryfonas, T., & Li, H. (2016). The Internet of Things: A security point of view. *Internet Research*.

Li, Z., Yin, X., Geng, Z., Zhang, H., Li, P., Sun, Y., ... Li, L. (2013, January). Research on PKI-like Protocol for the Internet of Things. In *2013 Fifth International Conference on Measuring Technology and Mechatronics Automation* (pp. 915-918). IEEE.

Lin, J., Yu, W., Zhang, N., Yang, X., Zhang, H., & Zhao, W. (2017). A survey on internet of things: Architecture, enabling technologies, security and privacy, and applications. *IEEE Internet of Things Journal*, *4*(5), 1125-1142.

Lin, J., Yu, W., Zhang, N., Yang, X., Zhang, H., & Zhao, W. (2017). A survey on internet of things: Architecture, enabling technologies, security and privacy, and applications. *IEEE Internet of Things Journal, 4*(5), 1125-1142.

Liu, X., Zhao, M., Li, S., Zhang, F., & Trappe, W. (2017). A security framework for the internet of things in the future internet architecture. *Future Internet, 9*(3), 27.

Liu, Y., Kuang, Y., Xiao, Y., & Xu, G. (2017). SDN-based data transfer security for Internet of Things. *IEEE Internet of Things Journal, 5*(1), 257–268. doi:10.1109/JIOT.2017.2779180

Lv, Z. (2020). Security of internet of things edge devices. *Software, Practice & Experience*, spe.2806. doi:10.1002pe.2806

Madakam, S., Lake, V., Lake, V., & Lake, V. (2015). Internet of Things (IoT): A literature review. *Journal of Computer and Communications, 3*(05), 164.

Madakam, S., Lake, V., Lake, V., & Lake, V. (2015). Internet of Things (IoT): A literature review. *Journal of Computer and Communications, 3*(05), 164.

Madakam, S., Lake, V., Lake, V., & Lake, V. (2015). Internet of Things (IoT): A literature review. *Journal of Computer and Communications, 3*(05), 164.

Mahmoud, R., Yousuf, T., Aloul, F., & Zualkernan, I. (2015, December). Internet of things (IoT) security: Current status, challenges and prospective measures. In *2015 10th International Conference for Internet Technology and Secured Transactions (ICITST)* (pp. 336-341). IEEE.

Makhdoom, I., Abolhasan, M., Lipman, J., Liu, R. P., & Ni, W. (2018). Anatomy of threats to the internet of things. *IEEE Communications Surveys and Tutorials, 21*(2), 1636–1675.

Maple, C. (2017). Security and privacy in the internet of things. *Journal of Cyber Policy, 2*(2), 155–184.

Maple, C. (2017). Security and privacy in the internet of things. *Journal of Cyber Policy, 2*(2), 155–184.

Mastorakis, G., Mavromoustakis, C. X., & Pallis, E. (2017). *Beyond the internet of things* (J. M. Batalla, Ed.). Springer.

Masud, M., Gaba, G. S., Alqahtani, S., Muhammad, G., Gupta, B. B., Kumar, P., & Ghoneim, A. (2020). *A lightweight and robust secure key establishment protocol for internet of medical things in COVID-19 patients care*. IEEE Internet of Things Journal.

Mattern, F., & Floerkemeier, C. (2010). From the Internet of Computers to the Internet of Things. In *From active data management to event-based systems and more* (pp. 242–259). Springer.

Mavropoulos, O., Mouratidis, H., Fish, A., & Panaousis, E. (2019). Apparatus: A framework for security analysis in internet of things systems. *Ad Hoc Networks, 92*, 101743.

McEwen, A., & Cassimally, H. (2013). *Designing the internet of things*. John Wiley & Sons.

Mendez, D. M., Papapanagiotou, I., & Yang, B. (2017). *Internet of things: Survey on security and privacy*. arXiv preprint arXiv:1707.01879.

Mendez Mena, D., Papapanagiotou, I., & Yang, B. (2018). Internet of things: Survey on security. *Information Security Journal: A Global Perspective, 27*(3), 162-182.

Miloslavskaya, N., & Tolstoy, A. (2019). Internet of things: Information security challenges and solutions. *Cluster Computing, 22*(1), 103–119.

Mirsadeghi, F., Rafsanjani, M. K., & Gupta, B. B. (2020). A trust infrastructure based authentication method for clustered vehicular ad hoc networks. *Peer-to-Peer Networking and Applications*, 1–17.

Mishra, A., Gupta, N., & Gupta, B. B. (2021). Defense mechanisms against DDoS attack based on entropy in SDN-cloud using POX controller. *Telecommunication Systems*, 1–16.

Misra, S., Maheswaran, M., & Hashmi, S. (2017). *Security challenges and approaches in internet of things*. Springer International Publishing.

Nandy, T., Idris, M. Y. I. B., Noor, R. M., Kiah, L. M., Lun, L. S., Juma'at, N. B. A., ... Bhattacharyya, S. (2019). Review on security of Internet of Things authentication mechanism. *IEEE Access: Practical Innovations, Open Solutions, 7*, 151054–151089.

Narendrakumar, S., Razaque, A., Patel, V., Almi'ani, M., Rizvi, S. S., & Hans, A. (2018). Token security for internet of things. *International Journal of Embedded Systems, 10*(4), 334–343.

Nurse, J. R., Creese, S., & De Roure, D. (2017). Security risk assessment in Internet of Things systems. *IT Professional, 19*(5), 20–26.

Obaidat, M. S., Rana, S. P., Maitra, T., Giri, D., & Dutta, S. (2019). Biometric security and internet of things (IoT). In *Biometric-Based Physical and Cybersecurity Systems* (pp. 477–509). Springer.

Ogonji, M. M., Okeyo, G., & Wafula, J. M. (2020). A survey on privacy and security of Internet of Things. *Computer Science Review, 38*, 100312.

Ongtang, M., McLaughlin, S., Enck, W., & McDaniel, P. (2012). Semantically rich application-centric security in Android. *Security and Communication Networks, 5*(6), 658–673.

Oracevic, A., Dilek, S., & Ozdemir, S. (2017, May). Security in internet of things: A survey. In *2017 International Symposium on Networks, Computers and Communications (ISNCC)* (pp. 1-6). IEEE. 10.1109/ISNCC.2017.8072001

Pajouh, H., Dehghantanha, A., Parizi, R. M., Aledhari, M., & Karimipour, H. (2019). A survey on internet of things security: Requirements, challenges, and solutions. *Internet of Things*, 100129.

Patwary, A. A. N., Fu, A., Battula, S. K., Naha, R. K., Garg, S., & Mahanti, A. (2020). FogAuthChain: A secure location-based authentication scheme in fog computing environments using Blockchain. *Computer Communications, 162*, 212–224.

Ray, P. P. (2018). A survey on Internet of Things architectures. *Journal of King Saud University-Computer and Information Sciences, 30*(3), 291–319.

Razzaq, M. A., Gill, S. H., Qureshi, M. A., & Ullah, S. (2017). Security issues in the Internet of Things (IoT): A comprehensive study. *International Journal of Advanced Computer Science and Applications, 8*(6), 383.

Razzaq, M. A., Gill, S. H., Qureshi, M. A., & Ullah, S. (2017). Security issues in the Internet of Things (IoT): A comprehensive study. *International Journal of Advanced Computer Science and Applications*, *8*(6), 383.

Ren, Z., Liu, X., Ye, R., & Zhang, T. (2017, July). Security and privacy on internet of things. In *2017 7th IEEE International Conference on Electronics Information and Emergency Communication (ICEIEC)* (pp. 140-144). IEEE.

Rizvi, S., Kurtz, A., Pfeffer, J., & Rizvi, M. (2018, August). Securing the internet of things (IoT): A security taxonomy for IoT. In *2018 17th IEEE International Conference On Trust, Security And Privacy In Computing And Communications/12th IEEE International Conference On Big Data Science And Engineering (TrustCom/BigDataSE)* (pp. 163-168). IEEE.

Robertazzi, T. G. (2017). Software-defined networking. In *Introduction to Computer Networking* (pp. 81–87). Springer.

Roman, R., Najera, P., & Lopez, J. (2011). Securing the internet of things. *Computer*, *44*(9), 51–58.

Sadeeq, M. A., Zeebaree, S. R., Qashi, R., Ahmed, S. H., & Jacksi, K. (2018, October). Internet of Things security: a survey. In *2018 International Conference on Advanced Science and Engineering (ICOASE)* (pp. 162-166). IEEE.

Sadeghi, A. R., Wachsmann, C., & Waidner, M. (2015, June). Security and privacy challenges in industrial internet of things. In *2015 52nd ACM/EDAC/IEEE Design Automation Conference (DAC)* (pp. 1-6). IEEE.

Saha, H. N., Mandal, A., & Sinha, A. (2017, January). Recent trends in the Internet of Things. In *2017 IEEE 7th annual computing and communication workshop and conference (CCWC)* (pp. 1-4). IEEE.

Sahmim, S., & Gharsellaoui, H. (2017). Privacy and security in internet-based computing: cloud computing, internet of things, cloud of things: a review. *Procedia Computer Science*, *112*, 1516–1522. doi:10.1016/j.procs.2017.08.050

Sain, M., Kang, Y. J., & Lee, H. J. (2017, February). Survey on security in Internet of Things: State of the art and challenges. In *2017 19th International conference on advanced communication technology (ICACT)* (pp. 699-704). IEEE.

Salam, A. (2020). Internet of things in agricultural innovation and security. In *Internet of Things for Sustainable Community Development* (pp. 71–112). Springer.

Salhi, D. E., Tari, A., & Kechadi, M. T. (2021). Using Clustering for Forensics Analysis on Internet of Things. *International Journal of Software Science and Computational Intelligence*, *13*(1), 56–71.

Salman, T., & Jain, R. (2019). *A survey of protocols and standards for internet of things*. arXiv preprint arXiv:1903.11549.

Samaila, M. G., Neto, M., Fernandes, D. A., Freire, M. M., & Inácio, P. R. (2017). Security challenges of the Internet of Things. In *Beyond the Internet of Things* (pp. 53–82). Springer.

Samaila, M. G., Neto, M., Fernandes, D. A., Freire, M. M., & Inácio, P. R. (2017). Security challenges of the Internet of Things. In *Beyond the Internet of Things* (pp. 53–82). Springer.

Sarma, A., Matos, A., Girao, J., & Aguiar, R. L. (2008). Virtual identity framework for telecom infrastructures. *Wireless Personal Communications*, *45*(4), 521–543.

Sfar, A. R., Natalizio, E., Challal, Y., & Chtourou, Z. (2018). A roadmap for security challenges in the Internet of Things. *Digital Communications and Networks*, *4*(2), 118–137. doi:10.1016/j.dcan.2017.04.003

Sfar, A. R., Natalizio, E., Challal, Y., & Chtourou, Z. (2018). A roadmap for security challenges in the Internet of Things. *Digital Communications and Networks*, *4*(2), 118–137.

Sha, K., Wei, W., Yang, T. A., Wang, Z., & Shi, W. (2018). On security challenges and open issues in Internet of Things. *Future Generation Computer Systems*, *83*, 326–337.

Sial, A., Singh, A., & Mahanti, A. (2019). Detecting anomalous energy consumption using contextual analysis of smart meter data. *Wireless Networks*, 1–18.

Sial, A., Singh, A., Mahanti, A., & Gong, M. (2018, April). Heuristics-Based Detection of Abnormal Energy Consumption. In *International Conference on Smart Grid Inspired Future Technologies* (pp. 21-31). Springer.

Sicari, S., Rizzardi, A., Grieco, L. A., & Coen-Porisini, A. (2015). Security, privacy and trust in Internet of Things: The road ahead. *Computer Networks*, *76*, 146–164.

Singh, N., & Vardhan, M. (2019). Distributed ledger technology based property transaction system with support for iot devices. *International Journal of Cloud Applications and Computing*, *9*(2), 60–78.

Sklavos, N., & Zaharakis, I. D. (2016, November). Cryptography and security in internet of things (iots): Models, schemes, and implementations. In *2016 8th IFIP International Conference on New Technologies, Mobility and Security (NTMS)* (pp. 1-2). IEEE.

Stankovic, J. A. (2014). Research directions for the internet of things. *IEEE Internet of Things Journal*, *1*(1), 3–9.

Stergiou, C. L., Psannis, K. E., & Gupta, B. B. (2020). IoT-based big data secure management in the fog over a 6G wireless network. *IEEE Internet of Things Journal*, *8*(7), 5164–5171.

Stergiou, C. L., Psannis, K. E., & Gupta, B. B. (2020). *IoT-based Big Data secure management in the Fog over a 6G Wireless Network. IEEE Internet of Things Journal*.

Sun, W., Cai, Z., Li, Y., Liu, F., Fang, S., & Wang, G. (2018). Security and privacy in the medical internet of things: A review. *Security and Communication Networks*.

Sun, W., Cai, Z., Li, Y., Liu, F., Fang, S., & Wang, G. (2018). Security and privacy in the medical internet of things: A review. *Security and Communication Networks*.

Sundaram, B. V., Ramnath, M., Prasanth, M., & Sundaram, V. (2015, March). Encryption and hash based security in Internet of Things. In *2015 3rd International Conference on Signal Processing, Communication and Networking (ICSCN)* (pp. 1-6). IEEE.

Suto, L. (2010). *Analyzing the accuracy and time costs of web application security scanners*. Academic Press.

Tahsien, S. M., Karimipour, H., & Spachos, P. (2020). Machine learning based solutions for security of Internet of Things (IoT): A survey. *Journal of Network and Computer Applications*, *161*, 102630.

Tankard, C. (2015). The security issues of the Internet of Things. *Computer Fraud & Security, 2015*(9), 11–14.

Tewari, A., & Gupta, B. B. (2017). A lightweight mutual authentication protocol based on elliptic curve cryptography for IoT devices. *International Journal of Advanced Intelligence Paradigms*, *9*(2-3), 111–121.

Tewari, A., & Gupta, B. B. (2020). Security, privacy and trust of different layers in Internet-of-Things (IoTs) framework. *Future Generation Computer Systems*, *108*, 909–920.

Tewari, A., & Gupta, B. B. (2020). Security, privacy and trust of different layers in Internet-of-Things (IoTs) framework. *Future Generation Computer Systems*, *108*, 909–920.

Tzafestas, S. G. (2018). Ethics and law in the internet of things world. *Smart Cities, 1*(1), 98-120.

Van Oorschot, P. C., & Smith, S. W. (2019). The internet of things: Security challenges. *IEEE Security and Privacy*, *17*(5), 7–9.

Vashi, S., Ram, J., Modi, J., Verma, S., & Prakash, C. (2017, February). Internet of Things (IoT): A vision, architectural elements, and security issues. In 2017 international conference on I-SMAC (IoT in Social, Mobile, Analytics and Cloud)(I-SMAC) (pp. 492-496). IEEE.

Vasilomanolakis, E., Daubert, J., Luthra, M., Gazis, V., Wiesmaier, A., & Kikiras, P. (2015, September). On the security and privacy of Internet of Things architectures and systems. In *2015 International Workshop on Secure Internet of Things (SIoT)* (pp. 49-57). IEEE.

Virat, M. S., Bindu, S. M., Aishwarya, B., Dhanush, B. N., & Kounte, M. R. (2018, May). Security and privacy challenges in internet of things. In *2018 2nd International Conference on Trends in Electronics and Informatics (ICOEI)* (pp. 454-460). IEEE.

Wang, N., Jiang, T., Li, W., & Lv, S. (2017). Physical-layer security in Internet of Things based on compressed sensing and frequency selection. *IET Communications*, *11*(9), 1431–1437.

Weber, R. H. (2010). Internet of Things–New security and privacy challenges. *Computer Law & Security Review*, *26*(1), 23–30.

Wei, W., Yang, A. T., Shi, W., & Sha, K. (2016, October). Security in internet of things: Opportunities and challenges. In *2016 International Conference on Identification, Information and Knowledge in the Internet of Things (IIKI)* (pp. 512-518). IEEE.

Wortmann, F., & Flüchter, K. (2015). Internet of things. *Business & Information Systems Engineering*, *57*(3), 221–224.

Yang, Y., Wu, L., Yin, G., Li, L., & Zhao, H. (2017). A survey on security and privacy issues in Internet-of-Things. *IEEE Internet of Things Journal*, *4*(5), 1250–1258.

Yaqoob, I., & Ahmed, E., ur Rehman, M. H., Ahmed, A. I. A., Al-garadi, M. A., Imran, M., & Guizani, M. (2017). The rise of ransomware and emerging security challenges in the Internet of Things. *Computer Networks*, *129*, 444–458.

Yousefi, A., & Jameii, S. M. (2017, May). Improving the security of internet of things using encryption algorithms. In *2017 International Conference on IoT and Application (ICIOT)* (pp. 1-5). IEEE. 10.1109/ICIOTA.2017.8073627

Yousefi, A., & Jameii, S. M. (2017, May). Improving the security of internet of things using encryption algorithms. In *2017 International Conference on IoT and Application (ICIOT)* (pp. 1-5). IEEE.

Yousuf, O., & Mir, R. N. (2019). *A survey on the internet of things security: State-of-art, architecture, issues and countermeasures*. Information & Computer Security.

Yu, Y., Li, Y., Tian, J., & Liu, J. (2018). Blockchain-based solutions to security and privacy issues in the internet of things. *IEEE Wireless Communications*, *25*(6), 12–18.

Chapter 10
SecBrain:
A Framework to Detect Cyberattacks Revealing Sensitive Data in Brain–Computer Interfaces

Enrique Tomás Martínez Beltrán

https://orcid.org/0000-0002-5169-2815

University of Murcia, Spain

Mario Quiles Pérez

University of Murcia, Spain

Sergio López Bernal

University of Murcia, Spain

Alberto Huertas Celdrán

University of Zürich, Switzerland

Gregorio Martínez Pérez

University of Murcia, Spain

ABSTRACT

In recent years, the growth of brain-computer interfaces (BCIs) has been remarkable in specific application fields, such as the medical sector or the entertainment industry. Most of these fields use evoked potentials, like P300, to obtain neural data able to handle prostheses or achieve greater immersion experience in videogames. The natural use of BCI involves the management of sensitive users' information as behaviors, emotions, or thoughts. In this context, new security breaches in BCI are offering cybercriminals the possibility of collecting sensitive data and affecting subjects' physical integrity, which are critical issues. For all these reasons, the fact of applying efficient cybersecurity mechanisms has become a main challenge. To improve this challenge, this chapter proposes a framework able to detect cyberattacks affecting one of the most typical scenarios of BCI, the generation of P300 through visual stimuli. A pool of experiments demonstrates the performance of the proposed framework.

DOI: 10.4018/978-1-7998-7789-9.ch010

Copyright © 2022, IGI Global. Copying or distributing in print or electronic forms without written permission of IGI Global is prohibited.

INTRODUCTION

Brain-Computer Interfaces History

Brain-Computer Interfaces (BCIs) are devices that enable two-way communication between an individual's brain and external devices. This bidirectional connection allows two different functionalities in terms of BCI usage. The first one is focused on the acquisition of neuronal activity produced by an individual and its transmission to a computer for analysis and processing. The second is given by the stimulation and inhibition of brain activity to regulate abnormal impulses or improve motor actions at a neuronal level.

Traditionally, the usage of BCI has been aligned with the medical field. With this technology, many advances have been made in neuropsychology and neurophysiology. BCI has contributed to the treatment of neurodegenerative diseases by analyzing the brain state, such as epilepsy and the autonomic nervous system (Liberati et al., 2012; Simon et al., 2011). Over the years, BCI technology has undergone significant technological evolution. Thanks to numerous studies, BCI has increased its application fields and has started to be used in other scenarios than medicine. One of these scenarios is the entertainment and video game industry (Ahn et al., 2014; Finke et al., 2009). Another sector exploring the use of BCI is the military one, where studies are aiming to allow the telepathic handling of multiple drones at a distance (Al-Nuaimi et al., 2020) or even exoskeletons (Crea et al., 2018).

Most of the scenarios functionality is based on capturing and processing the electroencephalography (EEG) signal and evoked potentials. Event-related potentials (ERPs) are signal patterns automatically generated by the brain when stimuli are presented to the person. Different types of potentials depend on the trigger action performed: visual, auditory, somatosensory, or cognitive. The study of these potentials has made it possible to obtain information about the subject, such as his/her emotional state, neurological problems, dependencies, or even private information.

One of the most well-known and used ERPs in brain recording is P300 (or P3). P300 is related to the visualization of stimuli known by the person. It is produced between 250-500 ms after the visualization of each known-stimulus and has a positive signal peak. One of the most common ways of provoking this potential is through the Oddball paradigm. The Oddball paradigm shows a series of known stimuli belonging to a more extensive set of unknown stimuli. At this point, it is important to mention that the captured EEG and the labeling of the P300 are susceptible for the user. This problem is aggravated due to the lack of frameworks that consider security aspects such as authentication, confidentiality, and data integrity. In this context, attackers could turn their attention to the BCIs to carry out malicious actions.

Motivating Cybersecurity Issues

This work is motivated by the limitations of current frameworks, which do not provide security mechanisms to ensure the integrity of transmitted data or users' privacy (Ghoneim et al., 2018). Many times, this leads to a malfunction of the actions carried out by the BCI or to leak sensitive information of the individual. Similarly, current EEG-based BCI frameworks do not provide authentication mechanisms, so an attacker could impersonate the legitimate user to adapt the BCI functionality with malicious data. Besides, there is no standard or specific protocol for the secure development of BCI applications, causing a significant weakness in the software and its interaction with the hardware in many current alternatives.

Contribution

To improve the previous challenges, this work designs and implements an intelligent and automatic framework, called from now SecBrain, that manages each phase of the BCI life cycle (communication and acquisition of EEG, data pre-processing, and P300 detection) to improve the limitations of existing BCI frameworks. SecBrain also considers the cybersecurity of the BCI life cycle, implementing security mechanisms to ensure the proper and secure framework functioning. The objective is to ensure data integrity and confidentiality throughout each phase of the BCI cycle and the secure storage of them afterward. For this purpose, the functionality is divided into several security layers. On the one hand, SecBrain encapsulates the EEG signal flows acquired by the BCI, ensuring the data confidentiality and integrity directly from the subject. This process is relevant since EEG travels from the headset equipped with electrodes to an external device where the data are acquired, processed, and stored, causing an attacker to manipulate the transmitted data or deliberately introduce new ones. On the other hand, SecBrain provides a secure scenario for BCI applications where visual stimuli predominate. The framework logic allows adapting the system in a personalized way according to the analysis purpose. It also guarantees the synchronization of stimuli with the EEG signal previously acquired by the BCI, including security mechanisms/capabilities. In this way, the aim is to avoid the materialization of malware in certain phases of the BCI cycle, affecting the acquired brain reading or denying the service in certain moments of the experiment. In order to measure the framework efficiency and effectiveness, this chapter proposes a scenario where an attacker performs different malware-based attacks on the proposed structure. The attacks contemplated are designed to affect the integrity of the data transmitted. In contrast, others are intended to infer the proper functioning of the BCI or manage the communication and interaction for the attacker's deliberation. These attack scenarios are applied to a specific use case, generating P300 potentials through the Oddball paradigm. This scenario is among the most common BCI applications as it provides a high level of neuronal information. This allows contrasting the security provided by SecBrain and the automatic detection measures.

The remainder of this chapter is structured as follows. The Background section presents the current state of the art regarding BCI, its benefits, and current cybersecurity issues. After that, the SecBrain Framework: Design and Deployments section introduces the design and implementation details of the proposed framework. In addition, a real experiment using SecBrain implementation is included. Section Future Research Directions highlights the current trend and future evolution of BCI, indicating possible opportunities in this area. Finally, the Conclusion section presents a summary of the chapter.

Background

Brain-Computer Interface (BCI) is a technology that establishes two-way communication between the brain and an external device. One of its applications is to capture the biometric signal produced by a subject's brain (Moreno et al., 2019). This signal is then interpreted and processed to give meaning to the information acquired. The main idea of this scenario is to analyze the signal produced and obtain its essential characteristics to finally transform it into a command or order that a computer can process and execute. Therefore, in many areas, such as medicine, it is considered a fundamental tool for treating patients.

Currently, other sectors, such as the leisure and entertainment sector, are taking great interest in using this technology. The interaction, the immersion provided, and, in short, the gameplay experience are fundamental pillars that BCI tries to improve by adapting its cycle to the purpose of the video game. Finkie et al. (2009) translated the brain signals into movements of a character within a video game. Alba et al. (2011) applied something like the previous one but in the mythical game "Pong" style. In recent years the use of BCI has been complemented with virtual reality. The main advantage is to improve the immersive visual experience of the subject and, consequently, enhancing the data obtained. In this sense, Fu et al. (2020) propose a cultural experience scenario, creating a room escape game using the EEG signal to interact virtually.

In cybersecurity, the use of this technology is also growing, intending to create new authentication mechanisms. Curran et al. (2016) used a commercial BCI, EarEEG, placed in the ear that allows for authentication based on tasks such as breathing with eyes closed, thinking of a song, or imagining a face. Rathi et al. (2021) proposed a robust authentication system based on EEG signals and the generation of the P300 potential during the visualization of different images, breaking with the traditional password and token schemes. The EEG signal generation is unique per subject making it a reliable and suitable system to protect assets. Finally, well-known cybersecurity attacks from network communications could be applied to BCI scenarios (Gupta et al., 2020).

BCI Lifecycle

The BCI maintains direct communication between the brain and a computer, opening a range of possibilities for interaction. Recording the brain signals using electrical activity is the most widely used technique in non-invasive systems. The electroencephalography technique or EEG is an excellent and inexpensive alternative (Badcock et al., 2013; Aydemir et al., 2015), with practically no risks and quite precise results (Millan et al., 2007; Polich et al., 1985). All this electrical activity produced will be transmitted to the computer, which will process and finally translate into a control command. A control command is a term given to a particular instruction that has been programmed or implemented in a computer. It carries out a functionality, for example, moving a prosthesis or a character within a video game. The literature gathers different proposals on structuring the phases or layers of the BCI life cycle. In this sense, López Bernal et al. (2021) proposed a bidirectional scheme, on the one hand, the neural data acquisition process and, on the other, brain stimulation. Both processes go through four phases: EEG signal generation, acquisition, processing, and end-user application.

Evoked Potentials

It is necessary to pay attention to the evoked potentials (Chiappa & Ropper, 1982, p. 1147) for reading brain signals. Event-related potentials (ERPs) are brain responses to sensory stimuli (visual, auditory, motor, or somesthetic) generated involuntarily by the brain. The normality or otherwise of these responses expresses the functional state of the visual, acoustic, motor, or somesthetic pathway examined. Since the signal is tiny (microvolts), it is necessary to give many stimuli to average the responses. These responses can reveal the cause of the discomfort suffered by a subject, which is why it has been considered necessary to carry out evoked potentials in their different modalities. In Alzheimer's disease, evoked potentials have been studied to determine the disease in patients. Na et al. (2020) have identified deficits in visual attention using pre-attentive ERPs in patients with the disease relative to a group of cognitively normal adults.

P300 and Utilities

One of the evoked potentials is the P300. The P300 wave is a positive deviation or increase in voltage directly related to the appearance of an event that provokes a subject's stimulus. This potential was first referred to as a long latency potential called the "text positive component". Later, Polich et al. (1996) defined it as P300 due to the 300ms latency in which the increase in voltage appeared in young subjects without psychic problems after the stimulation.

The Oddball paradigm is the technique that is usually used to obtain the P300 potential (Jang et al., 2011; Eligiusz Wronka et al., 2008). This procedure, located in the category of visual events, consists of showing a string of images to the subject with a frequency of approximately 250-500ms. About 10-20% are known or familiar.

This technique is based on a continuous sample of stimuli that could be cataloged as usual (Non-Target). Among these, one or more uncommon stimuli (Target) will appear (Donchin et al., 1979). The Oddball paradigm is based on the presentation of stimuli that are discordant to what is usually presented. These stimuli can be both sound (Cass et al., 1997) and visual (Choo & May, 2014). This procedure allows detecting when a trigger is recognized by the subject, creating a characteristic wave, the P300, instead of neutral waves generated by unfamiliar stimuli. With this premise, applications can be made that range from authentication by known images, spellers, or even to detect people with attention deficiencies.

Evoked potentials have been well studied to provide solutions to various problems. This research will be shown below, explaining what the P300 is about and how it is used. One of these investigations is that of "authentication", where it is intended to use the P300 potential for subject authentication using cognitive biometrics. It uses a series of letters, images, or colors, which only this subject knows. This work aims to protect, together with other methods, applications that need a high-security level.

Something similar aims to "authenticate faces", developing a system based on showing a series of human faces, both unknown and known, and studying the subject's response to them. In this way, it is possible to identify the individual who is trying to authenticate himself. Other interesting articles on this subject are Gupta et al. (2012) and Kaongoen et al. (2020). Another of the most widespread uses given to the evoked potential P300 is to detect neurodegenerative diseases by studying the latency and amplitude of the P300 wave. Some of the disorders can be Alzheimer's, schizophrenia, or Parkinson's.

Finally, some of the more varied uses that have been made of the potential evoked by P300 are subsequently commented. For example, Nurseitov et al. (2017) proposed the control of a robot, based on P300, which gave the possibility of ordering the robot to move in any of the four directions (left, right, forward, or backward). This can be extrapolated to the improvement of the quality of life of people with locomotion problems or reduced mobility, offering the possibility of moving a wheelchair (Iturrate et al., 2019) if necessary, or the opportunity to control a robot to assist these people as reduced mobility Arrichiello et al. (2017).

BCI Frameworks

This section compares the existing BCI frameworks, giving an overview of the characteristics of each solution (Table 1). The two main aspects that have been considered are (1) implementing one or more communications for the reception of data from the BCI platform and (2) the inclusion of a wide variety of filtering and signal processing applications in a personalized and straightforward way.

OpenBCI GUI (*The OpenBCI GUI*, 2020) is compatible with OpenBCI hardware. It implements substantial improvements in the final data representation, and it is compatible with LSL communications. Additionally, it provides the program source code and the ability to create custom modules that integrate with the desktop application. OpenViBe (*OpenViBE*, 2020) is the best alternative to launch pre-set experiments related to the Oddball paradigm. It offers schemes and customizable modules. Python MNE is the most used alternative in EEG signal processing, offering a high degree of modification. It also allows the use of complementary Python libraries to treat the data, apply filtering functions or noise applications to the signal for further study. Letswave (*Letswave7*, 2018), EEGLab (*EEGLAB*, 2020), and BCILab (*BCI Lab*, 2020) are complements to the Matlab (*MATLAB*, 2020) application. They are the most used alternatives for treating the data with Matlab, offering compatibility of import and export of the data. The most remarkable feature of these options is the pre-configuration already done of most of the filters.

Cybersecurity on BCI

Any device interconnected with another or towards the Internet is subject to possible attacks questioning cybersecurity. Several cyberattacks appear to extract sensitive information such as passwords, religious beliefs, political orientations, phone numbers, or credit card numbers (Lopez Bernal et al., 2020). According to the stimulus presented, most of these attacks are based on provoking a specific response in the brain. In this sense, Martinovic et al. (2012) carried out some experiments to steal critical subject information such as the bank 4-digit PIN code, data, and even the person's place of residence, in all of them using the generation of the P300 potential through visual stimuli.

The literature has not dealt in depth with the materialization of this kind of attacks, leading to insufficient protection and detection of threats. Meng et al. (2019) leave aside obtaining personal information from the subject to focus on the integrity of the captured data, applying deliberate modifications to alter them. Similarly, Sundararajan (2018) developed a laboratory scenario that executed tests with different attacks. These attacks were: 1) passive listening, which intercepted the data without the user being aware, 2) active interception, where it collected the data and could discard or resend it, 3) denial of service and 4) data modification, where it ordered the data, modified it and resent it to obtain a different response.

As can be seen, all of them addressed possible attacks on these devices to steal information or corrupt the interaction. The implementation of security mechanisms for BCI devices is scarcely addressed theoretically in the literature. In this context, Ajrawi et al. (2021) proposed a theoretical framework based on RFID to identify the subject's brain activity in real-time. The study focuses on the medical sector, deploying a scenario of EEG acquisition in patients. In short, it defines a theoretical approach that could improve and provide secure BCI applications. However, there is an absence of works presenting a practical implementation of active or proactive attack detection mechanisms and considering aspects such as the integrity of the transmitted data or the subject's privacy. In this sense, recent studies have reiterated the lack of cybersecurity in BCI devices and developed applications. Chaudhary et al. (2018) detailed the ethical and safety issues of commercial BCIs such as BioSemi Active or Emotiv EPOC. In particular, the authors analyzed the BCI development process and possible security measures needed to mitigate threats to end-user privacy.

Table 1. Comparative table between different frameworks in BCI.

Software	Programming language	Operating systems			Features	🔓
		Windows	Linux	Mac		
OpenBCI GUI	Java, Python, NodeJS	✔	✔	✔	1. Ease of use, representation, and obtaining the data. 2. High compatibility with OpenBCI Cyton. 3. Export to CSV or BDF+. 4. LSL and TCP/IP communication. 5. Friendly and straightforward GUI.	✘
OpenViBE	C++	✔	✔	✘	1. Education, high precision in mental commands, metrics, and facial expressions. 2. Compatibility with most BCI systems. 3. Export to CSV or OV. 4. Pre-established schemes to make P300 Speller, among other experiments.	✘
Python MNE	Python	✔	✔	✔	1. High degree of customization and modification of the signal, applied jointly with other scientific libraries like SciPy. 2. Complexity in signal alterations. 3. Ease of data segmentation in the function of the events produced. 4. An organization of the data is necessary to import/export. 5. Ability to introduce Machine Learning.	✘
Letswave	Matlab Toolbox	✔	✔	✔	1. Easy to use graphic interface. 2. Support for EEG/MEG measurements. 3. Import/Export of data from different sources (CSV, BDF, EDF, EEGLAB,...). 4. Statistical analysis of data and generation of adapted graphics.	✘
EEGLab	Matlab Toolbox	✔	✔	✔	1. EEG and MEG data processing. 2. ICA analysis tools. 3. Processing by time and frequency. 4. Export data in 20 different binary formats.	✘
BCILab	Matlab Toolbox	✔	✔	✔	1. Design, prototyping, testing, experimentation, and evaluation of BCI systems. 2. Extraction of signal characteristics. 3. Model-based machine learning prediction.	✘
SecBrain	Python	✔	✔	✔	1. Creation of secure scenarios adapted to the purpose of the BCI. 2. Analysis and processing of the EEG signal efficiently and synchronized with the stimuli of the experiments. 3. Use of the best pre-processing techniques and adaptation of the data provided by libraries such as MNE or SciPy. 4. Automatic detection of evoked potentials like P300. 5. Detection of threats affecting the confidentiality and integrity of transmitted and stored data.	✔

SECBRAIN FRAMEWORK: DESIGN, DEPLOYMENT AND EXPERIMENTS

The main objective of this section is to explain the design and implementation details of SecBrain, our framework able to capture the EEG signal through the BCI, pre-process it, and detect the P300. A use case is also presented to demonstrate the added-value and feasibility of SecBrain. Finally, this section also carries out adverse attacks on the EEG to examine its implications and the possibility of detecting them by SecBrain at any stage.

Use Case

The proposed use case presents a subject watching visual stimuli that are part of a video. As seen throughout this section, SecBrain monitors, acquires, and analyzes the EEG when the subject watches the video (containing known and unknown stimuli). Finally, through the P300, SecBrain automatically detects if each presented stimulus is known (Target) or not (Non-Target). For the creation of the video, the Oddball paradigm has been implemented, and two types of images are shown:

- Target image: it is shown at the beginning of the experiment and is the known stimulus. It will be repeated during the video, with a probability indicated at the beginning.
- Non-Target images: rest of the pictures shown in the video and represent the unknown stimuli. They generate the Non-Target signal in the capture of the EEG signal. This signal differs from that produced by the potential evoked by a viewing of the Target image.

The Non-Target images used in the creation of the video are random and meaningless for the subject. They belong to the categories of landscapes, animals, or unknown subjects. One of them is obtained as a target image and is shown at the beginning of the video. The Target image is the only one that is repeated several times randomly during the display.

In the previous scenario setup, the authors have performed three different experiments. In each experiment, wholly random and additional images are added, and another visual stimulus organization is established. SecBrain obtains random images, with the following implementation has been carried out with two different modes:

- Manual mode (Mode 1 onwards) allows the possibility of including the images that the framework administrator deems appropriate. This mode considers the dimensions of the monitor where the experiment so that they all have the same aspect ratio.
- Automatic mode (Mode 2 onwards). It allows obtaining different images to include in the experiment. This mode downloads some random images indicated as a parameter in the framework, one of which will be selected as Target, while the others will be included as Non-Target

For the implementation of Mode 2, *Unsplash* API (Unsplash, 2020) has been used to obtain random images of specific dimensions. All the photos have a random order along with the display. The proportion given to the type of target image is the determining factor for its appearance in the experiment developed. A ratio of 0.1 in an experiment with ten images implies one Target image and nine Non-Target images. To conclude, it is important to mention that the previous configuration setup is flexible and can be modified and configured at the beginning of the experiment.

Framework

This section details the design and implementation of SecBrain, whose objective is to create a secure and stable environment to develop scenarios based on the detection of P300 generated through visual stimuli. For that, the following phases of the BCI cycle (EEG acquisition, signal processing, and the identification of the P300) and the detection of possible threats during the process are considered. The conceptual design of the framework is shown in Figure 1.

Figure 1. A high-level diagram of SecBrain

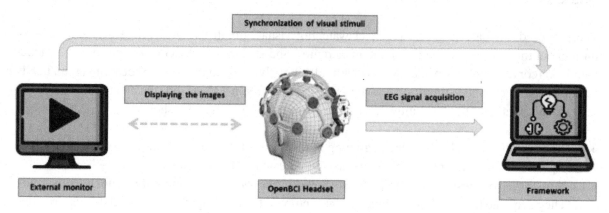

Signal Acquisition Component

The use of the Oddball paradigm in the experiments implies the recording of how each stimulus is shown to the subject and what type of stimulus has been shown (Target or Non-Target) to make later a detailed study of the generation of the P300. This section deals with the details of signal acquisition and its corresponding synchronization.

The EEG signal acquisition is performed through electrodes placed on the scalp thanks to a non-invasive BCI. This work has used the OpenBCI Headset, whose communication is performed via an external module provided by the OpenBCI software. The primary function of this module is to derive the data stream from the BCI controller and obtained by the USB Dongle (Figure 2) to an LSL communication. This adaptation allows the independence of the framework from the hardware used, with the possibility of using other BCIs different from the one used in this chapter. The framework controls each data flow originated by the BCI so that the acquisition phase will be closely related to the framework implementation. The framework generates an independent thread that remains listening to any EEG data stream for the reception of the EEG signal via LSL.

The Python library PyLSL is handy for this part of the acquisition. When it detects incoming data (Inlet), it receives it and stores it in a structured and organized way. The structure of Table 2 allows it to be correctly matched with the information received, so the acquisition of data for subsequent analysis is straightforward. The first two columns indicate time marks for each acquired sample, the first relative to the beginning of the experiment and the second one absolute (both in seconds). The following columns represent the value obtained per channel at each instant of time. The last column represents the Stream Stimulus, which maintains the synchronization of visual stimuli concerning each sample of the data, being the value 0 by default, 1 for a Target image, and 2 for a Non-Target image. The structure creation has been based on the definition of the ASCII standard in the representation of EEG data, the same format as when exporting raw data, stored in a *.txt* file, from the OpenBCI GUI. When the experiment starts, the framework proceeds to the synchronization of the visual elements shown on the screen with the EEG signal received by the thread through LSL. The signal-stimulus synchronization is done at run time, saving the synchronized data in internal structures.

Figure 2. OpenBCI Cyton hardware: left, different elements of the Cyton hardware; right, placement of the eight channels for acquisition

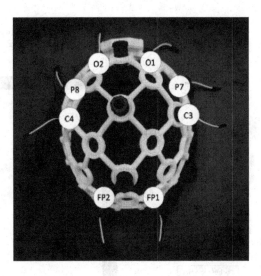

Table 2. Extract with the defined structure to store the EEG capture data

Time	Timestamp	FP1	...	O2	Stimuli type
82.435	1594894785.1193922	14415.1533203125	...	17168.91015625	0
82.439	1594894785.1193976	14379.2568359375	...	17215.15625	1
82.447	1594894785.5996578	14589.876953125	...	17114.439453125	0

SecBrain uses the epoch elements to synchronize the signal with each of the events produced during the experiment. Therefore, an epoch is a data structure that stores in a standard and synchronized way the following aspects: 1) EEG signal of each channel acquired by the computer and 2) events produced during the experiment display. The main advantage it offers is the representation of specific sections of the signal. Each segment will contain the event produced for further analysis. The framework has been initialized to obtain portions of the EEG signal that take as start 0.1 seconds before the event occurs and 0.8 seconds after (Figure 4). Also, it incorporates rejection parameters based on peak-to-peak amplitude. By default, a rejection parameter with a value of 100e-6 is applied to each electrode that intervenes at each time (Figure 5). A representation scheme is created to assign a value of 1 for Target and 2 for Non-Target; the value 0 will be the default for each one of the samples with no relation to the events. This procedure allows the different events produced to be differentiated and studied individually or compared between them. Figure 4 shows the first 20 of the 96 total periods stored by the framework in one of the acquisitions made. This type of independent representation will also help determine if the filters and treatments applied over the signal have reduced noise.

The attack scenario presented in Figure 3 focuses on the conceptual design of the framework. The figure details those areas that are vulnerable due to the use of malware. The first of these can be materialized in the communication between the BCI headset and the receiver placed in an external device. The second one is between the receiving device and the framework, where the external device infection

Figure 3. The proposed architecture and its possible attack regions in the acquired data—deployment of threat detection systems

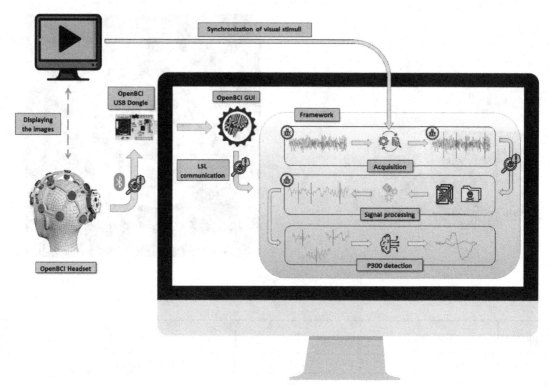

could cause severe data integrity and confidentiality problems. The third of these can occur during the process of synchronization and storage of the data.

The signal acquisition component is one of the main functionalities of the infrastructure. Therefore, it is compulsory to guarantee a minimum level of security on the device and during communication. Two different types of threats can occur. The first one materializes when the attackers know everything about the BCI application and know how they can affect its functionality. The second of these occurs when the attacker uses generic malware that attempts to spoil existing communication without considering the nature of the data transmitted and stored.

Regarding the first perspective, a more comprehensive range of possibilities is opened. In this sense, an attacker can deploy a system like the one provided by the BCI and generate an intermediate entity that negotiates the different BCI parameters. The BCI device would transmit information directly to an entity that is not legitimate, the definition of Man-in-the-Middle attacks. The receiving computer is infected with malware that passes itself off as legitimate software for receiving the data. This malware will capture all the data that the BCI sends, and along with the flow of images, the attacker could link the P300 provoked and obtain sensitive information from the subject. The modification of the data can be a triggering event in both scenarios. However, only in the first perspective, the attacker will enter the data needed to compromise the system to gain total control. The total system hijacking occurs when the attacker knows the process to be followed and what exactly would be the parameter that disturbs the proper functioning. Careful preparation of malware for the P300 scenario described above could lead to the generation of false P300s or the attenuation of these. In the same way that the data can be modified,

Figure 4. First twenty times of the EEG tagged signal: "1" for Target event and "2" for non-target

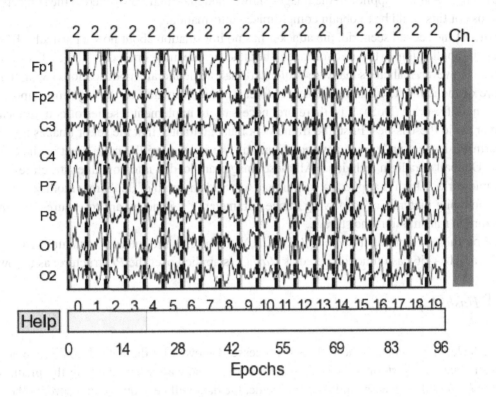

Figure 5. Times rejected by each channel of the EEG signal

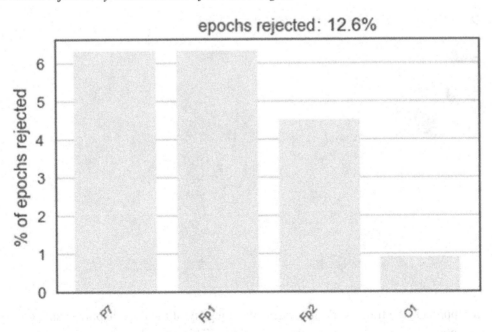

specific changes could be applied to the images shown, and the stimuli provoked in the subjects studied. The purpose of this could be to obtain compromised information.

In terms of the second scenario, the attacker has no information about how a particular BCI system works and its application. In this circumstance, the attackers are more limited in their ability to break into the system. However, malicious malware could start making deliberate modifications (without knowing the nature of the data). The main objective is to cause a malfunction of the legitimate application or even a denial of service (DoS). It is, therefore, necessary to implement a series of countermeasures to mitigate or avoid these issues. First, the framework must guarantee that the set of images introduced in the experiment has not undergone any modification. The images are the main asset of the experiment using the Oddball paradigm technique. All these images are loaded into container structures internally in the framework. A hash is applied to each image to avoid any kind of deliberate modification (adding images, removing pictures, or modifying image parameters). It is necessary to ensure the integrity of the structure in transmission and storage.

Based on these requirements, $PI = I_1, I_2, I_3, I_4, \ldots, N_N$ represents the internal structure of images. Additionally, a SHA-256 hash function noted as *Hash()*, is applied over the *PI* structure, as follows:

$$EI = \bigcup_1^n Hash(I_n)$$

Figure 6 shows graphically the flow and processes followed by the data. Initially, the acquisition module generates the *hash* of the set of images. In the same way, when showing the pictures on the screen, the *hash* will be generated. If both coincide, the data will be acquired and saved; otherwise, an alert will be generated.

Figure 6. Detect malware that attacks the integrity of images

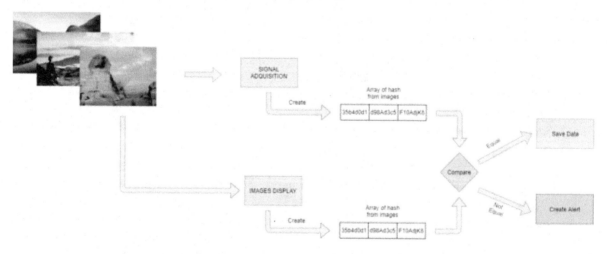

With this approach, the framework guarantees the integrity of the data displayed and, consequently, warns of any modification in the data to alert the subject. This procedure increases security in the use of BCI applications, as well as warns of the presence of any threat.

As a second procedure, the confidentiality of transmitted and received data is guaranteed. To this end, cryptographic processes are incorporated at the socket level. The framework gets information through the LSL protocol (Section Signal acquisition component). This protocol does not include security mechanisms, so it is convenient to treat the received data in such a way as to guarantee the clear reading of the data during the development of the experiment or in later phases of the BCI cycle, once the data have been stored.

The mechanism to be used is based on encrypting the data flows on reception. When the BCI obtains the voltage from each of the electrodes located on the scalp, the data collected from each electrode are sent to an external device that acquires the data. Sometimes the external device is simply an intermediate device that allows reaching the final device. The data encryption must be taken into account to avoid malware that allows sniffing of the data from contact with the first device.

In particular, the symmetric key algorithm, AES 256, has been used. Symmetric keys can be preselected by the user. The socket encryption functionality for received and transmitted data are also done in Python, as is the rest of the framework. The *Crypto library* of Python is used to generate random values employing the generator implemented in the *Random module* and all the related functionality for encryption and decryption in AES.

```python
def encrypt(self, data):
    raw = pad(data)
    iv = Random.new().read(AES.block_size)
    cipher = AES.new(self.key, AES.MODE_CBC, iv)
    return base64.b64encode(iv + cipher.encrypt(data))

def decrypt(self, data_enc):
    enc = base64.b64decode(data_enc)
    iv = enc[:AES.block_size]
    cipher = AES.new(self.key, AES.MODE_CBC, iv)
    return unpad(cipher.decrypt(data_enc[AES.block_size:]))
```

The encryption function receives the parameter data, which contains a received data stream. At the same time, *decrypt* receives the data encrypted for decryption and manipulation by the various processing and malware detection modules of SecBrain.

Padding is used as a filler system in each encrypted message. The aim is to hide identical patterns between different messages, eventually leading to security problems when carrying out statistical studies on the information exchanged.

The framework implementation also guarantees the user's privacy, protecting data visualization from entities external to the BCI headset and framework communication. The proposal has been identified as a feasible and necessary solution that can be used in addition to existing protocols such as LSL.

Signal Processing Component

Once the signal has been captured, the framework pre-processes it. This phase is crucial because once the raw data has been acquired, it is practically unreadable. Thus, it is necessary to use a series of methods to help make it easier to detect the P300. First, a noise filter is applied to the frequency 50Hz. Interference caused by the power supply on this frequency is avoided (the power supply operates at 50Hz in Europe). The next step is to apply a bandpass filter to limit the frequencies at which the P300 potential appears. A bandpass filter is used with the IIR method in the frequency range of 1-17 Hz. The documentation provided by the literature for its application has been followed, and the objective of obtaining a clean signal without eliminating vital information to capture the P300 potential.

To supplement the signal processing, ICA is used to separate the components that make up the EEG signal individually. The primary purpose is to reduce further the effect of noise on the data obtained. ICA suppresses those artifacts that remain in the signal after applying the previous filters (notch, bandpass) and affect the different channels, such as the flickers made during the experiment. Its operation is based on finding projections with high non-gaussianity. In this way, a decomposition of the signal is obtained, obtaining independent components.

Finally, to make the signal easier, a reduction of the signal samples is made (also called downsampling). The framework reduces the number of samples for each second. The downsampling ratio used to the EEG signal in this experiment has been 5. The signal will go from having 250 samples every second (250 Hz) to 50 samples every second (50 Hz).

Figure 7 shows a fragment of the same recently captured EEG signal and the one resulting from applying all the processing functions mentioned in this subsection.

Figure 7. EEG signal before and after applying all the functions of the signal processing component

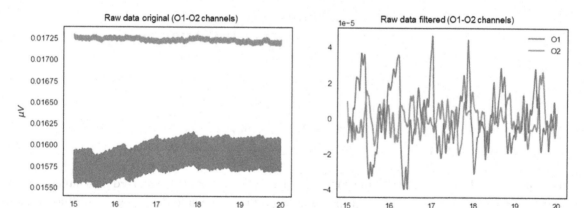

Although this process is a critical step in the BCI cycle functioning, the focus will be on the security risks involved. As in the previous phase, data can be compromised by third-party software or malware. For this reason, it is necessary to apply methods that offer integrity and confidentiality and prevent data from being stolen or modified.

It is necessary to check that the *hash* corresponds to the one generated in the acquisition phase. If it does not match, processing will be completed, and an alert will be displayed for a possible attack.

P300 Automatic Detection Component

In general, most applications involving BCI devices are aimed at detecting the P300, creating robust processes with various utilities. With its detection, it allows the development of robust applications for a variety of purposes. For this reason, it is essential to determine if one or more P300 potentials have been detected but even more so to determine if the signal has been compromised by introducing or attenuating these potentials. Therefore, the fundamental solution principle is to make a good and reliable detection of the P300 in specific EEG signal segments. In this way, SecBrain detects any deliberate manipulation of the signal that could affect the application functionality and, consequently, the device or person using the BCI.

SecBrain makes use of classifiers to carry out an automatic process and address this functionality. Classifiers belong to supervised computer-based learning that attempts to predict the outcome based on previous training models. If extrapolating the above definition to detect P300, these are classifiers explicitly trained to detect P300.

SecBrain uses several classifiers with specific correlation analysis algorithms for the detection of evoked potentials: Classifier I, use of scalar standardization algorithms and regressions; Classifier II, a model with a linear decision limit, generated by adjusting conditional class densities to the data and using Bayes' rule; Classifier III, the same operation as Classifier II but adding xDAWN as a spatial filter; Classifier IV, estimation of the covariance matrix of the possible potentials, spatial projection of the tangent and regressions; and Classifier V, with an analysis of the covariance matrix and classification by Minimum to Medium Distance.

A manual division of the labeled EEG signal data is made into two different sets to train the classifiers: training data and test, with proportions of 75% and 25%, respectively. The training data set (75%) has been cross-validated and stratified (due to the unbalance dataset). The *StratifiedShuffleSplit generator* (*StratifiedShuffleSplit, 2020*) determines the cross-validation split strategy. This strategy allows making ten partitions of the input data, forming ten different combinations. Each combination is divided into two data sets: training data and test data (with the same proportions as the previous division). While the first ones are used to train the classifiers, the latter is used to evaluate the accuracy of the given predictions. Figure 8 shows the supervised learning scheme followed. At this point, the cross-validator returns a set of scores obtained for each iteration and combination generated (10 scores per qualifier).

Figure 8. Supervised learning scheme on P300 detection.

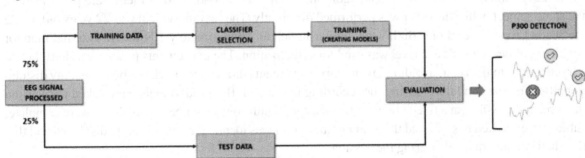

Having trained models allows identifying P300 evoked potentials in any experiment carried out automatically. Together with appropriate security measures, such as those implemented in SecBrain, the correct use of the BCI and the functionality it offers can be guaranteed.

Experiments

This section details a real experiment carried out to test the functionality of the SecBrain framework. After that, it will analyze that each phase of the framework has carried out its task correctly. In other words, it will check that a correct acquisition, processing, and detection of the P300 is performed.

The performed experiment follows the Oddball Paradigm technique to o2btain the P300 (Section Use case). The images used in the video creation are random and without any special meaning for the subject. They belong to the categories of landscapes, animals, or unknown subjects. One of them is obtained as a target image and is shown at the beginning of the video. Then, all the photos are organized, guaranteeing a brief and similar interval between them. The Target image is the only one that is repeated many times randomly during the display. Table 3 includes the parameters used in the construction and deployment of the experiment.

Table 3. Parameters used in the deployment of the experiment

Experiment parameter	Value
External monitor size	1920x1080
Approximate distance between subject and monitor	67 cm
Number of images used	150
Probability of appearance of the target image	6%
Display time of the target image at the beginning of the experiment	5 seconds
Interval time between images	0.250 seconds
Offset of each image	0.150 seconds
Variable jitter time	0.2

Three different experiments are carried out, in all of which the parameters mentioned above are applied. In each experiment, wholly random and additional images are added. Two of them were performed on the same subject, while the other was performed differently. The first individual was 22 years old, while the second was 23 years old. Both were similar in height, approximately 1.80m. An external monitor (Figure 1) at the subject's eye level was used for visualization. The participants posture was upright and perpendicular to the floor, avoiding involuntary movements or an uncomfortable position. Any distraction affecting the conditions during the recording is avoided. Both individuals were asked to focus on the screen, if possible, at a fixed point on the monitor. Finally, once the images displayed were complete, subjects were asked to say aloud the total number of images identical to that initially displayed and that they had counted mentally during the session.

It should be noted that during the experiment, SecBrain generates logs with the internal structure that is created to store the images in memory, the status of the security policies used during transmission as well as any error or alert during the acquisition process. From the beginning of the experiment, the data will be exchanged between the different components of the framework, producing the detection of the P300 always within the generated security perspective. Therefore, the results will be reliable, considering that no type of attacker has affected the data.

Once the experiment details have been described, it will be checked whether the framework has worked correctly. For this purpose, the Area Under the Curve (AUC) metric is used. This metric returns a score for each classifier indicating how well or poorly the classifier predicts new P300s that the classifiers have not used for training. Finally, the AUC values are averaged by the classifier, obtaining an average value AUC representing the classifier performance. Figure 9 shows the AUC value obtained when supplying the test assembly to each classifier.

The training results have been outstanding (Figure 8); it can detect P300 with an acceptable percentage (around 80% of AUC) of the P300 generated thanks to the set of images shown during the acquisition phase. Of all the classifiers, classifiers I and V (with AUC values of 0.812 and 0.817, respectively) stand out as the most promising.

Figure 9. AUC results of each classifier on the uncompromised signal.

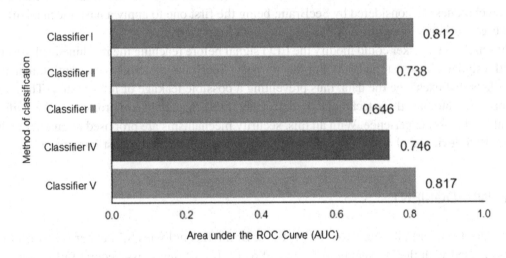

FUTURE RESEARCH DIRECTIONS

The BCI trend is to have an interconnected world where many BCI will share thoughts, feelings, or experiences. That is why cybersecurity is essential in the field of BCI. Possible future research could raise new malware applications with different behaviors whose purpose is to determine the accuracy in the detection of attacks. Another possibility would be to improve the existing infrastructure to provide scenarios with more sophisticated perimeter security scenarios.

The proposed solution provides a significant advance in cybersecurity on BCIs, which is currently almost non-existent. However, the viability of the future is notoriously low. The growth of distributed attack vectors and robust implementations in terms of offensive attacks means that potential attackers could overtake the proposed framework security.

Therefore, future research could pose new malware applications with different dynamics whose purpose is to determine the accuracy of threat detection. The use of more current malware-based attacks could be used to determine the framework potential for detection. Similarly, it could involve a renewal of the system to adapt to new requirements. Another possibility would be to improve the existing infrastructure to provide more sophisticated perimeter security scenarios. Therefore, cybersecurity opens an opportunity to enhance the BCI hardware to offer new types of more secure connections or the possibility of storing or generating cryptographic keys.

CONCLUSION

The benefits provided by BCIs are very varied, ranging from improving people's well-being to entertainment and leisure and security by providing new authentication techniques. However, these devices continuously deal with such compromised user's data and certain security aspects. The most relevant elements are mainly centered on the theft of sensitive data or the BCI control and its applications. In this context, the main contribution of this chapter is to design and implement an intelligent and secure framework, called SecBrain, for the detection of P300s generated by visual stimuli. For this purpose, different techniques are considered by SecBrain, being the first one to apply a hash mechanism to both the data used for image sampling and the data received from the EEG.

Additionally, an attacker could modify the EEG signal before reaching the machine in charge of processing the signal and detect the P300. For this purpose, SecBrain implements encryption mechanisms to the sockets that exchange the data, thus preventing a possible leakage of information. The SecBrain framework will automate these techniques to detect any threat that could compromise the BCI life cycle, deteriorating the user experience. With all this, security mechanisms are proposed to guarantee the safe use of the BCI devices and allow a first approach to a more reliable and robust infrastructure.

ACKNOWLEDGMENT

This work has been partially supported by (a) Bit & Brain Technologies S.L. under the project Cyber-Brain, associated with the University of Murcia (Spain), by (b) the Swiss Federal Office for Defense Procurement (armasuisse) with the CyberSpec (CYD-C-2020003) project, and by (c) the University of Zürich UZH.

REFERENCES

Ahn, M., Lee, M., Choi, J., & Jun, S. (2014). A Review of Brain-Computer Interface Games and an Opinion Survey from Researchers, Developers, and Users. *Sensors (Basel)*, *14*(8), 14601–14633. doi:10.3390140814601 PMID:25116904

Ajrawi, S., Rao, R., & Sarkar, M. (2021). Cybersecurity in Brain-Computer Interfaces: RFID-based design-theoretical framework. *Informatics in Medicine Unlocked*, *22*, 100489. doi:10.1016/j.imu.2020.100489

Al-Nuaimi, F. A., Al-Nuaimi, R. J., Al-Dhaheri, S. S., Ouhbi, S., & Belkacem, A. N. (2020). Mind Drone Chasing Using EEG-based Brain Computer Interface. *2020 16th International Conference on Intelligent Environments (IE)*, 1. 10.1109/IE49459.2020.9154926

Arrichiello, F., Di Lillo, P., Di Vito, D., Antonelli, G., & Chiaverini, S. (2017). Assistive robot operated via P300-based brain computer interface. *2017 IEEE International Conference on Robotics and Automation (ICRA)*, 1. 10.1109/ICRA.2017.7989714

Aydemir, O. (2015). Improving classification accuracy of EEG based brain computer interface signals. *2015 23nd Signal Processing and Communications Applications Conference (SIU)*, 1. 10.1109/SIU.2015.7130442

Badcock, N. A., Mousikou, P., Mahajan, Y., de Lissa, P., Thie, J., & McArthur, G. (2013). Validation of the Emotiv EPOC® EEG gaming system for measuring research quality auditory ERPs. *PeerJ*, *1*, e38. doi:10.7717/peerj.38 PMID:23638374

BCI Lab | Universidad de Granada. (2020). *BCI Lab*. http://www.ugr.es/%7Ebcilab/

Chaudhary, P., & Agrawal, R. (2018). Emerging Threats to Security and Privacy in Brain Computer Interface *International Journal of Advanced Studies of Scientific Research, 3*(12). https://ssrn.com/abstract=3326692

Chiappa, K. H., & Ropper, A. H. (1982). Evoked Potentials in Clinical Medicine. *The New England Journal of Medicine*, *306*(19), 1140–1150. doi:10.1056/NEJM198205133061904 PMID:7040957

Choo, A., & May, A. (2014). Virtual mindfulness meditation: Virtual reality and electroencephalography for health gamification. *2014 IEEE Games Media Entertainment*, 1. doi:10.1109/GEM.2014.7048076

Crea, S., Nann, M., Trigili, E., Cordella, F., Baldoni, A., Badesa, F. J., Catalán, J. M., Zollo, L., Vitiello, N., Aracil, N. G., & Soekadar, S. R. (2018). Feasibility and safety of shared EEG/EOG and vision-guided autonomous whole-arm exoskeleton control to perform activities of daily living. *Scientific Reports*, *8*(1), 1. doi:10.103841598-018-29091-5 PMID:30018334

Curran, M. T., Yang, J., Merrill, N., & Chuang, J. (2016). Passthoughts authentication with low cost EarEEG. *2016 38th Annual International Conference of the IEEE Engineering in Medicine and Biology Society (EMBC)*, 1979-1982. 10.1109/EMBC.2016.7591112

Donchin, E. (1979). Event-related Brain Potentials: A Tool in the Study of Human Information Processing. *Evoked Brain Potentials and Behavior*, 13–88. doi:10.1007/978-1-4684-3462-0_2

EEGLAB. (2020). https://sccn.ucsd.edu/eeglab/index.php

Finke, A., Lenhardt, A., & Ritter, H. (2009). The MindGame: A P300-based brain–computer interface game. *Neural Networks*, *22*(9), 1329–1333. doi:10.1016/j.neunet.2009.07.003 PMID:19635654

Fu, H.-L., Fang, P.-H., Chi, C.-Y., Kuo, C., Liu, M.-H., Hsu, H. M., Hsieh, C.-H., Liang, S.-F., Hsieh, S., & Yang, C.-T. (2020). Application of Brain-Computer Interface and Virtual Reality in Advancing Cultural Experience. *2020 IEEE International Conference on Visual Communications and Image Processing (VCIP)*, 351–354. 10.1109/VCIP49819.2020.9301801

Ghoneim, A., Muhammad, G., Amin, S. U., & Gupta, B. (2018). Medical image forgery detection for smart healthcare. *IEEE Communications Magazine*, *56*(4), 33–37. doi:10.1109/MCOM.2018.1700817

Gupta, B. B., Perez, G. M., Agrawal, D. P., & Gupta, D. (2020). *Handbook of computer networks and cyber security*. Springer. doi:10.1007/978-3-030-22277-2

Gupta, C. N., Palaniappan, R., & Paramesran, R. (2012). Exploiting the P300 paradigm for cognitive biometrics. *International Journal of Cognitive Biometrics*, *1*(1), 26. doi:10.1504/IJCB.2012.046513

Iturrate, I., Antelis, J. M., Kubler, A., & Minguez, J. (2009). A Non-invasive Brain-Actuated Wheelchair Based on a P300 Neurophysiological Protocol and Automated Navigation. *IEEE Transactions on Robotics*, *25*(3), 614–627. doi:10.1109/TRO.2009.2020347

Jang, Y. S., Ryu, S. A., & Park, K. C. (2011). Analysis of P300 Related Target Choice in Oddball Paradigm. *Journal of Information and Communication Convergence Engineering*, *9*(2), 125–128. doi:10.6109/jicce.2011.9.2.125

Kaongoen, N., Yu, M., & Jo, S. (2020). Two-Factor Authentication System Using P300 Response to a Sequence of Human Photographs. *IEEE Transactions on Systems, Man, and Cybernetics. Systems*, *50*(3), 1178–1185. doi:10.1109/TSMC.2017.2756673

Letswave7 | Letswave.cn. (2018, July 17). https://letswave.cn/

Liberati, G., da Rocha, J. L. D., van der Heiden, L., Raffone, A., Birbaumer, N., Olivetti Belardinelli, M., & Sitaram, R. (2012). Toward a Brain-Computer Interface for Alzheimer's Disease Patients by Combining Classical Conditioning and Brain State Classification. *Journal of Alzheimer's Disease*, *31*(s3), S211–S220. doi:10.3233/JAD-2012-112129 PMID:22451316

López Bernal, S., Huertas Celdrán, A., Martínez Pérez, G., Barros, M. T., & Balasubramaniam, S. (2021). Security in Brain-Computer Interfaces: State-of-the-Art, Opportunities, and Future Challenges. *ACM Computing Surveys*, *54*(1), 35. doi:10.1145/3427376

Martinovic, I., Davies, D., & Frank, M. (2012). On the feasibility of side-channel attacks with brain-computer interfaces. *Proceedings of the 21st USENIX Security Symposium*, 143-158.

MATLAB - El lenguaje del cálculo técnico. (2020). *MATLAB & Simulink*. https://es.mathworks.com/products/matlab.html

Moreno, I., Batista, E., Serracin, S., Moreno, R., Gómez, L., Serracin, J., Quintero, J., & Boya, C. (2019). Los sistemas de interfaz cerebro-computadora basado en EEG: características y aplicaciones. *I+D Tecnológico, 15*(2), 13–26. doi:10.33412/idt.v15.2.2230

Na, E., Lee, K., Kim, E. J., Bae, J. B., Suh, S. W., Byun, S., Han, J. W., & Kim, K. W. (2021). Pre-attentive Visual Processing in Alzheimer's Disease: An Event-related Potential Study. *Current Alzheimer Research*, *17*(13), 1195–1207. doi:10.2174/1567205018666210216084534 PMID:33593259

Nurseitov, D., Serekov, A., Shintemirov, A., & Abibullaev, B. (2017). Design and evaluation of a P300-ERP based BCI system for real-time control of a mobile robot. *2017 5th International Winter Conference on Brain-Computer Interface (BCI)*, 1. 10.1109/IWW-BCI.2017.7858177

OpenViBE | Software for Brain Computer Interfaces and Real Time Neurosciences. (2020, December 10). *OpenViBE*. http://openvibe.inria.fr/

Polich, J., & Heine, M. (1996). P300 topography and modality effects from a single-stimulus paradigm. *Psychophysiology*, *33*(6), 747–752. doi:10.1111/j.1469-8986.1996.tb02371.x PMID:8961797

Polich, J., Howard, L., & Starr, A. (1985). Effects of Age on the P300 Component of the Event-related Potential From Auditory Stimuli: Peak Definition, Variation, and Measurement. *Journal of Gerontology*, *40*(6), 721–726. doi:10.1093/geronj/40.6.721 PMID:4056328

Rathi, N., Singla, R. & Tiwari, S. (2021). A novel approach for designing authentication system using a picture based P300 speller. *Cogn Neurodyn*. doi:10.1007/s11571-021-09664-3

Simon, A. J., Bernstein, A., Hess, T., Ashrafiuon, H., Devilbiss, D., & Verma, A. (2011). P1-112: A brain computer interface to detect Alzheimer's disease. *Alzheimer's & Dementia*, *7*(4S_Part_4), S145–S146. doi:10.1016/j.jalz.2011.05.391

StratifiedShuffleSplit — scikit-learn 0.24.0 documentation. (2020). *Scikit-Learn*. https://scikit-learn.org/stable/modules/generated/sklearn.model_selection.StratifiedShuffleSplit.html

Sundararajan, K. (2017). *Privacy and security issues in Brain Computer Interface* [Unpublished master's thesis]. Auckland University of Technology, Auckland, New Zealand.

The OpenBCI GUI · OpenBCI Documentation. (2020). *OpenBCI*. https://docs.openbci.com/docs/06Software/01-OpenBCISoftware/GUIDocs

Unsplash. (2020). *Unsplash API Documentation*. https://unsplash.com/documentation

Wronka, E., Kaiser, J., & Coenen, A. M. (2008). The auditory P3 from passive and active three-stimulus oddball paradigm. *Acta Neurobiologiae Experimentalis*, *68*(3), 362–372. PMID:18668159

KEY TERMS AND DEFINITIONS

Brain-Computer Interface: BCI is a direct communication pathway between an enhanced or wired brain and an external device.

Electroencephalographic Signal: It is a test that detects brain electrical activity using small metal discs (electrodes) fixed on the scalp.

Event-Related Potential: Evoked potentials are diagnostic techniques that, using sensory stimuli (visual, auditory, or tactile electrical) and the recording of the brain responses that they provoke, assess the stimulated sensory pathways' integrity.

Framework: It is a standardized set of concepts, practices, and criteria for addressing a particular problem that serves as a reference for tackling and resolving new issues of a similar nature.

Hash Function: It is a mathematical function that converts a given input into a compressed output; the generated value is unique for the same data.

P300 ERP: An evoked potential that can be recorded by electroencephalography as a positive voltage deflection with a latency of about 300 ms in the EEG.

Visual Stimuli: This test is used to assess the functional state of the visual system. It records the variations in potential in the occipital cortex caused by a trigger on the retina.

Chapter 11
A Study on Data Sharing Using Blockchain System and Its Challenges and Applications

Santosh Kumar Smmarwar

National Institute of Technology, Raipur, India

Govind P. Gupta

 https://orcid.org/0000-0002-0456-1572
National Institute of Technology, Raipur, India

Sanjay Kumar

National Institute of Technology, Raipur, India

ABSTRACT

Blockchain since 2009 has been gaining more popularity in various fields to use in numerous applications to overcome the security issues such as privacy, transparency, and mutability of data in the process of data sharing. Process of data sharing has many addressed and unaddressed challenges such as information encryption and decryption, data authentication, storage security, latency time, transfer speed of data, detecting malicious nodes, prevent the computer system from attacks, trust in the sharing process. In this chapter, the authors have reviewed the data sharing paper based on blockchain technology and presented the analysis of various techniques used in the information sharing process. The comprehensive analysis is categorizing in the following areas like incentive mechanism-based work, IoT-based data sharing, healthcare data sharing, and internet of vehicle data sharing using blockchain.

INTRODUCTION

In the recent era of Big Data development with the advancement in information and communication technology the rate of growing data and digital resources has been grown exponentially. Storing these data has become important for customer and business organizations (Feng et al., 2019). One of the ways to control the growth rate of data to reduce the same information creation is through the data sharing

DOI: 10.4018/978-1-7998-7789-9.ch011

Copyright © 2022, IGI Global. Copying or distributing in print or electronic forms without written permission of IGI Global is prohibited.

process in various organizations such as health care, academic, financial sector, etc. Data sharing has many uses in various fields such as healthcare, the internet of things, smart devices, and internet of vehicles, supply chains, and logistic networks. In data sharing, secure data sharing is necessary to achieve security goals like confidentiality, integrity, availability, authentication, transparency, and privacy of the data. These problems can be overcome by using blockchain technology in making data sharing transparent, immutable, decentralized storage, integrity protected, and confidentiality. The feature of transparency and immutability of blockchain made it most popular to deploy or integrate into secure data sharing. Blockchain technology is based on the three pillars that are distributed ledger, peer-to-peer communication, and consensus protocol. These are the core of this technology that makes it more secure and transparent (McGhin et al., 2019). In this survey study, we have reviewed the blockchain used data sharing papers and analyses various methods used by the early researcher for secure data sharing to resolve the privacy concern by using some cryptographic techniques.

OUR CONTRIBUTION

In this research paper we have reviewed the work of data sharing using blockchain technology, to get a research trends of various security mechanism used in blockchain for information sharing. We found that in our study most of the author described comprehensive overview of secure data sharing by proposed method such as incentive mechanism, privacy preserving scheme, dynamic data access control policy, secret sharing schemes and some attribute based encryption technique. In this paper we demonstrated the summary of existing work and methods used in blockchain to secure data sharing. Shown existing work, pros and cons of early research work in areas of healthcare data sharing and IoT device-based data sharing, incentive-based data sharing and various industrial application.

MOTIVATION

As mentioned above security challenges faced by centralized authority such as single point of failure may lead to the collapse of all data, high sharing cost, reduce manual verification (Goyal et al., 2018), reduce wastage of time, brings transparency and immutability in the system encourage us to work on secure data sharing among the peer to peer or decentralize environment by integrating blockchain technology and smart contact functionality (Mohanta et al., 2019). Since the inception of blockchain technology came into existence these have brought some potential solutions that may be overcome by using blockchain in various emerging fields of information technology.

OVERVIEW OF BLOCKCHAIN TECHNOLOGY

Blockchain is distributed ledger technology initially developed for cryptocurrency purposes like bitcoin by an unknown person named Satoshi Nakamoto in 2009(Feng et al., 2019), (McGhin et al., 2019). It is a decentralized system of digital ledger stored the synchronized copy of data. The blockchain system is based on asymmetric cryptography where two keys, a public key for device identification and a private key for signing transactions used (Goyal et al., 2018),. Blockchain is a chain of the block, each block linked to the next block via hash value in chronological order. Blockchain is supported by a combination of three technologies that are distributed ledger technology, peer-to-peer network, and consensus protocol among all nodes (Mohanta et al., 2019). In decentralized, ledger block is added through consensus mechanism among nodes in the blockchain network. There is some of the popular consensus protocol used in blockchain mining as proof of work (POW), Proof of stake (PoS), and Practical Byzantine Fault Tolerance (PBFT) protocol. This is the most popular technology in recent times used by industry and academia nowadays. It has the characteristics of transparency, immutability, decentralization, anonymity (Hasselgren et al., 2019). The simple blockchain diagram has depicted below where every block is added from its previous block through hash value in a chronological way.

Figure 1. Structure of blockchain

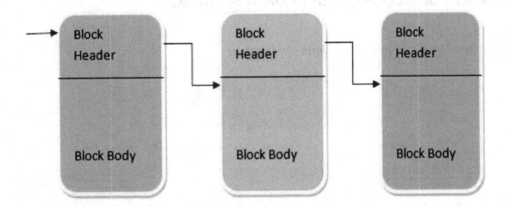

CLASSIFICATION OF BLOCKCHAIN

- **Public Blockchain**: Public blockchain is decentralizing networks to have more security. In this, ledgers are visible to all users who are connected to public networks. Anyone is free to join the network and add a block to the ledger (Xu et al., 2017). The most frequently used example is bitcoin and ethereum.
- **Private Blockchain:** In a private blockchain only selected nodes are allowed to join the network and add the data to the digital ledger. This allows anyone to view the ledger of data for example hyperledger fabric (Dinh et al., 2017).
- **Consortium Blockchain**: It is a combination of a group of the organization located at a different location (Dib et al., 2018). Only predefined organizations communicate, verify, and append-only transactions to the distributed digital ledger (Gai et al., 2019).

PROPERTIES OF BLOCKCHAIN

There are the following properties of blockchain technology that make it a powerful system to use in various fields as a solution (Liu et al, 2019).

- **Autonomous**: Autonomous property of blockchain makes it free from third party's control. Anyone can enter into the network verify and append transactions to the blockchain database.
- **Distributed**: in this, once the block confirms by all the peer's entities by some proof of mechanism then it is added only to the ledger. It works based on peer-to-peer infrastructure.
- **Immutability**: Immutability means no modification is possible in the block, once the block happened to the ledger. It would reflect all nodes in the global ledger.
- **Decentralize**: decentralization property makes the elimination of third parties involved in processing the transaction, reduces the cost, time and brings transparency among the nodes.
- **Anonymity**: this property hides the user identity in the blockchain network so that no node in the network trusts other nodes or its peer node.

APPLICATION OF BLOCKCHAIN IN DATA SHARING

Figure 2. Generalize diagram of blockchain applications

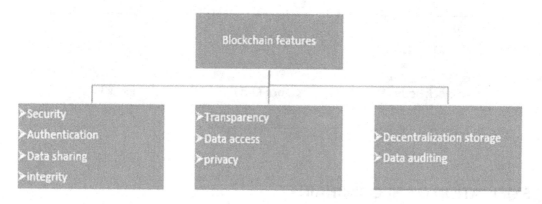

Blockchain technology has potential industrial application in many fields such healthcare industry, smart transportation, finance sectors, E-governance, food supply chain and many more in data sharing to brings the transparency, immutability, traceability and integrity as well. Blockhain technology can be useful in reducing the cost of production by using integrated smart contract facility and eliminates the central control of data. In healthcare sector it may provide the secure access of data sharing with greater transparency among different hospital globally to provide quick treatment to the patients. The finance sector can be achieved with less number fraudulent activities by using blockchain in transactional process. In smart transportation blockchain can support transparent, secure tracking of vehicles and brings transparency in insurance work to prevent illegal claim. The E-governance sector suffered from lack of transparency, so it also has wide applicability in this sector to provide secure authentication, data privacy and prevent fake data auditing. Similarly for other sectors also blockchain has various industrial application in terms of transparence, security, decentralization storage, integrity and immutability (Dubovitskaya et al., 2020).

THE ARCHITECTURE OF BLOCKCHAIN IN DATA SHARING

Figure 3. Simple architecture of blockchain data sharing

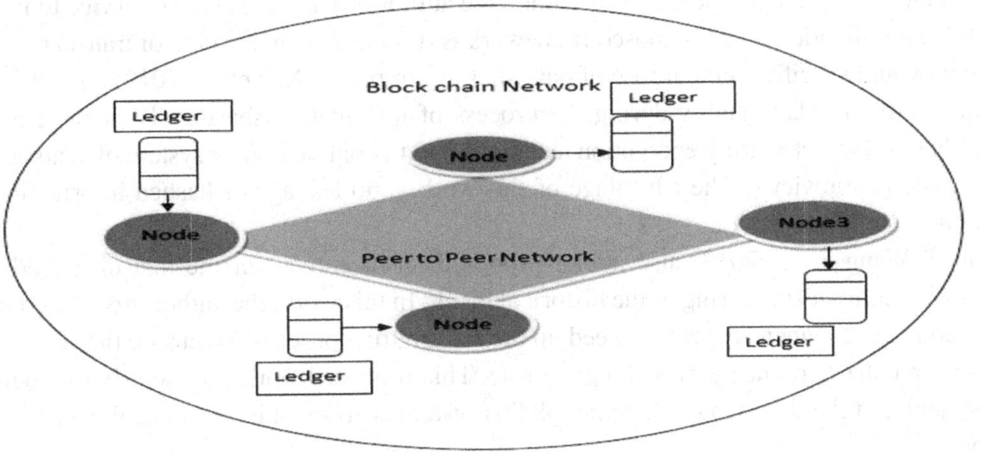

Figure 3 is showing the generalized representation of blockchain-based data sharing. Communication among peer-to-peer nodes is being done through the Node1, Node2, Node3, and Node4. Each node has its own ledger to store the data and installed with a software protocol is known as the smart contract which is automatic executable software code that runs after the condition is satisfied. The architecture is consisting of four users each having their local database to share data into the blockchains distributed ledgers. In the further section, we have mentioned the summary of our study of previous work done in the field of data sharing and made the pros and cons of used techniques in their work. Table 1 shows that papers related to blockchain-based data sharing, table 2 shows that the summary of blockchain used in the healthcare domain, table 3 indicates that blockchain is used in IoT data sharing.

LITERATURE SURVEY

In this survey of data sharing based on a blockchain platform, we have comprehensively reviewed papers on data sharing based on cloud data computing, Internet of Things (IoT), healthcare data, internet of vehicles, and blockchain-based platform for secure data sharing.

SURVEY BASED ON INCENTIVE MECHANISM

In paper (Bhaskaran et al., 2018) the work of the author has based on a user-associated consent-driven mechanism, in which a double-blind data-sharing approach is used for KYC (know your customer) validation using a blockchain system for banking institutions. This provides the dynamic access control of data sharing. It reduces the time and cost of manual verification. It has some drawbacks such as scalability issues, limited storage, and low transactional throughput.

In the paper (Shrestha et al., 2018) author proposed a decentralized data sharing framework based on blockchain for incentivizing data owners with digital tokens, author introduced blockchain with a smart contract concept for incentivizing participants in sharing their data and reward digital tokens. This approach of data sharing allows only the interested data seekers and ensures the data owner of misusing their data by illegal users. In this model, the author brought the escrow service to manage the user with legal obligations. The proposed framework is designed with due care of transparency, access control policy and specifies the purpose of data sharing. In paper (Naz et al., 2019) author focused on data authenticity and data quality during the process of information sharing. To achieve this author used the Shamir's secret sharing encryption technique and the online review system of Watson analyzer to identify the fake reviews. The advantage of this work is no leakage of hashed information, lowest computation time in encryption.

In paper (Wang et al., 2019) also author proposed an incentive scheme that discussed boosting blockchain-based IoT data sharing of the historical block. In this work, the author used the coin-locking strategy and micro-payment system to speed up the transmitting process. To ensure the security of data Shamir's secret sharing scheme played a great role. This proposed work can identify the malicious or dishonest nature of the sharing nodes. Although this system is efficient it has some high bandwidth cost limitations.

In the paper (Xuan et al., 2020) author presented an incentive mechanism for secure data sharing. This incentive method is based on evolutionary game theory which encourages participants to share their data securely and establish trust among the user who wants to share data to the blockchain-based secure platform. In addition to the game, theory the author applied the evolutionarily stable strategy and symmetric game theory to predict the most trustable sharing node among the various participants. However, this method has some limitations of data size and quality of data obtains by the recipient.

SURVEY BASED ON ACCESS CONTROL AND ENCRYPTION METHOD

In (Wang et al., 2017) author addressed the problem of conventional resource sharing in government departments such as efficiency, reliability, and security. These issues could be solved by the emerging blockchain technology. In this work, the author proposed the blockchain concept on government information, asset detail, resource sharing system to improve its reliability and security through the features of transparency, immutability, and traceability, and decentralization network of blockchain. This technology reduces the cost of implementation of sharing process than the traditional approach. However, this technology needs to be enhanced for the large scalable network in government setup and optimize the efficiency as well as the performance of the system. The work (Gupta & Gupta, 2017) has been discussed about the web application threats and vulnerabilities that may cause the major disruption in using the web application among various organizations. The proposed work concerns the potential security flaws and measures the threat.

In paper (Nakasumi et al., 2017) author presented the solution to solve the problem of double marginalization and information inconsistency in supply chain management. This system uses blockchain and homomorphic encryption techniques to provide transparency, immutability, traceability to user data. In this system author also added legal and authentic regulatory decisions of collecting data, storing, and sharing sensitive information. With the use of blockchain technology at supply chain it minimizes complex problem such as capacity risk in supply chain and improves the supply chain efficiency. It also increases the demand forecasting of consumers up to some extent. In the future, this solution needs to be bringing some incentive mechanism to handle the capacity risk and encourage users in sharing information.

In paper (Zhang et al., 2018) author focused on the privacy threat of data stored on the cloud due to the lack of processing power and storage capacity of IoT devices. To overcome these threats of data stealing and security author proposed architecture combined with the functionality of privacy preservation and authorized fine-grained user control access. In this work author used two types of method that is the attribute-based signature (ABS) and ciphertext-policy attribute-based encryption (CP-ABE). The ABS is used to provide fine-grained access control that identifies users or devices and attribute of signature instead of other signature schemes like ECDSA (Elliptic curve digital signature algorithm).

In the paper (Wang et al., 2018), the author discussed issues in existing data sharing models such as transparency and traceability methods. To improve these issues author presented the blockchain technology as a new data-sharing scheme. In which the author introduced the concept of the double-chain structure of blockchain, these double structure concepts differentiate between original data storage and transaction data. The first structure is responsible for storing original data and the second is for transaction data. To make reliable and safe sharing author used the proxy re-encryption technique.

In (Rawat et al., 2018) author presented the information sharing framework for cybersecurity infrastructure to prevent, detect, and respond to cyber attackers. The Cyberspace world is facing the ongoing challenge of safeguard confidential information and critical assets from potential future attacks. The proposed architecture known as ishare uses blockchain technology to share cyber threat information securely, reliably, and transparently among multiple organizations. The ishare framework is captured constantly high-resolution cyber-attack information to prevent IT resources from being compromised by an attacker. The proposed framework aimed at providing the procedure of transaction in ishare, cyber-attack detection and sharing information, deploying cyber-defense solutions and updates. To analyzes, the proposed framework author used the one-way-attack, two-way attack, and Stackelberg game for cyber-attack and defense analysis approach for security performance.

In (Cash et al., 2018) author presented a two-tier blockchain model consist of permission and permission-less blockchain to analyze the computing power of proof of work consensus algorithm and Proof of Authority protocol algorithm on ethereum platform. The environment used in work is Mac OS and Ubuntu Linux operating system. the result analysis shows the better performance of PoA algorithm on permissioned blockchain in term of constant or no change in block count on both operating systems when the number of nodes increases. In permission, blockchain required less computation power for consensus algorithm than permission-less. However, the less computation of permissioned blockchain may possess the threat of malicious users due to its less computing power required by consensus protocol. So this needs to establish reliable and strong trust among nodes.

In paper (Wang et al., 2019) author addressed the problem of data sharing flexibility where some of the public-key encryption with access control (PEAC) schemes are not able to control the encryption easily on both sides by the data owner. So in this work author proposed the functional broadcast encryption (FBE) to control the file-based encryption and receiver-based encryption simultaneously. This FBE technique can share the set of the file to a group of users. FBE is an expansion of the PEAC scheme. It is more efficient, flexible, feasible in terms of technically, economically and cloud storage performance while PEAC has storage overhead costs.

In (Shrestha et al., 2019) author has shown the concern over online services used by a user in the travel domain, addressed the privacy concern of user's data collected by travel agencies. In this paper, the author proposed the framework of user-controlled privacy-preserving to user's data while using online services of hotel booking systems through blockchain technology. This model is developed on a multichain framework to control the user profile data like name, nationality, birth date, contact phone number, address of the user, and purpose of travel. The multichain framework relies on the public key encryption technique. Multichain is used to restrict access to data by authorized users only. Multichain is a kind of private blockchain to maintain the privacy and access policy of data

In (Wu et al., 2019) author presented the efficient, effective, and user-controlled privacy-preserving traceable attribute-based encryption scheme in blockchain environment to protect the data integrity and non-repudiation of transactions. The data-sharing environment poses some security threats of cracking the secret key and leakage of sensitive information in a distributed environment, so to prevent these challenges author proposed the pre-encryption technology to improve the efficiency of attribute-based encryption (ABE), this pre-encryption technique does the necessary pre-calculation before the message to be encrypted is well known. The attribute bloom filter (ABF) is used in this scheme to determine the existence of an attribute or element in the set and hide the attributes in an anonymous access control scheme. To prevent the cracking of the secret key author combined the user's signature and the main master secret key of Attribute Authority in the user's master secret key.

In (Samuel et al., 2019) author presented the privacy and security concern to achieve efficient services by service providers in data sharing. Because huge data is generated by multiple smart home appliances that possess privacy and security threats and lacking fair data sharing which reduces the transparent participation of users. so given the author of the above issue proposed a fair data sharing scheme to encourage user participation based on their reputation score by using the PageRank mechanism in this work, the Pagerank mechanism provides the authenticity of node and adds block into the ledger.

In paper (Eltayieb et al., 2020) author has pointed out the drawback of the traditional cloud storage system of data sharing that poses the service availability, centralize information database, high running operational cost, and privacy concerns. To come out of this concern author proposed the integrated concept of blockchain consists of attribute-based encryption to make the secure cloud environment for information exchange. In this survey work, the concept of a smart contract is used to provide storage efficiency in the cloud atmosphere. In this work, the author achieved the confidentiality and integrity of data by using the concept of a secret sharing scheme and access tree.

In (Rahman et al., 2020) author proposed a framework based on Accountable cross-border data sharing, in this work author, presented a global cloud platform connected to the security gateway of different regions that allows data sharing among different countries securely. This framework has the feature of penalty for misbehaving nodes or entities in the sharing process. The authenticity of data is verified by the Elliptic curve digital signature algorithm. The framework consisted of three entities such as data sender, data receiver, and any entity or party. This platform allows the sharing based on the under relaxed trust assumption on sender and receiver. The author in (Sumathi, & Sangeetha, 2020) provides the concepts of blockchain in banking system to make efficient and secure storage with distributed ledger property of blockchain. Author highlights the risk of data center failure can be overcome by using decentralize system of blockchain and it provides the immutability in data modification. The author in (Mohan, & Gladston, 2020) proposed the work for cloud data auditing with help of merkle tree and blockchain to maintain the integrity, transparency and immutability. The blockchain store transaction in distributed form, so that it is difficult to modify the data by unauthorized users.

SURVEY BASED ON HEALTHCARE DATA SHARING SCHEME

In the paper (Amofa et al., 2018) author has shown challenges for health information exchanges and the inability to control the data once has been transmitted such as privacy and integrity. The problem of data access control discourages the participants from sharing the health data. For this author proposed a blockchain-based system framework for secure control and sharing data among different hospitals. This is done by pairing-based user-generated acceptable use policies by using the smart contract. This framework minimizes the threat to data after sharing. In this work, the author used the cryptographic key method and smart contract to define the access level of a person's data. By this approach, the author reduced the financial cost of managing data, improve the efficiency of accessing health data, provide secure distribution of data, and has low latency. However, this proposed model has scalability problems.

In (Guo et al., 2018) author address, the issues of authenticity of electronic health record (EHR) placed inside on blockchain. So to prove the validity or authenticity of EHR, the author presented the secured attribute-based ensured signature scheme with more than one authority. In this scheme, the secret pseudorandom function seeds are used among the multiple entities that prevent the collision attack. The computational bilinear Diffie-Hellman technique is used to achieve no modification and complete privacy, the integrity of attribute signer. The ABS is secure in the random oracle model. This scheme improves the performance and cost of medical data sharing among many authorities. The prime objective of the ABS scheme is to prove the validity of EHR data.

In (Wang et al., 2018) author presented the framework of a secure cloud-assisted EHR system by using Attribute cryptosystem along with blockchain to reach confidentiality, integrity, authentication, and fine-grained access control of data. This model integrates attribute-based encryption followed by identity-based encryption (IBE) to encrypt the patient secret data. The identity-based signature (IBS) is used to provide the digital signature for the authenticity of EHR data. This scheme combined all the techniques into a single one to achieve different functionality this known as attribute-based/identity-based encryption and signature(C-AB/IB-ES). Cloud storage provides fast transmission, file sharing, data storing space, minimum cost, and efficient access.

In paper (Thwin et al., 2018) author analyzed the personal health record system (PHR) in regards to blockchain properties that may arise the concern of privacy, integrity as well as confidentiality due to the transparency property of blockchain. The author also described some of the other issues of blockchain such as concern of storage, privacy aspect, user consent revocation, model performance, energy cost, and scalability. To resolve some of the above-mentioned problems such as on-chain data privacy; limited storage author used the Shamir's secret sharing data scheme by using the concept of proxy re-encryption technique to ensure the privacy concern of PHR. the authenticity is ensured by verified signature before storing data on the blockchain and all the data are inclusive with the signature of gateway server on the blockchain. This model also considered the availability of data by storing only meta-data on blockchain nodes and privacy concerns by using a fine-grained access control policy. In this access control policy, the encryption is done only by the data owner by using proxy re-encryption and the keys are known to the gateway server.

In paper (Liu et al., 2018) author focused on the concern regarding privacy and security of files stored on the cloud server. For this author used ciphertext-policy attribute-based encryption (CP-ABE). The CP-ABE provides a secure access control policy to a user, a secure decentralized environment, and provide user-friendly service. The confidentiality of data and efficiency of the model are guaranteed by the symmetrical encryption algorithm. The secure access control is provided by the CP-ABE technique and with an access tree structure. It also ensures anti-collision attack and data integrity by using the cryptographic hash value. This model has the advantage of the higher efficiency with symmetrical encryption for files as well as CP-ABE fork, increased reliability, data security, and integrity. However, the model has some limitation like computation time increase as the number of attribute increase in the policy.

In paper (Theodouli et al., 2018) author has pointed out the concern regarding privacy and security needs in healthcare data sharing. For this concern author presented the potential use of blockchain to address these issues through the smart contract feature of blockchain technology. The smart contract further categorizes into three contracts for different functions such as registry contract for users registry, patient data smart contract contains the hashed data of health information and permission contract for access control of data. This work aimed at private data sharing and access permission of healthcare information. The blockchain-based architecture has achieved the security goal while sharing healthcare information such as integrity, user identity and provides accountability and auditing. However, this architecture is not suitable for the large-scale network.

In (Liu et al., 2019) author aimed at the nature of medical data privacy and sensitivity during sharing and provides a protection scheme for patient data. In this scheme, the author used private blockchain to address the security and privacy concern. The private blockchain is more secure than the public blockchain to ensure the security of electronic health records. This blockchain-based scheme satisfies security requirements such as transparency, tamper proofness, immutability. In this system for mutual authentication and generating session key author used the symptom matching algorithm for communication of two same type disease patients about their illness in future. In this work, the Author used delegated proof of stake (DPoS) mechanism to prevent dishonest nodes participation in the data sharing process.

In (Wang et al., 2019) author has shown the security threat to cloud-based stored medical data such as privacy and security issues. In this regard author used blockchain technology as a solution to provide data privacy and security to cloud-based stored information. The cloud manages for storing the EHR ciphertext and hybrid blockchain contain the indexes of electronic health record (EHR). The framework proposed is reliable, secure, and effective efficient privacy-preserving EHR sharing protocol by using the searchable encryption and conditional proxy re-encryption technique. This framework uses the proof of authority consensus protocol as the authenticity of the nodes in the decentralized network that is consortium blockchain. The cryptographic primitives such as bilinear map, public-key encryption with conjunctive keyword search technique, and conditional proxy re-encryption are implemented on ethereum blockchain platform.

In (Nguyen et al., 2019) author discuss the concern of storage security of electronic health records(EHR) on mobile-based cloud environment that having the security and privacy concern while sharing information among patients, healthcare providers, and third party. Given the above issues, the author presented a novel EHRs sharing model which integrates blockchain ledger and decentralizes interplanetary file system (IPFS) with mobile cloud network. To provide secure access control and EHR sharing to medical data we use the smart contract. In this model proof of concept, the mechanism is used to provide decentralized access control of EHR data sharing on mobile cloud framework to analyze the proposed scheme. The advantage of this model is to provide the minimum network latency and data security as compared to other existing information-sharing models and it is feasible for various e-health applications.

The work (Gupta et al., 2021) proposed the blockchain based secure concept for healthcare by using the cloud assisted system and make the data sharing efficient by using the attribute based encryption method. The proposed method is computationally efficient and storage efficient as well as robust.

SURVEY BASED ON IOT DATA SHARING

In (Liu et al., 2018) author discussed the issues related to collecting high-quality data from IoT mobile terminals and how securely share these data among mobile terminals, prevent device failure and communication failure. To overcome these above challenges, blockchain technology is proposed for data sharing and data collection efficiently. In this paper author combined ethereum platform with deep reinforcement learning to make an efficient, secure environment for data sharing and exchange. Reinforcement learning facilitates the collection of a large amount of data while blockchain provides reliability, security, and efficiently sharing data. Ethereum node stores the data and creates a private blockchain to share data. This private network has two nodes named mining node and non-mining node. The mining node checks the validity of blocks and adds them into the ledger while the non-mining node is used as receiving and broadcasting e data sharing among nodes. The objective of this proposed system is to support the mobile terminal to sense surrounding personal of interest devices to gain an edge in higher data collection, geographic transparency, impartiality, and minimum power consumption. After the simulation test, this scheme is feasible to higher security, reliability, and anti-collusion to DoS, DDoS in data sharing. However, this system is not extendable to every blockchain node and executes multiple tasks at the same time on each mobile terminal.

In paper (Si et al., 2018) author proposed the lightweight IoT information sharing security framework by using decentralize platform. The author used the double chain model that combines the data blockchain and transaction, which protects source data storage and is responsible for storing the indexes of transaction data respectively. The double-chain concept is used to maintain data consistency and avoid tampering with IoT data. The practical Byzantine fault-tolerant consensus mechanism increases the registration efficiency of nodes, higher the transactional throughput and privacy of sharing data by using the partial blind signature method. In This paper author used the dynamic game method which provides the cooperation among the node and detect the malicious behavior of a node, this dynamic game method find out the state of an unauthorized node and estimate the reputation value by using PageRanker algorithm, higher reputation value provides trust in sharing the data. The loss of private keys is secured by secret sharing.

In (Pham et al., 2019) author addressed the issues of time and cost in data collection from sensor devices in IoT environments for intelligent systems. These data collections also have security challenges like data leakage, privacy, and integrity. This author proposed the blockchain-based architecture which ensures integrity, authorization, confidentiality, and transparency in the data sharing process. The data collection is being done through the IoT gateway. After receiving data the IoT gateway encrypts these data and stores them at off-chain storage, asymmetric encryption technique used on ethereum blockchain ensuring data security and integrity to overcome these security issues. So that to get higher transaction speed and provides reliable service availability. However, this has scalability concerns to include large peers at the network.

In (Hofman et al., 2019) author addressed the demand of customers in manufacturer, retailer, and supplier like food security and safety, sustainability. For this author proposed a methodological approach in a complex organization such as supply chain and logistic network for development and deployment of data sharing by using the blockchain technology with smart contract. This approach of data sharing in supply chain and logistic networks use blockchain technology to reduce the implementation time in commodity trading in the supply chain. In this work, the technology used by the author is distributed ledger technology that creates data sharing reference model for supply and logistic network, informatics principles as a Turing machine, ontologies

In the paper (Cech et al., 2019) author discussed the creation of a huge amount of data from IoT devices and sensor nodes, collecting and securely sharing these data is the biggest challenge. The author developed an expanded fog computing model with the integration of blockchain to share sensor data among fog computing nodes. The new model is known as HCL-BaFog (Hypriot Cluster Lab) to collect data and provide secure sharing of information to other fog nodes. The proof of concept that usages the total virtualize function of the blockchain platform to ensure fairness in data sharing and the round-robin block creation schedule method. The feasibility of the data-sharing model is tested by a testbed of Raspberry Pi SBC (single board computer). This model uses the multichain framework to enhance the performance of fog computing nodes and enable trust among peer nodes. However, this proposed scheme is platform-dependent on the behavior of blockchain.

In (Lu et al., 2019) author address, the potential threat of data sharing that is data leakage and the security of the network. given the author of the above issue presented the blockchain-based secure file sharing model among different parties, Then introduced the information-sharing problem at machine learning problems by bringing privacy secured federated learning. To maintain privacy this model uses sharing model of machine learning instead of actual data. The blockchain-based collaborative architecture is used to reduce the risk of data leakage in sharing the data among multiple entities. Federated learning uses the concept of differential privacy to more strengthen data security. The normalized weighted graph is used to generate the structure data instead of unstructured. The proof of training quality algorithm converts the data-sharing problem in model sharing, this protects the privacy of the data owner. The purpose of federated learning provides training to a data model that may provide correct responses for information sharing request entities. This federated model used various machine learning algorithms such as a random tree, random forest.

In (Manzoor et al., 2019) author discussed the issues of cloud-based data sharing centralize system which requires third-party services to pay some fee for services. To overcome these scalability and trust issues blockchain technology is used as a solution in IoT data sharing that uses the proxy re-encryption technique to facilitate secured data transmission and visibility only to the data owner and intended user into the blockchain network. The data is stored on the distributed cloud after passing through the encryption process. The secure sharing is performed by a smart contract between the data owner and the data requester. The whole framework is implemented on the ethereum virtualize platform to increase the performance, reliability as well security features. The proposed architecture consists of four entity includes IoT devices, data users, cloud-enabled service providers, and blockchain platforms. From the security point of view, the author applied a certificate-based proxy re-encryption (CP-PRE) scheme that consists of seven polynomial-time algorithms. The feasibility of the model is shown on permissioned ethereum blockchain with the sensor of devices and cloud server for storing data. However this system is not scalable to distributed cloud storage, so this will be the future enhancement of this proposed system.

In (Liang et al., 2019) author addresses the issues of previous data transmission techniques such as low security, the higher management cost of data, lack of proper monitoring in the industrial Internet of Things. These concerns may lead to tampering of data, unauthorized access in IoT devices. This decreases the quality, consistency, and efficiency of quality data. In the view of above issues, the author presented a secure blockchain-enabled data transmission model for the Industrial Internet of Things, which using the dynamic secret sharing technique to provide secure transmission. The dynamic secret sharing protects the private key. Key-value of private and public key sign the intelligent data transaction as well as prove its validity of own transaction. In this paper author secured the data transmission by blockchain sharing model that protects the decentralized system from attack. This model used the docker virtualization technique for creating the power blockchain network sharing model. The experiment shows that this model has achieved high security and efficient reliability, improves the transmission rate and packet receiving rate. However this model needs a lot of enhancement in the future to introduce power blockchain in large scalable networks, needs to remove data redundancies in the file storage system.

The paper (Stergiou et al., 2020) is related to provide the security and management of big data in fog based environment for 6G wireless networks. This work provides the secure and efficient platform for using internet and sharing information as well as provide scalability for large big data.

SUMMARY OF EXISTING WORK ON DATA SHARING WITH BLOCKCHAIN

Table 1. Comparison of existing papers on blockchain-based data sharing

Reference	Focused area	Method	Pros	Cons	Tools
Xu et al., 2017	Fine-grained access control and privacy preservation	Bilinear pairing method ABS CP-ABE	Privacy-preserving User control Data access policy	The limited computational power of IoT devices	Hyper ledger Pairing based and GNU library
Dinh et al., 2017	Focused on attribute-based signcryption scheme and confidentiality and access control	Bilinear mapping function Secret data sharing scheme Access tree method	Establish trust Lowest keysize and signcryption cost Computation and communication overhead overcome	Risk of DDoS attack	VC++ PBC library
Goyal et al., 2018	KYC validation using blockchain	Double-blind data sharing	Provide dynamic access control of data Reduce manual verification, time, and cost	Not scalable limited storage Slow transaction speed	Hyper ledger fabric Private network blockchain
Feng et al., 2019	Data sharing incentive mechanism	Evolutionary game theory Evolutionary stable strategy Symmetric Property of the game theory	Enhanced user participation	Data size and data quality limitations	Ethereum network MATLAB
McGhin et al., 2019	Proposed incentive schemes for boosting IoT data sharing	Coin-locking strategy Shamir's secret sharing scheme	Identification of malicious nodes behavior The enhanced motivation of nodes to share data	High bandwidth cost Slow data sharing.	Ethereum framework Microsoft Azure
Mohanta et al., 2019	Data authentication and data quality	Shamir's secret sharing Online review system RSA algorithm	Data integrity Less computation time in encryption	Not scalable	Ethereum network
Gai et al., 2019	Focused on encryption scheme to control simultaneous data sharing of data to a group of users.	Functional broadcast encryption Probabilistic polynomial-time algorithm(PPT)	FBE is storage efficient FBE is feasible in terms of technically and economically	Obsfucation program is not efficient in practical applications	C language

Table 2. Comparison based on healthcare data sharing

Reference	Focused area	Method	Pros	Cons	Tools
Fukumitsu et al., 2017	Secure cloud file sharing	CP-ABE, Access tree structure, ECB model, Symmetric encryption algorithm	Increased reliability of data security and integrity,	Encryption time increased with file size increase	Ethereum network and JPBC library
Wang et al., 2017	Health care data sharing using blockchain	Blockchain with smart contract	Provide auditing and accountability, Automatic workflow	Not scalable	Private blockchain
Wang et al., 2019	Medical data sharing and protection scheme	Delegated proof of stake	Better security performance	Low throughput and scalable	Private blockchain
Shrestha et al., 2019	Proposed secret data-sharing model for PHR	Proxy re-encryption, AFGH algorithm	Privacy of on-chain data Improved storage capacity	Energy consumption Not Scalable	Ethereum network
Rahman et al., 2020	Based on personal health data and sharing framework	Cryptographic key and smart contract	Reduce the financial cost of managing data, Low latency,	Not scalable	Ethereum VM

Table 3. Comparison based on IoT data sharing

Reference	Focused area	Method	Pros	Cons	Tools
Shrestha et al., 2018	Data sharing in supply chain and logistic network	Distributed ledger technology, Turing machine, ontologies	Reduce implementation time in commodity trading in the supply chain	scalability	Ethereum and DLT
Zhang et al., 2018	Proposed expanded fog computing model by integrating blockchain to share sensor data.	Proof of concept, PKI method, Round-robin block creation schedule method	Huge data processing capability to advance IoT applications	The proposed scheme is platform-dependent on blockchain	Private blockchain Fog computing, Multichain framework
Bhaskaran et al., 2018	Enhancing security in IoT devices data sharing	Blockchain and smart contract	Ensured data integrity and security, Ensure service availability	Not scalable	Ethereum TestNet Truffle framework
Naz et al., 2019	Incentive mechanism with on-chain and off-chain data that creates trust	DQDA algorithm, EM algorithm, Marginal social welfare greedy auction(MSWG)	Trust in sharing of off-chain data, Data quality is high at low cost	Not suitable for higher energy consumption devices.	Consortium blockchain
Eltayieb et al., 2020	secure data sharing among internet of vehicle by using blockchain	The fair blind signature scheme, Multi-signature and threshold mechanism, Threshold secret sharing scheme	Provide security and privacy of vehicle, Communication and storage cost-efficient	High computational complexity	Ethereum, Linux, MIRACL library

Table 4. System configuration of experimental environment

Reference	OS	CPU	Memory	Tools
Xu et al., 2017	Ubuntu 16.04	Intel (R) core(TM) i7-6700 CPU @ 3.4 GHz	3 GB RAM	• Go-ethereum • nodeJs • truffle
Dinh et al., 2017	Windows 10, 64 bit	Intel i5-7400, 3.00 GHz CPU	4 GB RAM	• VC++ 6.0 • PBC Library
Feng et al., 2019	Windows 7, 64 bit	Intel i5-3470 cpu@ 3.2GHz	4GB RAM	• MATLAB 6.5.0.1809139 release 13
Mohanta et al., 2019	64 bit OS and X64 based processor	Intel (R) core(TM) M3-7430 CPU @ 1.61 GHz	8 GB RAM	• Ethereum • Solidity • Vs code • Ganache • metamask
Gai et al., 2019	windows 10	Intel 2 core 8 i7-8565 CPU, 1.8 GHz & 1.99GHz	8 GB RAM	• C language

SECURITY CHALLENGES OF BLOCKCHAIN SYSTEM

- **Performance and scalability:** These are the significant feature of blockchain in terms of processing information. The performance depends upon the task the nodes perform like authentication, verification, running the consensus mechanism, and maintained the synchronized copy of the transaction to the global digital ledger (Croman et al., 2016). Another concern of blockchain is scalability when several users increase in the network the computational overhead also increased (Kosba et al., 2016).
- **Storage capacity and privacy:** As the blockchain is based on the decentralization concept to provide secure storage and access to transactions or data, store information on the ledger and maintain privacy among users for various services is the biggest challenge. The concern of decentralized systems is leakage of the public and private key used for encryption and decryption, limited storage capacity such as IoT devices (Xie et al., 2019). This needs to be improved in future work.
- **Energy consumption:** energy consumption is also associated with the above-mentioned issues. It may happen when more users are connected to network or IoT environment in solving puzzles the consensus algorithm like PoW requires hard computational resources in the mining process to overcome these energy constraints many researchers presented the energy-efficient algorithm such as proof of stake (PoS), delegated proof of stake (DpoS), practical byzantine fault tolerance (PBFT), etc.(Xie et al., 2019).

CONCLUSION

Recently blockchain has gained a lot of recognition because of its features such as transparency, immutability, decentralized environment, peer-to-peer node communication, and distributed ledger. It can be used in diverse fields like the internet of things, healthcare, cloud storage, supply chain, smart cities, etc. It is accompanied by transparency to the ledger's data and transactions. In this survey, we have summarized the existing work based on data sharing techniques using blockchain platforms in areas of IoT, healthcare, and the internet of vehicles. Most of the authors proposed the security model that provides an incentive mechanism for secure data sharing by using different Cryptographic algorithm and achieved the protection of data up to some extent of security goal. However, there is still some hidden security threat and challenges that need to improve more accurately in future work like scalability, energy consumption, privacy and security of decentralize storage as well as integration of blockchain for fog computing to provide better security, data integrity at fog layer, as fog layer help to provide better services with low latency and to utilize full bandwidth.

REFERENCES

Amofa, S., Sifah, E. B., Kwame, O. B., Abla, S., Xia, Q., Gee, J. C., & Gao, J. (2018, September). A blockchain-based architecture framework for secure sharing of personal health data. In *2018 IEEE 20th International Conference on e-Health Networking, Applications and Services (Healthcom)* (pp. 1-6). IEEE. 10.1109/HealthCom.2018.8531160

Bhaskaran, K., Ilfrich, P., Liffman, D., Vecchiola, C., Jayachandran, P., Kumar, A., ... Teo, E. G. (2018, April). Double-blind consent-driven data sharing on blockchain. In *2018 IEEE International Conference on Cloud Engineering (IC2E)* (pp. 385-391). IEEE. 10.1109/IC2E.2018.00073

Cash, M., & Bassiouni, M. (2018, September). Two-tier permission-ed and permission-less blockchain for secure data sharing. In *2018 IEEE International Conference on Smart Cloud (SmartCloud)* (pp. 138-144). IEEE. 10.1109/SmartCloud.2018.00031

Cech, H. L., Großmann, M., & Krieger, U. R. (2019, June). A fog computing architecture to share sensor data by means of blockchain functionality. In *2019 IEEE International Conference on Fog Computing (ICFC)* (pp. 31-40). IEEE. 10.1109/ICFC.2019.00013

Croman, K., Decker, C., Eyal, I., Gencer, A. E., Juels, A., Kosba, A., & Song, D. (2016, February). On scaling decentralized blockchains. In *International conference on financial cryptography and data security* (pp. 106-125). Springer.

Dib, O., Brousmiche, K. L., Durand, A., Thea, E., & Hamida, E. B. (2018). Consortium blockchains: Overview, applications and challenges. *International Journal on Advances in Telecommunications, 11*(1-2).

Dinh, T. T. A., Wang, J., Chen, G., Liu, R., Ooi, B. C., & Tan, K. L. (2017, May). Blockbench: A framework for analyzing private blockchains. In *Proceedings of the 2017 ACM International Conference on Management of Data* (pp. 1085-1100). 10.1145/3035918.3064033

Dubovitskaya, A., Novotny, P., Xu, Z., & Wang, F. (2020). Applications of blockchain technology for data-sharing in oncology: Results from a systematic literature review. *Oncology, 98*(6), 403–411. doi:10.1159/000504325 PMID:31794967

Eltayieb, N., Elhabob, R., Hassan, A., & Li, F. (2020). A blockchain-based attribute-based signcryption scheme to secure data sharing in the cloud. *Journal of Systems Architecture, 102*, 101653. doi:10.1016/j.sysarc.2019.101653

Feng, Q., He, D., Zeadally, S., Khan, M. K., & Kumar, N. (2019). A survey on privacy protection in blockchain system. *Journal of Network and Computer Applications*, *126*, 45–58. doi:10.1016/j.jnca.2018.10.020

Gai, K., Wu, Y., Zhu, L., Qiu, M., & Shen, M. (2019). Privacy-preserving energy trading using consortium blockchain in smart grid. *IEEE Transactions on Industrial Informatics*, *15*(6), 3548–3558. doi:10.1109/TII.2019.2893433

Goyal, S. (2018). *The History of Blockchain Technology: Must Know Timeline*. Academic Press.

Guo, R., Shi, H., Zhao, Q., & Zheng, D. (2018). Secure attribute-based signature scheme with multiple authorities for blockchain in electronic health records systems. *IEEE Access: Practical Innovations, Open Solutions*, *6*, 11676–11686. doi:10.1109/ACCESS.2018.2801266

Gupta, B. B., Li, K. C., Leung, V. C., Psannis, K. E., & Yamaguchi, S. (2021). Blockchain-assisted secure fine-grained searchable encryption for a cloud-based healthcare cyber-physical system. *IEEE/CAA Journal of Automatica Sinica*.

Gupta, S., & Gupta, B. B. (2017). Detection, avoidance, and attack pattern mechanisms in modern web application vulnerabilities: Present and future challenges. *International Journal of Cloud Applications and Computing*, *7*(3), 1–43. doi:10.4018/IJCAC.2017070101

Hasselgren, A., Kralevska, K., Gligoroski, D., Pedersen, S. A., & Faxvaag, A. (2019). Blockchain in healthcare and health sciences–a scoping review. *International Journal of Medical Informatics*, 104040. PMID:31865055

Hofman, W. J. (2019). A Methodological Approach for Development and Deployment of Data Sharing in Complex Organizational Supply and Logistics Networks with Blockchain Technology. *IFAC-PapersOnLine*, *52*(3), 55–60. doi:10.1016/j.ifacol.2019.06.010

Kosba, A., Miller, A., Shi, E., Wen, Z., & Papamanthou, C. (2016, May). Hawk: The blockchain model of cryptography and privacy-preserving smart contracts. In *2016 IEEE symposium on security and privacy (SP)* (pp. 839-858). IEEE.

Liang, W., Tang, M., Long, J., Peng, X., Xu, J., & Li, K. C. (2019). A secure fabric blockchain-based data transmission technique for industrial Internet-of-Things. *IEEE Transactions on Industrial Informatics*, *15*(6), 3582–3592. doi:10.1109/TII.2019.2907092

Liu, C. H., Lin, Q., & Wen, S. (2018). Blockchain-enabled data collection and sharing for industrial IoT with deep reinforcement learning. *IEEE Transactions on Industrial Informatics*, *15*(6), 3516–3526. doi:10.1109/TII.2018.2890203

Liu, X., Wang, Z., Jin, C., Li, F., & Li, G. (2019). A Blockchain-Based Medical Data Sharing and Protection Scheme. *IEEE Access: Practical Innovations, Open Solutions*, *7*, 118943–118953. doi:10.1109/ACCESS.2019.2937685

Liu, Y., Zhang, J., & Gao, Q. (2018, October). A Blockchain-Based Secure Cloud Files Sharing Scheme with Fine-Grained Access Control. In *2018 International Conference on Networking and Network Applications (NaNA)* (pp. 277-283). IEEE. 10.1109/NANA.2018.8648778

Lu, Y., Huang, X., Dai, Y., Maharjan, S., & Zhang, Y. (2019). Blockchain and Federated Learning for Privacy-preserved Data Sharing in Industrial IoT. *IEEE Transactions on Industrial Informatics*.

Manzoor, A., Liyanage, M., Braeke, A., Kanhere, S. S., & Ylianttila, M. (2019, May). Blockchain based proxy re-encryption scheme for secure IoT data sharing. In *2019 IEEE International Conference on Blockchain and Cryptocurrency (ICBC)* (pp. 99-103). IEEE. 10.1109/BLOC.2019.8751336

McGhin, T., Choo, K. K. R., Liu, C. Z., & He, D. (2019). Blockchain in healthcare applications: Research challenges and opportunities. *Journal of Network and Computer Applications*, *135*, 62–75. doi:10.1016/j.jnca.2019.02.027

Mohan, A. P., & Gladston, A. (2020). Merkle tree and Blockchain-based cloud data auditing. *International Journal of Cloud Applications and Computing*, *10*(3), 54–66. doi:10.4018/IJCAC.2020070103

Mohanta, B. K., Jena, D., Panda, S. S., & Sobhanayak, S. (2019). Blockchain Technology: A Survey on Applications and Security Privacy Challenges. *Internet of Things*, 100107.

Nakasumi, M. (2017, July). Information sharing for supply chain management based on block chain technology. In *2017 IEEE 19th Conference on Business Informatics (CBI)* (Vol. 1, pp. 140-149). IEEE. 10.1109/CBI.2017.56

Naz, M., Al-zahrani, F. A., Khalid, R., Javaid, N., Qamar, A. M., Afzal, M. K., & Shafiq, M. (2019). A Secure Data Sharing Platform Using Blockchain and Interplanetary File System. *Sustainability*, *11*(24), 7054. doi:10.3390u11247054

Nguyen, D. C., Pathirana, P. N., Ding, M., & Seneviratne, A. (2019). Blockchain for secure EHRs sharing of mobile cloud based e-Health systems. *IEEE Access: Practical Innovations, Open Solutions*, 7, 66792–66806. doi:10.1109/ACCESS.2019.2917555

Pham, H. A., Le, T. K., & Le, T. V. (2019, September). Enhanced Security of IoT Data Sharing Management by Smart Contracts and Blockchain. In *2019 19th International Symposium on Communications and Information Technologies (ISCIT)* (pp. 398-403). IEEE. 10.1109/ISCIT.2019.8905219

Rahman, M. S., Al Omar, A., Bhuiyan, M. Z. A., Basu, A., Kiyomoto, S., & Wang, G. (2020). Accountable cross-border data sharing using blockchain under relaxed trust assumption. *IEEE Transactions on Engineering Management*.

Rawat, D. B., Njilla, L., Kwiat, K., & Kamhoua, C. (2018, March). iShare: Blockchain-based privacy-aware multi-agent information sharing games for cybersecurity. In *2018 International Conference on Computing, Networking and Communications (ICNC)* (pp. 425-431). IEEE. 10.1109/ICCNC.2018.8390264

Samuel, O., Javaid, N., Awais, M., Ahmed, Z., Imran, M., & Guizani, M. (2019, July). A blockchain model for fair data sharing in deregulated smart grids. In *IEEE Global Communications Conference (GLOBCOM 2019)*. 10.1109/GLOBECOM38437.2019.9013372

Shrestha, A. K., Deters, R., & Vassileva, J. (2019). *User-controlled privacy-preserving user profile data sharing based on blockchain*. arXiv preprint arXiv:1909.05028.

Shrestha, A. K., & Vassileva, J. (2018, June). Blockchain-based research data sharing framework for incentivizing the data owners. In *International Conference on Blockchain* (pp. 259-266). Springer. 10.1007/978-3-319-94478-4_19

Si, H., Sun, C., Li, Y., Qiao, H., & Shi, L. (2019). IoT information sharing security mechanism based on blockchain technology. *Future Generation Computer Systems*, *101*, 1028–1040. doi:10.1016/j.future.2019.07.036

Stergiou, C. L., Psannis, K. E., & Gupta, B. B. (2020). IoT-based big data secure management in the fog over a 6G wireless network. *IEEE Internet of Things Journal*, *8*(7), 5164–5171. doi:10.1109/JIOT.2020.3033131

Sumathi, M., & Sangeetha, S. (2020). Blockchain based sensitive attribute storage and access monitoring in banking system. *International Journal of Cloud Applications and Computing*, *10*(2), 77–92. doi:10.4018/IJCAC.2020040105

Theodouli, A., Arakliotis, S., Moschou, K., Votis, K., & Tzovaras, D. (2018, August). On the design of a Blockchain-based system to facilitate Healthcare Data Sharing. In *2018 17th IEEE International Conference on Trust, Security And Privacy In Computing And Communications/12th IEEE International Conference On Big Data Science And Engineering (TrustCom/BigDataSE)* (pp. 1374-1379). IEEE. 10.1109/TrustCom/BigDataSE.2018.00190

Thwin, T. T., & Vasupongayya, S. (2018, August). Blockchain based secret-data sharing model for personal health record system. In *2018 5th International Conference on Advanced Informatics: Concept Theory and Applications (ICAICTA)* (pp. 196-201). IEEE. 10.1109/ICAICTA.2018.8541296

Wang, H., & Song, Y. (2018). Secure cloud-based EHR system using attribute-based cryptosystem and blockchain. *Journal of Medical Systems*, *42*(8), 152. doi:10.100710916-018-0994-6 PMID:29974270

Wang, H., Zhang, Y., Chen, K., Sui, G., Zhao, Y., & Huang, X. (2019). Functional broadcast encryption with applications to data sharing for cloud storage. *Information Sciences*, *502*, 109–124. doi:10.1016/j.ins.2019.06.028

Wang, L., Liu, W., & Han, X. (2017, December). Blockchain-based government information resource sharing. In *2017 IEEE 23rd International Conference on Parallel and Distributed Systems (ICPADS)* (pp. 804-809). IEEE. 10.1109/ICPADS.2017.00112

Wang, Y., Zhang, A., Zhang, P., & Wang, H. (2019). Cloud-Assisted EHR Sharing With Security and Privacy Preservation via Consortium Blockchain. *IEEE Access: Practical Innovations, Open Solutions*, *7*, 136704–136719. doi:10.1109/ACCESS.2019.2943153

Wang, Z., Tian, Y., & Zhu, J. (2018, August). Data sharing and tracing scheme based on blockchain. In *2018 8th International Conference on Logistics, Informatics and Service Sciences (LISS)* (pp. 1-6). IEEE. 10.1109/LISS.2018.8593225

Wang, Z., & Wu, Q. (2019, October). Incentive for Historical Block Data Sharing in Blockchain. In *2019 IEEE 10th Annual Information Technology, Electronics and Mobile Communication Conference (IEMCON)* (pp. 0913-0919). IEEE. 10.1109/IEMCON.2019.8936209

Wu, A., Zhang, Y., Zheng, X., Guo, R., Zhao, Q., & Zheng, D. (2019). Efficient and privacy-preserving traceable attribute-based encryption in blockchain. *Annales des Télécommunications*, 74(7-8), 401–411. doi:10.100712243-018-00699-y

Xie, J., Tang, H., Huang, T., Yu, F. R., Xie, R., Liu, J., & Liu, Y. (2019). A survey of blockchain technology applied to smart cities: Research issues and challenges. *IEEE Communications Surveys and Tutorials*, 21(3), 2794–2830. doi:10.1109/COMST.2019.2899617

Xu, L., Shah, N., Chen, L., Diallo, N., Gao, Z., Lu, Y., & Shi, W. (2017, April). Enabling the sharing economy: Privacy respecting contract based on public blockchain. In *Proceedings of the ACM Workshop on Blockchain, Cryptocurrencies and Contracts* (pp. 15-21). 10.1145/3055518.3055527

Xuan, S., Zheng, L., Chung, I., Wang, W., Man, D., Du, X., & Guizani, M. (2020). An incentive mechanism for data sharing based on blockchain with smart contracts. *Computers & Electrical Engineering*, 83, 106587. doi:10.1016/j.compeleceng.2020.106587

Zhang, Y., He, D., & Choo, K. K. R. (2018). BaDS: Blockchain-based architecture for data sharing with ABS and CP-ABE in IoT. Wireless Communications and Mobile Computing, 2018, 2018. doi:10.1155/2018/2783658

Chapter 12
Fruit Fly Optimization– Based Adversarial Modeling for Securing Wireless Sensor Networks (WSN)

Priyanka Ahlawat
National Institute of Technology, Kurukshetra, India

Mukul Goyal
National Institute of Technology, Kurukshetra, India

Rishabh Sethi
National Institute of Technology, Kurukshetra, India

Nitish Gupta
National Institute of Technology, Kurukshetra, India

ABSTRACT

Node capture attack is one of the crucial attacks in wireless sensor networks (WSN) that seizes the node physically and withdraws the confidential data from the node's memory. The chapter exploits the adversarial behavior during a node capture to build an attack model. The authors also propose a fruit fly optimization algorithm (FFOA) that is a multi-objective optimization algorithm that consists of a number of objectives for capturing a node in the network: maximum node contribution, maximum key contributions are some examples of the same. The aim is to demolish the maximum part of the network while minimizing the cost and maximizing attacking efficiency. Due to the multi-objective function, the authors attain a maximum fraction of compromised traffic, lower attacking rounds, and lower energy cost as contrasted with other node capture attack algorithms. They have developed an algorithm, which is an enhanced version of FFOA and has even better efficiency than FFOA.

DOI: 10.4018/978-1-7998-7789-9.ch012

Copyright © 2022, IGI Global. Copying or distributing in print or electronic forms without written permission of IGI Global is prohibited.

INTRODUCTION

Node capture attack is a comprehensive attack in which the intruder physically captures the sensor node by extracting keys and confidential data. With technological advances in the field of wireless sensor technology, various operations such as catastrophic and defense monitoring can be painlessly and quickly deployed to wireless sensor networks (WSN)(Lin, C,2016) . The scattered nodes communicate wirelessly to a central gateway, which connects to the wired world where users can collect, process, analyze, and present the measured physical data. Though WSNs have their advantages as the nodes are autonomous, they still need to be addressed. Some of the most common and important challenges are coverage, scalability, QoS, and security. Amidst the challenges listed, security is a major issue to be addressed in WSNs. Sensor networks is extremely vulnerable to node capture attacks. WSN is a group of a huge number of low price, low control, and self-organizing specialized sensor nodes (Lin, C,2015). It is very much vulnerable to different physical attacks due to limited resource capacity and screened to the external atmosphere for circulating network data. The node capture attack is one of the major attacks in WSN in which the attacker physically captures the node and can remove the secret information from the node's memory or misuse the confidential data (Lin.2013). With technological advances in wireless sensor technology, various operations such as the health and defense monitoring can be quickly deployed to WSN. We focus on developing a multi-objective function using which we can compromise the network efficiently and quickly, unlike random attack (RA), maximum key attack (MKA), maximum link attack (MLA). WSN is a wireless network comprising a large number of self-operative and self-sufficient nodes, which comprises low cost, less control, and self-organizing qualities(Lin.2013). This type of network uses sensors for catastrophic and defense monitoring of physical and environmental situations. When such self-governing nodes are used with routers and gateways, it creates a wireless sensor network system. This technology has its applications in various fields, including military, medical, defense, environmental, and many more.There are various issues to be addressed in WSNs. Some of them are scalability, quality of service, size, security, and many more (Tague, P,2008). Out of all these, security is the biggest challenge. Due to tight resource capacity and its exposure to the outer environment, it is prone to various kinds of physical attacks. Broadly, attacks can be of two types: active attacks, including routing attacks, eavesdropping, and passive attacks, which include all attacks against privacy. The performance is measure with other methods, and thus gives the improved resilience in order capturing node, hash computations decreased, compromise probability for proxy nodes also reduced with a revoked link (Ahlawat,2018) . The result matrix is examined with old strategies in order of the number attacking rounds, capturing cost and traffic compromised.. The performance validated by number of path compromise, path length, and route ratio (Ahlawat,2018). With this analysis of keys and linear automated theory, develop a model that effectively describes the behaviour of that network with attack. Optimal control theory method design a response for the network, which provide a network with secure stability(Bonaci,2010).Node capture attacks are one of the most major attacks in WSN. Node Capture Attack is a kind of attack in which the intruder can access the entire network and perform any operation on the network. The attacker captures the sensor node by gaining access to cryptographic keys and secret information like key pre-distribution model(Shukla,2015). Earlier, node capture attacks were having limitations like a lack of attacking methods and low attack efficiency. There are different types of node capture attacks. The next stage of the internet's development i.e. the internet of things which makes the internet a physical network requires the objects to communicate with minimal human interference. This type of network made of mobile sensor nodes communicating with each other and working synchronously in a controlled envirnments .It is a wireless network that comprises a great number of dynamic, self-directed, small, self operative, low powered devices named sensor nodes called 'motes'. A large number of battery-operated, spatially separated and minute devices are networked to collect, process, and transfer data to the operators in these networks. It has also controlled the ability to compute and to process the received data. It finds its application in numerous fields such as - Home Applications, Commercial Applications, Forest fire detection, Area monitoring, Air pollution monitoring, Military Applications, Health care monitoring, Health Applications, Environmental Applications, Earth/Environmental sensing, Water quality monitoring, Landslide detection, Industrial monitoring, and many more applications. Thus, so many applications of WSN make its security a prime concern. Henceforth, it aims to find out the vulnerability and weak points in WSN by simulating multiple attacks and concludes to point out where a WSN must be made more robust. Thus, to make the next generation of the internet, i.e., IoT, more reliable and secured, it is important to find out the most probable and destructive attacks prone to affect WSN's security. To conclude, we have simulated the most advanced attack, i.e., FFOA on node capture attack (Bhatt,2020). Further, a comparative study is provided by plotting graphs for FFOA and its improved version. Therefore, to enhance the attack efficiency of node capture attack, we propose an attacking approach using the Fruit Fly Optimization Algorithm (FFOA), which overcomes these limitations. We aim to develop a multi-objective function using which we can compromise the network efficiently and quickly. We would then compare the performance with few similar competing strategies to show that the FFOA outperforms its competitor.

MOTIVATION

The next stage of the internet's development i.e. the Internet of things which makes the internet a physical network requires the objects to communicate with minimal human interference. This type of network made of mobile sensor nodes communicating with each other and working synchronously is known as WSN. As it is a wireless network that comprises a great number of dynamic, self-directed, small, low powered devices named sensor nodes called motes. A huge number of battery-operated, spatially separated and minute devices are networked to collect, process, and transfer data to the operators in these networks. It also has controlled the ability to compute and to process the received data. It finds its application in numerous fields such as - Home Applications, Commercial Applications, Air pollution monitoring, Forest fire detection, Area monitoring, Military Applications, Health Applications, Environmental Applications, Health care monitoring, Environmental/Earth sensing, Landslide detection, Water quality monitoring, Industrial monitoring. Thus, such a vast application of WSN makes its security a prime concern. Hence, we aim to find out the vulnerability and weak points in a WSN by simulating multiple attacks and plotting a comparison graph to point out the fields or parts where a WSN must be made more secure. Thus, to make the next generation of internet i.e. IoT more trustworthy and secure we aim to find out the most probable and devastating attack which can affect WSN seriously. To achieve this, we simulate various attacks such as Random attack, Maximum Key Attack, Maximum Link attack, and applying FFOA on node capture attack. Further, we provide a comparative study by plotting graphs for each of the above attacks.

LITERATURE SURVEY

This section details the various schemes proposed to increase the attacking efficiency of attacker. WSN is a wireless network, comprising of large number of self-governing nodes, which are of low cost, less control and are self-organizing. This type of network uses sensors for catastrophic and defense monitoring of physical and environmental situations. When such self-governing nodes are used with routers and gateways, it creates a Wireless sensor network system. Currently, these types of network are in the initial stage of being deployed. But, in next few years, one would find these networks throughout the world, having access to them via Internet. This technology has its applications in various fields including military, medical, defense, environmental and many more.

Figure 1. Typical wireless sensor network

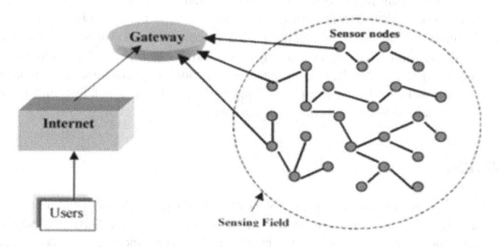

Node capture is a kind of attack in which the intruder can gain the access over entire network and perform any operation on the network. In this, the attacker physically captures the sensor node by gaining access to cryptographic keys and secret information. Earlier, node capture attacks were having limitations like lack of attacking methods and low attack efficiency. There are different types of node capture attacks which are given below:

1. Random Attack (RA)
    In this, nodes are captured independently of each other. In every round, the intruder selects a vertex to be captured. As attacker capture the nodes casually, the attacking efficiency is O(1).
2. Maximum Key Attack (MKA)
    In this kind of attack, in every round, nodes with highest number of keys are compromised. So, even if the node is not belonging to any route, then also, it is likely to be confined if it has if it has maximum number of keys. Its complexity is $O(N^2)$.
3. Maximum Link Attack (MLA)
    In this attack, in every round, nodes having highest number of links are compromised. In this also, even if the node does not belong to any route, then also it is likely to be captured. Its complexity is $O(N^4)$.

4. Maximum Traffic Attack (MTA)

    Here, the fraction of the attacked traffic to the whole traffic is calculated and nodes having highest value of this ratio are captured in each round. The number of attacking rounds is highest in this attack. Its complexity is $O(N^2)$.

5. Greedy Node capture Approximation using Vulnerability Evaluation (GNAVE)

    This takes susceptibility as the criteria for seizing nodes. Nodes, having highest susceptibility are captured first. However, it considers only those nodes which belong to the path and ignore all the other nodes. The metrics calculated by this are not perfect. Its complexity is $O(N^5)$.

6. Matrix Based Node Capture Attack (MA)

    In this method, a matrix is created which shows the relation between vertices and path. This is used to gain access over the complete network. The energy cost is least in this and it causes maximum destruction. However, it does not consider attacking competency. Its complexity is $O(N^2)$.

7. Full Graph Attack (FGA)

    It is used to cause more destruction to the network. But it has huge overhead in terms of computation. Its complexity is $O(N^2)$.

8. Opti-Graph Attack (OGA) and Path Covering Attack (PCA)

    These methods are used to enhance the effectiveness of FGA. However, these methods do not measure the energy cost. Its complexity is $O(N^2)$.

9. Minimum Resource Expenditure node capture Attack (MREA)

    It calculates the energy cost of the attacker. It causes maximum destruction with minimum resource expenditure. Its complexity is $O(N^2)$.

The attacks mentioned above were not efficient enough and they had some major issues, due to which the attack efficiency of these attacks was low. Some of these issues are addresses below.

1. Basically, susceptibility is defined as a number, and it cannot specifically describe the level of destruction in wireless sensor networks.
2. The attack efficiency of node capture attack is minimum, because it desires to capture the maximum amount of nodes in network.
3. The domain of many of these approaches is limited and is therefore not suitable for providing appropriate results.
4. The most important problem is that most of these methods focused only on single criteria like lowest cost, maximum keys or any such criteria.

So, to improve the attack efficiency in node capture attack, an approach should be developed which focus on multiple objectives, like lowest cost, maximum key contribution, degree of nodes, and similarly, we can include many more. This method can be used to find out the optimal nodes using optimization algorithms (Genetic algorithm or Fruit Fly Optimization algorithm). Several node capture attack algorithms have been given by the researchers to increase the capability of attacker in WSN. This kind of attack models can be exploited by the network designers to improve the security of complete network. The node capture attack is one of the foremost attacks in WSN. In this attack, the intruder physically captures the sensor node and eradicates the secret keying information from the node's memory. Several optimizations algorithms are also applied to increase the capability of adversary. A Fruit Fly Optimization Algorithm (FFOA) is used to increase the attacker capacity which consists of several objectives namely maximum node contribution, maximum node key contribution, least resource expenses, minimum energy cost to determine the set of optimal nodes. These optimal nodes are the nodes to be captured to destroy the complete network. It will result in destroying the maximum part of the network with minimum energy cost and maximum attacking efficiency. The performance parameters are compromised traffic, number of attacking rounds, and energy cost. The attacking models given above are still not very efficient, due to which their attacking efficiency is very low. The following issues need to be addressed during a design of attacking model:

- To overcome the problem of vulnerability based approaches and thus, to improve the attacking effectiveness or efficiency of the node capture attacking model.
- To design an effective model based on optimization algorithm that may have multiple objectives such as least number of sensor nodes, highest node key contribution, and minimum number of network resources, energy cost to find out an optimal set of node using Optimization Algorithms (like Fruit Fly Optimization).
- To construct algorithm that may cause higher destructiveness in the WSN with least number of resource expenses.

Following are the models that are used to design an effective node capture attack:

1. Network Model

   WSN is represented by the directed network graph G = (N, L), where N is the nodes number and L is the links number.

2. Key Distribution Model

   The cryptographic keys represent a key group set K and every sensor node $N_x \in N$ is randomly assigned a subset of keys $K_x \subset K$ from a key group set. Two sensor nodes N_x and N_y share a set of cryptographic keys $K_{x,y} = K_x \cap K_y$. These nodes are located in each other transmission range r and can communicate with each other. The set of $K_{x,y}$ encrypt the messages transferred between N_x and N_y. For example: $K_x = \{K1,K5,K8,K4\}$ and $Kb = \{K3,K5,K7,K8\}$, then $K_{x,y} = K_x \subset K_y = \{K5,K8\}$

3. Link Model

   A link $L_{x,y}$ is reliable and confined if it is encrypted by $K_{x,y}$. The information or messages can thus be sent between N_x and N_y without revealing it to other nodes. The security strength of the link $L_{x,y}$ is directly dependent on the size of $K_{x,y}$. The larger the overlapping value, higher is the strength. We specify the set of all the links in WSN by L, where $L = \{L_{x,y} | N_x \in N, N_y \in N\}$.

4. **Adversary Model**

   This model is described from the view of an attacker's and it is theoretical that the intruder can get the access to the information transmitting through the WSN. The intruder's focus is to do attack to capture the complete network by achieving more than one objective. It results in lower resource expenses, a large number of captured keys and least number of nodes.

To discover the optimal nodes to be captured, an optimization algorithm must be used. There are various optimization algorithms available. The Fruit Fly Optimization Algorithm (FOA) is a bio inspired algorithm for discovering global optimization based on the food searching performance of the fruit fly. The fruit fly is better than other species in sensing and perception, particularly, in vision. The fruit fly flies from one fruit to another using its sensitive visualization to discover the fruit which appears to be the best at the moment and then it flies in that path. FFOA works in a similar manner by computing the multi objective function, this algorithm is initiated to learn optimal nodes from the existing set of node, which minimize the multi objective function to produce the optimal results. We know that there are different methods to perform node capture attack in WSN. Our aim to is to enhance the attack efficiency of node capture attack in these networks. Different approaches have different efficiencies in terms of number of attacking round, cost required in compromising the network, and other parameters too. So, we propose to find out the best approach which would compromise the complete network in minimum attacking rounds and least cost. Different routing paths that contain multiple paths, are used for compromising the complete network traffic. The following matrices are used to find out the most destructiveness sensor node.

- **Key Route Matrix (KR):** This matrix determines the relationship between the cryptographic keys that are stored in every sensor node and the different routes that connect source node to the destination node.
- **Vertex (Sensor Node)-Key Matrix (VK):** This matrix represents the relationship between the keys that are stored in every sensor node. It is the number of keys stored in sensor node.
- **Key-Number Matrix (KN):** This matrix represent the relationship between the cryptographic keys that are associated with every sensor node..
- **VLR:** To assess on the partial keying relationship between nodes and the routes, we calculate another matrix VLR. It is used to demonstrate the ratio of overlapping keys captured by the adversary during a node capture attack.
- **Vertex (Sensor Node)- Route Matrix(VR):** This matrix gives the relationship between the sensor node and the different routes that connect source node to the destination node.

Where VR = VK * KR.

$KR = [KR_{a,b}]_{K*R}$, where: K=keys R=paths

$$KR_{a,b} = \begin{cases} 1 & \text{if } Ka \text{ can coperate } Kb \\ 0 & \text{otherwise} \end{cases} \tag{1}$$

$$VK_{b,a} = \begin{cases} 1 & \text{if } Ka \in b \\ 0 & \text{otherwise} \end{cases} \tag{2}$$

$$KN_b = \begin{cases} \sum_{a=1}^{k} VK_{b,a} & \text{if } Ka \in b \\ 0 & \text{otherwise} \end{cases} \tag{3}$$

$$VR = VK * KR \tag{4}$$

$$MM = \beta * VR + (1 - \beta) * VLR \qquad (5)$$

$$MM_b = \begin{cases} \displaystyle\sum_{a=1}^{R} MM_{b,a} & \text{participation of node } Nb \\ 0 & \text{otherwise} \end{cases} \qquad (6)$$

$$CS_{b,a} = \frac{CS_{b,a}}{W_b} \qquad (7)$$

$$CS_b = \begin{cases} \displaystyle\sum_{a=1}^{R} CS_{b,a} & \text{Cost node } Nb \\ 0 & \text{otherwise} \end{cases} \qquad (8)$$

$$F_{b=} \sum_{b=1}^{N} \sum_{a=1}^{R} \left\{ \frac{1}{MMb} + \frac{1}{KNb} + CS_b \right\} \qquad (9)$$

To discover the optimal nodes to be captured, an optimization algorithm must be used. There are various optimization algorithms available. Here, one of them is discussed.

Figure 2. The food searching behavior of the fruit fly

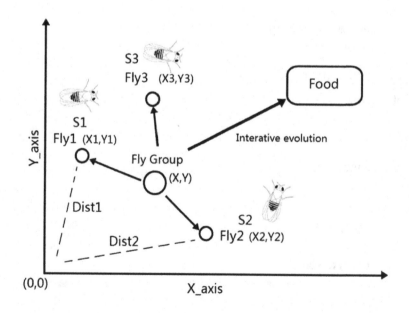

The Fruit Fly Optimization Algorithm (FOA) is a bio-inspired algorithm for finding global optimization based on the food searching behavior of the fruit fly. The fruit fly is better than other species in sensing and perception, particularly, in vision. The fruit fly flies from one fruit to another using its sensitive visualization to discover the fruit which appears to be the best at the moment and then it flies in that path. FFOA works in a similar manner by estimating multi objective function, this algorithm is used to discover optimal nodes from the existing node, which minimize the multi objective function to produce the optimal results (Bhatt,2020).

Different techniques for node capture attack have been discussed. Fruit Fly Optimization Algorithm has also been discussed here. They have shown that using Fruit Fly Optimization algorithm, the attack efficiency can be increased. Node capture techniques are classified as centralized and distributed schemes. MA, FGA, MREA are examples of distributed attack whereas random key predistribution is an example of centralized attack (Changlani et al., 2020).

Authors have given a matrix approach for implementing node capture attack. They have shown that Matrix approach is better than random attack, maximum link attack and maximum node attack (Lin & Wu 2013).

In this technique, various matrices are created to store the vulnerability value of every node of the network. The node with highest value of destructiveness is selected in each round. After every round, the values of matrices are modified. It includes a high complexity. MA has lesser number of captured nodes thus least energy cost. However MA has not well addressed the energy cost and attacking efficiency(Lin, C,2016)

Authors have discussed about node capture attack and have given different approaches to detect the node capture attack in WSN. But these approaches are also not efficient, some more methods need to be developed (Selvamani et al., 2012)

Authors have used flow of current from an electric circuit to represent a compromise traffic. It is used to quantify the vulnerability of network. A metric named vulnerability is given and it is calculated based on routing path. A minimum cost node capture attack model is given that is based on greedy heuristic. It results in lesser energy cost and maximum destructiveness in the network (Poovendran et al., 2008).

Authors have discussed about FFOA and its improved versions and hybrid FOA approaches. We know that there are different methods to perform node capture attack in WSN. Our aim to is to enhance the attack efficiency of node capture attack in these networks. Different approaches have different efficiencies in terms of number of attacking round, cost required in compromising the network, and other parameters too. So, we propose to find out the best approach which would compromise the complete network in minimum attacking rounds and least cost. For this purpose, we would create a random network and simulate different techniques of node capture attack on it. Then, we would do a comparative study of the results generated by these attacks. But as theoretical studies propose, these attacks have several drawbacks. So, we would run optimization algorithms on top of these attacks, to generate optimal results. Firstly, we have performed three basic attacks on our network, namely, Random Attack, Maximum Key Attack and Maximum Link Attack. We have provided the pseudo codes for these attack algorithms (Iscan & Gunduz, 2015).

WSNs are generally placed in hostile areas thus node capture is one of the critical attack. an adversarial model is given based on different vulnerability factors of the network such as node density, placement of sink node, neighbor influence factor that enhances the capability of attacker (Dave et al., 2018).

In data aggregation, node capture can significantly reduce the performance . It exposes the network to leakage of confidentiality. In this technique the cluster head selects the set of nodes. During data transfer, portions of data are transferred encrypted by authenticated keys. When a node receives the data portions then, it combines them and send to cluster head. Thus, it is able to mitigate the effect of node capture impact on the network (Bhoopathy & Parvathi 2012).

Authors presented multiple objective such as maximum node compromise, key participation, resource expenditure. It is used to find the optimal set of nodes to capture the complete network. PSO and GA are used to find this optimal set. It is shown that FiRAO-PG has higher destructiveness than MA (Tantubay et al., 2015).

Authors emphasized the maintenance of network connectivity in net centric warfare. In this paper several factors that can influence the connectivity are studied such as key predistribution. A relationship between network connectivity and key predistribution is given . An expression is formulated to find out the required communication radius for such kind of applications (Chan & Fekri, 2007).

Pseudo Code 1: Random Attack (nodes, paths, VK, cost)
```
1:   Initialize arrays to store performance of attack.
2:   while network is not compromised do
3:   Select a random node.
4:   Attack the selected node.
5:   Update the cost and keys acquired.
6:   Compromise the network using the nodes captured.
7:   end while
8:   return attack statistics.
```

Pseudo Code 2: Maximum Key Attack (nodes, paths, VK, cost)
```
1:   Initialize arrays to store performance of attack.
2:   while network is not compromised do
3:   Select the node having maximum keys.
4:   Attack the selected node.
5:   Update cost and keys acquired.
6:   Compromise the network using the nodes captured.
7:   end while
8:   return attack statistics.
```

Pseudo Code 3: Maximum Link Attack (nodes, paths, VK, cost, adjList)
```
1.   Initialize the arrays to store performance of attack.
2.   While network is not compromised do
3.   Select the node having maximum neighbors.
4.   Attack the selected node.
5.   Update the cost and keys acquired.
6.   Compromise the network using the nodes captured.
7.   End while
8.   Return attack statistics.
```

After performing these three basic attacks, we have implemented Fruit Fly Optimization Algorithm, which needs different matrices to be calculated upon which it performs optimization. These matrices show the relation of nodes with keys and routes.

Pseudo Code 4: FFOA (nodes, paths, VK, cost, keys)
1. Initialize the arrays to store performance of attack.
2. Pre-process the attack data (Generate matrices)
3. While network is not compromised do
4. Select the node having minimum aggregate cost.
5. Attack the selected node.
6. Update the cost and keys acquired.
7. Compromise the network using the nodes captured.
8. Re-evaluate the aggregate cost.
9. End while
10. Return attack statistics.

After performing these attacks, we have developed an algorithm which is an optimization over the Fruit Fly Optimization Algorithm (FFOA), where, after capturing a node we are re-evaluating the matrices over the network again by considering the already captured keys and not using them again for the remaining un captured nodes. This way the results produced are more optimal and hence, the number of rounds and the energy cost are minimized.

Pseudo Code 5: Enhanced FFOA (nodes, paths, VK, cost, keys):
1. Initialize the arrays to store performance of attack.
2. While network is not compromised do
3. Generate the network parameters.
4. Select the node having minimum network cost.
5. Attack the selected node.
6. Update the cost and keys acquired.
7. Compromise the network using the keys captured.
8. Re-evaluate the network links.
9. End while
10. Return attack statistics.

After implementing all these approaches, we have provided a comparative result in the form of different plots over different parameters.

DATA FLOW DIAGRAM

This section details the data flow diagram of proposed approach.

1 Level 0 DFD

Figure 3. Level 0 DFD

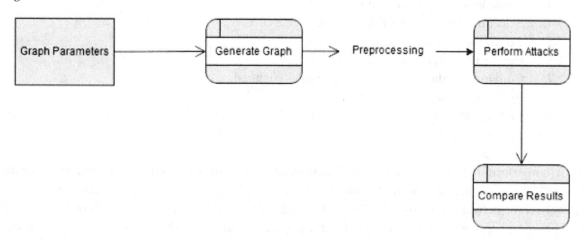

2 Level 1 DFD.

Figure 4. Level 1 DFD

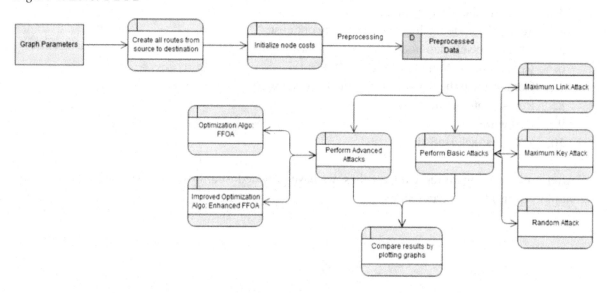

3 Level 2 DFD

Figure 5. Level 2 DFD

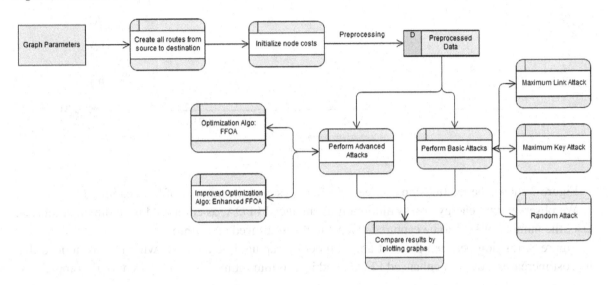

IMPLEMENTATION DETAILS

Initially, we create a random network of predetermined number of nodes (here, we have taken number of nodes to be 25). Then we allocate some number of keys randomly to each node (here, we have taken a total of 500 keys, and to each node, we have randomly allocated 3 to 15 keys), and we are storing this network using adjacency matrices. We have selected a node as the source vertex and a node as destination vertex. We have created all routes from source to destination. We have assumed that the attacker has information about the key pre-distribution model and routing mechanism used in the WSN. Also, we have allocated some predefined cost of capturing each vertex. Then, we have implemented 3 basic attacks, namely, Random Attack, Maximum Key Attack and Maximum Link Attack. After these three basic attacks, we have implemented fruit fly optimization algorithm, which requires some matrices to be computed that store the relations between nodes, routes and keys. Finally, we have developed an efficient algorithm, which is an optimized version of FFOA.

RESULTS AND OBSERVATIONS

By performing different attacks on the randomly created network, we have gathered sufficient information about different parameters, by which we can compare the efficiency of these attacks.

If we notice the number of nodes to be captured to compromise the whole network, we observed that the proposed algorithm outperforms the other algorithms, particularly in this aspect. It requires minimum number of nodes to be captured to compromise the complete traffic. It is shown in Fig 6. It is due the fact we have improved the basic FFOA to further minimize the number of captured nodes.

Figure 6. Fraction of traffic compromised v/s number of captured nodes

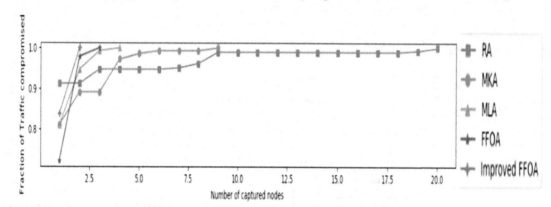

Figure 7 shows the relationship between the final cost and the number of keys captured.

We observed that energy cost is minimum in enhanced FFOA, as compared with the other attacks. Also, the number of keys to be captured is least in this improved algorithm.

Figure 8, relation between the cost and number of captured nodes is shown and it is noticed that the cost increases slowly in enhanced FFOA, and is also minimum, when compared to its competitors.

Figure 7 Energy Cost v/s Number of keys captured

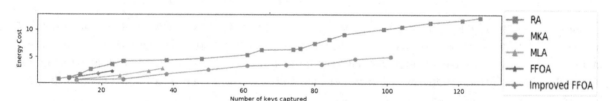

Figure 8 Cost v/s Number of Captured Nodes

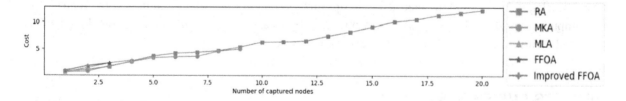

CONCLUSION AND FUTURE PLAN

This chapter concludes that the enhanced node capture attack outperforms the basic attacks like MLA, MKA and RA in almost all perspectives. The reason for such improved performance of FFOA as compared to other algorithms is its consideration to multiple objectives at every point whereas the simpler algorithms mostly work on a single objective which is either capturing node with maximum key, maximum links or minimum cost. But FFOA takes note of all these parameters and captures the node which yields maximum damage in terms of links and keys with keeping minimum cost in mind. The improved FFOA works even better due to its dynamic nature towards current network and hence predicting more precisely the node which yields maximum damage. The multiple objective function in advanced algorithms can also be adjusted in reference to contribution of keys and links and hence provides more dynamic and adjusting way to perform an efficient attack. The main problem with advanced or improved attacks is their time complexity with respect to number of nodes and paths. These algorithms take way longer time as compared to basic algorithms and hence can be improved further by inculcating dynamic behavior along with consideration to time taken. Though the results were promising there is still scope of enhancement in future. Firstly, the time taken to attack a network is currently very large so we can work on the time complexity aspect of the improved FFOA. The other thing we can work on is making our attack model responsive to the changes in WSN. As WSN is a mobile network therefore the topology and hence the connectivity of the network keeps changing with time as new nodes are added to network and existing nodes leave network but our assumption of fixed nodes with fixed locations doesn't allow us to incorporate these changes. The other thing we can experiment upon is changing the criteria of selection of node. Currently the node to be attacked in improved FFOA is searched over the entire network which can be changed to some subset of nodes instead of searching over the entire network. As a future work, this algorithm can be applied to clustered senor networks and WSN with mobile nodes. Further, optimization algorithms like simulated annealing, binary PSO, genetic algorithm may also be used to minimize the number of captured nods of the network.

REFERENCES

Ahlawat, P., & Dave, M. (2018). An attack model based highly secure key management scheme for wireless sensor networks. *Procedia Computer Science*, *125*, 201–207. doi:10.1016/j.procs.2017.12.028

Ahlawat, P., & Dave, M. (2018). An attack resistant key predistribution scheme for wireless sensor networks. *Journal of King Saud University-Computer and Information Sciences*.

Bharathi, Tanguturi, JayaKumar, & Selvamani. (2012). Node capture attack in Wireless Sensor Network: A survey. *2012 IEEE International Conference on Computational Intelligence and Computing Research, ICCIC 2012*, 1-3. 10.1109/ICCIC.2012.6510237

Bhatt, R., Maheshwary, P., Shukla, P., Shukla, P., Shrivastava, M., & Changlani, S. (2020). Implementation of Fruit Fly Optimization Algorithm (FFOA) to escalate the attacking efficiency of node capture attack in Wireless Sensor Networks (WSN). *Computer Communications*, *149*, 134–145. doi:10.1016/j.comcom.2019.09.007

Bonaci, T., Bushnell, L., & Poovendran, R. (2010, December). Node capture attacks in wireless sensor networks: A system theoretic approach. In *49th IEEE Conference on Decision and Control (CDC)* (pp. 6765-6772). IEEE. 10.1109/CDC.2010.5717499

Chan, H., Perrig, A., & Song, D. (2003, May). Random key predistribution schemes for sensor networks. In *2003 Symposium on Security and Privacy*, 2003 (pp. 197-213). IEEE. 10.1109/SECPRI.2003.1199337

Chan, K., & Fekri, F. (2007, May). Node compromise attacks and network connectivity. In *Defense Transformation and Net-Centric Systems 2007* (Vol. 6578, p. 65780W). International Society for Optics and Photonics.

Chhabra, Gupta, & Almomani. (2013). *A novel solution to handle DDOS attack in MANET*. Academic Press.

De, P., Liu, Y., & Das, S. K. (2006, June). Modeling node compromise spread in wireless sensor networks using epidemic theory. In *2006 International Symposium on a World of Wireless, Mobile and Multimedia Networks (WoWMoM'06)*. IEEE. 10.1109/WOWMOM.2006.74

Du, W., Deng, J., Han, Y. S., Chen, S., & Varshney, P. K. (2004, March). A key management scheme for wireless sensor networks using deployment knowledge. In *IEEE INFOCOM 2004* (Vol. 1). IEEE.

Ehdaie, M., Alexiou, N., Ahmadian, M., Aref, M. R., & Papadimitratos, P. (2017). Mitigating Node Capture Attack in Random Key Distribution Schemes through Key Deletion. *Journal of Communication Engineering*, *6*(2), 99–109.

Eschenauer, L., & Gligor, V. D. (2002, November). A key-management scheme for distributed sensor networks. In *Proceedings of the 9th ACM conference on Computer and communications security* (pp. 41-47). 10.1145/586110.586117

Iscan, H., & Gunduz, M. (2015, November). A survey on fruit fly optimization algorithm. In *2015 11th International Conference on Signal-Image Technology & Internet-Based Systems (SITIS)* (pp. 520-527). 10.1109/SITIS.2015.55

Jain, A. K., & Gupta, B. B. (2019). A machine learning based approach for phishing detection using hyperlinks information. *Journal of Ambient Intelligence and Humanized Computing*, *10*(5), 2015–2028. doi:10.100712652-018-0798-z

Lin, C., Qiu, T., Obaidat, M. S., Yu, C. W., Yao, L., & Wu, G. (2016). MREA: A minimum resource expenditure node capture attack in wireless sensor networks. *Security and Communication Networks*, *9*(18), 5502–5517. doi:10.1002ec.1713

Lin, C., Wu, G., Yu, C. W., & Yao, L. (2015). Maximizing destructiveness of node capture attack in wireless sensor networks. *The Journal of Supercomputing*, *71*(8), 3181–3212. doi:10.100711227-015-1435-7

Lin & Guowei Wu. (2013). Enhancing the attacking efficiency of the node captureattack in WSN: a matrix approach. *J Supercomput, Springer Science &Business Media*, 1-19.

Qin, T., & Chen, H. (2012). An Enhanced Scheme against Node Capture Attack using Hash-Chain for Wireless Sensor Networks. *Journal of Information Technology*, *11*(1), 102–109. doi:10.3923/itj.2012.102.109

Shaila, K., Manjula, S. H., Thriveni, J., Venugopal, K. R., & Patnaik, L. M. (2011). Resilience against node capture attack using asymmetric matrices in key predistribution scheme in wireless sensor networks. *International Journal on Computer Science and Engineering*, *3*(10), 3490.

Shukla, P. K., Goyal, S., Wadhvani, R., Rizvi, M. A., Sharma, P., & Tantubay, N. (2015). Finding robust assailant using optimization functions (FiRAO-PG) in wireless sensor network. *Mathematical Problems in Engineering*, *2015*, 2015. doi:10.1155/2015/594345

Tague, P., Slater, D., Rogers, J., & Poovendran, R. (2008, April). Vulnerability of network traffic under node capture attacks using circuit theoretic analysis. In *IEEE INFOCOM 2008-The 27th Conference on Computer Communications* (pp. 161-165). IEEE 10.1109/INFOCOM.2008.41

Wang, Z., Zhou, C., & Liu, Y. (2017). *Efficient hybrid detection of node replication attacks in mobile sensor networks*. Mobile Information Systems.

Zhu, Q., Bushnell, L., & Başar, T. (2012, December). Game-theoretic analysis of node capture and cloning attack with multiple attackers in wireless sensor networks. In *2012 IEEE 51st IEEE Conference on Decision and Control (CDC)* (pp. 3404-3411). IEEE. 10.1109/CDC.2012.6426481

KEY TERMS AND DEFINITIONS

Collusion Resistant: It is the property of key management in which the keys generated by key server are distinct. No two nodes are assigned same set of cryptographic keys.

Key Management: It is the process of creating, distributing to the senor nodes before they are deployed in sensor field. Later, it also includes the key refreshment process where cryptographic keys are changed to make the scheme secure against node capture attack.

Key Predistribution: It is one of the phase of the key management in which the cryptographic keys are created by the key distribution server. The generated keys should be collusion resistant.

Node Capture Attack: It is one of the prominent attack in WSN due to its hostile placement. During this attack, the adversary physically captures the node and steals the keying information stored in them by the network designer. It is used to launch future attacks in network.

Resistance Against Node Capture: It is the ability of the network to survive during node capture attack. It is the number of valid links of non-captured nodes are compromised when n nodes are captured by the adversary.

Chapter 13
Cybersecurity Risks Associated With Brain–Computer Interface Classifications

Sergio López Bernal
University of Murcia, Spain

Alberto Huertas Celdrán
University of Zürich, Switzerland

Gregorio Martínez Pérez
University of Murcia, Spain

ABSTRACT

Brain-computer interfaces (BCIs) have experienced a considerable evolution in the last decade, expanding from clinical scenarios to sectors such as entertainment or video games. Nevertheless, this popularization makes them a target for cyberattacks like malware. Current literature lacks comprehensive works focusing on cybersecurity applied to BCIs and, mainly, publications performing a rigorous analysis of the risks and weaknesses that these interfaces present. If not studied properly, these potential vulnerabilities could dramatically impact users' data, service availability, and, most importantly, users' safety. Because of that, this work introduces an evaluation of the risk that each BCI classification already defined in the literature presents to raise awareness between the readers of this chapter about the potential threat that BCIs can generate in the next years if comprehensive measures, based on standard mechanisms, are not adopted. Moreover, it seeks to alert academic and industrial stakeholders about the impact these risks could have on future BCI hardware and software.

DOI: 10.4018/978-1-7998-7789-9.ch013

Copyright © 2022, IGI Global. Copying or distributing in print or electronic forms without written permission of IGI Global is prohibited.

INTRODUCTION

Application Scenarios

Brain-Computer Interfaces (BCIs) are bidirectional devices that allow communication between the brain and external systems, such as computers. On the one hand, BCI systems permit the acquisition of neuronal data, study the status of the brain, and control external devices such as wheelchairs or prosthetic devices (Lebedev et al., 2017). On the other hand, they are used for neurostimulation procedures to stimulate targeted regions of the brain (Edwards et al., 2017). These separate approaches can be unified under the concept of bidirectional BCIs, which can alternate recording and stimulation actions to verify that the stimulation actions have the desired effect within the brain or offer feedback to BCI users through stimulation (Rao, 2019).

BCI technologies are mainly used in medical scenarios for the diagnosis and treatment of neurological diseases. Focusing on the acquisition perspective, BCIs are extensively used to detect various conditions, such as epilepsy, which allow the detection of anomalous neural activity (Sowndhararajan et al., 2018). They have also been used as mental speech systems, where the BCI can analyze the user's neural activity to determine each spelled letter (Guan et al., 2004). Additionally, technologies such as fMRI based on magnetic fields allow the visualization of the whole brain to detect damaged tissue, extensively used nowadays in most hospitals worldwide. Regarding neural stimulation, a wide variety of technologies is currently accepted by health agencies such as the American FDA to treat different illnesses. For example, Deep Brain Stimulation (DBS) is a BCI technology used to treat several conditions, such as Parkinson's Disease, essential tremor, or obsessive-compulsive disorders (Edwards et al., 2017).

Although BCIs are commonly used for medical purposes, these systems have gained popularity in other economic sectors. One of the most relevant is the military scenario, where the application of BCIs is studied in multiple scenarios (Binnendijk et al., 2020). One of these application scenarios is systems able to monitor soldiers' mental state, assessing the cognitive and emotional response against complex situations. They are also being researched to augment soldiers' mental capabilities in physical, cognitive, and emotional dimensions. Additionally, they could serve as systems to mentally transmit commands between individuals, improving the telecommunication systems on the battlefield. Finally, these devices are interesting for controlling exoskeletons, aiming to restore lost motor functionality or even improve natural human strength.

Another emerging application sector for BCIs is the entertainment and video game industries, where BCI systems have been used for controlling the avatar of the game with the mind (Ahn et al., 2014). The application of BCI technologies could generate a revolution in this field, similar to introducing virtual reality technologies in recent years. Despite these recreational purposes, the application of BCIs in video games also positively benefits neurorehabilitation therapies, where these systems can improve lost motor abilities (McMahon et al., 2018).

Moreover, new technologies and application scenarios have emerged in recent years, presenting considerable engineering challenges. First, invasive BCIs are moving to the miniaturization of their electrodes, aiming to reduce the damage caused by surgical procedures, and a better resolution and coverage of the brain (Musk, 2019). Furthermore, BCIs are incipiently used to allow users to access the Internet with their minds (Saboor et al., 2018) or even allow direct mental communication between subjects (Pais-Vieira et al., 2013).

The evolution and diversification of these technologies have derived in a differentiation of BCIs based on multiple classifications. One of these classifications is the invasiveness of BCI devices, differentiating those placed within the skull from those applied externally (Bonaci et al., 2015a; Lebedev et al., 2017). A second classification is based on the BCI design, which indicates how the acquisition or stimulation process is initiated, either by the user or the BCI (Wahlstrom et al., 2016; Ramadan et al., 2017). Based on these differentiations, multiple technologies have emerged in recent years, aiming to satisfy requirements not covered by the existing ones for both acquisition and stimulation procedures. The technology used represents the third classification analyzed in this chapter (Ramadan et al., 2017; Polanía et al., 2018). Another interesting classification consists in the synchronization of the BCIs, indicating who controls the processes (An et al., 2016; Ramadan et al., 2017). The last studied classification lies in the application scenario, such as neuromedical or gaming and entertainment (Li et al., 2015).

Motivation

Although BCI technologies present enormous benefits and future potential, in the past few years, the academic literature has addressed cybersecurity in BCIs, detecting attacks that can have a negative effect on these technologies. These works have identified cryptographic attacks aiming to disrupt the encryption mechanisms used to protect the transmitted data between BCI devices and computers, being essential to implement robust cryptographic systems (Gupta et al., 2016). They also indicated that jamming attacks focused on emitting electromagnetic noise could prevent the electrodes from acquiring neural data (Bonaci et al., 2015a; Ienca et al., 2016). Additionally, Bonaci et al. (2015a) detected that attackers could use malware strategies to affect data integrity and data confidentiality, compromising the normal functioning of the system. However, these works only focused on particular aspects of BCI systems, without an in-depth coverage of the situation. Based on this lack of comprehensive studies, Lopez-Bernal et al. (2019) reviewed the state of the art of cybersecurity applied to BCIs, analyzing attacks, impacts, and countermeasures applicable over both the BCI functioning cycle and common architectural deployments. However, that research does not cover the cybersecurity analysis from the perspective of BCI classifications. Based on that, this chapter detects an opportunity in the academic literature to perform a risk evaluation of existing BCI systems.

Contributions

Considering the absence of literature analyzing the cybersecurity aspects related to BCI classifications, the main contribution of this chapter is a review of the most critical risks associated with each particular classification from the data integrity, data confidentiality, data and service availability, and safety perspectives. This classification analysis highlights the most relevant cybersecurity impacts of each BCI family, aiming to alert about the vulnerabilities present in BCI technologies.

The remainder of this chapter is structured as follows. The Background section presents the current state of the art regarding cybersecurity on BCIs, and introduces the most common BCI classifications defined in the literature. After that, the Risk assessment of BCI classifications section presents an analysis of the risks existing for BCI classification. Section Future research directions highlights the current trend and future evolution of BCIs, indicating possible opportunities in this area. Finally, the Conclusion section presents a summary of the chapter.

BACKGROUND

This section first focuses on the analysis of cyberthreats proposed by the current academic literature. After that, it presents the most common BCI classifications proposed in the literature, indicating the BCI families included in each classification.

Cybersecurity on BCIs

Research focusing on cybersecurity applied to BCIs has gained importance in recent years, where the literature has documented threats against these technologies. Among the identified cyberattacks, Martinovic et al. (2012) documented that the presentation of malicious visual stimuli to BCI users using the P300 paradigm could extract sensitive information such as PIN numbers, the user's month of birth, area of living, or bank-related data. Frank et al. (2017) extended this study, considering the idea of subliminal visual stimuli, where the user is not aware of the attack, and determining that this approach could be feasible.

Li et al. (2015) and Landau et al. (2020) identified the applicability of replay and spoofing attacks over BCI systems, where the attacker acquires legitimate neuronal signals from a user, later retransmitting them to the medium. These could be particularly damaging in BCI authentication scenarios, where the attacker obtains the neural signals able to authenticate a user, used later to gain control over the protected assets. Additionally, the literature has detected the feasibility of jamming attacks (Ienca et al., 2016; Landau et al., 2020), preventing the BCI from acquiring neural signals from the brain by transmitting electromagnetic noise to the medium.

One of the most damaging attacks in computer systems is malware (Gupta et al., 2018), which is also one of the most harmful threats over BCI systems. Bonaci et al. (2015a) documented that current BCI applications and app stores do not implement security standards, not consider privacy or security measures. Based on that, a malicious developer could create an application containing malware, defining two attack strategies. The first one would focus on hijacking the legitimate components and algorithms of the BCI, changing the behavior of the feature extraction and decoding phases of the BCI functioning cycle. The second attack could focus on adding or replacing legitimate BCI components. In summary, malware attacks could alter the integrity of the BCI, making them vulnerable to malicious actions.

Inspired by the previous attacks, López Bernal et al. (2020a) identified vulnerabilities over emerging BCI solutions focused on stimulating individual neurons, such as Neuralink. They indicated that, based on these vulnerabilities, an attacker could take advantage of these vulnerabilities to control the BCI to disrupt the neurostimulation and alter spontaneous neural behavior. They defined the concepts of Neuronal Flooding and Neuronal Scanning cyberattacks as mechanisms able to disrupt neural behavior, inspired by computer communication attacks and mechanisms. The experimentation presented indicated that these threats can reduce the number of neuronal spikes produced, generating an increment in the temporal dispersion of these spikes as well.

Although the literature has addressed specific cybersecurity threats against BCIs, there was a necessity for academic works gathering all the knowledge about the topic. Based on that, López Bernal et al. (2019) introduced a fist identification of cyberattacks and countermeasures applicable to the phases of the BCI cycle. After that, López Bernal et al. (2020b) comprehensively reviewed the state of the art of cybersecurity on BCIs, analyzing the attacks applicable to each phase of the BCI functioning cycle, the impacts that they generate, and the possible countermeasures to mitigate them. Additionally, that work also reviewed the attacks, impacts, and countermeasures of the most common architectural deployments. In summary, the authors determined a lack of comprehensive works and solutions addressing cybersecurity issues in the BCI field.

BCI Classifications

This subsection presents the different classifications studied in the chapter, previously defined in the academic literature, studying the design of the BCIs, the technology that they use, their level of invasiveness, the synchronization approach used between the user and the BCI, and finally, the BCI application scenario.

Design of BCIs

The first classification studied in this work is the design of BCIs, which indicates who is responsible for initiating the neural data acquisition process and how the process is performed. In other words, this classification indicates if the user or the BCI triggers the process and how the interaction is done to perform the intended actions (Zander et al., 2010; Wahlstrom et al., 2016; Hong et al., 2017; Lebedev et al., 2017; Ramadan et al., 2017). According to this categorization, four BCI families have been defined in the literature: active, passive, reactive, and hybrid.

In active BCIs, also known as independent (Lebedev et al., 2017) or spontaneous (Ramadan et al., 2017), users intentionally initiate a predefined action that generates brain activity, such as imaging limb movements, which is then captured by the BCI (Zander et al., 2010; Lebedev et al., 2017). An example of an action is the imagination of limb movements (Lebedev et al., 2017). Active BCIs have been used by Gilja et al. (2012) for the control of a computer cursor in rhesus monkeys.

Passive BCIs, in contrast to active BCIs, focus on the acquisition of spontaneous and non-evoked brain activity, typically generated during complex real-world tasks, such as the actions performed by a pilot during a flight (Zander et al., 2010, Wahlstrom et al., 2016). Passive BCIs have been used to measure mental states such as attention, stress, workload, or emotions (Aricò et al., 2018).

The third family is termed Reactive BCIs, also identified as dependent (Lebedev et al., 2017) or evoked (Ramadan et al., 2017). This family depends on external stimuli presented to the users and the neural responses generated by their brains as a response. Reactive BCIs are used, for example, to detect situations in which the user recognizes known external stimuli from a set of unknown stimuli.

Finally, Hybrid BCIs can be considered from two perspectives. On the one hand, they are BCI systems that receive different types of brain signals as input (Lebedev et al., 2017). Focusing on this approach, Ramadan et al. (2017) and Hong et al. (2017) showed different possibilities and their purpose. For example, a combination of EEG and EMG to improve accuracy and enhance application performance. On the other hand, Wahlstrom et al. (2016) defined hybrid BCIs as a combination of at least one active, passive, or reactive BCI system with non-BCI technologies to improve system performance (e.g., a combination of an active BCI and a finite-state automaton to control a robot).

BCI Technology

The technology used by the BCI is the second classification, where two additional subclassifications arise depending on if they are intended for acquiring neural data or for brain stimulation. The most representative technologies considering the acquisition of brain waves are Electroencephalography (EEG), Functional Magnetic Resonance Imaging (fMRI), Magnetoencephalography (MEG), Electrocorticography (ECoG), and neural dust. On the other hand, focusing on brain stimulation techniques, the most relevant ones are Transcranial Magnetic Stimulation (TMS), Transcranial Electrical Stimulation(tES), Transcranial Focused Ultrasound (tFUS), Deep Brain Stimulation (DBS), and neural dust (Tyler et al., 2017; Polanía et al., 2018).

Related to neural activity recording, EEG is a non-invasive technology that uses electrodes placed on the scalp (Ramadan et al., 2017). This technology highlights for being easy to use, cheap, portable, and with a high temporal resolution, in the order of milliseconds (vanGerven et al., 2009; Ramadan et al., 2017). It is the most widely used non-invasive technology, mainly in video games and entertainment (Ahn et al., 2014; McMahon et al., 2018). However, it has a poor spatial resolution, and the acquired brain waves can be distorted by other neural activity, such as the movements of muscles and eyes, known as artifacts (vanGerven et al., 2009).

fMRI is another non-invasive technology used to measure the variation of blood hemoglobin concentrations during brain activity. It has better spatial resolution than EEG and MEG, identifying active zones throughout the brain. However, it has a low temporal resolution, between one and two seconds (vanGerven et al., 2009; Lebedev et al., 2017; Ramadan et al., 2017). The resolution of fMRI is also affected by head movements (Ramadan et al., 2017). This technology is useful in clinical scenarios to treat neurological conditions such as stroke or mental disorders, although it does not apply to everyday use (Lebedev et al., 2017).

Continuing with non-invasive recording technologies, MEG uses functional neuroimaging over magnetic fields produced by the electric current generated by cortical neurons. This method has an excellent temporal and spatial resolution. Despite these benefits, MEG can only be used in magnetically shielded installations, and it is not portable. This technology is widely used to detect regions with abnormal brain functions and in tetraplegic and stroke patients (Lebedev et al., 2017; Ramadan et al., 2017).

Finally, ECoG is a partial-invasive method in which a grid of electrodes is placed on the brain surface (Lebedev et al., 2017). It offers an SNR superior to non-invasive systems, such as EEG, and higher spatial and temporal resolution. Besides, it allows better detection of high-frequency oscillatory activity (vanGerven et al., 2009). Despite the above advantages, ECoG cannot be used to detect single-neuron spikes (Lebedev et al., 2017), and it is very challenging to use these devices outside an operating room (Ramadan et al., 2017).

Regarding the stimulation of neurons, TMS is a technology that generates electrical fields within the brain, reaching the cortex and aiming to modulate brain activity and behavior. This technology obtained FDA approval in 2018 to treat depression and headaches (Tyler et al., 2017). TMS has also been used for testing dynamic communication between interconnected areas of the brain (Polanía et al., 2018) and cognitive aging (Gomes-Osman et al., 2018). Although TMS has a good temporal resolution, it presents an inadequate spatial precision (Lebedev et al., 2017).

tES is another stimulation technique that uses weak, painless currents applied to the scalp (Polanía et al., 2018). It can be based on direct current stimulation (tDCS) or alternating current stimulation (tACS). tDCS is a simple method that stimulates the cortex and affects relatively large areas, presenting a low spatial and temporal resolution. In contrast, tACS presents good temporal precision (Polanía et al., 2018). It has been reported that tES can enhance and perturb cognitive processes, such as creative problem solving or working memory, when applied to different brain regions. Furthermore, it can improve working memory performance and motor behavior (Tyler et al., 2017; Polanía et al., 2018). Although these technologies are promising, they are not mature enough for their use in humans in terms of reliability and reproducibility (Tyler et al., 2017; Bikson et al., 2018).

tFUS is a novel neuromodulation technique that offers a high spatial resolution, being the only non-invasive technology able to penetrate the skull and stimulate specific circuits deep in the brain (Kubanek et al., 2018, Legon et al., 2018). It has been used to stimulate the activity of cortical, thalamic, and hippocampal circuits in animals (Tyler et al., 2017), and it may be useful to identify and treat neurological and psychiatric disorders in humans, such as neuropathic pain or depression, due to its potential to induce plastic changes in aberrant brain circuits (Kubanek et al., 2018).

Finally, DBS is an invasive neurostimulation technique that involves a surgical procedure for implanting electrodes deep within the brain. This invasiveness provides DBS with acceptable spatial and temporal resolution. Focusing on their functioning, the implanted device sends electric currents into targeted subcortical areas to increase, suppress, or distort neural activity. This method has been used to treat conditions such as Parkinson's disease, dystonia, and chronic pain syndromes (Denning et al., 2009; Ienca et al., 2016; Khabarova et al.; 2018, Kubanek et al., 2018). Despite the benefits of DBS, the associated surgeries required may have complications such as infection or hemorrhage (Kubanek et al., 2018).

Neural nanonetworks comprise several technologies to record and stimulate neural activity through the use of nanodevices. In particular, neural dust is a solution to acquire neural data relying on nanodevices allocated into the cortex, beneath the skull, and below the dura mater (Seo et al., 2013; Lebedev et al., 2017). An interrogator is powered by an external transceiver using radio frequency power transfer (Seo et al., 2013), and it establishes wireless power and communication with the neural dust using ultrasounds (Seo et al., 2013, Neely et al., 2018). This nanotechnology offers some advantages, as it does not use microelectrode shafts that can damage the nervous tissue, it records very enclosed areas within the brain, and it can work as a closed-loop system based on real-time adaptation, offering high spatial and temporal resolution (Lebedev et al., 2017). It is also an interesting alternative to electromagnetic systems due to its lower attenuation and higher efficiency (Neely et al., 2018). Wirdatmadja et al. (2017) used the neural dust model defined by Seo et al. (2013) to propose a stimulation system based on optogenetic nanonetworks and the definition of different firing patterns (e.g., brain regions, frequencies, temporal synchronization) to interact with the devices. Zheng et al. (2019) developed an implantable device based on optogenetic stimulation for peripheral nerves, focused on activating limb muscles. Lee et al. (2019) defined the concept of Neurograin sensors, implementing a network of nanodevices that uses wireless energy harvesting, and validated in both ex vivo and in vivo rodent tests. Despite the advantages of these technologies, they are experimental, and they have not yet been tested in humans (Lebedev et al., 2017). Additionally, the architecture of neural dust has been identified as vulnerable by López Bernal et al. (2020a).

Level of Invasiveness

The invasiveness level classification indicates whether the BCI device is implanted in the user's body or placed externally. This classification has been widely studied in the literature (vanGerven et al., 2009; Bonaci et al., 2015a; Li et al., 2015; Vaid et al., 2015; Ienca et al., 2016; Wahlstrom et al., 2016; Frank et al., 2017; Ramadan et al., 2017; Lebedev et al., 2017; Polania et al., 2018), where the following three families have been proposed: invasive, partial-invasive and non-invasive.

Invasive systems require a neurosurgery process involving opening the scalp, the skull and placing the BCI components in the brain tissue to record or stimulate neurons. This technology has been used mainly in the medical field because it allows measuring neural activity with very little noise. In the last decades, they allow direct interaction with the brain, enabling the stimulation of individual neurons (Lebedev et al., 2017; Wirdatmadja et al., 2017).

The second family of this category is called partial-invasive, and the BCI components are placed on the brain surface without penetrating the nervous tissue. This family is used in medicine, for example, with subdural electrodes aiming to identify the location of epileptic seizures (vanGerven et al., 2009; Yang et al., 2014). This type of BCIs has lower temporal and spatial resolution than the previous one, affecting its applicability in some application scenarios.

Finally, non-invasive BCIs are applied outside the skull, directly on the scalp. They present lower temporal and spatial resolution than the previous two families due to the attenuation and filter provoked by the bone and skin. However, they have an essential role in the health field, where non-invasive neural stimulation systems are gaining popularity (Ramadan et al., 2017). Additionally, these technologies are the most extended systems due to their simplicity and applicability in entertainment scenarios, where final users benefit from their advantages (Li et al., 2015; Ramadan et al., 2017).

Synchronization

The fourth classification considered in this work is the synchronization of BCIs, focused on the interaction between the BCIs and the users. It determines who controls the recording and stimulation processes and in which time slots. Based on that, two families of BCIs have been documented in the literature (An et al., 2016; Ramadan et al., 2017): synchronous and asynchronous.

In synchronous (or cue-paced) BCI systems, the interaction between the user and the BCI occurs during specific periods (Ramadan et al., 2017). This planning is imposed by the BCI, which controls the communication. Outside these periods, the BCI is not able to communicate with the user. They are easier to implement than asynchronous BCIs, but they are not suitable for acquiring users' mental intentions (An et al., 2016). Bentabet et al. (2016) used synchronous BCIs to control domotic devices, extracting features from P300 waves.

In contrast, in asynchronous (or self-paced) systems, users can generate brain signals at any time, and the BCI will react to these events. Ramadan et al. (2017) highlighted the complexity of detecting idle states and proposed using a button to activate or deactivate the acquisition of stimuli. An et al. (An et al., 2016) proposed an asynchronous BCI to control a virtual avatar in a game. In this game, the avatar competes with other users in a race, running continuously and, when a control command is received, an action on the avatar is performed. As can be seen, these systems depend on the moment and the action performed by the user, without control imposed from the BCI.

Usage Scenario

The application scenario is another well-known BCI classification. It was proposed by Li et al. (2015), and they highlighted the following four types: neuromedical, user authentication, gaming and entertainment, and smartphone-based BCIs.

The field of neuromedical applications has been the center of research in BCI for decades. The applications developed within this field range from the control of prosthetic limbs and wheelchairs (Denning et al., 2009; Li et al., 2015; Ienca et al., 2016) to the use in brain stimulation procedures (Lebedev et al., 2017; Wirdatmadja et al., 2017; Polanía et al., 2018). Besides, Chaudhary et al. (2017) used BCIs to establish a simple communication system with wholly paralyzed patients. Nowadays, current research on BCIs focuses on novel mechanisms and technologies to analyze and stimulate the brain.

The second scenario is the use of BCIs as authentication systems. The authentication process consists in recording the user's brain waves while performing a previously established task. The acquired neural data is then validated against the entity, containing the authentication data to validate the user. Brain signals are an excellent biometric element since each brain generates unique patterns (Bonaci et al., 2015a, Takabi et al., 2016b), and the mental action that triggers the authentication process can be modified, enabling an adaptive and flexible authentication mechanism. Finally, brain signals can be easily affected, and it is difficult to reproduce them under the effects of stress, anxiety, or drugs (Martinovic et al., 2012).

The third family, gaming and entertainment, arose due to the utility of BCIs in the video game industry to control the actions transmitted to the game with the mind. The development tasks allowing their creation have been facilitated by using standard APIs (Takabi et al., 2016b). Ahn et al. (2014) reviewed BCI games, highlighting games such as Bacteria Hunt, and performed a survey involving researchers, game developers, and users. McMahon et al. (2018) focused on virtual reality and created a low-cost open-source development environment prototype for BCI games.

Finally, the smartphone-based BCIs are based on the relationship between BCIs and user applications stored in smartphones, where it is the most common usage scenario in commercial BCI brands, such as Emotive or Neurosky (Takabi et al., 2016b). Additionally, Pycroft et al. (2016) identified that computational devices, such as smartphones, introduce new risks and security problems. In this sense, Li et al. (2015) indicated that most of the issues existing in smartphones could also be applied to smartphone-based BCI applications. For example, gain access to data stored in the SD card, or transfer sensitive data to remote servers using malware attacks.

RISK ASSESSMENT OF BCI CLASSIFICATIONS

This section presents a quantitative analysis of the risks present in each classification introduced in the previous section, from the data integrity, data confidentiality, data and service availability, and safety perspectives. To facilitate the lecture of this section, Figure 1 presents a summary of the classifications studied, also included the different families included in each classification.

Design of BCIs

Regarding the cybersecurity risks associated with each family of this classification, this chapter identifies malicious external stimuli as the most damaging ones. They are exploited by misleading stimuli attacks (López Bernal et al., 2020b) by presenting malicious inputs to the user or the BCI to obtain a benefit. An example of this benefit is the use of subliminal visual stimuli to generate specific brain signals that imply sensitive data leakages, such as acquiring thoughts or personals beliefs. In this context, Wahlstrom et al. (2016) indicated that if users with active BCIs can stop the BCI functioning and they have given consent to acquire such data, there is no risk of confidentiality attacks. However, the authors of this chapter identify that misleading stimuli attacks applied to these BCIs generate data confidentiality concerns, as the conditions mentioned above do not prevent BCIs from suffering vulnerabilities.

Figure 1.BCI classifications studied and their associated families.

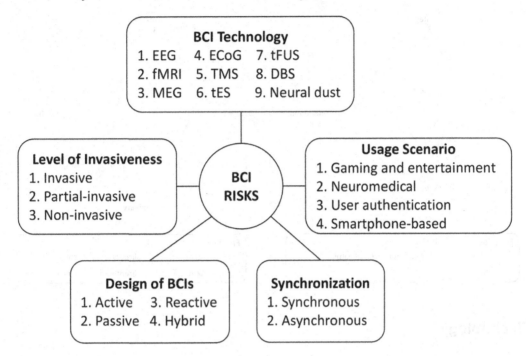

Additionally, Wahlstrom et al. (2016) documented that passive BCIs are at risk of data confidentiality attacks since users do not control the BCI. Moreover, they highlighted that in reactive BCIs, confidentiality issues are unlikely to arise if the neural activity is filtered, users are in a controlled environment, and consent to the procedure. In contrast, based on the subliminal visual principles mentioned above, misleading stimuli attacks have been detected in the literature for this kind of BCIs (Martinovic et al., 2012; Frank et al., 2017). Related to hybrid BCIs, Wahlstrom et al. (2016) identified that the risk of these technologies is the combination of the risks of each of their parts. Considering these aspects, the authors of this chapter also detect data integrity and data availability concerns in all BCI designs since misleading stimuli attacks can alter the data acquired by the BCI or even disrupt the data acquisition process. Besides, the authors identify safety issues generated from these problems. Based on the above concerns, hybrid BCIs have the highest risk, followed by reactive BCIs, passive BCIs, and finally active BCIs.

Figure 2 summarizes the risks described in this classification. Each family has been represented by a line color with a particular line style, while a number indicates the risks documented in this section. The severity of these risks has been considered based on four different types of impacts (integrity, confidentiality, availability, and safety), represented in the vertex of each radar chart. This severity is quantified on a scale between zero and three, where a zero value defines an absence of risk, and three represents a critical high risk.

Figure 2. Cybersecurity and safety risks associated with the design of BCIs

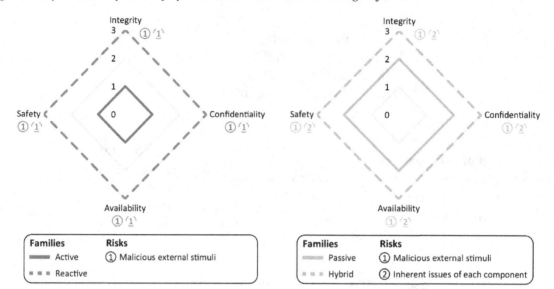

BCI Technology

The authors identify that both temporal and spatial resolutions generate significant cybersecurity risks. In particular, BCI technologies such as DBS, neural dust, ECoG, or MEG present higher risks in data confidentiality and safety than those with lower resolutions, like EEG, fMRI, or TMS. It is also important to highlight that the invasiveness of these methods also impacts the severity of the risks associated with each family. Because of that, DBS and neural dust have a higher risk than ECoG due to their invasiveness, and all of them are more damaging than MEG, as it is a non-invasive technology. In contrast, technologies with low resolutions present concerns on data and service availability since they transmit a reduced amount of data affected more easily by electromagnetic interference.

According to the inherent functioning of acquisition and stimulation systems, two more risks arise. On the one hand, since acquisition technologies aim to record neural data, they generate data integrity and confidentiality risks, where attacks can impersonate or gather users' neural data. On the other hand, stimulation systems mainly present safety issues, where attackers can cause brain damage. Several works in the literature review the safety concerns of stimulation technologies. According to Glannon et al. (2014), ECoG has a risk of infection and hemorrhage, and the microelectrode arrays used present potential problems of biocompatibility with neural tissue. Besides, Polanía et al. (2018) indicated that TMS pulses applied to particular areas could induce suppression of visual perception or speech arrest, which serve as an opportunity for attackers. Finally, the authors of the chapter identify electromagnetic noise as a risk directed over the physical aspects of non-invasive transmission systems. Technologies such as EEG acquire electrical currents, while fMRI and MEG acquire magnetic fields emitted from the brain. These specific aspects can serve as an opportunity for attackers to override the legitimate information generated by the brain, creating concerns in data integrity and availability.

Finally, Figure 3 indicates the risks that affect each of the BCI technologies documented in this classification. It is important to note that the invasiveness of these technologies also influences the risks associated with precision and electromagnetic noise. Because of that, invasive systems offer higher risks than non-invasive methods.

Figure 3. Cybersecurity and safety risks associated with the BCI technology

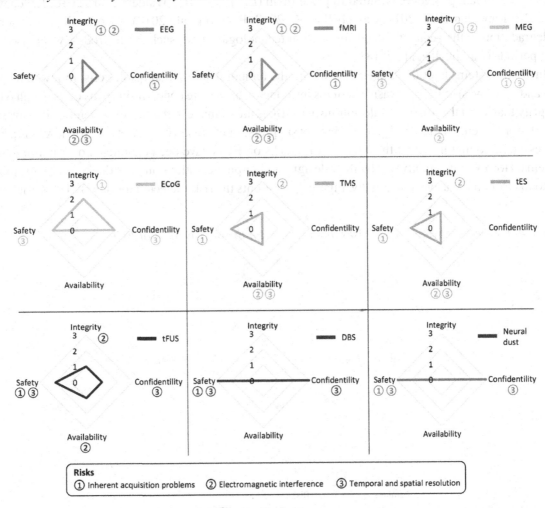

Level of Invasiveness

Analyzing the previous three families from the cybersecurity point of view, the authors have identified that two of the most severe risks are temporal and spatial resolutions. In this context, BCIs with higher spatial resolution can access more precise neural data or stimulate more specific brain regions than those with lower precision (Lebedev et al., 2017; Ramadan et al., 2017). A high temporal resolution allows attackers to perform more complex attacks since the communication delay is reduced. In this context, invasive systems have access to neural-level data, whereas less invasive systems acquire aggregated data with less resolution. That increase of precision generates concerns in data confidentiality, where systems with higher resolution have access to more precise and detailed information (e.g., thoughts or beliefs). Besides, the BCI precision can impact users' physical safety, where a high precision can increase the damage of attacks during neurostimulation processes. However, a reduction of the precision produces the transmission of a reduced quantity of data that can be insufficient for the correct functioning of BCIs in specific scenarios, impacting service availability. The level of intrusiveness is another risk detected in the literature. Invasive and partial-invasive BCIs are at risk of tissue damage, infection, and rejection due to the surgical procedure required to place them (Li et al., 2015; Waldert et al., 2016; Lebedev et al., 2017; Ramadan et al., 2017; Campbell et al., 2018; Pycroft et al., 2018). Also, both present a risk of degradation in the acquisition and stimulation technologies used, such as electrodes, when used for long periods (Campbell et al., 2018).

Invasive systems have the highest risk within the temporal and spatial resolutions, followed by partial- and non-invasive BCIs. Invasive systems introduce more severe concerns in terms of users' physical integrity than partial-invasive, while non-invasive BCIs are immune to them. Nevertheless, non-invasive stimulation systems significantly reduce, but not suppress, safety risks (Polanía et al., 2018). At this point, it is essential to highlight that the majority of attacks on BCIs have been conducted over non-invasive systems. However, it is motivated by their designs and implementations and not due to problems inherent to the level of invasiveness. Finally, Figure 4 represents the risks detected for this BCI classification.

Figure 4. Cybersecurity and safety risks associated with the invasiveness of BCIs

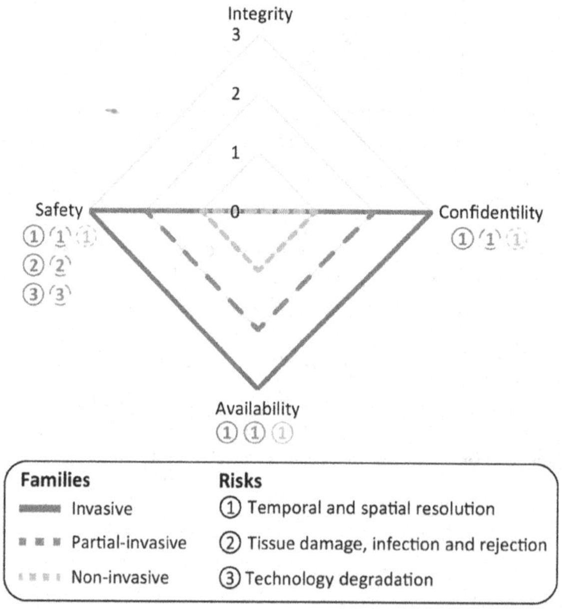

Synchronization

Considering the cybersecurity risks generated by these two families of BCIs, no risks have been documented in the literature. However, the authors identify that their main issue is losing control over the communication between a BCI and its user. In this context, the authors detected that synchronous BCIs, which control the communication, originate data integrity and confidentiality concerns, where attackers taking control over the BCI can gather and alter the neural data. Moreover, Ienca et al. (2018) highlighted the third parties with access to brain waves could extract private information from subjects. In this sense, we consider that, although this issue is extensible to all BCI families, synchronous systems could have a higher impact since more sensitive information could be acquired. Additionally, availability issues are possible, where attackers disable the data acquisition process, even without the users' knowledge. Finally, this lack of control can generate safety impacts, where attackers managing the functionality of BCIs can produce critical physical harm, such as malicious movements of a wheelchair or damaging stimulation patterns.

On the other hand, since asynchronous BCIs have fewer decision capabilities and awareness over the acquisition process, this chapter identifies that this BCI family has a risk of malicious external stimuli aiming to perform misleading stimuli attacks. These stimuli originate data integrity concerns, where attackers impersonate the neural data generated that is communicated to the BCI. Moreover, they generate data and service availability issues since these stimuli can impact the acquisition process and, thus, the normal functioning of the communication. Finally, the authors consider that asynchronous BCIs have a high risk of confidentiality problems, where the BCIs are constantly acquiring brain activity, and therefore sensitive information is gathered. The previous attacks and concerns also generate safety problems.

Considering the above, asynchronous BCIs present greater data integrity and availability issues due to their more extensive temporal exposition to neural data. However, considering the user's awareness and control capabilities over the communication, synchronous BCIs have more serious concerns over both issues. Although both synchronous and asynchronous BCIs share common concerns, the authors detect that the first family has a higher risk since attacks over BCIs are more probable than those based on user neural data impersonation. This situation is summarized in Figure 5, which highlights the difference of severity between these BCI families.

Figure 5. Cybersecurity and safety risks associated with the synchronization of BCIs

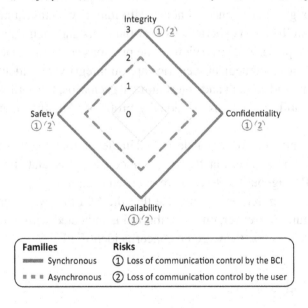

Usage Scenario

The cybersecurity risks of each BCI family vary considerably according to the usage scenario. These risks generate data confidentiality concerns in medical scenarios, where attackers can gather sensitive information (Li et al., 2015; Sempreboni et al., 2018). Moreover, users are at risk of physical harm since BCIs are used to improve patients' health conditions. Denning et al. (2009) identified safety concerns based on malicious neural stimulation actions, whereas Li et al. (2015) detected service integrity issues if users modify the parameters that control prosthetic limbs to gain a personal benefit. The authors of this chapter also identify that neuromedical scenarios risk the management of sensitive information of patients, such as their personal data, medical history, and neural activity data, affecting users' confidentiality.

Li et al. (2015) identified data confidentiality concerns based on the acquisition of the authentication data regarding authentication scenarios. The authors of the present chapter detect that they are at risk of malicious external stimuli aiming to alter the neural data used for the authentication process and thus impact the data integrity and availability. On the other hand, this chapter identifies that the gaming and entertainment scenario has a risk of malicious external stimuli, as this family is based on audiovisual systems that serve as an opportunity for attackers to perform adversarial attacks. The authors highlight data confidentiality issues, where attackers present malicious stimuli to acquire sensitive data taking advantage of these multimedia resources. The authors also identify that this situation affects data integrity and availability. Finally, smartphone-based scenarios present several risks. First, they rely on systems with potential problems, such as a lack of updates of the Operating System (OS) and applications (Martinovic et al., 2012; Bonaci et al., 2015b; Li et al., 2015; Sundararajan, 2017). The authors of the chapter also detect that the heterogeneity of the hardware, OS, applications used, and versions of each specific smartphone can also produce cybersecurity risks (StatCounter Global Stats, 2020). Based on that, Takabi et al. (Takabi et al., 2016b) analyzed several smartphone applications developed with the NeuroSky platform (NeuroSky, 2020). They detected that some third-party applications required access to the phone book and permissions to read the call logs, which was not the objective of the applications, generating confidentiality concerns. Moreover, this chapter detects that this lack of control over the smartphone elements generates concerns about data integrity, data availability, and safety, where attackers could perform well-known cyberattacks over the users and their data (Agrawal et al., 2018).

In conclusion, Figure 6 provides an overview of the previous concerns. Due to their inherent critical actions, the highest risks of neuromedical scenarios are on integrity, confidentiality, and safety issues. For authentication systems and gaming and entertainment scenarios, the authors consider that integrity, confidentiality, and availability concerns are equally probable. Finally, smartphone-based scenarios present all four concerns.

Finally, Table 1 groups all the information described in the section. It indicates, for each classification and BCI family, the general references that treat relevant concepts associated with each BCI family. The four concerns analyzed throughout the section are exposed (i.e., integrity, confidentiality, availability, and safety), where one or more references indicate that the BCI family presents a concern previously documented in the literature. Moreover, our contribution is indicated with a red X icon (✗). Finally, a green check icon (✓) indicates that there are no concerns identified.

Figure 6. Cybersecurity and safety risks associated with the BCI usage scenario

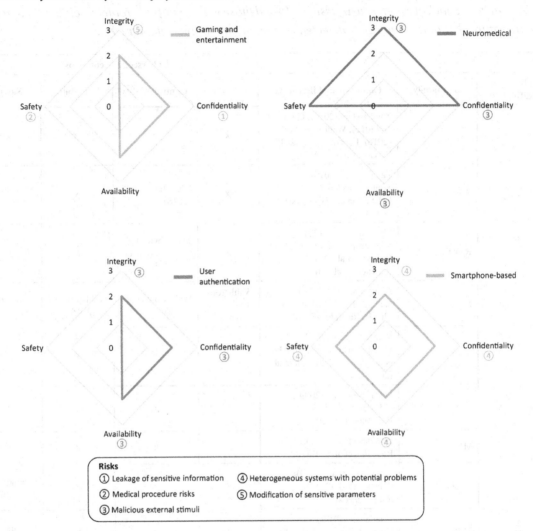

FUTURE RESEARCH DIRECTIONS

The BCI field has presented a considerable development in recent years, moving from medical and research scenarios to commercial ones. This growth defines emerging and promising application scenarios, such as the connection of BCIs to the Internet, allowing the transfer and storage of neural data to cloud environments. Another interesting scenario is the communication between brains, known as brain-to-brain (BtB) communication, where two or more BCI users mentally share information.

Although these advances in the BCI field are promising, they introduce new challenges and risks, especially by applying well-known cyberattacks. An example of this situation is malware, where attackers could affect the integrity, confidentiality, and availability of data and services, also causing physical damage to these users. The application of new communication mechanisms and the use of cloud computing strategies augment the number of elements potentially vulnerable in the architecture of the services, easing the tasks of finding vulnerabilities and exploiting them to perform malware attacks.

Table 1. Cybersecurity risks and concerns based on BCI classifications, differentiating between those families that have a lack of cybersecurity issues (✔) and those with identified problems, either documented in the literature (list of references) or detected by the authors of this chapter (✗).

BCI classification	BCI family	Family-related literature	Cybersecurity concerns			
			Integrity	Confidentiality	Availability	Safety
Design of BCIs	Active	Zander et al. (2010); Gilja et al. (2012); Wahlstrom et al. (2016); Lebedev et al. (2017); Ramadan et al. (2017)	✗	✗	✗	✗
	Passive	Zander et al. (2010); Wahlstrom et al. (2016); Lebedev et al. (2017); Aricò et al. (2018)	✗	Wahlstrom et al. (2016)	✗	✗
	Reactive	Martinovic et al. (2012); Wahlstrom et al. (2016); Lebedev et al. (2017); Ramadan et al. (2017)	✗	Martinovic et al. (2012); Frank et al. (2017)	✗	✗
	Hybrid	Hong et al. (2017); Wahlstrom et al. (2016); Lebedev et al. (2017); Ramadan et al. (2017)	Wahlstrom et al. (2016)	Wahlstrom et al. (2016)	Wahlstrom et al. (2016)	Wahlstrom et al. (2016)
BCI Technology	EEG	Ramadan et al. (2017); vanGerven et al. (2009); Ahn et al. (2014); McMahon et al., (2018)	✗	✗	✗	✔
	fMRI	vanGerven et al. (2009); Lebedev et al. (2017); Ramadan et al. (2017)	✗	✗	✗	✔
	MEG	Lebedev et al. (2017); Ramadan et al. (2017)	✗	✗	✗	✗
	ECoG	vanGerven et al. (2009); Lebedev et al. (2017); Ramadan et al. (2017)	✗	✗	✔	Glannon et al. (2014)
	TMS	Tyler et al. (2017), Gomes-Osman et al. (2018), Polanía et al. (2018)	✗	✔	✗	Polanía et al. (2018)
	tES	Tyler et al. (2017); Bikson et al. (2018); Polanía et al. (2018)	✗	✔	✗	✗
	tFUS	Tyler et al. (2017); Kubanek et al. (2018); Legon et al. (2018)	✗	✗	✗	✗
	DBS	Denning et al. (2009); Ienca et al. (2016) Khabarova et al. (2018); Kubanek et al. (2018)	✔	✗	✔	Kubanek et al. (2018)
	Neural dust	Seo et al. (2013); Lebedev et al. (2017); Wirdatmadja et al. (2017); Neely et al. (2018)	✔	✗	✔	✗

continues on following page

Table 1. Continued

BCI classification	BCI family	Family-related literature	Cybersecurity concerns			
			Integrity	Confidentiality	Availability	Safety
Level of invasiveness	Invasive	Lebedev et al. (2017); Ramadan et al. (2017); Wirdatmadja et al. (2017)	✓	✗	✗	Campbell et al. (2018)
	Partial-invasive	vanGerven et al. (2009); Yang et al. (2014)	✓	✗	✗	Campbell et al. (2018)
	Non-invasive	Li et al. (2015); Ramadan et al. (2017)	✓	✗	✗	Polanía et al. (2018)
Synchronization	Synchronous	An et al. (2016); Bentabet et al. (2016); Ramadan et al. (2017)	✗	✗	✗	✗
	Asynchronous	An et al. (2016); Ramadan et al. (2017)	✗	✗	✗	✗
Usage scenario	Neuromedical	Denning et al. (2009); Li et al. (2015); Ienca et al. (2016); Lebedev et al. (2017); Polanía et al. (2018)	Li et al. (2015)	Li et al. (2015); Sempreboni et al. (2018)	✓	Denning et al. (2009)
	User authentication	Martinovic et al. (2012); Bonaci et al. (2015a); Li et al. (2015); Takabi (2016a); Takabi et al. (2016b); Gavas et al. (2017); Sundararajan (2017)	✗	Li et al. (2015)	✗	✓
	Gaming and entertainment	Ahn et al. (2014); Li et al. (2015); McMahon et al. (2018)	✗	✗	✗	✓
	Smartphone based	Li et al. (2015); Bonaci et al. (2014a); Bonaci et al. (2014b); Takabi et al. (2016b)	✗	Takabi et al. (2016b)	✗	✗

This chapter identifies the importance of performing comprehensive risk assessment actions over BCI, applying well-known methodologies from cybersecurity scenarios. In particular, the authors highlight the relevance of using standard methodologies such as the one defined by the ISO 27001 to unify the study of BCI risks and vulnerabilities, allowing to contrast the results obtained by future works in the literature.

This chapter also detects an opportunity to analyze the risks and vulnerabilities of commercial BCI brands and their products, aiming to extend the risk analysis performed in this chapter. As indicated in the present work, the literature has identified vulnerabilities in consumer-grade BCI products, although a comprehensive analysis of the most used BCI devices is required. It is essential to ensure that a considerable amount of BCI technologies in the market are previously reviewed by external cybersecurity experts, making it difficult to exploit vulnerabilities by potential attackers.

Among the risks detected in this chapter, one of the most common to exploit is the acquisition of sensitive neural data and acquiring data concerning users' health status or private data from their medical records. These devices must be analyzed to verify that they comply with most data protection regulations, such as the legislation of the United States of America or the General Data Protection Regulation (GDPR) in the European Union (Huertas et al., 2019; Huertas et al., 2020). If BCI devices are not manufactured considering security-by-design and privacy-by-design principles, the possibility of attacks over data confidentiality alarmingly increases.

CONCLUSION

This chapter has presented the analysis of risk existing in the most common BCI classifications from the academic literature. The authors have studied these risks from the perspective of data and service integrity, confidentiality and availability, and BCI users' physical safety. These risks are motivated by the inherent vulnerabilities present in each classification and the possibility of applying well-known cyberattacks, such as malware. Particularly, malware has been identified in the literature as one of the most damaging threats against BCI, where attackers can control the BCI to perform malicious actions or serve as a mechanism to obtain sensitive information.

This chapter also highlights that all families within each classification present vulnerabilities, identifying that the BCI design determined for a device considerably determines the type and severity of the risks. Particularly, both reactive and hybrid BCIs present higher risks than active and passive approaches. There are considerable differences in BCI technology as each technology is used in particular scenarios and solves different problems. In general, this chapter detects that those technologies with higher resolutions for both acquisition and stimulation procedures are the most vulnerable.

The invasiveness of the BCI, also related to the BCI technology classification, has a considerable influence over the risks of its families, where invasive technologies have the highest impact. The synchronization mechanisms of the BCI, which indicate if the actions are either initiated by the BCI or the user, are vulnerable, where synchronous BCIs present higher risks in terms of loss of communication control. Finally, the application scenario present high differences between its families, since each scenario have specific characteristics and requirements.

ACKNOWLEDGMENT

This work has been partially supported by (a) Bit & Brain Technologies S.L. under the project Cyber-Brain, associated with the University of Murcia (Spain), by (b) the Swiss Federal Office for Defense Procurement (armasuisse) with the CyberSpec (CYD-C-2020003) project, and by (c) the University of Zürich UZH.

REFERENCES

Agrawal, D. P., & Wang, H. (2018). *Computer and Cyber Security: Principles, Algorithm, Applications, and Perspectives* (B. B. Gupta, Ed.; 1st ed.). CRC Press. doi:10.1201/9780429424878

Ahn, M., Lee, M., Choi, J., & Jun, S. C. (2014). A Review of Brain-Computer Interface Games and an Opinion Survey from Researchers, Developers and Users. *Sensors (Basel)*, *14*(8), 14601–14633. doi:10.3390140814601 PMID:25116904

An, H., Kim, J., & Lee, S. (2016). Design of an asynchronous brain-computer interface for control of a virtual Avatar. *2016 4th International Winter Conference on Brain-Computer Interface (BCI)* (pp. 1-2). 10.1109/IWW-BCI.2016.7457463

Aricò, P., Borghini, G., Di Flumeri, G., Sciaraffa, N., & Babiloni, F. (2018). Passive BCI beyond the lab: Current trends and future directions. *Physiological Measurement, 39*(8), 08TR02. Advance online publication. doi:10.1088/1361-6579/aad57e PMID:30039806

Bentabet, N., & Berrached, N. (2016). Synchronous P300 based BCI to control home appliances. *2016 8th International Conference on Modelling, Identification and Control (ICMIC)* (pp. 835-838). 10.1109/ICMIC.2016.7804230

Bikson, M., Brunoni, A. R., Charvet, L. E., Clark, V. P., Cohen, L. G., Deng, Z. D., Dmochowski, J., Edwards, D. J., Frohlich, F., Kappenman, E. S., Lim, K. O., Loo, C., Mantovani, A., McMullen, D. P., Parra, L. C., Pearson, M., Richardson, J. D., Rumsey, J. M., Sehatpour, P., ... Losanby, S. H. (2018). Rigor and reproducibility in research with transcranial electrical stimulation: An NIMH-sponsored workshop. *Brain Stimulation, 11*(3), 465–480. doi:10.1016/j.brs.2017.12.008 PMID:29398575

Binnendijk, A., Marler, T., & Bartels, E. M. (2020). *Brain-Computer Interfaces: U.S. Military Applications and Implications, An Initial Assessment*. RAND Corporation. doi:10.7249/RR2996

Bonaci, T., Calo, R., & Chizeck, H. J. (2015). App Stores for the Brain: Privacy and Security in Brain-Computer Interfaces. *IEEE Technology and Society Magazine, 34*(2), 32–39. doi:10.1109/MTS.2015.2425551

Bonaci, T., Herron, J., Matlack, C., & Chizeck, H. J. (2015). Securing the Exocortex: A Twenty-First Century Cybernetics Challenge. *IEEE Technology and Society Magazine, 34*(3), 44–51. doi:10.1109/MTS.2015.2461152

Campbell, A., & Wu, C. (2018). Chronically Implanted Intracranial Electrodes: Tissue Reaction and Electrical Changes. *Micromachines, 9*(9), 430. doi:10.3390/mi9090430 PMID:30424363

Chaudhary, U., Xia, B., Silvoni, S., Cohen, L. G., & Birbaumer, N. (2017). Brain–Computer Interface–Based Communication in the Completely Locked-In State. *PLoS Biology, 15*(1), 1–25. doi:10.1371/journal.pbio.1002593 PMID:28141803

Chizeck, H. J., & Bonaci, T. (2014). *Brain-Computer Interface Anonymizer* (Patent application US20140228701A1). United States Patent and Trademark Office.

Denning, T., Matsuoka, Y., & Kohno, T. (2009). Neurosecurity: Security and privacy for neural devices. *Neurosurgical Focus FOC, 27*(1), E7. doi:10.3171/2009.4.FOCUS0985 PMID:19569895

Edwards, C., Kouzani, A., Lee, K. H., & Ross, E. K. (n.d.). Neurostimulation Devices for the Treatment of Neurologic Disorders. *Mayo Clinic Proceedings, 92*(9), 1427-1444. doi:10.1016/j.mayocp.2017.05.005

Frank, M., Hwu, T., Jain, S., Knight, R. T., Martinovic, I., Mittal, P., Perito, D., Sluganovic, I., & Song, D. (2017) Using EEG-Based BCI Devices to Subliminally Probe for Private Information. *Proceedings of the 2017 on Workshop on Privacy in the Electronic Society - WPES '17*, 133-136. 10.1145/3139550.3139559

Gilja, V., Nuyujukian, P., Chestek, C., Cunningham, J. P., Yu, B. M., Fan, J. M., Churchland, M. M., Kaufman, M. T., Kao, J. C., Ryu, S. I., & Shenoy, K. V. (2012). A high-performance neural prosthesis enabled by control algorithm design. *Nature Neuroscience*, *15*(12), 1752–1757. doi:10.1038/nn.3265 PMID:23160043

Glannon, G. (2014). Ethical issues with brain-computer interfaces. *Frontiers in Systems Neuroscience*, *8*, 136. doi:10.3389/fnsys.2014.00136 PMID:25126061

Gomes-Osman, J., Indahlastari, A., Fried, P. J., Cabral, D. L. F., Rice, J., Nissim, N. R., Aksu, S., McLaren, M. E., & Woods, A. J. (2018). Non-invasive Brain Stimulation: Probing Intracortical Circuits and Improving Cognition in the Aging Brain. *Frontiers in Aging Neuroscience*, *10*, 177. doi:10.3389/fnagi.2018.00177 PMID:29950986

Guan, C., Thulasidas, M., & Wu, J. (2004). High performance P300 speller for brain-computer interface. *IEEE International Workshop on Biomedical Circuits and Systems* (pp. S3/5/INV-S3/13). 10.1109/BIOCAS.2004.1454155

Gupta, B., Agrawal, D. P., & Yamaguchi, S. (2016). *Handbook of Research on Modern Cryptographic Solutions for Computer and Cyber Security*. IGI Global. doi:10.4018/978-1-5225-0105-3

Gupta, D., Gupta, B., & Mishra, A. (2018). Identity Theft, Malware, and Social Engineering in Dealing with Cybercrime. In B. B. G. Gupta (Ed.), *Computer and Cyber Security*. CRC Press.

Hong, K., & Khan, M. J. (2017). Hybrid Brain–Computer Interface Techniques for Improved Classification Accuracy and Increased Number of Commands: A Review. *Frontiers in Neurorobotics*, *11*, 35. doi:10.3389/fnbot.2017.00035 PMID:28790910

Huertas Celdrán, A., Gil Pérez, M., Mlakar, I., Alcaraz Calero, J. M., García Clemente, F. J., & Martínez Pérez, G. (2019). A Management Platform for Citizen's Data Protection Regulation. In G. Wang, A. El Saddik, X. Lai, G. Martinez Perez, & K. K. Choo (Eds.), *Smart City and Informatization. iSCI 2019. Communications in Computer and Information Science* (Vol. 1122). Springer. doi:10.1007/978-981-15-1301-5_6

Huertas Celdrán, A., Gil Pérez, M., Mlakar, I., Alcaraz Calero, J. M., García Clemente, F. J., Martínez Pérez, G., & Bhuiyan, Z. A. (2020). PROTECTOR: Towards the protection of sensitive data in Europe and the US. *Computer Networks*, *181*, 107448. doi:10.1016/j.comnet.2020.107448

Ienca, M., & Haselager, P. (2016). Hacking the brain: Brain–computer interfacing technology and the ethics of neurosecurity. *Ethics and Information Technology*, *18*(2), 117–129. doi:10.100710676-016-9398-9

Ienca, M., Haselager, P., & Emanuel, E. (2018). Brain leaks and consumer neurotechnology. *Nature Biotechnology*, *36*(9), 805–810. doi:10.1038/nbt.4240 PMID:30188521

Khabarova, E. A., Denisova, N. P., Dmitriev, A. B., Slavin, K. V., & Verhagen Metman, L. (2018). Deep Brain, Stimulation of the Subthalamic Nucleus in Patients with Parkinson Disease with Prior Pallidotomy or Thalamotomy. *Brain Sciences*, *8*(4), 66. doi:10.3390/brainsci8040066 PMID:29659494

Kubanek, J. (2018). Neuromodulation with transcranial focused ultrasound. *Neurosurgical Focus FOC*, *44*(2), E14. doi:10.3171/2017.11.FOCUS17621 PMID:29385924

Landau, O., Puzis, R., & Nissum, N. (2020). Mind Your Mind: EEG-Based Brain-Computer Interfaces and Their Security in Cyber Space. *ACM Computing Surveys*, *53*(1), 1–38. doi:10.1145/3372043

Lebedev, M. A., & Nicolelis, A. L. (2017). Brain-Machine Interfaces: From Basic Science to Neuroprostheses and Neurorehabilitation. *Physiological Reviews*, *97*(2), 767–837. doi:10.1152/physrev.00027.2016 PMID:28275048

Lee, J., Mok, E., Huang, J., Cui, L., Lee, A., Leung, V., Mercier, P., Shellhammer, S., Larson, L., Asbeck, P., Rao, R., Song, Y., Nurmikko, A., & Laiwalla, F. (2019) An Implantable Wireless Network of Distributed Microscale Sensors for Neural Applications. *2019 9th International IEEE/EMBS Conference on Neural Engineering (NER)* (pp. 871-874). 10.1109/NER.2019.8717023

Legon, W., Bansal, P., Tyshynsky, R., Ai, L., & Mueller, J. K. (2018). Transcranial focused ultrasound neuromodulation of the human primary motor cortex. *Scientific Reports*, *8*(1), 10007. doi:10.103841598-018-28320-1 PMID:29968768

Li, Q., Ding, D., & Conti, M. (2015). Brain-Computer Interface applications: Security and privacy challenges. *2015 IEEE Conference on Communications and Network Security (CNS)*, 663-666. 10.1109/CNS.2015.7346884

López Bernal, S., Huertas Celdrán, A., Fernández Maimó, L., Martínez Pérez, G., Barros, M. T., & Balasubramaniam, S. (2020). Cyberattacks on Miniature Brain Implants to Disrupt Spontaneous Neural Signaling. *IEEE Access: Practical Innovations, Open Solutions*, *8*, 152204–152222. doi:10.1109/ACCESS.2020.3017394

López Bernal, S., Huertas Celdrán, A., & Martínez Pérez, G. (2019). Cybersecurity on Brain-Computer Interfaces: attacks and countermeasures. V Jornadas Nacionales de Investigación en Ciberseguridad (JNIC2019), 198-199.

López Bernal, S., Huertas Celdrán, A., Martínez Pérez, G., Barros, M. T., & Balasubramaniam, S. (2020). Security in Brain-Computer Interfaces: State-of-the-Art, Opportunities, and Future Challenges. *ACM Computing Surveys*, *54*(1), 35. doi:10.1145/3427376

Martinovic, I., Davies, D., & Frank, M. (2012) On the feasibility of side-channel attacks with brain-computer interfaces. *Proceedings of the 21st USENIX Security Symposium*, 143-158.

McMahon, M., & Schukat, M. (2018). A low-Cost, Open-Source, BCI- VR Game Control Development Environment Prototype for Game Based Neurorehabilitation. *IEEE Games, Entertainment, Media Conference (GEM)*, 1-9. 10.1109/GEM.2018.8516468

Musk, E. (2019). Neuralink An Integrated Brain-Machine Interface Platform With Thousands of Channels. *Journal of Medical Internet Research*, *21*(10), e16194. doi:10.2196/16194 PMID:31642810

Neely, R. M., Piech, D. K., Santacruz, S. R., Maharbiz, M. M., & Carmena, J. M. (2018). Recent advances in neural dust: Towards a neural interface platform. *Current Opinion in Neurobiology*, *50*, 64–71. doi:10.1016/j.conb.2017.12.010 PMID:29331738

NeuroSky. (2019). http://neurosky.com

Pais-Vieira, M., Lebedev, M., Kunicki, C., Wang, J., & Nicolelis, M. A. L. (2013). A Brain-to-Brain Interface for Real-Time Sharing of Sensorimotor Information. *Scientific Reports*, *3*(1), 1319. doi:10.1038rep01319 PMID:23448946

Pycroft, L., & Aziz, T. Z. (2018). Security of implantable medical devices with wireless connections: The dangers of cyber-attacks. *Expert Review of Medical Devices*, *15*(6), 403–406. doi:10.1080/174344 40.2018.1483235 PMID:29860880

Pycroft, L., Boccard, S. G., Owen, S. L. F., Stein, J. F., Fitzgerald, J. J., Green, A. L., & Aziz, T. Z. (2016). Brainjacking: Implant Security Issues in Invasive Neuromodulation. *World Neurosurgery*, *92*, 454–462. doi:10.1016/j.wneu.2016.05.010 PMID:27184896

Ramadan, R. A., & Vasilakos, A. V. (2017). Brain computer interface: Control signals review. *Neurocomputing*, *223*, 26–44. doi:10.1016/j.neucom.2016.10.024

Rao, R. P. N. (2019). Towards neural co-processors for the brain: Combining decoding and encoding in brain–computer interfaces. *Current Opinion in Neurobiology*, *55*, 142–151. doi:10.1016/j.conb.2019.03.008 PMID:30954862

Saboor, A., Gembler, F., Benda, M., Stawicki, P., Rezeika, A., Grichnik, R., & Volosyak, I. (2018). A Browser-Driven SSVEP-Based BCI Web Speller. *2018 IEEE International Conference on Systems, Man, and Cybernetics (SMC)*, 625–630. 10.1109/SMC.2018.00115

Sempreboni, D., & Viganò, L. (2018). *Privacy, Security and Trust in the Internet of Neurons*. arXiv.

Seo., D., Carmena, J. M., Rabaey, J. M., Alon, E., & Maharbiz, M. M. (2013). *Neural Dust: An Ultrasonic, Low Power Solution for Chronic Brain-Machine Interfaces*. arXiv.

Sowndhararajan, K., Minju, K., Ponnuvel, D., Se, P., & Songmun, K. (2018). Application of the P300 Event-Related Potential in the Diagnosis of Epilepsy Disorder: A Review. *Scientia Pharmaceutica*, *86*(2), 10. doi:10.3390cipharm86020010 PMID:29587468

StatCounter Global Stats. (2020). *Mobile & Tablet Android Version Market Share Worldwide*. https://gs.statcounter.com/android-version-market-share/mobile-tablet/worldwide

Sundararajan, K. (2017). *Privacy and security issues in Brain Computer Interface* [Unpublished master's thesis]. Auckland University of Technology, Auckland, New Zealand.

Takabi, H. (2016) Firewall for brain: Towards a privacy preserving ecosystem for BCI applications. *IEEE Conference on Communications and Network Security (CNS)*, 370-371. 10.1109/CNS.2016.7860516

Takabi, H., Bhalotiya, A., & Alohaly, M. (2016). Brain Computer Interface (BCI) Applications: Privacy Threats and Countermeasures. *2016 IEEE 2nd International Conference on Collaboration and Internet Computing (CIC)*, 102-111. 10.1109/CIC.2016.026

Tyler, W. J., Sanguinetti, J. L., Fini, M., & Hool, N. (2017). Non-invasive neural stimulation. *Micro- and Nanotechnology Sensors. Systems, and Applications*, *IX*, 280–290. doi:10.1117/12.2263175

Vaid, S., Singh, P., & Kaur, C. (2015). EEG Signal Analysis for BCI Interface: A Review. *2015 Fifth International Conference on Advanced Computing & Communication Technologies*, 143-147. 10.1109/ACCT.2015.72

Waldert, S. (2016). Invasive vs. Non-Invasive Neuronal Signals for Brain-Machine Interfaces: Will One Prevail? *Frontiers in Neuroscience*, 10, 295. doi:10.3389/fnins.2016.00295 PMID:27445666

Wirdatmadja, S. A., Barros, M. T., Koucheryavy, Y., Jornet, J. M., & Balasubramaniam, S. (2017). Wireless Optogenetic Nanonetworks for Brain Stimulation: Device Model and Charging Protocols. *IEEE Transactions on Nanobioscience*, 16(8), 859–872. doi:10.1109/TNB.2017.2781150 PMID:29364130

Yang, T., Hakimian, S., & Schwartz, T. H. (2014). Intraoperative ElectroCorticoGraphy (ECog): Indications, techniques, and utility in epilepsy surgery. *Epileptic Disorders*, 16(3), 271–279. doi:10.1684/epd.2014.0675 PMID:25204010

Zander, T. O., Kothe, C., Jatzev, S., & Gaertner, M. (2010). Enhancing Human-Computer Interaction with Input from Active and Passive Brain-Computer Interfaces. In D. Tan & A. Nijholt (Eds.), *Brain-Computer Interfaces. Human-Computer Interaction Series*. Springer. doi:10.1007/978-1-84996-272-8_11

Zheng, H., Zhang, Z., Jiang, S., Yan, B., Shi, X., Xie, Y., Huang, X., Yu, Z., Liu, H., Weng, S., Nurmikko, A., Zhang, Y., Peng, H., Xu, W., & Zhang, J. (2019). A shape-memory and spiral light-emitting device for precise multisite stimulation of nerve bundles. *Nature Communications*, 10(1), 2790. doi:10.103841467-019-10418-3 PMID:31243276

Compilation of References

Pande, A. S., & Thool, R. C. (2016, September). Survey on logical key hierarchy for secure group communication. *2016 International*.

Sherman, A. T., & McGrew, D. A. (2003). Key establishment in large dynamic groups using one-way function trees. *IEEE Transactions on Software Engineering, 29*(5), 444–458. doi:10.1109/TSE.2003.1199073

Kumar, N. S., & Lavanya, S. (2015). A novel scheme for secure group communication in multicast network. *International Journal of Security and Networks, 10*(2), 65–75. doi:10.1504/IJSN.2015.070409

Bao, X., Liu, J., She, L., & Zhang, S. (2014, June). A key management scheme based on grouping within cluster. In *Proceeding of the 11th World Congress on Intelligent Control and Automation* (pp. 3455- 3460). IEEE.

Kumar, S., Purusothaman, T. N. M., & Lavanya, S. (2013). Design and performance analysis of scalable and efficient group key Manage- ment scheme [SEGKMS] for group communication in multicast net- works. *Life Science Journal, 10*(2).

Albakri, A., Harn, L., & Song, S. (2019). Hierarchical key manage- ment scheme with probabilistic security in a wireless sensor network (WSN). *Security and Communication Networks*, 2019.

Vijayakumar, P., Bose, S., Kannan, A., & Jegatha Deborah, L. (2013). *Computation and Communication Efficient Key Distribution*. Academic Press.

Zhu, S., & Jajodia, S. (2003, December). Scalable group rekeying for secure multicast: A survey. In *International Workshop on Distributed Computing* (pp. 1-10). Springer. 10.1007/978-3-540-24604-6_1

Eltoweissy, M., Heydari, M. H., Morales, L., & Sudborough, I. H. (2004). Combinatorial optimization of group key management. *Journal of Network and Systems Management, 12*(1), 33–50. doi:10.1023/B:JONS.0000015697.38671.ec

Wong, C. K., Gouda, M., & Lam, S. S. (2000). Secure group communications using key graphs. *IEEE/ACM Transactions on Networking, 8*(1), 16–30. doi:10.1109/90.836475

He, X., Niedermeier, M., & De Meer, H. (2013). Dynamic key management in wireless sensor networks: A survey. *Journal of Network and Computer Applications, 36*(2), 611–622. doi:10.1016/j.jnca.2012.12.010

Dave, M. (2016, March). Storage as a parameter for classifying dynamic key management schemes proposed for WSNs. In *2016 International Conference on Computational Techniques in Information and Communication Technologies (ICCTICT)* (pp. 51-56). IEEE.

Eschenauer, L., & Gligor, V. D. (2002). A key-management scheme for distributed sensor networks. *Proceedings of the 9th ACM Conference on Computer and Communication Security*, 41–47. 10.1145/586110.586117

Chen, C. T., Huang, S. Y., & Lin, I. C. (2012). Providing perfect forward secrecy for location-aware wireless sensor networks. *EURASIP Journal on Wireless Communications and Networking, 2012*(1), 241. doi:10.1186/1687-1499-2012-241

Messai, M. L., Aliouat, M., & Seba, H. (2010). Tree based scheme for key Management in wireless sensor networks. *EURASIP Journal on Wireless Communications and Networking, 2010*(1), 1–10. doi:10.1155/2010/910695

Liu, D., & Ning, P. (2003, October). Location-based pairwise key establishments for static sensor networks. In *Proceedings of the 1st ACM workshop on Security of ad hoc and sensor networks* (pp. 72-82). 10.1145/986858.986869

Eltoweissy, M., Moharrum, M., & Mukkamala, R. (2006). Dynamic key management in sensor networks. *IEEE Communications Magazine, 44*(4), 122–130. doi:10.1109/MCOM.2006.1632659

Dutertre, B., Cheung, S., & Levy, J. (2004). *Lightweight key management in wireless sensor networks by leveraging initial trust*. Technical Report SRI-SDL-04-02, SRI International.

Du, W., Deng, J., Han, Y. S., Chen, S., & Varshney, P. K. (2004, March). A key management scheme for wireless sensor networks using deployment knowledge. In *IEEE INFOCOM 2004* (Vol. 1). IEEE.

Xu, Y., & Sun, Y. (2005, December). A new group rekeying method in secure multicast. In *International Conference on Computational and Information Science* (pp. 155-160). Springer. 10.1007/11596981_23

Wallner, D., Harder, E., & Agee, R. (1999). *Key management for multicast: Issues and architectures*. RFC 2627.

Yousefpoor, M. S., & Barati, H. (2019). Dynamic key management algorithms in wireless sensor networks: A survey. *Computer Communications, 134*, 52–69. doi:10.1016/j.comcom.2018.11.005

Seetha, R., & Saravanan, R. (2015). A survey on group key management schemes. *Cybernetics and Information Technologies, 15*(3), 3–25. doi:10.1515/cait-2015-0038

Chen, C. Y., & Chao, H. C. (2014). A survey of key distribution in wireless sensor networks. *Security and Communication Networks, 7*(12), 2495–2508. doi:10.1002ec.354

Barskar, R., & Chawla, M. (2016). A survey on efficient group key management schemes in wireless networks. *Indian Journal of Science and Technology, 9*(14), 1–16. doi:10.17485/ijst/2016/v9i14/87972

Rahman, M., & Sampalli, S. (2015). An efficient pairwise and group key management protocol for wireless sensor network. *Wireless Personal Communications, 84*(3), 2035–2053. doi:10.100711277-015-2546-4

netlab. (2017). *Warning: Satori, a Mirai Branch Is Spreading in Worm Style on Port 37215 and 52869*. Retrieved from https://blog.netlab.360.com/warning-satori-a-new-mirai-variant-is-spreading-in-worm-style-on-port-37215-and-52869-en/

Jain, A. K., & Gupta, B. B. (2019). A machine learning based approach for phishing detection using hyperlinks information. *Journal of Ambient Intelligence and Humanized Computing, 10*(5), 2015–2028. doi:10.100712652-018-0798-z

Ouaguid, A., Abghour, N., & Ouzzif, M. (2018). A novel security framework for managing android permissions using blockchain technology. *International Journal of Cloud Applications and Computing, 8*(1), 55–79. doi:10.4018/IJCAC.2018010103

Stergiou, C., Psannis, K. E., Gupta, B. B., & Ishibashi, Y. (2018). Security, privacy & efficiency of sustainable cloud computing for big data & IoT. *Sustainable Computing: Informatics and Systems, 19*, 174–184. doi:10.1016/j.suscom.2018.06.003

Zheng, Q., Wang, X., Khan, M. K., Zhang, W., Gupta, B. B., & Guo, W. (2017). A lightweight authenticated encryption scheme based on chaotic scml for railway cloud service. *IEEE Access: Practical Innovations, Open Solutions, 6*, 711–722. doi:10.1109/ACCESS.2017.2775038

Rafaeli, S., & Hutchison, D. (2003). A survey of key management for secure group communication. *ACM Computing Surveys*, *35*(3), 309–329. doi:10.1145/937503.937506

Ng, W. H. D., Howarth, M., Sun, Z., & Cruickshank, H. (2007). Dynamic balanced key tree management for secure multicast communications. *IEEE Transactions on Computers*, *56*(5), 590–605. doi:10.1109/TC.2007.1022

Ng, W. H. D., Cruickshank, H., & Sun, Z. ((2006) Scalable balanced batch rekeying for secure group communication. *Computers & Security, 25*(4), 265-273.

Tiloca, M., Dini, G., Rizki, K., & Raza, S. (2019). Group rekeying based on member join history. *International Journal of Information Security*, 1–39. doi:10.100710207-019-00451-0

Howarth, M. P., Iyengar, S., Sun, Z., & Cruickshank, H. (2004). Dynamics of key management in secure satellite multicast. *IEEE Journal on Selected Areas in Communications*, *22*(2), 308–319. doi:10.1109/JSAC.2003.819978

Bilal, M., & Kang, S. G. (2017). A secure key agreement protocol for dynamic group. *Cluster Computing*, *20*(3), 2779–2792. doi:10.100710586-017-0853-0

Duma, C., Shahmehri, N., & Lambrix, P. (2003, June). A hybrid key tree scheme for multicast to balance security and efficiency requirements. In *WET ICE 2003. Proceedings. Twelfth IEEE International Workshops on Enabling Technologies: Infrastructure for Collaborative Enterprises, 2003* (pp. 208-213). IEEE.

Ab Malek, M. S. B., Ahmadon, M. A. B., Yamaguchi, S., & Gupta, B. B. (2016, October). On privacy verification in the IoT service based on PN 2. In *2016 IEEE 5th Global Conference on Consumer Electronics* (pp. 1-4). IEEE.

Adat, V., & Gupta, B. B. (2018). Security in Internet of Things: Issues, challenges, taxonomy, and architecture. *Telecommunication Systems*, *67*(3), 423–441. doi:10.100711235-017-0345-9

Adepu, S., Kandasamy, N. K., & Mathur, A. (2018). Epic: An electric power testbed for research and training in cyber physical systems security. In *Computer Security* (pp. 37–52). Springer.

Aghajari, E., & Chandrashekhar, G. D. (2017). Self-organizing map based extended fuzzy C-means (SEEFC) algorithm for image segmentation. *Applied Soft Computing*, *54*, 347–363. doi:10.1016/j.asoc.2017.01.003

Agrawal, D. P., & Wang, H. (2018). *Computer and Cyber Security: Principles, Algorithm, Applications, and Perspectives* (B. B. Gupta, Ed.; 1st ed.). CRC Press. doi:10.1201/9780429424878

Ahlawat, P., & Dave, M. (2018). An attack resistant key predistribution scheme for wireless sensor networks. *Journal of King Saud University-Computer and Information Sciences*.

Ahlawat, P., & Dave, M. (2018). An attack model based highly secure key management scheme for wireless sensor networks. *Procedia Computer Science*, *125*, 201–207. doi:10.1016/j.procs.2017.12.028

Ahmadian, M. M., Shajari, M., & Shafiee, M. A. (2020). Industrial control system security taxonomic framework with application to a comprehensive incidents survey. *International Journal of Critical Infrastructure Protection*, *29*, 100356. doi:10.1016/j.ijcip.2020.100356

Ahmadi, M., Ulyanov, D., Semenov, S., Trofimov, M., & Giacinto, G. (2016, March). Novel feature extraction, selection and fusion for effective malware family classification. In *Proceedings of the sixth ACM conference on data and application security and privacy* (pp. 183-194). ACM.

Ahmadlou, M., Al-Fugara, A. K., Al-Shabeeb, A. R., Arora, A., Al-Adamat, R., Pham, Q. B., Al-Ansari, N., Linh, N. T. T., & Sajedi, H. (2021). Flood susceptibility mapping and assessment using a novel deep learning model combining multilayer perceptron and autoencoder neural networks. *Journal of Flood Risk Management*, *14*(1), e12683. doi:10.1111/jfr3.12683

Ahn, M., Lee, M., Choi, J., & Jun, S. (2014). A Review of Brain-Computer Interface Games and an Opinion Survey from Researchers, Developers, and Users. *Sensors (Basel)*, *14*(8), 14601–14633. doi:10.3390140814601 PMID:25116904

Airehrour, D., Gutierrez, J., & Ray, S. K. (2017). A trust-aware RPL routing protocol to detect blackhole and selective forwarding attacks. *Journal of Telecommunications and the Digital Economy*, *5*(1), 50–69.

Ajrawi, S., Rao, R., & Sarkar, M. (2021). Cybersecurity in Brain-Computer Interfaces: RFID-based design-theoretical framework. *Informatics in Medicine Unlocked*, *22*, 100489. doi:10.1016/j.imu.2020.100489

Al Shuhaimi, F., Jose, M., & Singh, A. V. (2016, September). Software defined network as solution to overcome security challenges in IoT. In *2016 5th International Conference on Reliability, Infocom Technologies and Optimization (Trends and Future Directions)(ICRITO)* (pp. 491-496). IEEE.

Alaba, F. A., Othman, M., Hashem, I. A. T., & Alotaibi, F. (2017). Internet of Things security: A survey. *Journal of Network and Computer Applications*, *88*, 10–28. doi:10.1016/j.jnca.2017.04.002

Aldowah, H., Rehman, S. U., & Umar, I. (2018, June). Security in internet of things: issues, challenges and solutions. In *International Conference of Reliable Information and Communication Technology* (pp. 396-405). Springer.

Al-Garadi, M. A., Mohamed, A., Al-Ali, A. K., Du, X., Ali, I., & Guizani, M. (2020). A survey of machine and deep learning methods for internet of things (IoT) security. *IEEE Communications Surveys and Tutorials*, *22*(3), 1646–1685.

Alghamdi, T. A. (2019). Convolutional technique for enhancing security in wireless sensor networks against malicious nodes. *Human-centric Computing and Information Sciences*, *9*(1), 38. doi:10.118613673-019-0198-1

Ali, I., Sabir, S., & Ullah, Z. (2019). *Internet of things security, device authentication and access control: a review.* arXiv preprint arXiv:1901.07309.

Almogren, A. S. (2020). Intrusion detection in Edge-of-Things computing. *Journal of Parallel and Distributed Computing*, *137*, 259–265. doi:10.1016/j.jpdc.2019.12.008

Al-Nuaimi, F. A., Al-Nuaimi, R. J., Al-Dhaheri, S. S., Ouhbi, S., & Belkacem, A. N. (2020). Mind Drone Chasing Using EEG-based Brain Computer Interface. *2020 16th International Conference on Intelligent Environments (IE)*, 1. 10.1109/IE49459.2020.9154926

Alomari, E., Manickam, S., Gupta, B. B., Anbar, M., Saad, R. M., & Alsaleem, S. (2016). A survey of botnet-based ddos flooding attacks of application layer: Detection and mitigation approaches. In *Handbook of research on modern cryptographic solutions for computer and cyber security* (pp. 52–79). IGI Global.

Al-Qerem, A., Alauthman, M., Almomani, A., & Gupta, B. B. (2020). IoT transaction processing through cooperative concurrency control on fog–cloud computing environment. *Soft Computing*, *24*(8), 5695–5711.

Alrawais, A., Alhothaily, A., Hu, C., & Cheng, X. (2017). Fog computing for the internet of things: Security and privacy issues. *IEEE Internet Computing*, *21*(2), 34–42.

Altaweel, M., Bone, C., & Abrams, J. (2019). Documents as data: A content analysis and topic modeling approach for analyzing responses to ecological disturbances. *Ecological Informatics*, *51*, 82–95. doi:10.1016/j.ecoinf.2019.02.014

Aly, M., Khomh, F., Haoues, M., Quintero, A., & Yacout, S. (2019). Enforcing security in Internet of Things frameworks: A systematic literature review. *Internet of Things*, *6*, 100050. doi:10.1016/j.iot.2019.100050

Ammar, M., Russello, G., & Crispo, B. (2018). Internet of Things: A survey on the security of IoT frameworks. *Journal of Information Security and Applications*, *38*, 8–27.

Amofa, S., Sifah, E. B., Kwame, O. B., Abla, S., Xia, Q., Gee, J. C., & Gao, J. (2018, September). A blockchain-based architecture framework for secure sharing of personal health data. In *2018 IEEE 20th International Conference on e-Health Networking, Applications and Services (Healthcom)* (pp. 1-6). IEEE. 10.1109/HealthCom.2018.8531160

An, H., Kim, J., & Lee, S. (2016). Design of an asynchronous brain-computer interface for control of a virtual Avatar. *2016 4th International Winter Conference on Brain-Computer Interface (BCI)* (pp. 1-2). 10.1109/IWW-BCI.2016.7457463

Ande, R., Adebisi, B., Hammoudeh, M., & Saleem, J. (2020). Internet of Things: Evolution and technologies from a security perspective. *Sustainable Cities and Society*, *54*, 101728.

Andrea, I., Chrysostomou, C., & Hadjichristofi, G. (2015, July). Internet of Things: Security vulnerabilities and challenges. In 2015 IEEE symposium on computers and communication (ISCC) (pp. 180-187). IEEE.

Anusha, K., & Sathiyamoorthy, E. (2016). A decision tree-based rule formation with combined PSO-GA algorithm for intrusion detection system. *International Journal of Internet Technology and Secured Transactions*, *6*(3), 186–202. doi:10.1504/IJITST.2016.080399

Arghire, I. (2017). *Mirai Variant Has Bitcoin Mining Capabilities*. Retrieved from https://www.securityweek.com/mirai-variant-has-bitcoin-mining-capabilities

Arias, O., Wurm, J., Hoang, K., & Jin, Y. (2015). Privacy and security in internet of things and wearable devices. *IEEE Transactions on Multi-Scale Computing Systems*, *1*(2), 99–109.

Aricò, P., Borghini, G., Di Flumeri, G., Sciaraffa, N., & Babiloni, F. (2018). Passive BCI beyond the lab: Current trends and future directions. *Physiological Measurement*, *39*(8), 08TR02. Advance online publication. doi:10.1088/1361-6579/aad57e PMID:30039806

Arıs, A., Oktug, S. F., & Voigt, T. (2018). *Security of internet of things for a reliable internet of services*. Academic Press.

Arrichiello, F., Di Lillo, P., Di Vito, D., Antonelli, G., & Chiaverini, S. (2017). Assistive robot operated via P300-based brain computer interface. *2017 IEEE International Conference on Robotics and Automation (ICRA)*, 1. 10.1109/ICRA.2017.7989714

Arzamendi, P., Bing, M., & Soluk, K. (2018). *The ARC of Satori*. Retrieved from https://www.netscout.com/blog/asert/arc-satori

ASERT Team. (2018). *OMG - Mirai Minions are Wicked*. Retrieved from https://www.netscout.com/blog/asert/omg-mirai-minions-are-wicked

Ashfahani, A., Pratama, M., Lughofer, E., & Ong, Y. S. (2020). DEVDAN: Deep evolving denoising autoencoder. *Neurocomputing*, *390*, 297–314. doi:10.1016/j.neucom.2019.07.106

Athiwaratkun, B., & Stokes, J. W. (2017, March). Malware classification with LSTM and GRU language models and a character-level CNN. In *2017 IEEE International Conference on Acoustics, Speech and Signal Processing (ICASSP)* (pp. 2482-2486). IEEE.

Aydemir, O. (2015). Improving classification accuracy of EEG based brain computer interface signals. *2015 23nd Signal Processing and Communications Applications Conference (SIU)*, 1. 10.1109/SIU.2015.7130442

Badcock, N. A., Mousikou, P., Mahajan, Y., de Lissa, P., Thie, J., & McArthur, G. (2013). Validation of the Emotiv EPOC® EEG gaming system for measuring research quality auditory ERPs. *PeerJ*, *1*, e38. doi:10.7717/peerj.38 PMID:23638374

Bailey, M., Cooke, E., Jahanian, F., Xu, Y., & Karir, M. (2009). A Survey of Botnet Technology and Defenses. In Proc. of the 2009 Cybersecurity Applications & Technology Conference for Homeland Security (pp.299-304). Academic Press.

Ballano, M. (2015). *Is there an Internet-of-Things vigilante out there?* Retrieved from https://www.symantec.com/connect/blogs/there-internet-things-vigilante-out-there

BCI Lab | Universidad de Granada. (2020). *BCI Lab*. http://www.ugr.es/%7Ebcilab/

Beaver, J. M., Borges-Hink, R. C., & Buckner, M. A. (2013, December). An evaluation of machine learning methods to detect malicious SCADA communications. In *2013 12th international conference on machine learning and applications* (Vol. 2, pp. 54-59). IEEE. 10.1109/ICMLA.2013.105

Belavagi, M. C., & Muniyal, B. (2016). Performance evaluation of supervised machine learning algorithms for intrusion detection. *Procedia Computer Science*, *89*, 117–123. doi:10.1016/j.procs.2016.06.016

Bentabet, N., & Berrached, N. (2016). Synchronous P300 based BCI to control home appliances. *2016 8th International Conference on Modelling, Identification and Control (ICMIC)* (pp. 835-838). 10.1109/ICMIC.2016.7804230

Berman, D. S., Buczak, A. L., Chavis, J. S., & Corbett, C. L. (2019). A survey of deep learning methods for cyber security. *Information (Basel)*, *10*(4), 122. doi:10.3390/info10040122

Bernard, Y., Hueber, N., & Girau, B. (2020, September). A fast algorithm to find Best Matching Units in Self-Organizing Maps. In *International Conference on Artificial Neural Networks* (pp. 825-837). Springer.

Bertino, E., & Islam, N. (2017). Botnets and internet of things security. *Computer*, *50*(2), 76–79.

Bezerra, V. H., da Costa, V. G. T., Barbon, J., Miani, R. S., & Zarpelão, B. B. (2019). IoTDS: A One-Class Classification Approach to Detect Botnets in Internet of Things Devices. *Sensors (Basel)*, *19*(14), 3188.

Bharathi, Tanguturi, JayaKumar, & Selvamani. (2012). Node capture attack in Wireless Sensor Network: A survey. *2012 IEEE International Conference on Computational Intelligence and Computing Research, ICCIC 2012*, 1-3. 10.1109/ICCIC.2012.6510237

Bhaskaran, K., Ilfrich, P., Liffman, D., Vecchiola, C., Jayachandran, P., Kumar, A., ... Teo, E. G. (2018, April). Double-blind consent-driven data sharing on blockchain. In *2018 IEEE International Conference on Cloud Engineering (IC2E)* (pp. 385-391). IEEE. 10.1109/IC2E.2018.00073

Bhattarai, S., & Wang, Y. (2018). End-to-end trust and security for Internet of Things applications. *Computer*, *51*(4), 20–27. doi:10.1109/MC.2018.2141038

Bhatt, R., Maheshwary, P., Shukla, P., Shukla, P., Shrivastava, M., & Changlani, S. (2020). Implementation of Fruit Fly Optimization Algorithm (FFOA) to escalate the attacking efficiency of node capture attack in Wireless Sensor Networks (WSN). *Computer Communications*, *149*, 134–145. doi:10.1016/j.comcom.2019.09.007

Bhatt, S., & Ragiri, P. R. (2021). Security trends in Internet of Things: A survey. *SN Applied Sciences*, *3*(1), 1–14.

Bhushan, K., & Gupta, B. B. (2019). Distributed denial of service (DDoS) attack mitigation in software defined network (SDN)-based cloud computing environment. *Journal of Ambient Intelligence and Humanized Computing*, *10*(5), 1985–1997.

Bikson, M., Brunoni, A. R., Charvet, L. E., Clark, V. P., Cohen, L. G., Deng, Z. D., Dmochowski, J., Edwards, D. J., Frohlich, F., Kappenman, E. S., Lim, K. O., Loo, C., Mantovani, A., McMullen, D. P., Parra, L. C., Pearson, M., Richardson, J. D., Rumsey, J. M., Sehatpour, P., ... Losanby, S. H. (2018). Rigor and reproducibility in research with transcranial electrical stimulation: An NIMH-sponsored workshop. *Brain Stimulation, 11*(3), 465–480. doi:10.1016/j.brs.2017.12.008 PMID:29398575

Binbusayyis, A., & Vaiyapuri, T. (2020). Comprehensive analysis and recommendation of feature evaluation measures for intrusion detection. *Heliyon, 6*(7), e04262. doi:10.1016/j.heliyon.2020.e04262 PMID:32685709

Binnendijk, A., Marler, T., & Bartels, E. M. (2020). *Brain-Computer Interfaces: U.S. Military Applications and Implications, An Initial Assessment*. RAND Corporation. doi:10.7249/RR2996

Blei, D. M., Ng, A. Y., & Jordan, M. I. (2003). Latent dirichlet allocation. *The Journal of Machine Learning Research, 3*, 993-1022.

Bonaci, T., Bushnell, L., & Poovendran, R. (2010, December). Node capture attacks in wireless sensor networks: A system theoretic approach. In *49th IEEE Conference on Decision and Control (CDC)* (pp. 6765-6772). IEEE. 10.1109/CDC.2010.5717499

Bonaci, T., Calo, R., & Chizeck, H. J. (2015). App Stores for the Brain: Privacy and Security in Brain-Computer Interfaces. *IEEE Technology and Society Magazine, 34*(2), 32–39. doi:10.1109/MTS.2015.2425551

Bonaci, T., Herron, J., Matlack, C., & Chizeck, H. J. (2015). Securing the Exocortex: A Twenty-First Century Cybernetics Challenge. *IEEE Technology and Society Magazine, 34*(3), 44–51. doi:10.1109/MTS.2015.2461152

Bonderud, D. (2016). *Leaked Mirai Malware Boosts IoT Insecurity Threat Level*. Retrieved from https://securityintelligence.com/news/leaked-mirai-malware-boosts-iot-insecurity-threat-level/

Bormann, C., Castellani, A. P., & Shelby, Z. (2012). Coap: An application protocol for billions of tiny internet nodes. *IEEE Internet Computing, 16*(2), 62–67.

Boyer, S. A. (1999). *SCADA: Supervisory control and data acquisition* (Vol. 3). ISA.

Boyes, H., Hallaq, B., Cunningham, J., & Watson, T. (2018). The industrial internet of things (IIoT): An analysis framework. *Computers in Industry, 101*, 1–12. doi:10.1016/j.compind.2018.04.015

Brakerski, Z., & Vaikuntanathan, V. (2014). Efficient fully homomorphic encryption from (standard) LWE. *SIAM Journal on Computing, 43*(2), 831–871.

Burnap, P., French, R., Turner, F., & Jones, K. (2018). Malware classification using self organising feature maps and machine activity data. *Computers & Security, 73*, 399–410. doi:10.1016/j.cose.2017.11.016

Butun, I., Österberg, P., & Song, H. (2019). Security of the Internet of Things: Vulnerabilities, attacks, and countermeasures. *IEEE Communications Surveys and Tutorials, 22*(1), 616–644.

Cabău, G., Buhu, M., & Oprişa, C. (2016). Malware classification using filesystem footprints. *2016 IEEE International Conference on Automation, Quality and Testing, Robotics (AQTR)*, 1-6. 10.1109/AQTR.2016.7501294

Campbell, A., & Wu, C. (2018). Chronically Implanted Intracranial Electrodes: Tissue Reaction and Electrical Changes. *Micromachines, 9*(9), 430. doi:10.3390/mi9090430 PMID:30424363

Canfora, G., Mercaldo, F., Visaggio, C. A., & Di Notte, P. (2014). Metamorphic malware detection using code metrics. *Information Security Journal: A Global Perspective, 23*(3), 57-67.

Cash, M., & Bassiouni, M. (2018, September). Two-tier permission-ed and permission-less blockchain for secure data sharing. In *2018 IEEE International Conference on Smart Cloud (SmartCloud)* (pp. 138-144). IEEE. 10.1109/SmartCloud.2018.00031

Cech, H. L., Großmann, M., & Krieger, U. R. (2019, June). A fog computing architecture to share sensor data by means of blockchain functionality. In *2019 IEEE International Conference on Fog Computing (ICFC)* (pp. 31-40). IEEE. 10.1109/ICFC.2019.00013

Centre for Research in Cyber Security. (n.d.). *iTrust*. https://itrust.sutd.edu.sg/

Ceron, J. M., Steding-Jessen, K., Hoepers, C., Granville, L. Z., & Margi, C. B. (2019). Improving IoT Botnet Investigation Using an Adaptive Network Layer. *Sensors (Basel)*, *19*(3), 727.

Chahid, Y., Benabdellah, M., & Azizi, A. (2017, April). Internet of things security. In *2017 International Conference on Wireless Technologies, Embedded and Intelligent Systems (WITS)* (pp. 1-6). IEEE. doi:10.1109/ICOASE.2018.8548785

Chandola, V., Banerjee, A., & Kumar, V. (2009). Anomaly detection: A survey. *ACM computing surveys (CSUR)*, *41*(3), 1-58.

Chan, H., Perrig, A., & Song, D. (2003, May). Random key predistribution schemes for sensor networks. In *2003 Symposium on Security and Privacy*, 2003 (pp. 197-213). IEEE. 10.1109/SECPRI.2003.1199337

Chan, K., & Fekri, F. (2007, May). Node compromise attacks and network connectivity. In *Defense Transformation and Net-Centric Systems 2007* (Vol. 6578, p. 65780W). International Society for Optics and Photonics.

Chasaki, D., & Mansour, C. (2015). Security challenges in the internet of things. *International Journal of Space-Based and Situated Computing*, *5*(3), 141–149.

Chaudhary, P., & Agrawal, R. (2018). Emerging Threats to Security and Privacy in Brain Computer Interface *International Journal of Advanced Studies of Scientific Research, 3*(12). https://ssrn.com/abstract=3326692

Chaudhary, P., Gupta, B. B., Chang, X., Nedjah, N., & Chui, K. T. (2021). Enhancing big data security through integrating XSS scanner into fog nodes for SMEs gain. *Technological Forecasting and Social Change*, *168*, 120754. doi:10.1016/j.techfore.2021.120754

Chaudhary, U., Xia, B., Silvoni, S., Cohen, L. G., & Birbaumer, N. (2017). Brain–Computer Interface–Based Communication in the Completely Locked-In State. *PLoS Biology*, *15*(1), 1–25. doi:10.1371/journal.pbio.1002593 PMID:28141803

Chegini, H., & Mahanti, A. (2019, December). A Framework of Automation on Context-Aware Internet of Things (IoT) Systems. In *Proceedings of the 12th IEEE/ACM International Conference on Utility and Cloud Computing Companion* (pp. 157-162). IEEE.

Chen, Y. K. (2012, January). Challenges and opportunities of internet of things. In *17th Asia and South Pacific design automation conference* (pp. 383-388). IEEE.

Chen, H., Perrig, A., & Song, D. (2003) Random Key Predistribution Schemes for Sensor Networks. *Proceedings of the 2003 IEEE symposium on security and privacy*, 197–213.

Chen, K., Zhang, S., Li, Z., Zhang, Y., Deng, Q., Ray, S., & Jin, Y. (2018). Internet-of-things security and vulnerabilities: Taxonomy, challenges, and practice. *Journal of Hardware and Systems Security*, *2*(2), 97–110.

Chhabra, Gupta, & Almomani. (2013). *A novel solution to handle DDOS attack in MANET*. Academic Press.

Chhabra, M., Gupta, B., & Almomani, A. (2013). *A novel solution to handle DDOS attack in MANET*. Academic Press.

Chhabra, M., Gupta, B., & Almomani, A. (2013). A novel solution to handle DDOS attack in MANET. *Journal of Information Security*, *4*(3), 34631. Advance online publication. doi:10.4236/jis.2013.43019

Chiappa, K. H., & Ropper, A. H. (1982). Evoked Potentials in Clinical Medicine. *The New England Journal of Medicine*, *306*(19), 1140–1150. doi:10.1056/NEJM198205133061904 PMID:7040957

Chizeck, H. J., & Bonaci, T. (2014). *Brain-Computer Interface Anonymizer* (Patent application US20140228701A1). United States Patent and Trademark Office.

Choi, S. (2020). Combined kNN Classification and hierarchical similarity hash for fast malware detection. *Applied Sciences*, *10*(15), 5173.

Choo, A., & May, A. (2014). Virtual mindfulness meditation: Virtual reality and electroencephalography for health gamification. *2014 IEEE Games Media Entertainment*, 1. doi:10.1109/GEM.2014.7048076

Chouhan, L., Chauhan, N., Mahapatra, A. S., & Agarwal, V. (2020). A survey on the applications of machine learning in wireless sensor networks. *International Journal of High Performance Computing and Networking*, *16*(4), 197–220. doi:10.1504/IJHPCN.2020.113779

Chow, J. K., Su, Z., Wu, J., Tan, P. S., Mao, X., & Wang, Y. H. (2020). Anomaly detection of defects on concrete structures with the convolutional autoencoder. *Advanced Engineering Informatics*, *45*, 101105. doi:10.1016/j.aei.2020.101105

Chui, K. T., Vasant, P., & Liu, R. W. (2019). Smart city is a safe city: information and communication technology–enhanced urban space monitoring and surveillance systems: the promise and limitations. In Smart Cities: Issues and Challenges (pp. 111-124). Elsevier. doi:10.1016/B978-0-12-816639-0.00007-7

Chui, K. T., Liu, R. W., Zhao, M., & De Pablos, P. O. (2020). Predicting students' performance with school and family tutoring using generative adversarial network-based deep support vector machine. *IEEE Access: Practical Innovations, Open Solutions*, *8*, 86745–86752. doi:10.1109/ACCESS.2020.2992869

Cimpanu, C. (2018). *New Mirai Variant Focuses on Turning IoT Devices into Proxy Servers*. Retrieved from https://www.bleepingcomputer.com/news/security/new-mirai-variant-focuses-on-turning-iot-devices-into-proxy-servers/

Cisco. (2020). *Cisco Annual Internet Report (2018–2023) White Paper*. Retrieved from https://www.cisco.com/c/en/us/solutions/collateral/executive-perspectives/annual-internet-report/white-paper-c11-741490.html

Conti, M., Dehghantanha, A., Franke, K., & Watson, S. (2018). *Internet of Things security and forensics: Challenges and opportunities*. Academic Press.

Crea, S., Nann, M., Trigili, E., Cordella, F., Baldoni, A., Badesa, F. J., Catalán, J. M., Zollo, L., Vitiello, N., Aracil, N. G., & Soekadar, S. R. (2018). Feasibility and safety of shared EEG/EOG and vision-guided autonomous whole-arm exoskeleton control to perform activities of daily living. *Scientific Reports*, *8*(1), 1. doi:10.103841598-018-29091-5 PMID:30018334

Croman, K., Decker, C., Eyal, I., Gencer, A. E., Juels, A., Kosba, A., & Song, D. (2016, February). On scaling decentralized blockchains. In *International conference on financial cryptography and data security* (pp. 106-125). Springer.

Curran, M. T., Yang, J., Merrill, N., & Chuang, J. (2016). Passthoughts authentication with low cost EarEEG. *2016 38th Annual International Conference of the IEEE Engineering in Medicine and Biology Society (EMBC)*, 1979-1982. 10.1109/EMBC.2016.7591112

Cvitić, I., Peraković, D., Periša, M., & Gupta, B. (2021). Ensemble machine learning approach for classification of IoT devices in smart home. *International Journal of Machine Learning and Cybernetics*, 1-24. https://www.ll.mit.edu/r-d/datasets/1998-darpa-intrusion-detection-evaluation-dataset

Cvitić, I., Peraković, D., Periša, M., & Gupta, B. (2021). Ensemble machine learning approach for classification of IoT devices in smart home. *International Journal of Machine Learning and Cybernetics*, 1–24.

da Costa, K. A., Papa, J. P., Lisboa, C. O., Munoz, R., & de Albuquerque, V. H. C. (2019). Internet of Things: A survey on machine learning-based intrusion detection approaches. *Computer Networks*, *151*, 147–157. doi:10.1016/j.comnet.2019.01.023

Dabbagh, M., & Rayes, A. (2019). Internet of things security and privacy. In *Internet of Things from hype to reality* (pp. 211–238). Springer.

Dadoun, A., & Troncy, R. (2020). *Many-to-one Recurrent Neural Network for Session-based Recommendation*. arXiv preprint arXiv:2008.11136.

Dahiya, A., & Gupta, B. B. (2021). A reputation score policy and Bayesian game theory based incentivized mechanism for DDoS attacks mitigation and cyber defense. *Future Generation Computer Systems*, *117*, 193–204.

Dahl, G. E., Stokes, J. W., Deng, L., & Yu, D. (2013, May). Large-scale malware classification using random projections and neural networks. In *2013 IEEE International Conference on Acoustics, Speech and Signal Processing* (pp. 3422-3426). IEEE.

Das, S., Koperski, M., Bremond, F., & Francesca, G. (2018, November). Deep-temporal lstm for daily living action recognition. In *2018 15th IEEE International Conference on Advanced Video and Signal Based Surveillance (AVSS)* (pp. 1-6). IEEE. 10.1109/AVSS.2018.8639122

Das, A. K., Zeadally, S., & He, D. (2018). Taxonomy and analysis of security protocols for Internet of Things. *Future Generation Computer Systems*, *89*, 110–125.

DatasetN. S. L.-K. D. D. (n.d.). https://www.unb.ca/cic/datasets/nsl.html

David, O. E., & Netanyahu, N. S. (2015, July). Deepsign: Deep learning for automatic malware signature generation and classification. In *2015 International Joint Conference on Neural Networks (IJCNN)* (pp. 1-8). IEEE. 10.1109/IJCNN.2015.7280815

Denning, T., Matsuoka, Y., & Kohno, T. (2009). Neurosecurity: Security and privacy for neural devices. *Neurosurgical Focus FOC*, *27*(1), E7. doi:10.3171/2009.4.FOCUS0985 PMID:19569895

De, P., Liu, Y., & Das, S. K. (2006, June). Modeling node compromise spread in wireless sensor networks using epidemic theory. In *2006 International Symposium on a World of Wireless, Mobile and Multimedia Networks (WoWMoM'06)*. IEEE. 10.1109/WOWMOM.2006.74

Devry, J. (2016). *Mirai Botnet Infects Devices in 164 Countries*. Retrieved from https://www.cybersecurity-insiders.com/mirai-botnet-infects-devices-in-164-countries/

Dhillon, A., & Verma, G. K. (2020). Convolutional neural network: A review of models, methodologies and applications to object detection. *Progress in Artificial Intelligence*, *9*(2), 85–112. doi:10.100713748-019-00203-0

Diallo, B., Hu, J., Li, T., Khan, G. A., Liang, X., & Zhao, Y. (2021). Deep embedding clustering based on contractive autoencoder. *Neurocomputing*, *433*, 96–107. doi:10.1016/j.neucom.2020.12.094

Dib, O., Brousmiche, K. L., Durand, A., Thea, E., & Hamida, E. B. (2018). Consortium blockchains: Overview, applications and challenges. *International Journal on Advances in Telecommunications*, *11*(1-2).

Dinh, T. T. A., Wang, J., Chen, G., Liu, R., Ooi, B. C., & Tan, K. L. (2017, May). Blockbench: A framework for analyzing private blockchains. In *Proceedings of the 2017 ACM International Conference on Management of Data* (pp. 1085-1100). 10.1145/3035918.3064033

Donchin, E. (1979). Event-related Brain Potentials: A Tool in the Study of Human Information Processing. *Evoked Brain Potentials and Behavior*, 13–88. doi:10.1007/978-1-4684-3462-0_2

Dong, A., Du, Z., & Yan, Z. (2019). Round trip time prediction using recurrent neural networks with minimal gated unit. *IEEE Communications Letters*, 23(4), 584–587. doi:10.1109/LCOMM.2019.2899603

Dubovitskaya, A., Novotny, P., Xu, Z., & Wang, F. (2020). Applications of blockchain technology for data-sharing in oncology: Results from a systematic literature review. *Oncology*, 98(6), 403–411. doi:10.1159/000504325 PMID:31794967

Dwivedi, R. K., Kumar, R., & Buyya, R. (2021). Secure healthcare monitoring sensor cloud with attribute-based elliptical curve cryptography. *International Journal of Cloud Applications and Computing*, 11(3), 1–18. doi:10.4018/IJCAC.2021070101

Dwivedi, S., Vardhan, M., Tripathi, S., & Shukla, A. K. (2020). Implementation of adaptive scheme in evolutionary technique for anomaly-based intrusion detection. *Evolutionary Intelligence*, 13(1), 103–117. doi:10.100712065-019-00293-8

Edwards, C., Kouzani, A., Lee, K. H., & Ross, E. K. (n.d.). Neurostimulation Devices for the Treatment of Neurologic Disorders. *Mayo Clinic Proceedings*, 92(9), 1427-1444. doi:10.1016/j.mayocp.2017.05.005

Edwards, S., & Profetis, I. (2016). *Hajime: Analysis of a Decentralized Internet Worm for IoT Devices.* http://security.rapiditynetworks.com/publications/2016-10-16/Hajime.pdf

EEGLAB. (2020). https://sccn.ucsd.edu/eeglab/index.php

Ehdaie, M., Alexiou, N., Ahmadian, M., Aref, M. R., & Papadimitratos, P. (2017). Mitigating Node Capture Attack in Random Key Distribution Schemes through Key Deletion. *Journal of Communication Engineering*, 6(2), 99–109.

Ehrenfeld, J. M. (2017). Wannacry, cybersecurity and health information technology: A time to act. *Journal of Medical Systems*, 41(7), 104. doi:10.100710916-017-0752-1 PMID:28540616

Elhag, S., Fernández, A., Bawakid, A., Alshomrani, S., & Herrera, F. (2015). On the combination of genetic fuzzy systems and pairwise learning for improving detection rates on intrusion detection systems. *Expert Systems with Applications*, 42(1), 193–202. doi:10.1016/j.eswa.2014.08.002

Elhoseny, M., Shankar, K., Lakshmanaprabu, S. K., Maseleno, A., & Arunkumar, N. (2020). Hybrid optimization with cryptography encryption for medical image security in Internet of Things. *Neural Computing & Applications*, 32(15), 10979–10993.

Elnour, M., Meskin, N., Khan, K., & Jain, R. (2020). A dual-isolation-forests-based attack detection framework for industrial control systems. *IEEE Access: Practical Innovations, Open Solutions*, 8, 36639–36651. doi:10.1109/ACCESS.2020.2975066

Eltayieb, N., Elhabob, R., Hassan, A., & Li, F. (2020). A blockchain-based attribute-based signcryption scheme to secure data sharing in the cloud. *Journal of Systems Architecture*, 102, 101653. doi:10.1016/j.sysarc.2019.101653

Fabio Ceschini, G., Gatta, N., Venturini, M., Hubauer, T., & Murarasu, A. (2018). Optimization of statistical methodologies for anomaly detection in gas turbine dynamic time series. *Journal of Engineering for Gas Turbines and Power*, 140(3), 032401. doi:10.1115/1.4037963

Fang, Z., Wang, J., Geng, J., & Kan, X. (2019). Feature Selection for Malware Detection Based on Reinforcement Learning. *IEEE Access: Practical Innovations, Open Solutions, 7,* 176177–176187. doi:10.1109/ACCESS.2019.2957429

Farnaaz, N., & Jabbar, M. A. (2016). Random forest modeling for network intrusion detection system. *Procedia Computer Science, 89,* 213–217. doi:10.1016/j.procs.2016.06.047

Farooq, M., Waseem, M., Mazhar, S., Khairi, A., & Kamal, T. (2015). A Review on Internet of Things (IoT). *International Journal of Computers and Applications, 113*(1), 1–7.

Feizollah, A., Anuar, N. B., Salleh, R., Suarez-Tangil, G., & Furnell, S. (2017). Androdialysis: Analysis of android intent effectiveness in malware detection. *Computers & Security, 65,* 121-134.

Feizollah, A. (2014). *Comparative study of k-means and mini batch k-means clustering algorithms in android malware detection using network traffic analysis. In 2014 international symposium on biometrics and security technologies (ISBAST).* IEEE.

Feng, Q., He, D., Zeadally, S., Khan, M. K., & Kumar, N. (2019). A survey on privacy protection in blockchain system. *Journal of Network and Computer Applications, 126,* 45–58. doi:10.1016/j.jnca.2018.10.020

Ficco, M., Esposito, C., Xiang, Y., & Palmieri, F. (2017). Pseudo-dynamic testing of realistic edge-fog cloud ecosystems. *IEEE Communications Magazine, 55*(11), 98–104. doi:10.1109/MCOM.2017.1700328

Finke, A., Lenhardt, A., & Ritter, H. (2009). The MindGame: A P300-based brain–computer interface game. *Neural Networks, 22*(9), 1329–1333. doi:10.1016/j.neunet.2009.07.003 PMID:19635654

Firdausi, I., Erwin, A., & Nugroho, A. S. (2010, December). Analysis of machine learning techniques used in behavior-based malware detection. In *2010 second international conference on advances in computing, control, and telecommunication technologies* (pp. 201-203). IEEE. 10.1109/ACT.2010.33

Fischer, T., & Krauss, C. (2018). Deep learning with long short-term memory networks for financial market predictions. *European Journal of Operational Research, 270*(2), 654–669. doi:10.1016/j.ejor.2017.11.054

Florea, I., Ruse, L. C., & Rughinis, R. (2017, September). Challenges in security in Internet of Things. In *2017 16th RoEduNet Conference: Networking in Education and Research (RoEduNet)* (pp. 1-5). IEEE.

Frank, C., Nance, C., Jarocki, S., & Pauli, W. E. (2018). Protecting IoT from Mirai botnets; IoT device hardening. *Journal of Information Systems Applied Research, 11*(2), 33–44.

Frank, M., Hwu, T., Jain, S., Knight, R. T., Martinovic, I., Mittal, P., Perito, D., Sluganovic, I., & Song, D. (2017) Using EEG-Based BCI Devices to Subliminally Probe for Private Information. *Proceedings of the 2017 on Workshop on Privacy in the Electronic Society - WPES '17,* 133-136. 10.1145/3139550.3139559

Fu, H.-L., Fang, P.-H., Chi, C.-Y., Kuo, C., Liu, M.-H., Hsu, H. M., Hsieh, C.-H., Liang, S.-F., Hsieh, S., & Yang, C.-T. (2020). Application of Brain-Computer Interface and Virtual Reality in Advancing Cultural Experience. *2020 IEEE International Conference on Visual Communications and Image Processing (VCIP),* 351–354. 10.1109/VCIP49819.2020.9301801

Gai, K., Wu, Y., Zhu, L., Qiu, M., & Shen, M. (2019). Privacy-preserving energy trading using consortium blockchain in smart grid. *IEEE Transactions on Industrial Informatics, 15*(6), 3548–3558. doi:10.1109/TII.2019.2893433

Ganesh, M. (2017). CNN-based android malware detection. In *2017 International Conference on Software Security and Assurance (ICSSA).* IEEE. 10.1109/ICSSA.2017.18

Gangadharan, V., & Gupta, D. (2020). Recognizing Named Entities in Agriculture Documents using LDA based Topic Modelling Techniques. *Procedia Computer Science, 171,* 1337–1345. doi:10.1016/j.procs.2020.04.143

Garcia, S., Grill, M., Stiborek, J., & Zunino, A. (2014). An empirical comparison of botnet detection methods. *Computers & Security, 45*, 100-123.

Gaurav, A., Gupta, B. B., Hsu, C. H., Yamaguchi, S., & Chui, K. T. (2021, January). Fog Layer-based DDoS attack Detection Approach for Internet-of-Things (IoTs) devices. In *2021 IEEE International Conference on Consumer Electronics (ICCE)* (pp. 1-5). IEEE.

Gavriluţ, D., Cimpoeşu, M., Anton, D., & Ciortuz, L. (2009). Malware detection using machine learning. *2009 International Multiconference on Computer Science and Information Technology*, 735-741. 10.1109/IMCSIT.2009.5352759

Gelenbe, E., Domanska, J., Czàchorski, T., Drosou, A., & Tzovaras, D. (2018, June). Security for internet of things: The seriot project. In *2018 International Symposium on Networks, Computers and Communications (ISNCC)* (pp. 1-5). IEEE.

Ge, M., Hong, J. B., Guttmann, W., & Kim, D. S. (2017). A framework for automating security analysis of the internet of things. *Journal of Network and Computer Applications, 83*, 12–27.

Ghoneim, A., Muhammad, G., Amin, S. U., & Gupta, B. (2018). Medical image forgery detection for smart healthcare. *IEEE Communications Magazine, 56*(4), 33–37.

Gibert, D., Mateu, C., & Planes, J. (2019, July). A hierarchical convolutional neural network for malware classification. In *2019 International Joint Conference on Neural Networks (IJCNN)* (pp. 1-8). IEEE.

Gibert, D., Mateu, C., & Planes, J. (2020). The rise of machine learning for detection and classification of malware: Research developments, trends and challenges. *Journal of Network and Computer Applications, 153*, 102526. doi:10.1016/j.jnca.2019.102526

Gibert, D., Mateu, C., Planes, J., & Vicens, R. (2019). Using convolutional neural networks for classification of malware represented as images. *Journal of Computer Virology and Hacking Techniques, 15*(1), 15–28.

Gilja, V., Nuyujukian, P., Chestek, C., Cunningham, J. P., Yu, B. M., Fan, J. M., Churchland, M. M., Kaufman, M. T., Kao, J. C., Ryu, S. I., & Shenoy, K. V. (2012). A high-performance neural prosthesis enabled by control algorithm design. *Nature Neuroscience, 15*(12), 1752–1757. doi:10.1038/nn.3265 PMID:23160043

Glannon, G. (2014). Ethical issues with brain-computer interfaces. *Frontiers in Systems Neuroscience, 8*, 136. doi:10.3389/fnsys.2014.00136 PMID:25126061

Gomes-Osman, J., Indahlastari, A., Fried, P. J., Cabral, D. L. F., Rice, J., Nissim, N. R., Aksu, S., McLaren, M. E., & Woods, A. J. (2018). Non-invasive Brain Stimulation: Probing Intracortical Circuits and Improving Cognition in the Aging Brain. *Frontiers in Aging Neuroscience, 10*, 177. doi:10.3389/fnagi.2018.00177 PMID:29950986

Gong, J., Xu, X., & Lei, Y. (2020). Unsupervised specific emitter identification method using radio-frequency fingerprint embedded InfoGAN. *IEEE Transactions on Information Forensics and Security, 15*, 2898–2913. doi:10.1109/TIFS.2020.2978620

Gopal, T. S., Meerolla, M., Jyostna, G., Eswari, L., Reddy, P., & Magesh, E. (2018). Mitigating Mirai Malware Spreading in IoT Environment. In *Proc. of ICACCI 2018* (pp.2226-2230). Academic Press.

Gou, Z., & Yamaguchi, S. (2017). Analysis of various security issues and challenges in cloud computing environment: a survey. In Identity Theft: Breakthroughs in Research and Practice (pp. 221-247). IGI Global.

Gou, Z., Yamaguchi, S., & Gupta, B. B. (2017). Analysis of various security issues and challenges in cloud computing environment: a survey. In Identity Theft: Breakthroughs in Research and Practice (pp. 221-247). IGI Global.

Gou, Z., Yamaguchi, S., & Gupta, B. B. (2017). Analysis of various security issues and challenges in cloud computing environment: a survey. In Identity Theft: Breakthroughs in Research and Practice (pp. 221-247). IGI global. doi:10.4018/978-1-5225-0808-3.ch011

Goyal, S. (2018). *The History of Blockchain Technology: Must Know Timeline*. Academic Press.

Grammatikis, P. I. R., Sarigiannidis, P. G., & Moscholios, I. D. (2019). Securing the Internet of Things: Challenges, threats and solutions. *Internet of Things*, *5*, 41–70.

Granjal, J., Monteiro, E., & Silva, J. S. (2015). Security for the internet of things: A survey of existing protocols and open research issues. *IEEE Communications Surveys and Tutorials*, *17*(3), 1294–1312.

Gruber, N., & Jockisch, A. (2020). Are GRU cells more specific and LSTM cells more sensitive in motive classification of text? *Frontiers in Artificial Intelligence*, *3*, 40. doi:10.3389/frai.2020.00040 PMID:33733157

Guan, C., Thulasidas, M., & Wu, J. (2004). High performance P300 speller for brain-computer interface. *IEEE International Workshop on Biomedical Circuits and Systems* (pp. S3/5/INV-S3/13). 10.1109/BIOCAS.2004.1454155

Gubbi, J., Buyya, R., Marusic, S., & Palaniswami, M. (2013). Internet of things (IoT): A vision, architectural elements, and future directions. *Future Generation Computer Systems*, *29*(7), 1645–1660.

Gulzar, M., & Abbas, G. (2019, February). Internet of things security: a survey and taxonomy. In *2019 International Conference on Engineering and Emerging Technologies (ICEET)* (pp. 1-6). IEEE.

Guo, C., Huang, D., Dong, N., Zhang, J., & Xu, J. (2021). Callback2Vec: Callback-aware hierarchical embedding for mobile application. *Information Sciences*, *542*, 131–155. doi:10.1016/j.ins.2020.06.058

Guo, R., Shi, H., Zhao, Q., & Zheng, D. (2018). Secure attribute-based signature scheme with multiple authorities for blockchain in electronic health records systems. *IEEE Access: Practical Innovations, Open Solutions*, *6*, 11676–11686. doi:10.1109/ACCESS.2018.2801266

Gupta, B. B., Li, K. C., Leung, V. C., Psannis, K. E., & Yamaguchi, S. (2021). Blockchain-assisted secure fine-grained searchable encryption for a cloud-based healthcare cyber-physical system. *IEEE/CAA Journal of Automatica Sinica*.

Gupta, B. B., Gupta, S., Gangwar, S., Kumar, M., & Meena, P. K. (2015). Cross-site scripting (XSS) abuse and defense: Exploitation on several testing bed environments and its defense. *Journal of Information Privacy and Security*, *11*(2), 118–136.

Gupta, B. B., Perez, G. M., Agrawal, D. P., & Gupta, D. (2020). *Handbook of computer networks and cyber security*. Springer. doi:10.1007/978-3-030-22277-2

Gupta, B. B., & Quamara, M. (2020). An overview of Internet of Things (IoT): Architectural aspects, challenges, and protocols. *Concurrency and Computation*, *32*(21), e4946.

Gupta, B. B., & Sheng, Q. Z. (Eds.). (2019). *Machine learning for computer and cyber security: principle, algorithms, and practices*. CRC Press. doi:10.1201/9780429504044

Gupta, B. B., Yadav, K., Razzak, I., Psannis, K., Castiglione, A., & Chang, X. (2021). A novel approach for phishing URLs detection using lexical based machine learning in a real-time environment. *Computer Communications*, *175*, 47–57. doi:10.1016/j.comcom.2021.04.023

Gupta, B., Agrawal, D. P., & Yamaguchi, S. (2016). *Handbook of Research on Modern Cryptographic Solutions for Computer and Cyber Security*. IGI Global. doi:10.4018/978-1-5225-0105-3

Gupta, C. N., Palaniappan, R., & Paramesran, R. (2012). Exploiting the P300 paradigm for cognitive biometrics. *International Journal of Cognitive Biometrics*, *1*(1), 26. doi:10.1504/IJCB.2012.046513

Gupta, D., Gupta, B., & Mishra, A. (2018). Identity Theft, Malware, and Social Engineering in Dealing with Cybercrime. In B. B. G. Gupta (Ed.), *Computer and Cyber Security*. CRC Press.

Gupta, K., & Shukla, S. (2016, February). Internet of Things: Security challenges for next generation networks. In *2016 International Conference on Innovation and Challenges in Cyber Security (ICICCS-INBUSH)* (pp. 315-318). IEEE.

Gupta, S., & Gupta, B. B. (2015, May). PHP-sensor: a prototype method to discover workflow violation and XSS vulnerabilities in PHP web applications. In *Proceedings of the 12th ACM International Conference on Computing Frontiers* (pp. 1-8). ACM.

Gupta, S., & Gupta, B. B. (2016). JS-SAN: Defense mechanism for HTML5-based web applications against javascript code injection vulnerabilities. *Security and Communication Networks*, *9*(11), 1477–1495.

Gupta, S., & Gupta, B. B. (2016). XSS-SAFE: A server-side approach to detect and mitigate cross-site scripting (XSS) attacks in JavaScript code. *Arabian Journal for Science and Engineering*, *41*(3), 897–920.

Gupta, S., & Gupta, B. B. (2017). Detection, avoidance, and attack pattern mechanisms in modern web application vulnerabilities: Present and future challenges. *International Journal of Cloud Applications and Computing*, *7*(3), 1–43. doi:10.4018/IJCAC.2017070101

HaddadPajouh, H., Dehghantanha, A., Khayami, R., & Choo, K.-K. R. (2018). A deep recurrent neural network based approach for internet of things malware threat hunting. *Future Generation Computer Systems*, *85*, 88–96. doi:10.1016/j.future.2018.03.007

Hallappanavar, V. L., & Birje, M. N. (2021). A reliable trust computing mechanism in fog computing. *International Journal of Cloud Applications and Computing*, *11*(1), 1–20. doi:10.4018/IJCAC.2021010101

Hameed, S., Khan, F. I., & Hameed, B. (2019). Understanding security requirements and challenges in Internet of Things (IoT): A review. *Journal of Computer Networks and Communications*.

Hao, X., Wang, Z., Shan, Z., & Zhao, Y. (2019). Prediction of electricity consumption in cement production: A time-varying delay deep belief network prediction method. *Neural Computing & Applications*, *31*(11), 7165–7179. doi:10.100700521-018-3540-z

Harbi, Y., Aliouat, Z., Harous, S., Bentaleb, A., & Refoufi, A. (2019). A review of security in internet of things. *Wireless Personal Communications*, *108*(1), 325–344.

Hasan, M., Islam, M. M., Zarif, M. I. I., & Hashem, M. M. A. (2019). Attack and anomaly detection in IoT sensors in IoT sites using machine learning approaches. *Internet of Things*, *7*, 100059. doi:10.1016/j.iot.2019.100059

Hassan, M. M., Gumaei, A., Alsanad, A., Alrubaian, M., & Fortino, G. (2020). A hybrid deep learning model for efficient intrusion detection in big data environment. *Information Sciences*, *513*, 386–396. doi:10.1016/j.ins.2019.10.069

Hassan, W. H. (2019). Current research on Internet of Things (IoT) security: A survey. *Computer Networks*, *148*, 283–294. doi:10.1016/j.comnet.2018.11.025

Hasselgren, A., Kralevska, K., Gligoroski, D., Pedersen, S. A., & Faxvaag, A. (2019). Blockchain in healthcare and health sciences–a scoping review. *International Journal of Medical Informatics*, 104040. PMID:31865055

Hastie, T., Tibshirani, R., & Friedman, J. (2009). *The elements of statistical learning: data mining, inference, and prediction.* Springer Science & Business Media. Industrial Control System (ICS) Cyber Attack Datasets. https://sites.google.com/a/uah.edu/tommy-morris-uah/ics-data-sets

Hiraishi, K. (2001). A Petri-net-based model for the mathematical analysis of multi-agent systems. *IEICE Trans. on Fundamentals, E84-A*(11), 2829–2837.

Hofman, W. J. (2019). A Methodological Approach for Development and Deployment of Data Sharing in Complex Organizational Supply and Logistics Networks with Blockchain Technology. *IFAC-PapersOnLine, 52*(3), 55–60. doi:10.1016/j.ifacol.2019.06.010

Hong, J., & Liu, C. C. (2017). Intelligent electronic devices with collaborative intrusion detection systems. *IEEE Transactions on Smart Grid, 10*(1), 271–281. doi:10.1109/TSG.2017.2737826

Hong, K., & Khan, M. J. (2017). Hybrid Brain–Computer Interface Techniques for Improved Classification Accuracy and Increased Number of Commands: A Review. *Frontiers in Neurorobotics, 11*, 35. doi:10.3389/fnbot.2017.00035 PMID:28790910

Hossain, K., Rahman, M., & Roy, S. (2019). Iot data compression and optimization techniques in cloud storage: Current prospects and future directions. *International Journal of Cloud Applications and Computing, 9*(2), 43–59.

Hossain, M. M., Fotouhi, M., & Hasan, R. (2015, June). *Towards an analysis of security issues, challenges, and open problems in the internet of things. In 2015 IEEE world congress on services.* IEEE.

Hou, J., Qu, L., & Shi, W. (2019). A survey on internet of things security from data perspectives. *Computer Networks, 148*, 295–306.

Hu, C., Zhang, J., & Wen, Q. (2011, October). An identity-based personal location system with protected privacy in IoT. In *2011 4th IEEE International Conference on Broadband Network and Multimedia Technology* (pp. 192-195). IEEE.

Huang, W., & Stokes, J. W. (2016, July). MtNet: a multi-task neural network for dynamic malware classification. In *International conference on detection of intrusions and malware, and vulnerability assessment* (pp. 399-418). Springer. 10.1007/978-3-319-40667-1_20

Huertas Celdrán, A., Gil Pérez, M., Mlakar, I., Alcaraz Calero, J. M., García Clemente, F. J., & Martínez Pérez, G. (2019). A Management Platform for Citizen's Data Protection Regulation. In G. Wang, A. El Saddik, X. Lai, G. Martinez Perez, & K. K. Choo (Eds.), *Smart City and Informatization. iSCI 2019. Communications in Computer and Information Science* (Vol. 1122). Springer. doi:10.1007/978-981-15-1301-5_6

Huertas Celdrán, A., Gil Pérez, M., Mlakar, I., Alcaraz Calero, J. M., García Clemente, F. J., Martínez Pérez, G., & Bhuiyan, Z. A. (2020). PROTECTOR: Towards the protection of sensitive data in Europe and the US. *Computer Networks, 181*, 107448. doi:10.1016/j.comnet.2020.107448

Husamuddin, M., & Qayyum, M. (2017, March). Internet of Things: A study on security and privacy threats. In *2017 2nd International Conference on Anti-Cyber Crimes (ICACC)* (pp. 93-97). IEEE.

Idika, N., & Mathur, A. P. (2007). A survey of malware detection techniques. Purdue University.

Ienca, M., & Haselager, P. (2016). Hacking the brain: Brain–computer interfacing technology and the ethics of neurosecurity. *Ethics and Information Technology, 18*(2), 117–129. doi:10.100710676-016-9398-9

Ienca, M., Haselager, P., & Emanuel, E. (2018). Brain leaks and consumer neurotechnology. *Nature Biotechnology, 36*(9), 805–810. doi:10.1038/nbt.4240 PMID:30188521

Imad, J., Mohammed, F., Jaroodi, J. A., & Mohamed, N. (2016). TRAS: a trust-based routing protocol for ad hoc and sensor networks. *IEEE 2nd international conference on big data security on cloud, IEEE international conference on high performance and smart computing, IEEE international conference on intelligent data and security*, 382–387.

Inoue, J., Yamagata, Y., Chen, Y., Poskitt, C. M., & Sun, J. (2017, November). Anomaly detection for a water treatment system using unsupervised machine learning. In *2017 IEEE International Conference on Data Mining Workshops (ICDMW)* (pp. 1058-1065). IEEE. http://kdd.ics.uci.edu/databases/kddcup99/kddcup99.html

Iscan, H., & Gunduz, M. (2015, November). A survey on fruit fly optimization algorithm. In *2015 11th International Conference on Signal-Image Technology & Internet-Based Systems (SITIS)* (pp. 520-527). 10.1109/SITIS.2015.55

Iturrate, I., Antelis, J. M., Kubler, A., & Minguez, J. (2009). A Non-invasive Brain-Actuated Wheelchair Based on a P300 Neurophysiological Protocol and Automated Navigation. *IEEE Transactions on Robotics, 25*(3), 614–627. doi:10.1109/TRO.2009.2020347

Jamali, S., & Jafarzadeh, P. (2017). An intelligent intrusion detection system by using hierarchically structured learning automata. *Neural Computing & Applications, 28*(5), 1001–1008. doi:10.100700521-015-2116-4

Jang, Y. S., Ryu, S. A., & Park, K. C. (2011). Analysis of P300 Related Target Choice in Oddball Paradigm. *Journal of Information and Communication Convergence Engineering, 9*(2), 125–128. doi:10.6109/jicce.2011.9.2.125

Jaramillo, L. E. S. (2018). Malware Detection and Mitigation Techniques: Lessons Learned from Mirai DDOS Attack. *Journal of Information Systems Engineering & Management, 3*(3), 19.

Jerbi, W., Guermazi, A., & Trabelsi, H. (2020). A novel secure routing protocol of generation and management cryptographic keys for wireless sensor networks deployed in internet of things. *International Journal of High Performance Computing and Networking, 16*(2-3), 87–94.

Jerlin, M. A., & Marimuthu, K. (2018). A new malware detection system using machine learning techniques for API call sequences. *Journal of Applied Security Research, 13*(1), 45–62. doi:10.1080/19361610.2018.1387734

Jindal, F., Jamar, R., & Churi, P. (2018). Future and challenges of internet of things. *International Journal of Computer Science & Information Technology, 10*(2), 13–25.

Jose, D. V., & Vijyalakshmi, A. (2018). An overview of security in Internet of Things. *Procedia Computer Science, 143*, 744–748. doi:10.1016/j.procs.2018.10.439

Kalyani, G., & Chaudhari, S. (2020). An efficient approach for enhancing security in Internet of Things using the optimum authentication key. *International Journal of Computers and Applications, 42*(3), 306–314.

Kancherla, K., & Mukkamala, S. (2013, April). Image visualization based malware detection. In *2013 IEEE Symposium on Computational Intelligence in Cyber Security (CICS)* (pp. 40-44). IEEE.

Kaongoen, N., Yu, M., & Jo, S. (2020). Two-Factor Authentication System Using P300 Response to a Sequence of Human Photographs. *IEEE Transactions on Systems, Man, and Cybernetics. Systems, 50*(3), 1178–1185. doi:10.1109/TSMC.2017.2756673

Kaspersky. (2021). *Machine Learning for Malware Detection*. Retrieved from https://media.kaspersky.com/en/enterprise-security/Kaspersky-Lab-Whitepaper-Machine-Learning.pdf

Kaur, J., Gill, S. S., & Dhaliwal, B. S. (2016). Secure trust based key management routing framework for wireless sensor networks. *Journal of Engineering (Stevenage, England), 2016*, 1–9.

Keyes, L., & Kaur, L. Gagnon, & Massicotte. (2021). EntropLyzer: Android Malware Classification and Characterization Using Entropy Analysis of Dynamic Characteristics. In Reconciling Data Analytics, Automation, Privacy, and Security: A Big Data Challenge (RDAAPS). IEEE.

Khabarova, E. A., Denisova, N. P., Dmitriev, A. B., Slavin, K. V., & Verhagen Metman, L. (2018). Deep Brain, Stimulation of the Subthalamic Nucleus in Patients with Parkinson Disease with Prior Pallidotomy or Thalamotomy. *Brain Sciences*, *8*(4), 66. doi:10.3390/brainsci8040066 PMID:29659494

Khalid, A., Kirisci, P., Ghrairi, Z., Thoben, K. D., & Pannek, J. (2017, July). Towards implementing safety and security concepts for human-robot collaboration in the context of Industry 4.0. In *39th International MATADOR Conference on Advanced Manufacturing (Manchester, UK)*.

Khalid, A., Kirisci, P., Khan, Z. H., Ghrairi, Z., Thoben, K. D., & Pannek, J. (2018). Security framework for industrial collaborative robotic cyber-physical systems. *Computers in Industry*, *97*, 132–145. doi:10.1016/j.compind.2018.02.009

Khan, M., Wang, H., & Ngueilbaye, A. (2021). Attention-Based Deep Gated Fully Convolutional End-to-End Architectures for Time Series Classification. *Neural Processing Letters*, 1–34.

Khan, Z. H., Khalid, A., & Iqbal, J. (2018). Towards realizing robotic potential in future intelligent food manufacturing systems. *Innovative Food Science & Emerging Technologies*, *48*, 11–24. doi:10.1016/j.ifset.2018.05.011

Khattak, H. A., Shah, M. A., Khan, S., Ali, I., & Imran, M. (2019). Perception layer security in Internet of Things. *Future Generation Computer Systems*, *100*, 144–164. doi:10.1016/j.future.2019.04.038

Kim. (2018). A multimodal deep learning method for android malware detection using various features. *IEEE Transactions on Information Forensics and Security*, *14*(3), 773-788.

Kolias, C., Kambourakis, G., Stavrou, A., & Voas, J. (2017). DDoS in the IoT: Mirai and other botnets. *IEEE Computer*, *50*(7), 80–84. doi:10.1109/MC.2017.201

Kolias, C., Stavrou, A., Voas, J., Bojanova, I., & Kuhn, R. (2016). Learning Internet-of-Things security" hands-on. *IEEE Security and Privacy*, *14*(1), 37–46.

Kolosnjaji, B., Zarras, A., Webster, G., & Eckert, C. (2016, December). Deep learning for classification of malware system call sequences. In *Australasian Joint Conference on Artificial Intelligence* (pp. 137-149). Springer. 10.1007/978-3-319-50127-7_11

Kosba, A., Miller, A., Shi, E., Wen, Z., & Papamanthou, C. (2016, May). Hawk: The blockchain model of cryptography and privacy-preserving smart contracts. In *2016 IEEE symposium on security and privacy (SP)* (pp. 839-858). IEEE.

Kouicem, D. E., Bouabdallah, A., & Lakhlef, H. (2018). Internet of things security: A top-down survey. *Computer Networks*, *141*, 199–221.

Kravchik, M., & Shabtai, A. (2018, January). Detecting cyber attacks in industrial control systems using convolutional neural networks. In *Proceedings of the 2018 Workshop on Cyber-Physical Systems Security and PrivaCy* (pp. 72-83). 10.1145/3264888.3264896

Kravchik, M., & Shabtai, A. (2021). Efficient cyber attack detection in industrial control systems using lightweight neural networks and PCA. *IEEE Transactions on Dependable and Secure Computing*, 1. doi:10.1109/TDSC.2021.3050101

Krčál, M., Švec, O., Bálek, M., & Jašek, O. (2018). *Deep convolutional malware classifiers can learn from raw executables and labels only*. Academic Press.

Krichen, M., Cheikhrouhou, O., Lahami, M., Alroobaea, R., & Maâlej, A. J. (2017, November). Towards a model-based testing framework for the security of internet of things for smart city applications. In *International Conference on Smart Cities, Infrastructure, Technologies and Applications* (pp. 360-365). Springer.

Kshetri, N., & Voas, J. (2017). Hacking power grids: A current problem. *Computer*, *50*(12), 91–95. doi:10.1109/MC.2017.4451203

Kubanek, J. (2018). Neuromodulation with transcranial focused ultrasound. *Neurosurgical Focus FOC*, *44*(2), E14. doi:10.3171/2017.11.FOCUS17621 PMID:29385924

Kumar, P., Gupta, G. P., & Tripathi, R. (2021). Toward Design of an Intelligent Cyber Attack Detection System using Hybrid Feature Reduced Approach for IoT Networks. *Arabian Journal for Science and Engineering*, *46*(4), 3749–3778. doi:10.100713369-020-05181-3

Kumar, S. (2020). An emerging threat Fileless malware: A survey and research challenges. *Cybersecurity*, *3*(1), 1–12. doi:10.118642400-019-0043-x

Landau, O., Puzis, R., & Nissum, N. (2020). Mind Your Mind: EEG-Based Brain-Computer Interfaces and Their Security in Cyber Space. *ACM Computing Surveys*, *53*(1), 1–38. doi:10.1145/3372043

Langner, R. (2011). Stuxnet: Dissecting a cyberwarfare weapon. *IEEE Security and Privacy*, *9*(3), 49–51. doi:10.1109/MSP.2011.67

Larochelle, H., Mandel, M., Pascanu, R., & Bengio, Y. (2012). Learning algorithms for the classification restricted boltzmann machine. *Journal of Machine Learning Research*, *13*(1), 643–669.

Lashkari, A. H. (2018). Toward developing a systematic approach to generate benchmark android malware datasets and classification. In *2018 International Carnahan Conference on Security Technology (ICCST)*. IEEE. 10.1109/CCST.2018.8585560

Lasi, H., Fettke, P., Kemper, H. G., Feld, T., & Hoffmann, M. (2014). Industry 4.0. *Business & Information Systems Engineering*, *6*(4), 239–242. doi:10.100712599-014-0334-4

Lavin, A., & Ahmad, S. (2015, December). Evaluating Real-Time anomaly detection algorithms--The Numenta anomaly benchmark. In *2015 IEEE 14th International Conference on Machine Learning and Applications (ICMLA)* (pp. 38-44). IEEE.

Learning-Based Security Technique for Selective Forwarding Attack in Clustered WSN. (n.d.). *Applied Soft Computing*, *108*, 107473. doi:10.1016/j.asoc.2021.107473

Lebedev, M. A., & Nicolelis, A. L. (2017). Brain-Machine Interfaces: From Basic Science to Neuroprostheses and Neurorehabilitation. *Physiological Reviews*, *97*(2), 767–837. doi:10.1152/physrev.00027.2016 PMID:28275048

Lee, J., Mok, E., Huang, J., Cui, L., Lee, A., Leung, V., Mercier, P., Shellhammer, S., Larson, L., Asbeck, P., Rao, R., Song, Y., Nurmikko, A., & Laiwalla, F. (2019) An Implantable Wireless Network of Distributed Microscale Sensors for Neural Applications. *2019 9th International IEEE/EMBS Conference on Neural Engineering (NER)* (pp. 871-874). 10.1109/NER.2019.8717023

Lee, J. H., & Kim, H. (2017). Security and privacy challenges in the internet of things [security and privacy matters]. *IEEE Consumer Electronics Magazine*, *6*(3), 134–136.

Lee, J., Park, D., & Lee, C. (2017). Feature selection algorithm for intrusions detection system using sequential forward search and random forest classifier. *Transactions on Internet and Information Systems (Seoul)*, *11*(10), 5132–5148.

Legon, W., Bansal, P., Tyshynsky, R., Ai, L., & Mueller, J. K. (2018). Transcranial focused ultrasound neuromodulation of the human primary motor cortex. *Scientific Reports*, *8*(1), 10007. doi:10.103841598-018-28320-1 PMID:29968768

Lei, Y., Yang, B., Jiang, X., Jia, F., Li, N., & Nandi, A. K. (2020). Applications of machine learning to machine fault diagnosis: A review and roadmap. *Mechanical Systems and Signal Processing*, *138*, 106587. doi:10.1016/j.ymssp.2019.106587

Letswave7 | Letswave.cn. (2018, July 17). https://letswave.cn/

Letteri, I., Penna, G. D., & Gasperis, G. D. (2019). Security in the internet of things: Botnet detection in software-defined networks by deep learning techniques. *International Journal of High Performance Computing and Networking*, *15*(3-4), 170–182.

Liang, W., Tang, M., Long, J., Peng, X., Xu, J., & Li, K. C. (2019). A secure fabric blockchain-based data transmission technique for industrial Internet-of-Things. *IEEE Transactions on Industrial Informatics*, *15*(6), 3582–3592. doi:10.1109/TII.2019.2907092

Liao, H. J., Lin, C. H. R., Lin, Y. C., & Tung, K. Y. (2013). Intrusion detection system: A comprehensive review. *Journal of Network and Computer Applications*, *36*(1), 16–24. doi:10.1016/j.jnca.2012.09.004

Liao, K., Lin, C., Zhao, Y., & Gabbouj, M. (2019). DR-GAN: Automatic radial distortion rectification using conditional GAN in real-time. *IEEE Transactions on Circuits and Systems for Video Technology*, *30*(3), 725–733. doi:10.1109/TCSVT.2019.2897984

Liberati, G., da Rocha, J. L. D., van der Heiden, L., Raffone, A., Birbaumer, N., Olivetti Belardinelli, M., & Sitaram, R. (2012). Toward a Brain-Computer Interface for Alzheimer's Disease Patients by Combining Classical Conditioning and Brain State Classification. *Journal of Alzheimer's Disease*, *31*(s3), S211–S220. doi:10.3233/JAD-2012-112129 PMID:22451316

Li, D., Chen, D., Jin, B., Shi, L., Goh, J., & Ng, S. K. (2019, September). MAD-GAN: Multivariate anomaly detection for time series data with generative adversarial networks. In *International Conference on Artificial Neural Networks* (pp. 703-716). Springer. 10.1007/978-3-030-30490-4_56

Lien, J., Amihood, P. M., Javidan, A. J., Karagozler, M. E., Olson, E. M., & Poupyrev, I. (2017). *Embedding Radars in Robots for Safety and Obstacle Detection*. Academic Press.

Li, F., Shi, Y., Shinde, A., Ye, J., & Song, W. (2019). Enhanced cyber-physical security in internet of things through energy auditing. *IEEE Internet of Things Journal*, *6*(3), 5224–5231.

Li, F., & Xiong, P. (2013). Practical secure communication for integrating wireless sensor networks into the internet of things. *IEEE Sensors Journal*, *13*(10), 3677–3684.

Li, J., Sun, L., Yan, Q., Li, Z., Srisa-An, W., & Ye, H. (2018). Significant permission identification for machine-learning-based android malware detection. *IEEE Transactions on Industrial Informatics*, *14*(7), 3216–3225. doi:10.1109/TII.2017.2789219

Lin & Guowei Wu. (2013). Enhancing the attacking efficiency of the node captureattack in WSN: a matrix approach. *J Supercomput, Springer Science &Business Media*, 1-19.

Lin, J., Yu, W., Zhang, N., Yang, X., Zhang, H., & Zhao, W. (2017). A survey on internet of things: Architecture, enabling technologies, security and privacy, and applications. *IEEE Internet of Things Journal, 4*(5), 1125-1142.

Lin, C., Qiu, T., Obaidat, M. S., Yu, C. W., Yao, L., & Wu, G. (2016). MREA: A minimum resource expenditure node capture attack in wireless sensor networks. *Security and Communication Networks*, *9*(18), 5502–5517. doi:10.1002ec.1713

Lin, C., Wu, G., Yu, C. W., & Yao, L. (2015). Maximizing destructiveness of node capture attack in wireless sensor networks. *The Journal of Supercomputing, 71*(8), 3181–3212. doi:10.100711227-015-1435-7

Li, P., Salour, M., & Su, X. (2008). A survey of internet worm detection and containment. *IEEE Communications Surveys and Tutorials, 10*(1), 20–35. doi:10.1109/COMST.2008.4483668

Li, Q., Ding, D., & Conti, M. (2015). Brain-Computer Interface applications: Security and privacy challenges. *2015 IEEE Conference on Communications and Network Security (CNS)*, 663-666. 10.1109/CNS.2015.7346884

Li, S., & Da Xu, L. (2017). *Securing the internet of things*. Syngress.

Li, S., Da Xu, L., & Zhao, S. (2015). The internet of things: A survey. *Information Systems Frontiers, 17*(2), 243–259.

Li, S., Tryfonas, T., & Li, H. (2016). The Internet of Things: A security point of view. *Internet Research*.

Liu, C. H., Lin, Q., & Wen, S. (2018). Blockchain-enabled data collection and sharing for industrial IoT with deep reinforcement learning. *IEEE Transactions on Industrial Informatics, 15*(6), 3516–3526. doi:10.1109/TII.2018.2890203

Liu, L., Wang, B., Yu, B., & Zhong, Q. (2017). Automatic malware classification and new malware detection using machine learning. *Frontiers of Information Technology & Electronic Engineering, 18*(9), 1336–1347. doi:10.1631/FITEE.1601325

Liu, Q., Sun, L., Kornhauser, A., Sun, J., & Sangwa, N. (2019). Road roughness acquisition and classification using improved restricted Boltzmann machine deep learning algorithm. *Sensor Review, 39*(6), 733–742. doi:10.1108/SR-05-2018-0132

Liu, X., Wang, Z., Jin, C., Li, F., & Li, G. (2019). A Blockchain-Based Medical Data Sharing and Protection Scheme. *IEEE Access: Practical Innovations, Open Solutions, 7*, 118943–118953. doi:10.1109/ACCESS.2019.2937685

Liu, X., Zhao, M., Li, S., Zhang, F., & Trappe, W. (2017). A security framework for the internet of things in the future internet architecture. *Future Internet, 9*(3), 27.

Liu, Y., Kuang, Y., Xiao, Y., & Xu, G. (2017). SDN-based data transfer security for Internet of Things. *IEEE Internet of Things Journal, 5*(1), 257–268. doi:10.1109/JIOT.2017.2779180

Liu, Y., Zhang, J., & Gao, Q. (2018, October). A Blockchain-Based Secure Cloud Files Sharing Scheme with Fine-Grained Access Control. In *2018 International Conference on Networking and Network Applications (NaNA)* (pp. 277-283). IEEE. 10.1109/NANA.2018.8648778

Li, X., Hu, Z., Xu, M., Wang, Y., & Ma, J. (2021). Transfer learning based intrusion detection scheme for Internet of vehicles. *Information Sciences, 547*, 119–135. doi:10.1016/j.ins.2020.05.130

Li, Z., Yin, X., Geng, Z., Zhang, H., Li, P., Sun, Y., ... Li, L. (2013, January). Research on PKI-like Protocol for the Internet of Things. In *2013 Fifth International Conference on Measuring Technology and Mechatronics Automation* (pp. 915-918). IEEE.

López Bernal, S., Huertas Celdrán, A., & Martínez Pérez, G. (2019). Cybersecurity on Brain-Computer Interfaces: attacks and countermeasures. V Jornadas Nacionales de Investigación en Ciberseguridad (JNIC2019), 198-199.

López Bernal, S., Huertas Celdrán, A., Fernández Maimó, L., Martínez Pérez, G., Barros, M. T., & Balasubramaniam, S. (2020). Cyberattacks on Miniature Brain Implants to Disrupt Spontaneous Neural Signaling. *IEEE Access: Practical Innovations, Open Solutions, 8*, 152204–152222. doi:10.1109/ACCESS.2020.3017394

López Bernal, S., Huertas Celdrán, A., Martínez Pérez, G., Barros, M. T., & Balasubramaniam, S. (2021). Security in Brain-Computer Interfaces: State-of-the-Art, Opportunities, and Future Challenges. *ACM Computing Surveys, 54*(1), 35. doi:10.1145/3427376

Lü, X., Meng, L., Chen, C., & Wang, P. (2019). Fuzzy removing redundancy restricted boltzmann machine: Improving learning speed and classification accuracy. *IEEE Transactions on Fuzzy Systems*, 28(10), 2495–2509. doi:10.1109/TFUZZ.2019.2940415

Lu, Y., Huang, X., Dai, Y., Maharjan, S., & Zhang, Y. (2019). Blockchain and Federated Learning for Privacy-preserved Data Sharing in Industrial IoT. *IEEE Transactions on Industrial Informatics*.

Lv, Z. (2020). Security of internet of things edge devices. *Software, Practice & Experience*, spe.2806. doi:10.1002pe.2806

Lyu, X., Ding, Y., & Yang, S. H. (2019). Safety and security risk assessment in cyber-physical systems. *IET Cyber-Physical Systems. Theory & Applications*, 4(3), 221–232.

Madakam, S., Lake, V., Lake, V., & Lake, V. (2015). Internet of Things (IoT): A literature review. *Journal of Computer and Communications*, 3(05), 164.

Mahdavifar, Fitriah Kadir, Fatemi, Alhadidi, & Ghorbani. (2020). Dynamic Android Malware Category Classification using Semi-Supervised Deep Learning. *The 18th IEEE International Conference on Dependable, Autonomic, and Secure Computing (DASC)*.

Mahmoud, R., Yousuf, T., Aloul, F., & Zualkernan, I. (2015, December). Internet of things (IoT) security: Current status, challenges and prospective measures. In *2015 10th International Conference for Internet Technology and Secured Transactions (ICITST)* (pp. 336-341). IEEE.

Makhdoom, I., Abolhasan, M., Lipman, J., Liu, R. P., & Ni, W. (2018). Anatomy of threats to the internet of things. *IEEE Communications Surveys and Tutorials*, 21(2), 1636–1675.

Ma, L., Liu, Y., Zhang, X., Ye, Y., Yin, G., & Johnson, B. A. (2019). Deep learning in remote sensing applications: A meta-analysis and review. *ISPRS Journal of Photogrammetry and Remote Sensing*, 152, 166–177. doi:10.1016/j.isprsjprs.2019.04.015

Mani, N., Moh, M., & Moh, T. S. (2021). Defending deep learning models against adversarial attacks. *International Journal of Software Science and Computational Intelligence*, 13(1), 72–89.

Manso, P., Moura, J., & Serrão, C. (2019). SDN-Based Intrusion Detection System for Early Detection and Mitigation of DDoS Attacks. *Information*, 10, 106.

Manzoor, A., Liyanage, M., Braeke, A., Kanhere, S. S., & Ylianttila, M. (2019, May). Blockchain based proxy re-encryption scheme for secure IoT data sharing. In *2019 IEEE International Conference on Blockchain and Cryptocurrency (ICBC)* (pp. 99-103). IEEE. 10.1109/BLOC.2019.8751336

Maple, C. (2017). Security and privacy in the internet of things. *Journal of Cyber Policy*, 2(2), 155–184.

Martinovic, I., Davies, D., & Frank, M. (2012). On the feasibility of side-channel attacks with brain-computer interfaces. *Proceedings of the 21st USENIX Security Symposium*, 143-158.

Mastorakis, G., Mavromoustakis, C. X., & Pallis, E. (2017). *Beyond the internet of things* (J. M. Batalla, Ed.). Springer.

Masud, M., Gaba, G. S., Alqahtani, S., Muhammad, G., Gupta, B. B., Kumar, P., & Ghoneim, A. (2020). *A lightweight and robust secure key establishment protocol for internet of medical things in COVID-19 patients care*. IEEE Internet of Things Journal.

Mathur, A. P., & Tippenhauer, N. O. (2016, April). SWaT: a water treatment testbed for research and training on ICS security. In *2016 international workshop on cyber-physical systems for smart water networks (CySWater)* (pp. 31-36). IEEE.

MATLAB - El lenguaje del cálculo técnico. (2020). *MATLAB & Simulink*. https://es.mathworks.com/products/matlab.html

Mattern, F., & Floerkemeier, C. (2010). From the Internet of Computers to the Internet of Things. In *From active data management to event-based systems and more* (pp. 242–259). Springer.

Mavropoulos, O., Mouratidis, H., Fish, A., & Panaousis, E. (2019). Apparatus: A framework for security analysis in internet of things systems. *Ad Hoc Networks*, *92*, 101743.

McEwen, A., & Cassimally, H. (2013). *Designing the internet of things*. John Wiley & Sons.

McGhin, T., Choo, K. K. R., Liu, C. Z., & He, D. (2019). Blockchain in healthcare applications: Research challenges and opportunities. *Journal of Network and Computer Applications*, *135*, 62–75. doi:10.1016/j.jnca.2019.02.027

McMahon, M., & Schukat, M. (2018). A low-Cost, Open-Source, BCI- VR Game Control Development Environment Prototype for Game Based Neurorehabilitation. *IEEE Games, Entertainment, Media Conference (GEM)*, 1-9. 10.1109/GEM.2018.8516468

Meidan, Y., Bohadana, M., Mathov, Y., Mirsky, Y., Shabtai, A., Breitenbacher, D., & Elovici, Y. (2018). N-BaIoT - Network-Based Detection of IoT Botnet Attacks Using Deep Autoencoders. *IEEE Pervasive Computing*, *17*(3), 12–22.

Mendez Mena, D., Papapanagiotou, I., & Yang, B. (2018). Internet of things: Survey on security. *Information Security Journal: A Global Perspective, 27*(3), 162-182.

Mendez, D. M., Papapanagiotou, I., & Yang, B. (2017). *Internet of things: Survey on security and privacy*. arXiv preprint arXiv:1707.01879.

Mienye, I. D., Sun, Y., & Wang, Z. (2020). Improved sparse autoencoder based artificial neural network approach for prediction of heart disease. *Informatics in Medicine Unlocked*, *18*, 100307. doi:10.1016/j.imu.2020.100307

Milić, J. (2019). *Mirai Botnet Continues to Plague IoT Space*. Retrieved from https://blog.reversinglabs.com/blog/mirai-botnet-continues-to-plague-iot-space

Miller, B., & Rowe, D. (2012, October). A survey SCADA of and critical infrastructure incidents. In *Proceedings of the 1st Annual conference on Research in information technology* (pp. 51-56). 10.1145/2380790.2380805

Miloslavskaya, N., & Tolstoy, A. (2019). Internet of things: Information security challenges and solutions. *Cluster Computing, 22*(1), 103–119.

Mirian, A., Ma, Z., Adrian, D., Tischer, M., Chuenchujit, T., & Yardley, T. (2016, December). An internet-wide view of ICS devices. In *2016 14th Annual Conference on Privacy, Security and Trust (PST)* (pp. 96-103). IEEE. 10.1109/PST.2016.7906943

Mirsadeghi, F., Rafsanjani, M. K., & Gupta, B. B. (2020). A trust infrastructure based authentication method for clustered vehicular ad hoc networks. *Peer-to-Peer Networking and Applications*, 1–17.

Mishra, A., Gupta, N., & Gupta, B. B. (2021). Defense mechanisms against DDoS attack based on entropy in SDN-cloud using POX controller. *Telecommunication Systems*, 1–16.

Misra, S., Maheswaran, M., & Hashmi, S. (2017). *Security challenges and approaches in internet of things*. Springer International Publishing.

Moffitt, T. (2016). *Source Code for Mirai IoT Malware Released*. Retrieved from https://www.webroot.com/blog/2016/10/10/source-code-Mirai-iot-malware-released/

Mohan, A. P., & Gladston, A. (2020). Merkle tree and Blockchain-based cloud data auditing. *International Journal of Cloud Applications and Computing*, *10*(3), 54–66. doi:10.4018/IJCAC.2020070103

Mohanta, B. K., Jena, D., Panda, S. S., & Sobhanayak, S. (2019). Blockchain Technology: A Survey on Applications and Security Privacy Challenges. *Internet of Things,* 100107.

Molesky, M. J., & Cameron, E. A. (2019). Internet of Things: An Analysis and Proposal of White Worm Technology. In *Proc. of IEEE ICCE 2019.* Academic Press.

Moore, D., Paxson, V., Savage, S., Shannon, C., Staniford, S., & Weaver, N. (2003). *The spread of the sapphire/slammer worm.* CAIDA, ICSI, Silicon Defense, UC Berkeley EECS and UC San Diego CSE.

Moreno, I., Batista, E., Serracin, S., Moreno, R., Gómez, L., Serracin, J., Quintero, J., & Boya, C. (2019). Los sistemas de interfaz cerebro-computadora basado en EEG: características y aplicaciones. *I+D Tecnológico, 15*(2), 13–26. doi:10.33412/idt.v15.2.2230

Morris, T., & Gao, W. (2014, March). Industrial control system traffic data sets for intrusion detection research. In *International Conference on Critical Infrastructure Protection* (pp. 65-78). Springer. 10.1007/978-3-662-45355-1_5

Morris, T., Srivastava, A., Reaves, B., Gao, W., Pavurapu, K., & Reddi, R. (2011). A control system testbed to validate critical infrastructure protection concepts. *International Journal of Critical Infrastructure Protection, 4*(2), 88–103. doi:10.1016/j.ijcip.2011.06.005

Movahedi, F., Coyle, J. L., & Sejdić, E. (2017). Deep belief networks for electroencephalography: A review of recent contributions and future outlooks. *IEEE Journal of Biomedical and Health Informatics, 22*(3), 642–652. doi:10.1109/JBHI.2017.2727218 PMID:28715343

Muna, A. H., Moustafa, N., & Sitnikova, E. (2018). Identification of malicious activities in industrial internet of things based on deep learning models. *Journal of Information Security and Applications, 41*, 1-11.

Munro, K. (2012). Deconstructing flame: The limitations of traditional defences. *Computer Fraud & Security, 2012*(10), 8–11. doi:10.1016/S1361-3723(12)70102-1

Murata, T. (1989). Petri nets: Properties, analysis and applications. *Proceedings of the IEEE, 77*(4), 541–580.

Musk, E. (2019). Neuralink An Integrated Brain-Machine Interface Platform With Thousands of Channels. *Journal of Medical Internet Research, 21*(10), e16194. doi:10.2196/16194 PMID:31642810

Na, E., Lee, K., Kim, E. J., Bae, J. B., Suh, S. W., Byun, S., Han, J. W., & Kim, K. W. (2021). Pre-attentive Visual Processing in Alzheimer's Disease: An Event-related Potential Study. *Current Alzheimer Research, 17*(13), 1195–1207. doi:10.2174/1567205018666210216084534 PMID:33593259

Nakahori, K., & Yamaguchi, S. (2017). A support tool to design IoT services with NuSMV. In *Proc. of IEEE ICCE 2017* (pp.84–87). IEEE.

Nakao, K. (2018). Proactive cyber security response by utilizing passive monitoring technologies. In *Proc. of IEEE ICCE 2018* (p. 1). 10.1109/ICCE.2018.8326061

Nakasumi, M. (2017, July). Information sharing for supply chain management based on block chain technology. In *2017 IEEE 19th Conference on Business Informatics (CBI)* (Vol. 1, pp. 140-149). IEEE. 10.1109/CBI.2017.56

Nandy, T., Idris, M. Y. I. B., Noor, R. M., Kiah, L. M., Lun, L. S., Juma'at, N. B. A., ... Bhattacharyya, S. (2019). Review on security of Internet of Things authentication mechanism. *IEEE Access: Practical Innovations, Open Solutions, 7*, 151054–151089.

Narendrakumar, S., Razaque, A., Patel, V., Almi'ani, M., Rizvi, S. S., & Hans, A. (2018). Token security for internet of things. *International Journal of Embedded Systems, 10*(4), 334–343.

Narudin, F. A., Feizollah, A., Anuar, N. B., & Gani, A. (2016). Evaluation of machine learning classifiers for mobile malware detection. *Soft Computing*, *20*(1), 343–357. doi:10.100700500-014-1511-6

Nataraj, L., Karthikeyan, S., Jacob, G., & Manjunath, B. S. (2011, July). Malware images: visualization and automatic classification. In *Proceedings of the 8th international symposium on visualization for cyber security* (pp. 1-7). Academic Press.

Naz, M., Al-zahrani, F. A., Khalid, R., Javaid, N., Qamar, A. M., Afzal, M. K., & Shafiq, M. (2019). A Secure Data Sharing Platform Using Blockchain and Interplanetary File System. *Sustainability*, *11*(24), 7054. doi:10.3390u11247054

Necla, B., & Ismail, E. (2012). WSNSec: A scalable data link layer security protocol forWSNs. *Ad Hoc Networks*, *10*(1), 37–45. doi:10.1016/j.adhoc.2011.04.013

Neely, R. M., Piech, D. K., Santacruz, S. R., Maharbiz, M. M., & Carmena, J. M. (2018). Recent advances in neural dust: Towards a neural interface platform. *Current Opinion in Neurobiology*, *50*, 64–71. doi:10.1016/j.conb.2017.12.010 PMID:29331738

NeuroSky. (2019). http://neurosky.com

Nguyen, D. C., Pathirana, P. N., Ding, M., & Seneviratne, A. (2019). Blockchain for secure EHRs sharing of mobile cloud based e-Health systems. *IEEE Access: Practical Innovations, Open Solutions*, *7*, 66792–66806. doi:10.1109/AC-CESS.2019.2917555

Nicholson, A., Webber, S., Dyer, S., Patel, T., & Janicke, H. (2012). SCADA security in the light of Cyber-Warfare. *Computers & Security*, *31*(4), 418–436. doi:10.1016/j.cose.2012.02.009

Noor, Z., Jung, L., Alsaadi, F., & Alghamdi, T. (2012). Wireless sensor network (WSN) routing security, reliability and energy efficiency. *J Appl Sci*, *12*(6), 593–59. doi:10.3923/jas.2012.593.597

Nurseitov, D., Serekov, A., Shintemirov, A., & Abibullaev, B. (2017). Design and evaluation of a P300-ERP based BCI system for real-time control of a mobile robot. *2017 5th International Winter Conference on Brain-Computer Interface (BCI)*, 1. 10.1109/IWW-BCI.2017.7858177

Nurse, J. R., Creese, S., & De Roure, D. (2017). Security risk assessment in Internet of Things systems. *IT Professional*, *19*(5), 20–26.

O'Brien, S. A. (2016). *Widespread cyberattack takes down sites world wide*. Retrieved from https://money.cnn.com/2016/10/21/technology/ddos-attack-popular-sites/index.html

Obaidat, M. S., Rana, S. P., Maitra, T., Giri, D., & Dutta, S. (2019). Biometric security and internet of things (IoT). In *Biometric-Based Physical and Cybersecurity Systems* (pp. 477–509). Springer.

Ogonji, M. M., Okeyo, G., & Wafula, J. M. (2020). A survey on privacy and security of Internet of Things. *Computer Science Review*, *38*, 100312.

Ongtang, M., McLaughlin, S., Enck, W., & McDaniel, P. (2012). Semantically rich application-centric security in Android. *Security and Communication Networks*, *5*(6), 658–673.

OpenViBE | Software for Brain Computer Interfaces and Real Time Neurosciences. (2020, December 10). *OpenViBE*. http://openvibe.inria.fr/

Oracevic, A., Dilek, S., & Ozdemir, S. (2017, May). Security in internet of things: A survey. In *2017 International Symposium on Networks, Computers and Communications (ISNCC)* (pp. 1-6). IEEE. 10.1109/ISNCC.2017.8072001

Ordóñez de Pablos, P., Almunawar, M. N., Chui, K. T., & Kaliannan, M. (Eds.). (2021). *Handbook of Research on Analyzing IT Opportunities for Inclusive Digital Learning.* IGI Global. doi:10.4018/978-1-7998-7184-2

Pais-Vieira, M., Lebedev, M., Kunicki, C., Wang, J., & Nicolelis, M. A. L. (2013). A Brain-to-Brain Interface for Real-Time Sharing of Sensorimotor Information. *Scientific Reports*, *3*(1), 1319. doi:10.1038rep01319 PMID:23448946

Pajouh, H., Dehghantanha, A., Parizi, R. M., Aledhari, M., & Karimipour, H. (2019). A survey on internet of things security: Requirements, challenges, and solutions. *Internet of Things*, 100129.

Pang, Y. (2019). A signature-based assistant random oversampling method for malware detection. In *2019 18th IEEE International conference on trust, security and privacy in computing and communications/13th IEEE international conference on big data science and engineering (TrustCom/BigDataSE).* IEEE. 10.1109/TrustCom/BigDataSE.2019.00042

Pan, S., Morris, T., & Adhikari, U. (2015). Developing a hybrid intrusion detection system using data mining for power systems. *IEEE Transactions on Smart Grid*, *6*(6), 3104–3113. doi:10.1109/TSG.2015.2409775

Pascanu, R., Stokes, J. W., Sanossian, H., Marinescu, M., & Thomas, A. (2015, April). Malware classification with recurrent networks. In *2015 IEEE International Conference on Acoustics, Speech and Signal Processing (ICASSP)* (pp. 1916-1920). IEEE. 10.1109/ICASSP.2015.7178304

Patwary, A. A. N., Fu, A., Battula, S. K., Naha, R. K., Garg, S., & Mahanti, A. (2020). FogAuthChain: A secure location-based authentication scheme in fog computing environments using Blockchain. *Computer Communications*, *162*, 212–224.

Peraković, D., Periša, M., Cvitić, I., & Zorić, P. (n.d.). *Information and communication technologies for the society 5.0 environment.* Academic Press.

Perakovic, D., Perisa, M., Cvitic, I., & Zoric, P. (2020). Identification of the relevant parameters for modeling the eco-system elements in Industry 4.0. In *4th EAI International Conference on Management of Manufacturing Systems* (pp. 111-123). Springer. 10.1007/978-3-030-34272-2_11

Perales Gómez, Á. L., Fernández Maimó, L., Huertas Celdrán, A., García Clemente, F. J., & Cleary, F. (2021). Crafting Adversarial Samples for Anomaly Detectors in Industrial Control Systems. In *The 4th International Conference on Emerging Data and Industry 4.0 (EDI40).*

Perales Gómez, Á. L., Fernández Maimó, L., Huertas Celdrán, A., & García Clemente, F. J. (2020). MADICS: A Methodology for Anomaly Detection in Industrial Control Systems. *Symmetry*, *12*(10), 1583. doi:10.3390ym12101583

Perales Gómez, Á. L., Fernández Maimó, L., Huertas Celdran, A., García Clemente, F. J., Cadenas Sarmiento, C., Del Canto Masa, C. J., & Méndez Nistal, R. (2019). On the generation of anomaly detection datasets in industrial control systems. *IEEE Access: Practical Innovations, Open Solutions*, *7*, 177460–177473. doi:10.1109/ACCESS.2019.2958284

Perales Gómez, Á. L., Fernández Maimó, L., Huertas Celdrán, A., García Clemente, F. J., Gil Pérez, M., & Martínez Pérez, G. (2020). SafeMan: A unified framework to manage cybersecurity and safety in manufacturing industry. *Software, Practice & Experience.*

Perrig, A., Szewczyk, R., Wen, V., Cullar, D., & Tygar, J. D. (2002). SPINS: Security protocols for sensor networks. *Int J Commun Comput Inform*, *8*(5), 521–534.

Pham, H. A., Le, T. K., & Le, T. V. (2019, September). Enhanced Security of IoT Data Sharing Management by Smart Contracts and Blockchain. In *2019 19th International Symposium on Communications and Information Technologies (ISCIT)* (pp. 398-403). IEEE. 10.1109/ISCIT.2019.8905219

Pillitteri, V. Y., & Brewer, T. L. (2014). *Guidelines for smart grid cybersecurity.* Academic Press.

Pinelli, M., Venturini, M., & Burgio, M. (2003, January). Statistical methodologies for reliability assessment of gas turbine measurements. In *Turbo Expo: Power for Land, Sea, and Air* (Vol. 36851, pp. 787-793). 10.1115/GT2003-38407

Polich, J., & Heine, M. (1996). P300 topography and modality effects from a single-stimulus paradigm. *Psychophysiology, 33*(6), 747–752. doi:10.1111/j.1469-8986.1996.tb02371.x PMID:8961797

Polich, J., Howard, L., & Starr, A. (1985). Effects of Age on the P300 Component of the Event-related Potential From Auditory Stimuli: Peak Definition, Variation, and Measurement. *Journal of Gerontology, 40*(6), 721–726. doi:10.1093/geronj/40.6.721 PMID:4056328

Prasse, P., Machlica, L., Pevný, T., Havelka, J., & Scheffer, T. (2017, September). Malware detection by analysing encrypted network traffic with neural networks. In *Joint European Conference on Machine Learning and Knowledge Discovery in Databases* (pp. 73-88). Springer. 10.1007/978-3-319-71246-8_5

Pycroft, L., & Aziz, T. Z. (2018). Security of implantable medical devices with wireless connections: The dangers of cyber-attacks. *Expert Review of Medical Devices, 15*(6), 403–406. doi:10.1080/17434440.2018.1483235 PMID:29860880

Pycroft, L., Boccard, S. G., Owen, S. L. F., Stein, J. F., Fitzgerald, J. J., Green, A. L., & Aziz, T. Z. (2016). Brainjacking: Implant Security Issues in Invasive Neuromodulation. *World Neurosurgery, 92*, 454–462. doi:10.1016/j.wneu.2016.05.010 PMID:27184896

Qin, T., & Chen, H. (2012). An Enhanced Scheme against Node Capture Attack using Hash-Chain for Wireless Sensor Networks. *Journal of Information Technology, 11*(1), 102–109. doi:10.3923/itj.2012.102.109

Qu, X., Yang, L., Guo, K., Ma, L., Sun, M., Ke, M., & Li, M. (2021). A survey on the development of self-organizing maps for unsupervised intrusion detection. *Mobile Networks and Applications, 26*(2), 808–829. doi:10.100711036-019-01353-0

Raff, E., Barker, J., Sylvester, J., Brandon, R., Catanzaro, B., & Nicholas, C. (2017). *Malware detection by eating a whole exe.* arXiv preprint arXiv:1710.09435.

Rahman, M. S., Al Omar, A., Bhuiyan, M. Z. A., Basu, A., Kiyomoto, S., & Wang, G. (2020). Accountable cross-border data sharing using blockchain under relaxed trust assumption. *IEEE Transactions on Engineering Management.*

Ramadan, R. A., & Vasilakos, A. V. (2017). Brain computer interface: Control signals review. *Neurocomputing, 223*, 26–44. doi:10.1016/j.neucom.2016.10.024

Ranjeetha, S., Renuga, N., & Sharmila, R. (2017) Secure zone routing protocol for MANET. *International conference on emerging trends in engineering, science and sustainable technology (ICETSST-2017)*, 67–76.

Rao, R. P. N. (2019). Towards neural co-processors for the brain: Combining decoding and encoding in brain–computer interfaces. *Current Opinion in Neurobiology, 55*, 142–151. doi:10.1016/j.conb.2019.03.008 PMID:30954862

Rathi, N., Singla, R. & Tiwari, S. (2021). A novel approach for designing authentication system using a picture based P300 speller. *Cogn Neurodyn.* doi:10.1007/s11571-021-09664-3

Rawat, D. B., Njilla, L., Kwiat, K., & Kamhoua, C. (2018, March). iShare: Blockchain-based privacy-aware multi-agent information sharing games for cybersecurity. In *2018 International Conference on Computing, Networking and Communications (ICNC)* (pp. 425-431). IEEE. 10.1109/ICCNC.2018.8390264

Ray, B. R., Abawajy, J., & Chowdhury, M. (2014). Scalable RFID security framework and protocol supporting Internet of Things. *Computer Networks, 67*, 89–103. doi:10.1016/j.comnet.2014.03.023

Ray, P. P. (2018). A survey on Internet of Things architectures. *Journal of King Saud University-Computer and Information Sciences, 30*(3), 291–319.

Razzaq, M. A., Gill, S. H., Qureshi, M. A., & Ullah, S. (2017). Security issues in the Internet of Things (IoT): A comprehensive study. *International Journal of Advanced Computer Science and Applications*, 8(6), 383.

Rege, A., & Bleiman, R. (2020, June). Ransomware Attacks Against Critical Infrastructure. In *ECCWS 2020 20th European Conference on Cyber Warfare and Security* (p. 324). Academic Conferences and Publishing Limited. https://www.risidata.com/

Ren, Z., Liu, X., Ye, R., & Zhang, T. (2017, July). Security and privacy on internet of things. In *2017 7th IEEE International Conference on Electronics Information and Emergency Communication (ICEIEC)* (pp. 140-144). IEEE.

Rendell, D. (2019). Understanding the evolution of malware. *Computer Fraud & Security*, 2019(1), 17–19. doi:10.1016/S1361-3723(19)30010-7

Ren, Z., Chen, G., & Lu, W. (2020). Malware visualization methods based on deep convolution neural networks. *Multimedia Tools and Applications*, 79(15), 10975–10993. doi:10.100711042-019-08310-9

Rezende, E., Ruppert, G., Carvalho, T., Ramos, F., & De Geus, P. (2017, December). Malicious software classification using transfer learning of resnet-50 deep neural network. In *2017 16th IEEE International Conference on Machine Learning and Applications (ICMLA)* (pp. 1011-1014). IEEE.

Richemond, P. H., & Guo, Y. (2019). *Combining learning rate decay and weight decay with complexity gradient descent-Part I.* arXiv preprint arXiv:1902.02881.

Riel, A., Kreiner, C., Macher, G., & Messnarz, R. (2017). Integrated design for tackling safety and security challenges of smart products and digital manufacturing. *CIRP Annals*, 66(1), 177–180. doi:10.1016/j.cirp.2017.04.037

Rizvi, S., Kurtz, A., Pfeffer, J., & Rizvi, M. (2018, August). Securing the internet of things (IoT): A security taxonomy for IoT. In *2018 17th IEEE International Conference On Trust, Security And Privacy In Computing And Communications/12th IEEE International Conference On Big Data Science And Engineering (TrustCom/BigDataSE)* (pp. 163-168). IEEE.

Robertazzi, T. G. (2017). Software-defined networking. In *Introduction to Computer Networking* (pp. 81–87). Springer.

Roman, R., Najera, P., & Lopez, J. (2011). Securing the internet of things. *Computer*, 44(9), 51–58.

Ronen, R., Radu, M., Feuerstein, C., Yom-Tov, E., & Ahmadi, M. (2018). *Microsoft malware classification challenge.* arXiv preprint arXiv:1802.10135.

Rose, G., Raghuram, P., Watson, S., & Wigley, E. (2021). Platform urbanism, smartphone applications and valuing data in a smart city. *Transactions of the Institute of British Geographers*, 46(1), 59–72. doi:10.1111/tran.12400

Saboor, A., Gembler, F., Benda, M., Stawicki, P., Rezeika, A., Grichnik, R., & Volosyak, I. (2018). A Browser-Driven SSVEP-Based BCI Web Speller. *2018 IEEE International Conference on Systems, Man, and Cybernetics (SMC)*, 625–630. 10.1109/SMC.2018.00115

Sadeeq, M. A., Zeebaree, S. R., Qashi, R., Ahmed, S. H., & Jacksi, K. (2018, October). Internet of Things security: a survey. In *2018 International Conference on Advanced Science and Engineering (ICOASE)* (pp. 162-166). IEEE.

Sadeghi, A. R., Wachsmann, C., & Waidner, M. (2015, June). Security and privacy challenges in industrial internet of things. In *2015 52nd ACM/EDAC/IEEE Design Automation Conference (DAC)* (pp. 1-6). IEEE.

Saha, H. N., Mandal, A., & Sinha, A. (2017, January). Recent trends in the Internet of Things. In *2017 IEEE 7th annual computing and communication workshop and conference (CCWC)* (pp. 1-4). IEEE.

Sahmim, S., & Gharsellaoui, H. (2017). Privacy and security in internet-based computing: cloud computing, internet of things, cloud of things: a review. *Procedia Computer Science*, 112, 1516–1522. doi:10.1016/j.procs.2017.08.050

Sain, M., Kang, Y. J., & Lee, H. J. (2017, February). Survey on security in Internet of Things: State of the art and challenges. In *2017 19th International conference on advanced communication technology (ICACT)* (pp. 699-704). IEEE.

Salam, A. (2020). Internet of things in agricultural innovation and security. In *Internet of Things for Sustainable Community Development* (pp. 71–112). Springer.

Salhi, D. E., Tari, A., & Kechadi, M. T. (2021). Using Clustering for Forensics Analysis on Internet of Things. *International Journal of Software Science and Computational Intelligence*, *13*(1), 56–71. doi:10.4018/IJSSCI.2021010104

Salman, T., & Jain, R. (2019). *A survey of protocols and standards for internet of things*. arXiv preprint arXiv:1903.11549.

Samaila, M. G., Neto, M., Fernandes, D. A., Freire, M. M., & Inácio, P. R. (2017). Security challenges of the Internet of Things. In *Beyond the Internet of Things* (pp. 53–82). Springer.

Samuel, O., Javaid, N., Awais, M., Ahmed, Z., Imran, M., & Guizani, M. (2019, July). A blockchain model for fair data sharing in deregulated smart grids. In *IEEE Global Communications Conference (GLOBCOM 2019)*. 10.1109/GLOBECOM38437.2019.9013372

Sarma, A., Matos, A., Girao, J., & Aguiar, R. L. (2008). Virtual identity framework for telecom infrastructures. *Wireless Personal Communications*, *45*(4), 521–543.

Sathyanarayan, V. S., Kohli, P., & Bruhadeshwar, B. (2008). Signature generation and detection of malware families. In *Australasian Conference on Information Security and Privacy*. Springer. 10.1007/978-3-540-70500-0_25

Saxe, J., & Berlin, K. (2015, October). Deep neural network based malware detection using two dimensional binary program features. In *2015 10th International Conference on Malicious and Unwanted Software (MALWARE)* (pp. 11-20). IEEE. 10.1109/MALWARE.2015.7413680

Saxe, J., & Sanders, H. (2018). *Malware Data Science: Attack Detection and Attribution*. No Starch Press.

Sempreboni, D., & Viganò, L. (2018). *Privacy, Security and Trust in the Internet of Neurons*. arXiv.

Seo., D., Carmena, J. M., Rabaey, J. M., Alon, E., & Maharbiz, M. M. (2013). *Neural Dust: An Ultrasonic, Low Power Solution for Chronic Brain-Machine Interfaces*. arXiv.

Sfar, A. R., Natalizio, E., Challal, Y., & Chtourou, Z. (2018). A roadmap for security challenges in the Internet of Things. *Digital Communications and Networks*, *4*(2), 118–137. doi:10.1016/j.dcan.2017.04.003

Shaila, K., Manjula, S. H., Thriveni, J., Venugopal, K. R., & Patnaik, L. M. (2011). Resilience against node capture attack using asymmetric matrices in key predistribution scheme in wireless sensor networks. *International Journal on Computer Science and Engineering*, *3*(10), 3490.

Sha, K., Wei, W., Yang, T. A., Wang, Z., & Shi, W. (2018). On security challenges and open issues in Internet of Things. *Future Generation Computer Systems*, *83*, 326–337.

Shalyga, D., Filonov, P., & Lavrentyev, A. (2018). *Anomaly detection for water treatment system based on neural network with automatic architecture optimization*. arXiv preprint arXiv:1807.07282.

Sharafaldin, I., Lashkari, A. H., & Ghorbani, A. A. (2018, January). Toward generating a new intrusion detection dataset and intrusion traffic characterization. In ICISSp (pp. 108-116). doi:10.5220/0006639801080116

Sharmeen, S., Huda, S., Abawajy, J. H., Ismail, W. N., & Hassan, M. M. (2018). Malware threats and detection for industrial mobile-IoT networks. *IEEE Access: Practical Innovations, Open Solutions*, *6*, 15941–15957. doi:10.1109/ACCESS.2018.2815660

Shhadat, I., Hayajneh, A., & Al-Sharif, Z. A. (2020). The use of machine learning techniques to advance the detection and classification of unknown malware. *Procedia Computer Science, 170,* 917–922. doi:10.1016/j.procs.2020.03.110

Shi, G., Zhang, J., Zhang, C., & Hu, J. (2020). A distributed parallel training method of deep belief networks. *Soft Computing, 24*(17), 1–12. doi:10.100700500-020-04754-6

Shrestha, A. K., Deters, R., & Vassileva, J. (2019). *User-controlled privacy-preserving user profile data sharing based on blockchain.* arXiv preprint arXiv:1909.05028.

Shrestha, A. K., & Vassileva, J. (2018, June). Blockchain-based research data sharing framework for incentivizing the data owners. In *International Conference on Blockchain* (pp. 259-266). Springer. 10.1007/978-3-319-94478-4_19

Shukla, P. K., Goyal, S., Wadhvani, R., Rizvi, M. A., Sharma, P., & Tantubay, N. (2015). Finding robust assailant using optimization functions (FiRAO-PG) in wireless sensor network. *Mathematical Problems in Engineering, 2015,* 2015. doi:10.1155/2015/594345

Sial, A., Singh, A., & Mahanti, A. (2019). Detecting anomalous energy consumption using contextual analysis of smart meter data. *Wireless Networks,* 1–18.

Sial, A., Singh, A., Mahanti, A., & Gong, M. (2018, April). Heuristics-Based Detection of Abnormal Energy Consumption. In *International Conference on Smart Grid Inspired Future Technologies* (pp. 21-31). Springer.

Sicari, S., Rizzardi, A., Grieco, L. A., & Coen-Porisini, A. (2015). Security, privacy and trust in Internet of Things: The road ahead. *Computer Networks, 76,* 146–164.

Siddiqui, M., Wang, M. C., & Lee, J. (2008). A survey of data mining techniques for malware detection using file features. *Proceedings of the 46th annual southeast regional conference.* 10.1145/1593105.1593239

Si, H., Sun, C., Li, Y., Qiao, H., & Shi, L. (2019). IoT information sharing security mechanism based on blockchain technology. *Future Generation Computer Systems, 101,* 1028–1040. doi:10.1016/j.future.2019.07.036

Sihwail, Omar, & Ariffin. (2018). A survey on malware analysis techniques: Static, dynamic, hybrid and memory analysis. *International Journal on Advanced Science, Engineering and Information Technology, 8*(4-2), 1662.

Simon, A. J., Bernstein, A., Hess, T., Ashrafiuon, H., Devilbiss, D., & Verma, A. (2011). P1-112: A brain computer interface to detect Alzheimer's disease. *Alzheimer's & Dementia, 7*(4S_Part_4), S145–S146. doi:10.1016/j.jalz.2011.05.391

Sinaović, H., & Mrdovic, S. (2017). Analysis of Mirai malicious software. In *Proc. of SoftCOM 2017* (pp. 1-5). HR.

Singh, A., & Kumar, R. (2021). A Two-Phase Load Balancing Algorithm for Cloud Environment. *International Journal of Software Science and Computational Intelligence, 13*(1), 38–55.

Singh, N., & Vardhan, M. (2019). Distributed ledger technology based property transaction system with support for iot devices. *International Journal of Cloud Applications and Computing, 9*(2), 60–78.

Sklavos, N., & Zaharakis, I. D. (2016, November). Cryptography and security in internet of things (iots): Models, schemes, and implementations. In *2016 8th IFIP International Conference on New Technologies, Mobility and Security (NTMS)* (pp. 1-2). IEEE.

Skobelev, P. O., & Borovik, S. Y. (2017). On the way from Industry 4.0 to Industry 5.0: from digital manufacturing to digital society. *Industry 4.0, 2*(6), 307-311.

Solis, D., & Vicens, R. (2017, October). Convolutional neural networks for classification of malware assembly code. In *Recent Advances in Artificial Intelligence Research and Development: Proceedings of the 20th International Conference of the Catalan Association for Artificial Intelligence, Deltebre, Terres de L'Ebre, Spain, October 25-27, 2017 (Vol. 300*, p. 221). IOS Press.

SonicWall. (2021). Annual number of malware attacks worldwide from 2015 to 2020 (in billions). In *Statista*. Retrieved 9 August 2021, from https://www.statista.com/statistics/873097/malware-attacks-per-year-worldwide/

Sowndhararajan, K., Minju, K., Ponnuvel, D., Se, P., & Songmun, K. (2018). Application of the P300 Event-Related Potential in the Diagnosis of Epilepsy Disorder: A Review. *Scientia Pharmaceutica, 86*(2), 10. doi:10.3390cipharm86020010 PMID:29587468

Stankovic, J. A. (2014). Research directions for the internet of things. *IEEE Internet of Things Journal, 1*(1), 3–9.

StatCounter Global Stats. (2020). *Mobile & Tablet Android Version Market Share Worldwide.* https://gs.statcounter.com/android-version-market-share/mobile-tablet/worldwide

Stein, G., Chen, B., Wu, A. S., & Hua, K. A. (2005, March). Decision tree classifier for network intrusion detection with GA-based feature selection. In *Proceedings of the 43rd annual Southeast regional conference-Volume 2* (pp. 136-141). 10.1145/1167253.1167288

Stergiou, C. L., Psannis, K. E., & Gupta, B. B. (2020). IoT-based big data secure management in the fog over a 6G wireless network. *IEEE Internet of Things Journal, 8*(7), 5164–5171. doi:10.1109/JIOT.2020.3033131

Stergiou, C. L., Psannis, K. E., & Gupta, B. B. (2020). *IoT-based Big Data secure management in the Fog over a 6G Wireless Network. IEEE Internet of Things Journal.*

StratifiedShuffleSplit — scikit-learn 0.24.0 documentation. (2020). *Scikit-Learn.* https://scikit-learn.org/stable/modules/generated/sklearn.model_selection.StratifiedShuffleSplit.html

Sumathi, M., & Sangeetha, S. (2020). Blockchain based sensitive attribute storage and access monitoring in banking system. *International Journal of Cloud Applications and Computing, 10*(2), 77–92. doi:10.4018/IJCAC.2020040105

Sundaram, B. V., Ramnath, M., Prasanth, M., & Sundaram, V. (2015, March). Encryption and hash based security in Internet of Things. In *2015 3rd International Conference on Signal Processing, Communication and Networking (IC-SCN)* (pp. 1-6). IEEE.

Sundararajan, K. (2017). *Privacy and security issues in Brain Computer Interface* [Unpublished master's thesis]. Auckland University of Technology, Auckland, New Zealand.

Sun, W., Cai, Z., Li, Y., Liu, F., Fang, S., & Wang, G. (2018). Security and privacy in the medical internet of things: A review. *Security and Communication Networks.*

Suto, L. (2010). *Analyzing the accuracy and time costs of web application security scanners.* Academic Press.

Tague, P., Slater, D., Rogers, J., & Poovendran, R. (2008, April). Vulnerability of network traffic under node capture attacks using circuit theoretic analysis. In *IEEE INFOCOM 2008-The 27th Conference on Computer Communications* (pp. 161-165). IEEE 10.1109/INFOCOM.2008.41

Taheri, A., & Lashkari. (2019). Extensible Android Malware Detection and Family Classification Using Network-Flows and API-Calls. *The IEEE (53rd) International Carnahan Conference on Security Technology.*

Tahsien, S. M., Karimipour, H., & Spachos, P. (2020). Machine learning based solutions for security of Internet of Things (IoT): A survey. *Journal of Network and Computer Applications, 161*, 102630.

Takabi, H., Bhalotiya, A., & Alohaly, M. (2016). Brain Computer Interface (BCI) Applications: Privacy Threats and Countermeasures. *2016 IEEE 2nd International Conference on Collaboration and Internet Computing (CIC)*, 102-111. 10.1109/CIC.2016.026

Takabi, H. (2016) Firewall for brain: Towards a privacy preserving ecosystem for BCI applications. *IEEE Conference on Communications and Network Security (CNS)*, 370-371. 10.1109/CNS.2016.7860516

Takase, T., Oyama, S., & Kurihara, M. (2018). Effective neural network training with adaptive learning rate based on training loss. *Neural Networks, 101*, 68–78. doi:10.1016/j.neunet.2018.01.016 PMID:29494873

Tankard, C. (2015). The security issues of the Internet of Things. *Computer Fraud & Security, 2015*(9), 11–14.

Taormina, R., Galelli, S., Tippenhauer, N. O., Salomons, E., Ostfeld, A., Eliades, D. G., Aghashahi, M., Sundararajan, R., Pourahmadi, M., Banks, M. K., Brentan, B. M., Campbell, E., Lima, G., Manzi, D., Ayala-Cabrera, D., Herrera, M., Montalvo, I., Izquierdo, J., Luvizotto, E. Jr, ... Ohar, Z. (2018). Battle of the attack detection algorithms: Disclosing cyber attacks on water distribution networks. *Journal of Water Resources Planning and Management, 144*(8), 04018048. doi:10.1061/(ASCE)WR.1943-5452.0000969

Tao, Y., Xiangyang, X., Tonghui, L., & Leina, P. (2018). A secure routing of wireless sensor networks based on trust evaluation model. *Procedia Computer Science, 131*, 1156–1163. doi:10.1016/j.procs.2018.04.289

Tavallaee, M., Bagheri, E., Lu, W., & Ghorbani, A. A. (2009, July). A detailed analysis of the KDD CUP 99 data set. In *2009 IEEE symposium on computational intelligence for security and defense applications* (pp. 1-6). IEEE.

Technology markets: Software, Revenue by segment. (2021). In *Statista*. Retrieved 9 August 2021, from https://www.statista.com/statistics/873097/malware-attacks-per-year-worldwide/

Tewari, A., & Gupta, B. B. (2017). A lightweight mutual authentication protocol based on elliptic curve cryptography for IoT devices. *International Journal of Advanced Intelligence Paradigms, 9*(2-3), 111–121.

Tewari, A., & Gupta, B. B. (2020). Secure Timestamp-Based Mutual Authentication Protocol for IoT Devices Using RFID Tags. *International Journal on Semantic Web and Information Systems, 16*(3), 20–34. doi:10.4018/IJSWIS.2020070102

Tewari, A., & Gupta, B. B. (2020). Security, privacy and trust of different layers in Internet-of-Things (IoTs) framework. *Future Generation Computer Systems, 108*, 909–920.

The OpenBCI GUI · OpenBCI Documentation. (2020). *OpenBCI*. https://docs.openbci.com/docs/06Software/01-OpenBCISoftware/GUIDocs

Theodouli, A., Arakliotis, S., Moschou, K., Votis, K., & Tzovaras, D. (2018, August). On the design of a Blockchain-based system to facilitate Healthcare Data Sharing. In *2018 17th IEEE International Conference on Trust, Security And Privacy In Computing And Communications/12th IEEE International Conference On Big Data Science And Engineering (TrustCom/BigDataSE)* (pp. 1374-1379). IEEE. 10.1109/TrustCom/BigDataSE.2018.00190

Thwin, T. T., & Vasupongayya, S. (2018, August). Blockchain based secret-data sharing model for personal health record system. In *2018 5th International Conference on Advanced Informatics: Concept Theory and Applications (ICAICTA)* (pp. 196-201). IEEE. 10.1109/ICAICTA.2018.8541296

Tyler, W. J., Sanguinetti, J. L., Fini, M., & Hool, N. (2017). Non-invasive neural stimulation. *Micro- and Nanotechnology Sensors. Systems, and Applications, IX*, 280–290. doi:10.1117/12.2263175

Tzafestas, S. G. (2018). Ethics and law in the internet of things world. *Smart Cities, 1*(1), 98-120.

Ucci, D., Aniello, L., & Baldoni, R. (2019). Survey of machine learning techniques for malware analysis. *Computers & Security*, *81*, 123–147. doi:10.1016/j.cose.2018.11.001

Unsplash. (2020). *Unsplash API Documentation.* https://unsplash.com/documentation

US-CERT. (2016). *Heightened DDoS threat posed by Mirai and other botnets.* Retrieved from https://www.us-cert.gov/ncas/alerts/TA16-288A

Vaid, S., Singh, P., & Kaur, C. (2015). EEG Signal Analysis for BCI Interface: A Review. *2015 Fifth International Conference on Advanced Computing & Communication Technologies*, 143-147. 10.1109/ACCT.2015.72

Van Oorschot, P. C., & Smith, S. W. (2019). The internet of things: Security challenges. *IEEE Security and Privacy*, *17*(5), 7–9.

Vardhana, M., Arunkumar, N., Lasrado, S., Abdulhay, E., & Ramirez-Gonzalez, G. (2018). Convolutional neural network for bio-medical image segmentation with hardware acceleration. *Cognitive Systems Research*, *50*, 10–14. doi:10.1016/j.cogsys.2018.03.005

Vashi, S., Ram, J., Modi, J., Verma, S., & Prakash, C. (2017, February). Internet of Things (IoT): A vision, architectural elements, and security issues. In 2017 international conference on I-SMAC (IoT in Social, Mobile, Analytics and Cloud) (I-SMAC) (pp. 492-496). IEEE.

Vasighi, M., & Amini, H. (2017). A directed batch growing approach to enhance the topology preservation of self-organizing map. *Applied Soft Computing*, *55*, 424–435. doi:10.1016/j.asoc.2017.02.015

Vasilomanolakis, E., Daubert, J., Luthra, M., Gazis, V., Wiesmaier, A., & Kikiras, P. (2015, September). On the security and privacy of Internet of Things architectures and systems. In *2015 International Workshop on Secure Internet of Things (SIoT)* (pp. 49-57). IEEE.

Vignali, G., Bottani, E., Guareschi, N., Di Donato, L., Ferraro, A., & Pirozzi, M. (2019, June). Development of a 4.0 industry application for increasing occupational safety: guidelines for a correct approach. In *2019 IEEE International Conference on Engineering, Technology and Innovation (ICE/ITMC)* (pp. 1-6). IEEE. 10.1109/ICE.2019.8792814

Vijayanand, R., Devaraj, D., & Kannapiran, B. (2018). Intrusion detection system for wireless mesh network using multiple support vector machine classifiers with genetic-algorithm-based feature selection. *Computers & Security*, *77*, 304–314. doi:10.1016/j.cose.2018.04.010

Vinayakumar, R., Alazab, M., Soman, K. P., Poornachandran, P., Al-Nemrat, A., & Venkatraman, S. (2019). Deep learning approach for intelligent intrusion detection system. *IEEE Access: Practical Innovations, Open Solutions*, *7*, 41525–41550. doi:10.1109/ACCESS.2019.2895334

Virat, M. S., Bindu, S. M., Aishwarya, B., Dhanush, B. N., & Kounte, M. R. (2018, May). Security and privacy challenges in internet of things. In *2018 2nd International Conference on Trends in Electronics and Informatics (ICOEI)* (pp. 454-460). IEEE.

Waldert, S. (2016). Invasive vs. Non-Invasive Neuronal Signals for Brain-Machine Interfaces: Will One Prevail? *Frontiers in Neuroscience*, *10*, 295. doi:10.3389/fnins.2016.00295 PMID:27445666

Wang, L., Liu, W., & Han, X. (2017, December). Blockchain-based government information resource sharing. In *2017 IEEE 23rd International Conference on Parallel and Distributed Systems (ICPADS)* (pp. 804-809). IEEE. 10.1109/ICPADS.2017.00112

Wang, Z., & Wu, Q. (2019, October). Incentive for Historical Block Data Sharing in Blockchain. In *2019 IEEE 10th Annual Information Technology, Electronics and Mobile Communication Conference (IEMCON)* (pp. 0913-0919). IEEE. 10.1109/IEMCON.2019.8936209

Wang, Z., Tian, Y., & Zhu, J. (2018, August). Data sharing and tracing scheme based on blockchain. In *2018 8th International Conference on Logistics, Informatics and Service Sciences (LISS)* (pp. 1-6). IEEE. 10.1109/LISS.2018.8593225

Wang, D., Vinson, R., Holmes, M., Seibel, G., Bechar, A., Nof, S., & Tao, Y. (2019). Early detection of tomato spotted wilt virus by hyperspectral imaging and outlier removal auxiliary classifier generative adversarial nets (OR-AC-GAN). *Scientific Reports*, *9*(1), 1–14. doi:10.103841598-019-40066-y PMID:30867450

Wang, H., Li, Z., Li, Y., Gupta, B. B., & Choi, C. (2020). Visual saliency guided complex image retrieval. *Pattern Recognition Letters*, *130*, 64–72.

Wang, H., Peng, M. J., Miao, Z., Liu, Y. K., Ayodeji, A., & Hao, C. (2021). Remaining useful life prediction techniques for electric valves based on convolution auto encoder and long short term memory. *ISA Transactions*, *108*, 333–342. doi:10.1016/j.isatra.2020.08.031 PMID:32891421

Wang, H., & Song, Y. (2018). Secure cloud-based EHR system using attribute-based cryptosystem and blockchain. *Journal of Medical Systems*, *42*(8), 152. doi:10.100710916-018-0994-6 PMID:29974270

Wang, H., Zhang, Y., Chen, K., Sui, G., Zhao, Y., & Huang, X. (2019). Functional broadcast encryption with applications to data sharing for cloud storage. *Information Sciences*, *502*, 109–124. doi:10.1016/j.ins.2019.06.028

Wang, N., Jiang, T., Li, W., & Lv, S. (2017). Physical-layer security in Internet of Things based on compressed sensing and frequency selection. *IET Communications*, *11*(9), 1431–1437.

Wang, W., Feng, Y., & Dai, W. (2018). Topic analysis of online reviews for two competitive products using latent Dirichlet allocation. *Electronic Commerce Research and Applications*, *29*, 142–156. doi:10.1016/j.elerap.2018.04.003

Wang, W., Li, Y., Wang, X., Liu, J., & Zhang, X. (2018). Detecting Android malicious apps and categorizing benign apps with ensemble of classifiers. *Future Generation Computer Systems*, *78*, 987–994. doi:10.1016/j.future.2017.01.019

Wang, W., Zhu, M., Zeng, X., Ye, X., & Sheng, Y. (2017, January). Malware traffic classification using convolutional neural network for representation learning. In *2017 International Conference on Information Networking (ICOIN)* (pp. 712-717). IEEE. 10.1109/ICOIN.2017.7899588

Wang, Y. R., Sun, G. D., & Jin, Q. (2020). Imbalanced sample fault diagnosis of rotating machinery using conditional variational auto-encoder generative adversarial network. *Applied Soft Computing*, *92*, 106333. doi:10.1016/j.asoc.2020.106333

Wang, Y., Zhang, A., Zhang, P., & Wang, H. (2019). Cloud-Assisted EHR Sharing With Security and Privacy Preservation via Consortium Blockchain. *IEEE Access: Practical Innovations, Open Solutions*, *7*, 136704–136719. doi:10.1109/ACCESS.2019.2943153

Wang, Z., Zhou, C., & Liu, Y. (2017). *Efficient hybrid detection of node replication attacks in mobile sensor networks.* Mobile Information Systems.

Water Distribution (WADI) Dataset. (n.d.). https://itrust.sutd.edu.sg/testbeds/water-distribution-wadi/

Weber, R. H. (2010). Internet of Things–New security and privacy challenges. *Computer Law & Security Review*, *26*(1), 23–30.

Wei, W., Yang, A. T., Shi, W., & Sha, K. (2016, October). Security in internet of things: Opportunities and challenges. In *2016 International Conference on Identification, Information and Knowledge in the Internet of Things (IIKI)* (pp. 512-518). IEEE.

Wirdatmadja, S. A., Barros, M. T., Koucheryavy, Y., Jornet, J. M., & Balasubramaniam, S. (2017). Wireless Optogenetic Nanonetworks for Brain Stimulation: Device Model and Charging Protocols. *IEEE Transactions on Nanobioscience*, *16*(8), 859–872. doi:10.1109/TNB.2017.2781150 PMID:29364130

Wortmann, F., & Flüchter, K. (2015). Internet of things. *Business & Information Systems Engineering*, *57*(3), 221–224.

Wroblewski, G. (2013). General method of program code obfuscation. In *The 5th Conference on Information and Knowledge Technology*. IEEE.

Wronka, E., Kaiser, J., & Coenen, A. M. (2008). The auditory P3 from passive and active three-stimulus oddball paradigm. *Acta Neurobiologiae Experimentalis*, *68*(3), 362–372. PMID:18668159

Wu, H., Schwab, S., & Peckham, R. L. (2008). *U.S. Patent No. 7,424,744*. Washington, DC: U.S. Patent and Trademark Office.

Wu, A., Zhang, Y., Zheng, X., Guo, R., Zhao, Q., & Zheng, D. (2019). Efficient and privacy-preserving traceable attribute-based encryption in blockchain. *Annales des Télécommunications*, *74*(7-8), 401–411. doi:10.100712243-018-00699-y

Wu, S., Roberts, K., Datta, S., Du, J., Ji, Z., Si, Y., Soni, S., Wang, Q., Wei, Q., Xiang, Y., Zhao, B., & Xu, H. (2020). Deep learning in clinical natural language processing: A methodical review. *Journal of the American Medical Informatics Association: JAMIA*, *27*(3), 457–470. doi:10.1093/jamia/ocz200 PMID:31794016

Xiang, W., Zhang, H., Cui, R., Chu, X., Li, K., & Zhou, W. (2018). Pavo: A rnn-based learned inverted index, supervised or unsupervised? *IEEE Access: Practical Innovations, Open Solutions*, *7*, 293–303. doi:10.1109/ACCESS.2018.2885350

Xie, J., Tang, H., Huang, T., Yu, F. R., Xie, R., Liu, J., & Liu, Y. (2019). A survey of blockchain technology applied to smart cities: Research issues and challenges. *IEEE Communications Surveys and Tutorials*, *21*(3), 2794–2830. doi:10.1109/COMST.2019.2899617

Xin, Y., Kong, L., Liu, Z., Chen, Y., Li, Y., Zhu, H., Gao, M., Hou, H., & Wang, C. (2018). Machine learning and deep learning methods for cybersecurity. *IEEE Access: Practical Innovations, Open Solutions*, *6*, 35365–35381. doi:10.1109/ACCESS.2018.2836950

Xuan, S., Zheng, L., Chung, I., Wang, W., Man, D., Du, X., & Guizani, M. (2020). An incentive mechanism for data sharing based on blockchain with smart contracts. *Computers & Electrical Engineering*, *83*, 106587. doi:10.1016/j.compeleceng.2020.106587

Xu, L., Shah, N., Chen, L., Diallo, N., Gao, Z., Lu, Y., & Shi, W. (2017, April). Enabling the sharing economy: Privacy respecting contract based on public blockchain. In *Proceedings of the ACM Workshop on Blockchain, Cryptocurrencies and Contracts* (pp. 15-21). 10.1145/3055518.3055527

Yamaguchi, S. (2021). A Basic Command and Control Strategy in Botnet Defense System. In *Proc. of IEEE ICCE 2021*. Academic Press.

Yamaguchi, S. (2020a). Botnet Defense System: Concept, Design, and Basic Strategy. *Information*, *11*, 516.

Yamaguchi, S. (2020b). White-Hat Worm to Fight Malware and Its Evaluation by Agent-Oriented Petri Nets. *Sensors (Basel)*, *20*, 556.

Yamaguchi, S., Bin Ahmadon, M. A., & Ge, Q. W. (2016). Introduction of Petri Nets: Its Applications and Security Challenges. In B. Gupta, D. P. Agrawal, & S. Yamaguchi (Eds.), *Handbook of Research on Modern Cryptographic Solutions for Computer and Cyber Security* (pp. 145–179). IGI Publishing.

Yamaguchi, S., & Gupta, B. (2019). Malware Threat in Internet of Things and Its Mitigation Analysis. In R. C. Joshi, B. Gupta, D. P. Agrawal, & S. Yamaguchi (Eds.), *Security, Privacy, and Forensics Issues in Big Data* (pp. 363–379). IGI Publishing.

Yamaguchi, S., & Gupta, B. (2021). Malware threat in Internet of Things and its mitigation analysis. In *Research Anthology on Combating Denial-of-Service Attacks* (pp. 371–387). IGI Global. doi:10.4018/978-1-7998-5348-0.ch020

Yamaguchi, S., Tanaka, H., & Bin Ahmadon, M. A. (2020). Modeling and Evaluation of Mitigation Methods against IoT Malware Mirai with Agent-Oriented Petri Net PN^2. *International Journal of Internet of Things and Cyber-Assurance*, *1*(3/4), 195–213.

Yang, K., Liu, D., Qu, Q., Sang, Y., & Lv, J. (2021). An automatic evaluation metric for Ancient-Modern Chinese translation. *Neural Computing & Applications*, *33*(8), 3855–3867. doi:10.100700521-020-05216-8

Yang, T., Hakimian, S., & Schwartz, T. H. (2014). Intraoperative ElectroCorticoGraphy (ECog): Indications, techniques, and utility in epilepsy surgery. *Epileptic Disorders*, *16*(3), 271–279. doi:10.1684/epd.2014.0675 PMID:25204010

Yang, Y., Wu, L., Yin, G., Li, L., & Zhao, H. (2017). A survey on security and privacy issues in Internet-of-Things. *IEEE Internet of Things Journal*, *4*(5), 1250–1258.

Yaqoob, I., & Ahmed, E., ur Rehman, M. H., Ahmed, A. I. A., Al-garadi, M. A., Imran, M., & Guizani, M. (2017). The rise of ransomware and emerging security challenges in the Internet of Things. *Computer Networks*, *129*, 444–458.

Yin, C., Zhang, S., Wang, J., & Xiong, N. N. (2020). Anomaly detection based on convolutional recurrent autoencoder for IoT time series. *IEEE Transactions on Systems, Man, and Cybernetics. Systems*, 1–11. doi:10.1109/TSMC.2020.2968516

Yousefi, A., & Jameii, S. M. (2017, May). Improving the security of internet of things using encryption algorithms. In *2017 International Conference on IoT and Application (ICIOT)* (pp. 1-5). IEEE. 10.1109/ICIOTA.2017.8073627

Yousefi-Azar, M., Varadharajan, V., Hamey, L., & Tupakula, U. (2017). Autoencoder-based feature learning for cyber security applications. *2017 International Joint Conference on Neural Networks (IJCNN)*, 3854-3861. 10.1109/IJCNN.2017.7966342

Yousuf, O., & Mir, R. N. (2019). *A survey on the internet of things security: State-of-art, architecture, issues and countermeasures*. Information & Computer Security.

Yuan, X., Li, L., & Wang, Y. (2019). Nonlinear dynamic soft sensor modeling with supervised long short-term memory network. *IEEE Transactions on Industrial Informatics*, *16*(5), 3168–3176. doi:10.1109/TII.2019.2902129

Yue, B., Fu, J., & Liang, J. (2018). Residual recurrent neural networks for learning sequential representations. *Information (Basel)*, *9*(3), 56. doi:10.3390/info9030056

Yu, Y., Li, Y., Tian, J., & Liu, J. (2018). Blockchain-based solutions to security and privacy issues in the internet of things. *IEEE Wireless Communications*, *25*(6), 12–18.

Zander, T. O., Kothe, C., Jatzev, S., & Gaertner, M. (2010). Enhancing Human-Computer Interaction with Input from Active and Passive Brain-Computer Interfaces. In D. Tan & A. Nijholt (Eds.), *Brain-Computer Interfaces. Human-Computer Interaction Series*. Springer. doi:10.1007/978-1-84996-272-8_11

Zarras, A. (2014). Automated generation of models for fast and precise detection of HTTP-based malware. In *2014 Twelfth Annual International Conference on Privacy, Security and Trust*. IEEE. 10.1109/PST.2014.6890946

Zavrak, S., & Iskefiyeli, M. (2020). Anomaly-based intrusion detection from network flow features using variational autoencoder. *IEEE Access: Practical Innovations, Open Solutions*, *8*, 108346–108358. doi:10.1109/ACCESS.2020.3001350

Zekri, El Kafhali, Aboutabit, & Saadi. (2017). *DDoS attack detection using machine learning techniques in cloud computing environments*. . doi:10.1109/CloudTech.2017.8284731

Zhang, Wu, & Cao. (2008). A Secret Sharing-Based Key Management in Hierarchical Wireless Sensor Network. In *Securing wireless sensor networks: A survey*. IEEE Communications Surveys and Tutorials.

Zhang, X., Zhao, J., & LeCun, Y. (2015). *Character-level convolutional networks for text classification*. arXiv preprint arXiv:1509.01626.

Zhang, Y., He, D., & Choo, K. K. R. (2018). BaDS: Blockchain-based architecture for data sharing with ABS and CP-ABE in IoT. *Wireless Communications and Mobile Computing*, *2018*, 2018. doi:10.1155/2018/2783658

Zhang, H., Sindagi, V., & Patel, V. M. (2019). Image de-raining using a conditional generative adversarial network. *IEEE Transactions on Circuits and Systems for Video Technology*, *30*(11), 3943–3956. doi:10.1109/TCSVT.2019.2920407

Zhang, Y., Wu, C., Cao, J., & Li, X. (2013). A secret sharing-based key management in a hierarchical wireless sensor network. *International Journal of Distributed Sensor Networks*, *2013*(6), 1–7. doi:10.1155/2013/406061

Zhang, Z., Sun, R., Zhao, C., Wang, J., Chang, C. K., & Gupta, B. B. (2017). CyVOD: A novel trinity multimedia social network scheme. *Multimedia Tools and Applications*, *76*(18), 18513–18529. doi:10.100711042-016-4162-z

Zheng, H., Zhang, Z., Jiang, S., Yan, B., Shi, X., Xie, Y., Huang, X., Yu, Z., Liu, H., Weng, S., Nurmikko, A., Zhang, Y., Peng, H., Xu, W., & Zhang, J. (2019). A shape-memory and spiral light-emitting device for precise multisite stimulation of nerve bundles. *Nature Communications*, *10*(1), 2790. doi:10.103841467-019-10418-3 PMID:31243276

Zhengwang, Y., Wen, T., Song, X., Liu, Z., & Fu, C. (2017). An efficient dynamic trust evaluation model for wireless sensor networks. *Journal of Sensors*, *2017*, 1–16.

Zhioua, S. (2013, July). The middle east under malware attack dissecting cyber weapons. In *2013 IEEE 33rd International Conference on Distributed Computing Systems Workshops* (pp. 11-16). IEEE. 10.1109/ICDCSW.2013.30

Zhu, Q., Bushnell, L., & Başar, T. (2012, December). Game-theoretic analysis of node capture and cloning attack with multiple attackers in wireless sensor networks. In *2012 IEEE 51st IEEE Conference on Decision and Control (CDC)* (pp. 3404-3411). IEEE. 10.1109/CDC.2012.6426481

Zizzo, G., Hankin, C., Maffeis, S., & Jones, K. (2019). *Intrusion detection for industrial control systems: Evaluation analysis and adversarial attacks*. arXiv preprint arXiv:1911.04278.

About the Contributors

Brij B. Gupta received a PhD degree from Indian Institute of Technology Roorkee, India in the area of Information and Cyber Security. In 2009, he was selected for the Canadian Commonwealth Scholarship award. He has published more than 380 research papers in International Journals and Conferences of high repute including IEEE, Elsevier, ACM, Springer, Wiley, Taylor & Francis, Inderscience, etc. Dr. Gupta also received the Sir Visvesvaraya Young Faculty Research Fellowship Award in 2017, Best Faculty Awards in 2018 and 2019 from the Ministry of Electronics and Information Technology, GoI and NIT Kurukshetra, respectively. He also received the 2020 and 2021 ICT Express Elsevier Best Reviewer Award. His Google scholar H-index is 57 (including i10 index: 187, Researchgate RG Score: 45.79) with over 11000 citations for his work. In addition, he is serving as a distinguished lecturer for IEEE Consumer Technology Society and also included in the list of Top 2% Scientists in the world which is created by the researchers from Stanford University. He is also working as principal investigator of various R&D projects sponsored by various government funding agencies. He is serving/served as Associate editor (or Guest Editor) of IEEE TII, IEEE Access, IEEE IoTM, ACM TOIT, IEEE IoT, FGCS, COMCOM, etc. Moreover, Dr. Gupta is also leading International Journal of Cloud Applications and Computing (IJCAC), IGI Global, USA and IJSSCI, and IJSWIS, IGI Global as Editor-in-Chief. He has also served as Technical program committee (TPC) member or in other capacities of more than 100 International conferences worldwide. Dr. Gupta received outstanding paper awards in both regular and student categories in 5th IEEE Global Conference on Consumer Electronics (GCCE) in Kyoto, Japan during Oct. 7-10, 2016. Dr. Gupta is senior member of IEEE, ACM, Life Member, International Association of Engineers (IAENG), Life Member, IACSIT. He also worked as a post-doctoral research fellow in UNB, Canada. He was also visiting researcher with Yamaguchi University, Japan, with Deakin University, Australia and with Swinburne University of Technology, Australia during January, 2015 and 2018, July 2017, and Mar-Apr. 2018, respectively. Moreover, he was also visiting Professor in University of Murcia, Spain in Jun.-Jul., 2018. Additionally, he was visiting professor with Temple university, USA and Staffordshire University, UK during June, 2019 and July 2020, respectively. At present, Dr. Gupta is group lead, Information and Cyber security, Programme coordinator, and Assistant Professor in the Department of Computer Engineering, National Institute of Technology Kurukshetra India. He is also working as honorary Associate Professor with Macquarie University, Australia and Adjunct Associate Professor with Asia University, Taiwan, respectively. His research interests include Information security, Cyber Security, Cloud Computing, Web security, Mobile/Smartphone, Intrusion detection, IoT Security, AI, Social media, Computer networks and Phishing.

* * *

Kwok Tai Chui received the B.Eng. degree in Electronic and Communication Engineering – Business Intelligence Minor, with first-class honor, and Ph.D. degree in Electronic Engineering from City University of Hong Kong. He was the recipient of international awards in several IEEE events. For instance, he received the 2nd Prize Award (Postgraduate Category) of 2014 IEEE Region 10 Student Paper Contest, and Best Paper Award in IEEE The International Conference on Consumer Electronics-China, in both 2014 and 2015. He has industry experience as a Senior Data Scientist with an Internet of Things (IoT) company. He is currently an Assistant Professor of the Department of Technology. He is specialized in artificial intelligence and data science/analytics for smart city applications including healthcare, smart grid, transportation, and education. He has served as Managing Editor of International Journal on Semantic Web and Information Systems, Associate Editors, Guest Editors, and Editorial Board Members for several ESCI/SCI journals.

Félix J. García Clemente received the Ph.D. degree in computer science from the University of Murcia, in 2006. He is currently an Associate Professor with the Department of Computer Engineering, University of Murcia. His research interests include cybersecurity and management of distributed communication networks. He is the coauthor of over 100 scientific publications and an active member on different national and international research projects.

Lorenzo Fernández Maimó is an associate professor in the Department of Computer Engineering of the University of Murcia. His research interests primarily focus on machine learning and deep learning applied to cybersecurity and computer vision. Fernández Maimó has a MSc and PhD in Computer Science from the University of Murcia.

Francisco José García-Peñalvo received his bachelor's degree in computing from the University of Valladolid (Spain), and his PhD. degree from the University of Salamanca, where he is currently the Head of the Research Group in Interaction and e-Learning (GRIAL). His main research interests focus on eLearning, computers and education and digital ecosystems. He is the Editor in Chief of the Education in the Knowledge Society journal and the Journal of Information Technology Research. He coordinates the Doctoral Program in Education in the Knowledge Society.

Govind P. Gupta received his Ph.D. degree from Indian Institute of Technology, Roorkee, India, in 2014. He is presently working as Assistant Professor in the Department of Information Technology at National Institute of Technology, Raipur, India. His current research interests include Internet of Things, Software-defined Networking, Network Security, Blockchain Application development for IoT, Enterprise Blockchain. He has published more than 50 research articles in peer reviewed Journals and reputed Conference proceedings. He is a professional member of the IEEE and ACM.

Alberto Huertas Celdrán received the M.Sc. and Ph.D. degrees in computer science from the University of Murcia, Spain. He is a Postdoctoral Researcher with the Department of Informatics, University of Zurich. His scientific interests include medical cyber-physical systems, brain–computer interfaces, cybersecurity, trust, data privacy, continuous authentication, semantic technology, context-aware systems, and computer networks.

Mavneet Kaur is a Senior student at NIT Kurukshetra, doing her research in information security under the guidance of Professor BB Gupta.

Anish Khan received a B.Tech. degree in 2018, in Electronics and Communication Engineering, and M.Tech. degree in 2020, in Electronics and Communication Engineering both from the Kurukshetra University, Kurukshetra. His field of interest is Wireless Sensor Networks and Internet of Things (IoT). He published 2 international conference papers and 1 book chapter in the Springer series. He holds IEEE Student Membership and IEEE Consumer Technology Society Membership.

Sanjay Kumar has completed his B.E. with specialization in Computer Science and Engineering from MNREC(now MNNIT) Allahabad, M. Tech. in Computer Science and Engineering from RGPV Bhopal and Ph.D. in Information Technology from NIT Raipur. He is having 14 years of experience in academia and 2 years of experience in industry. He is life member of IETE and CSI. He is senior member of IEEE.

Wen Liu received the B.Sc. degree (Hons.) in information and computing science from the Department of Mathematics, Wuhan University of Technology, Wuhan, China, in 2009, and the Ph.D. degree in mathematical imaging from The Chinese University of Hong Kong, Hong Kong, in 2015. He was a Visiting Scholar with the College of Computer Science and Software Engineering, Shenzhen University, Shenzhen, China, and also with the Agency for Science, Technology, and Research (A*STAR), Singapore. He is currently an Associate Professor with the School of Navigation, Wuhan University of Technology. His research interests include computer vision, trajectory data mining, machine learning, and computational navigation sciences. He is an Associate Editor of the International Journal on Semantic Web and Information Systems.

Sergio López Bernal received the B.Sc. and M.Sc. degrees in computer science from the University of Murcia, and the M.Sc. degree in architecture and engineering for the IoT from IMT Atlantique, France. He is currently pursuing the Ph.D. degree with the University of Murcia. His research interests include ICT security on brain–computer interfaces and network and information security.

Miltiadis D. Lytras is Associate Professor at Deree- ACG with a research focus on semantic web, knowledge management and e-learning, with more than 100 publications. He has co-edited more than 45 special issues in International Journals (IEEE Transaction on Knowledge and Data Engineering, IEEE Internet Computing, IEEE Transactions on Education, Computers in Human Behaviour, Interactive Learning Environments, Journal of Knowledge Management, Journal of Computer Assisted Learning) and has authored/[co-]edited 42 books [e.g. Open Source for Knowledge and Learning Management, Ubiquitous and Pervasive Knowledge Management, Intelligent Learning Infrastructures for Knowledge Intensive Organizations, Semantic Web Based Information Systems, China Information Technology Handbook, Real World Applications of Semantic Web and Ontologies, Web 2.0: The Business Model, etc]. He (has) serves(ed) as the (Co) Editor in Chief of 8 international journals (e.g. International Journal on Semantic Web and Information Systems, International Journal of Knowledge Society Research, International Journal of Knowledge and Learning, International Journal of Technology Enhanced Learning).

Enrique Tomás Martínez Beltrán is working towards a Ph.D. in Computer Science at the University of Murcia, Spain. He obtained a B.Sc. degree in Information and Communication Technologies and an M.Sc. degree in New Technologies, specializing in information security, networks, and telematics. His research interests include cybersecurity, Brain-Computer Interfaces, IoT, and Artificial Intelligence applied to different fields using Machine Learning and Deep Learning techniques.

Gregorio Martínez Pérez received the M.Sc. and Ph.D. degrees in computer science from the University of Murcia, Spain. He is currently a Full Professor with the Department of Information and Communications Engineering, University of Murcia. His research interests include cybersecurity, privacy, and networking, working on different national and European IST research projects on these topics.

Patricia Ordóñez de Pablos is a professor in the Department of Business Administration in the Faculty of Business and Economics at The University of Oviedo, Spain. She completed her education in The London School of Economics, UK. Her teaching and research interests focus on the areas of strategic management, knowledge management, organizational learning, human resource management, intellectual capital, information technologies, with special interest in Asia (Bhutan, China, Laos, Myanmar). She is Editor-in-Chief of the International Journal of Learning and Intellectual Capital (IJLIC) and International Journal of Asian Business and Information Management (IJABIM), respectively. She has edited books for IGI Global, Routledge, and Springer. In 2021, she earned placement on Stanford University's "Ranking of the World Scientists: World's Top 2% Scientists" list, which can be found here: https://econo.uniovi. es/noticias/-/asset_publisher/XiGH/content/enhorabuena-a-la-profesora-patricia-ordonez-de-pablos;jse ssionid=7DECA9C6930CC81559878BD6A43B8483?redirect=%2F.

Dragan Peraković received a B.Sc. degree in 1995, an M.Sc. degree in 2003, and a PhD in 2005, all at the University of Zagreb, Croatia, EU. Dragan is Head of the Department for Information and Communication Traffic and Head of Chair of Information Communication Systems and Services Management, all at the Faculty of Transport and Traffic Sciences, University of Zagreb, where he is currently a full professor. Dragan is visiting professor at the University of Mostar, Faculty of Science and Education Sciences, Mostar / Bosnia and Herzegovina. Area of scientific interests and activities is modelling of innovative communication ecosystems in the environment of the TELCO, transport system (ITS) and Industry 4.0; AI & ML in cybersecurity, DDoS, Internet of Things; AI in e-forensic of communication ecosystems (terminal devices/services); design and development of new innovative services and modules.

Ángel Luis Perales Gómez received the Ph.D. degree in Computer Science from the University of Murcia (Spain). He is currently a postdoctoral researcher with the Department of Computer Engineering, University of Murcia. His research interests include deep learning, cybersecurity of industrial control systems, and the security of distributed communication networks.

Mario Quiles Pérez is a B.Eng. student in Computer Engineering at the University of Murcia (UMU). Mention in Information and Communication Technologies. Currently in his last academic year, he is investigating the possible attacks that could be carried out on brain-machine interfaces. Interested and initiated in cybersecurity, he develops training scenarios for the detection of adversarial attacks on internal networks. In the future, he hopes to dedicate himself fully to the world of cybersecurity.

Chien-wen Shen is a Professor in the Department of Business Administration and the Division Director of the University Social Responsibility Office at the National Central University (NCU). He also serves as the Director of the Yunus Social Business Center and the Center for Media and Social Impact at NCU and the Executive Director of the Social Impact Institute of Taiwan. He received his M.S. and Ph.D. in Industrial Engineering and Management Sciences from Northwestern University. His research interests include big data analytics, information management, supply chain management, decision science, and social business.

Santosh Kumar Smmarwar is working towards a Ph.D. degree in Information Technology from, National Institute of Technology, Raipur, India. He earned his Ph.D. scholarship position as a talented student in 2019. He received B.E. with a specialization in Computer Science and Engineering in 2008 from SATI Vidisha(RGPV Bhopal) and an M.S. with a specialization in Cyber Law and Information Security from the Indian Institute of Information Technology, Allahabad, India, in 2011. His research interests include Cybersecurity and Network security areas like intrusion detection systems and malware detection systems, Internet of Things, Machine learning, Deep learning.

Shingo Yamaguchi is a Professor in the Graduate School of Sciences and Technology for Innovation Yamaguchi University, Japan. He received the B.E., M.E., and D.E. degrees from Yamaguchi University, Japan, in 1992, 1994, and 2002. He was a Visiting Scholar at the University of Illinois at Chicago, US, in 2007. He is currently the Director of Information and Data Science Education Center, Yamaguchi University. His research interests include AI, IoT, big data, and cybersecurity. He was the Executive Conference Chair of IEEE ICCE 2021. He is a Member of the Board of Governors of IEEE Consumer Technology Society. He is also the Editor-in-Chief of IEEE Consumer Electronics Magazine. He is a Senior Member of IEEE and IEICE.

Index

sensor 21, 57, 70, 73, 78, 87, 93-99, 103, 106, 110-111, 115, 123-126, 148-149, 154, 159, 169, 209-210, 214, 219-225, 233-235
signature 1, 3-4, 9, 14-15, 17, 46, 66, 69, 74, 95, 205-207, 209, 215
smart contract 199, 202-204, 206-210
Supervisory Control and Data Acquisition 75, 89, 93
systematic review 59, 61, 65

T

topic modeling 19-21, 23, 37

V

visual stimuli 176, 178, 181, 183-184, 194, 198, 239, 244
vulnerability 52-53, 57, 81-82, 85-86, 128-129, 176, 221, 223-224, 227, 235-236

W

Wireless Sensor Network (WSN) 96, 103, 106, 110-111, 123, 125, 148, 220, 222, 233-234
worm 20, 81-82, 90-91, 127, 129-132, 134, 136-139, 141-147

Recommended Reference Books

IGI Global's reference books are available in three unique pricing formats:
Print Only, E-Book Only, or Print + E-Book.

Shipping fees may apply.

www.igi-global.com

ISBN: 978-1-5225-9866-4
EISBN: 978-1-5225-9867-1
© 2020; 1,805 pp.
List Price: US$ **2,350**

ISBN: 978-1-5225-8876-4
EISBN: 978-1-5225-8877-1
© 2019; 141 pp.
List Price: US$ **135**

ISBN: 978-1-5225-7847-5
EISBN: 978-1-5225-7848-2
© 2019; 306 pp.
List Price: US$ **195**

ISBN: 978-1-5225-6313-6
EISBN: 978-1-5225-6314-3
© 2019; 349 pp.
List Price: US$ **215**

ISBN: 978-1-5225-1941-6
EISBN: 978-1-5225-1942-3
© 2017; 408 pp.
List Price: US$ **195**

ISBN: 978-1-5225-0808-3
EISBN: 978-1-5225-0809-0
© 2017; 442 pp.
List Price: US$ **345**

Do you want to stay current on the latest research trends, product announcements, news, and special offers?
Join IGI Global's mailing list to receive customized recommendations, exclusive discounts, and more.
Sign up at: **www.igi-global.com/newsletters.**

Publisher of Peer-Reviewed, Timely, and Innovative Academic Research

www.igi-global.com Sign up at www.igi-global.com/newsletters facebook.com/igiglobal twitter.com/igiglobal linkedin.com/igiglobal

Ensure Quality Research is Introduced to the Academic Community

Become an Evaluator for IGI Global Authored Book Projects

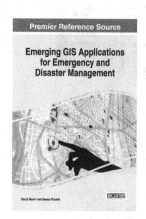
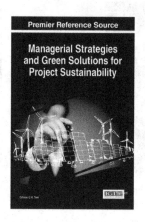

The overall success of an authored book project is dependent on quality and timely manuscript evaluations.

Applications and Inquiries may be sent to:
development@igi-global.com

Applicants must have a doctorate (or equivalent degree) as well as publishing, research, and reviewing experience. Authored Book Evaluators are appointed for one-year terms and are expected to complete at least three evaluations per term. Upon successful completion of this term, evaluators can be considered for an additional term.

If you have a colleague that may be interested in this opportunity, we encourage you to share this information with them.

IGI Global Author Services

Providing a high-quality, affordable, and expeditious service, IGI Global's Author Services enable authors to streamline their publishing process, increase chance of acceptance, and adhere to IGI Global's publication standards.

Benefits of Author Services:

- **Professional Service:** All our editors, designers, and translators are experts in their field with years of experience and professional certifications.

- **Quality Guarantee & Certificate:** Each order is returned with a quality guarantee and certificate of professional completion.

- **Timeliness:** All editorial orders have a guaranteed return timeframe of 3-5 business days and translation orders are guaranteed in 7-10 business days.

- **Affordable Pricing:** IGI Global Author Services are competitively priced compared to other industry service providers.

- **APC Reimbursement:** IGI Global authors publishing Open Access (OA) will be able to deduct the cost of editing and other IGI Global author services from their OA APC publishing fee.

Author Services Offered:

English Language Copy Editing
Professional, native English language copy editors improve your manuscript's grammar, spelling, punctuation, terminology, semantics, consistency, flow, formatting, and more.

Scientific & Scholarly Editing
A Ph.D. level review for qualities such as originality and significance, interest to researchers, level of methodology and analysis, coverage of literature, organization, quality of writing, and strengths and weaknesses.

Figure, Table, Chart & Equation Conversions
Work with IGI Global's graphic designers before submission to enhance and design all figures and charts to IGI Global's specific standards for clarity.

Translation
Providing 70 language options, including Simplified and Traditional Chinese, Spanish, Arabic, German, French, and more.

Hear What the Experts Are Saying About IGI Global's Author Services

"Publishing with IGI Global has been an amazing experience for me for sharing my research. The strong academic production support ensures quality and timely completion." – **Prof. Margaret Niess, Oregon State University, USA**

"The service was very fast, very thorough, and very helpful in ensuring our chapter meets the criteria and requirements of the book's editors. I was quite impressed and happy with your service." – **Prof. Tom Brinthaupt, Middle Tennessee State University, USA**

Learn More or Get Started Here:

For Questions, Contact IGI Global's Customer Service Team at cust@igi-global.com or 717-533-8845

IGI Global
PUBLISHER of TIMELY KNOWLEDGE
www.igi-global.com

www.igi-global.com

Celebrating Over 30 Years of Scholarly
Knowledge Creation & Dissemination

I InfoSci®-Books

A Database of Nearly 6,000 Reference Books Containing Over 105,000+ Chapters Focusing on Emerging Research

GAIN ACCESS TO **THOUSANDS** OF REFERENCE BOOKS AT **A FRACTION** OF THEIR INDIVIDUAL LIST **PRICE**.

InfoSci®-Books Database

The **InfoSci®-Books** is a database of nearly 6,000 IGI Global single and multi-volume reference books, handbooks of research, and encyclopedias, encompassing groundbreaking research from prominent experts worldwide that spans over 350+ topics in 11 core subject areas including business, computer science, education, science and engineering, social sciences, and more.

Open Access Fee Waiver (Read & Publish) Initiative

For any library that invests in IGI Global's InfoSci-Books and/or InfoSci-Journals (175+ scholarly journals) databases, IGI Global will match the library's investment with a fund of equal value to go toward **subsidizing the OA article processing charges (APCs) for their students, faculty, and staff** at that institution when their work is submitted and accepted under OA into an IGI Global journal.*

INFOSCI® PLATFORM FEATURES

- Unlimited Simultaneous Access
- No DRM
- No Set-Up or Maintenance Fees
- A Guarantee of No More Than a 5% Annual Increase for Subscriptions
- Full-Text HTML and PDF Viewing Options
- Downloadable MARC Records
- COUNTER 5 Compliant Reports
- Formatted Citations With Ability to Export to RefWorks and EasyBib
- No Embargo of Content (Research is Available Months in Advance of the Print Release)

*The fund will be offered on an annual basis and expire at the end of the subscription period. The fund would renew as the subscription is renewed for each year thereafter. The open access fees will be waived after the student, faculty, or staff's paper has been vetted and accepted into an IGI Global journal and the fund can only be used toward publishing OA in an IGI Global journal. Libraries in developing countries will have the match on their investment doubled.

To Recommend or Request a Free Trial:
www.igi-global.com/infosci-books

eresources@igi-global.com • Toll Free: 1-866-342-6657 ext. 100 • Phone: 717-533-8845 x100

www.igi-global.com

www.igi-global.com

Publisher of Peer-Reviewed, Timely, and
Innovative Academic Research Since 1988

IGI Global's Transformative Open Access (OA) Model:
How to Turn Your University Library's Database Acquisitions Into a Source of OA Funding

Well in advance of Plan S, IGI Global unveiled their OA Fee Waiver (Read & Publish) Initiative. Under this initiative, librarians who invest in IGI Global's InfoSci-Books and/or InfoSci-Journals databases will be able to subsidize their patrons' OA article processing charges (APCs) when their work is submitted and accepted (after the peer review process) into an IGI Global journal.

How Does it Work?

Step 1: **Library Invests in the InfoSci-Databases:** A library perpetually purchases or subscribes to the InfoSci-Books, InfoSci-Journals, or discipline/subject databases.

Step 2: **IGI Global Matches the Library Investment with OA Subsidies Fund:** IGI Global provides a fund to go towards subsidizing the OA APCs for the library's patrons.

Step 3: **Patron of the Library is Accepted into IGI Global Journal (After Peer Review):** When a patron's paper is accepted into an IGI Global journal, they option to have their paper published under a traditional publishing model or as OA.

Step 4: **IGI Global Will Deduct APC Cost from OA Subsidies Fund:** If the author decides to publish under OA, the OA APC fee will be deducted from the OA subsidies fund.

Step 5: **Author's Work Becomes Freely Available:** The patron's work will be freely available under CC BY copyright license, enabling them to share it freely with the academic community.

Note: This fund will be offered on an annual basis and will renew as the subscription is renewed for each year thereafter. IGI Global will manage the fund and award the APC waivers unless the librarian has a preference as to how the funds should be managed.

Hear From the Experts on This Initiative:

"I'm very happy to have been able to make one of my recent research contributions *freely available* along with having access to the *valuable resources* found within IGI Global's InfoSci-Journals database."

– Prof. Stuart Palmer,
Deakin University, Australia

"Receiving the support from IGI Global's OA Fee Waiver Initiative *encourages me to continue my research work without any hesitation.*"

– Prof. Wenlong Liu, College of Economics and Management at Nanjing University of Aeronautics & Astronautics, China

For More Information, Scan the QR Code or Contact:
IGI Global's Digital Resources Team at eresources@igi-global.com.

Printed in the United States
by Baker & Taylor Publisher Services